Voices in Flight:
Escaping Soldiers
and Airmen
of World War I

Martin W. Bowman

Pen & Sword
AVIATION

First Published in Great Britain in 2017 by
Pen & Sword Aviation
an imprint of
Pen & Sword Books Ltd
47 Church Street, Barnsley, South Yorkshire S70 2AS

Copyright © Pen & Sword Books 2017
ISBN 9781473863224

The right of Martin W Bowman to be identified as author of this work
has been asserted by him in accordance with the
Copyright, Designs and Patents Act 1988.

A CIP catalogue record for this book is
available from the British Library.

Typeset in 10/12pt Palatino
by GMS Enterprises PE3 8QQ

Printed and bound in England by
CPI Group (UK) Ltd, Croydon, CR0 4YY

Pen & Sword Books Ltd incorporates the Imprints of Pen & Sword
Aviation, Pen & Sword Family History, Pen & Sword Maritime, Pen & Sword
Military, Pen & Sword Discovery, Wharncliffe Local History, Wharncliffe
True Crime, Wharncliffe Transport, Pen & Sword Select, Pen & Sword
Military Classics, Leo Cooper, The Praetorian Press, Remember When,
Seaforth Publishing and Frontline Publishing.

For a complete list of Pen & Sword titles please contact
PEN & SWORD BOOKS LIMITED

47 Church Street, Barnsley, South Yorkshire, S70 2AS, England
E-mail: enquiries@pen-and-sword.co.uk
Website: www.pen-and-sword.co.uk

Contents

Acknowledgements

I am indebted to all the contributors for their words and photographs. Thanks also go to my fellow author, friend and colleague, Graham Simons, for getting the book to press ready standard and for his detailed work on the photographs; to Pen & Sword and in particular, Laura Hirst; and Jon Wilkinson, for his unique jacket design once again. Also, to The Norfolk & Suffolk Aviation Museum, the Shuttleworth Trust; and the Second Air Division Memorial Library, Norwich.

Part One: In Flight

Preface

It is very apparent that the airman, even flying a machine in peace time, must ever be on the alert if he would avoid meeting with sudden disaster. In war service the observer has to be a trained wireless operator, an expert photographer under difficulties and a crack shot with the intricacies of machine guns at his finger ends. The pilot, before he begins to learn the serious side of his arduous profession, must pass three tests. He has to fly solo in five figures of eight, which of necessity involves turning right and left and when he lands he has to stop within fifty yards of a given mark. He goes through this performance a second time and yet once again, but in his third descent he must switch off his engine when at a height of 350 feet and glide down to earth. The pilot then seriously begins his training, which largely covers the work of an observer too, in order to extend his usefulness when flying in a single-seater. Needless to say that being classed fit for general service is not sufficient guarantee of fitness for air service. Special tests for heart and sight and nerve have to be passed, for the flying man must have 'the heart of a lion and the eye of an eagle.'

At the end of the war British airmen night after night were dropping heavy bombs on strong points in the enemy's rear and were attacking places more than 250 miles away and dumping heavy loads of explosives on factories, aerodromes, railway stations and other places whose destruction would hamper the operations of the enemy. They were dropping smoke bombs in advance of our attacking troops in order to screen them from the foe. When our advance posts were temporarily cut off from their base of supplies the airmen would take them both food and ammunition. Fighting pilots, diving almost vertically at a speed of 200 mph, were firing bullets at the rate of 400 a minute at hostile 'planes and often our single machines would attack and drive off four or five enemy 'planes.

Thousands of our aerial fighters had never been in an aeroplane before the war. The Royal Air Force went into the hostilities without any traditions, for the service was too young to have any, but from end to end of the record of the greatest war the world has ever known, British airmen blazed a trail of glory that added lustre to the Flag for which they fought, earning undying fame by deeds that brought a thrill to the heart of every true Briton.

From the very beginning of the war British airmen always attacked even against superior numbers, whereas in similar circumstances the Hun generally put down his nose and drove his hardest for safety.

At one time organization and preparedness for war gave the Germans a huge advantage in pitting against us larger fighting machines, carrying a pilot and two machine gunners. Yet even then the Germans were acting largely on the defensive. Long observation flights in the worst air battles, which called for individual brilliance not only in manoeuvring the machine but in snatching at the opportunities that made for victory, they signally failed with few exceptions. In all probability German iron discipline did nothing to help to produce ideal aviators, who depend more upon personal initiative and instinctive resourcefulness that count far more than a more or less blind obedience to orders which may not best serve the urgencies of the situation that might arise.

It must be admitted that British persistence against the odds cost us dearly in machines and men; but aerial success is ever a matter of risk and the British airman set himself a lofty ideal and acted up to it in doing all and daring all, until we could turn out aeroplanes second to none in fighting qualities and in such numbers that our superiority in the air was beyond all argument.

The difference in the matter of rewards for airmen points its own moral. A German pilot got the Iron Cross first class automatically after about fifty hours' flying. The British pilot got nothing for fifty days' flying, unless he did something particularly out of the common and where the standard of fighting excellence was so uniformly high, it was not an easy matter for a British pilot to gain a Military Cross, while a VC went only to a super-flying man who performed some super deed that hall-marked him as one of the bravest of the brave.

Ernest Hanley Protheroe, a schoolmaster born in Dudley, Worcestershire in 1866, writing in 1923.

In the Italian-Turkish War (1911-12) the Italians used aeroplanes, airships and balloons against the Arabs in Tripoli, and Italy can claim the credit of putting the lessons learnt in manoeuvres to the first real practical test. Italian air scouts supplied their headquarters with most valuable information concerning the movements of bodies of the enemy preparing to make attacks on Italian positions. It was found that even when the wings of an aeroplane were riddled by shot there was generally sufficient supporting surface left to enable the machine to return home after making a reconnaissance. Upon several occasions Italian airmen acted upon the offensive to very good purpose; for example, from a height of 700 feet, Lieutenant Gavotti threw a bomb made of picrate of potash upon a mass of some 2,000 Arabs, who were scattered in all directions. In this first instance of bomb-dropping from aircraft the method in the light of later experience was quite primitive, for the pilot carried the bomb in a bag at his side and dropped it by hand over the side of the machine.

'The position of the aeroplane on the eve of the First World War is interesting' wrote M. J. B. Davy in Air Power and Civilisation. 'In 1914 the average speed was 70-80 mph and the maximum height attainable - the 'ceiling' - was only 7,000 feet. Great Britain possessed, by the end of the year, 300 service aeroplanes, whereas Germany had no less than 1,000 service machines and 450 which were privately owned. France possessed 1,500 and there were also 500 privately owned. By 30 November 1918 the Royal Air Force had no less than 22,647 service aircraft of all types on charge - a figure which shows vividly the degree of expansion due to the stimulus of war. Indeed warfare provided an incentive, for, from a tentative and generally untried military instrument, the aeroplane was developed into a highly scientific weapon and all this was done in less than four years; it was an example of rapid, technical progress hitherto unequalled. For instance, the average weight of aero-engines of air-cooled type was 4lb per horse-power in 1914 and this figure was reduced to 1.9lb per horse-power by the end of 1918; those of the water-cooled type were reduced from

4.05lb to 2.2lb per horse-power. By 1919 the average ceiling for certain service types had been increased to 30,000 feet, this being mainly due to the advance in engine design. In 1918 fighter aircraft were in use which had speeds of 140-155 mph (i.e. double those of 1914). This represented a very great advance. In 1914 the weight of a single-seater reconnaissance machine was about 20 to 25lb for each horse-power developed by the engine; by the end of 1918 this figure had been reduced to about 8lb per horse-power. Wing loadings increased from about 4lb to as much as 8lb per square feet during the same period and a rate of climb of 10,000 feet in five minutes was reached.'

On 3 August 1914 the British Foreign Secretary, Sir Edward Grey remarked that 'The lamps are going out all over Europe; we shall not see them lit again in our lifetime.' The following day, almost without warning, Britain and Germany were at war. General Count von Schlieffen, who had died the year before the war began, had spent his retirement years working on a grand operational strategy for a war between Germany on the one hand, Russia, France and Britain on the other... the Schlieffen Plan. An essential element of his plan was to outflank the strong French fortifications facing Germany by a scythe-like attack through Holland, Belgium and Luxembourg - ignoring the neutrality of those countries.

There was no single definitive factor that caused the start of the First World War. Tensions throughout Europe had been growing for many years - nationalism, an arms race, disputes over territories and spheres of influence, greed, fear, distrust and the division of Europe into two hostile alliances were all contributing factors. The assassination of Archduke Franz Ferdinand, heir to the Austro-Hungarian throne, by Serbian terrorists led to the Austro-Hungarian invasion of Serbia, on 29 July 1914. Russia mobilised troops to prevent Serbia being crushed. Germany declared war on Russia and, realising that France would support Russia, declared war on France as well. When Germany invaded neutral Belgium, Britain declared war on Germany. Japan, seeing the chance to seize German territory in China, also declared war on Germany. Bulgaria and Turkey sided with the Central Powers and soon most countries in Europe had become involved in the war.

At the start of the war the Royal Flying Corps (RFC), commanded by Brigadier-General Sir David Henderson, consisted of five squadrons - one observation balloon squadron (1 Squadron RFC) and four aeroplane squadrons. These were first used for aerial spotting on 13 September 1914, but only became efficient when they perfected the use of wireless communication at Aubers Ridge on 9 May 1915. Aerial photography was attempted during 1914, but again only became effective the next year. By 1918 photographic images could be taken from 15,000 feet and interpreted by over 3,000 personnel.

When the war had been in progress only a few weeks, Sir John French said of British airmen: 'Their skill, energy and perseverance have been beyond all praise. They have furnished me with the most complete and accurate information which has been of incalculable value in the conduct of the operations. Fired at constantly by friend and foe and not hesitating to fly in every kind of weather, they have remained undaunted throughout. Further, by actual fighting in the air they have destroyed five of the enemy's machines.' In a dispatch published in November 1915, Sir John French stated that the amount of flying had been doubled and that, in 240 aerial duels, our supremacy had been maintained. He specified one instance where an airman had carried on although his machine had been perforated by 300 bullets.

'Quite early in 1915', wrote Ernest Protheroe, 'we employed as many as thirty and forty aeroplanes at a time in raiding German submarine bases along the Belgian coast, where the enemy suffered never-ending losses and dislocations.

'One of the most impressive sights the writer saw, when he was accorded the privilege of visits to the Third and Fifth armies on the Western Front, was about fifty British aeroplanes like a flight of huge birds going over the German lines in the neighbourhood of Cambrai. Subconsciously there rose to the mind Tennyson's lines in *Locksley Hall: Heard the heavens fill with shouting and there rained a ghastly dew. From the nations' airy navies grappling in the central blue.*

Hitherto regarded as merely the imaginative fancy of the poet, events had proved that it was an accurate prophecy, as was to be realized not only by actual combatants, but by peaceable stay-at-home folk, who in that degree shared some of the horrors of the new warfare with their loved ones at the front.'

Parachutes were not available to pilots of the RFC's heavier than aircraft - nor were they used by the RAF during the war. With no parachute, many Allied airmen were forced to make a dreadful final choice. Some fliers carried a pistol with which to shoot themselves should they become a 'flamer'. Airmen often saw their victims die. A pilot or observer might slump into his cockpit; might jump in agony from a burning aircraft, his clothes aflame; or might be sent plunging to earth, unharmed but doomed, in a crippled machine (The Calthrop Guardian Angel parachute - 1916 model - was only officially adopted just as the war ended. By this time parachutes had been used by balloonists for three years).

When the war had been in progress ten months it was stated in Parliament that the men in the Air Service had been increased by five times and the pilots by ten times and yet the exigencies of the operations ever called for more and still more airmen. Apart from the constant casualties, not only in actual fighting but in inseparable accidents, the wearing life of an airman called for constant rests from duty and thus to keep only a hundred machines constantly in the air called for the services of about a thousand pilots.

Given the nature of warfare on the Western Front, it is not difficult to imagine why men would seek to transfer into the RFC. Many had experienced the misery and squalor of the trenches. An airman's existence was a curious one. Against the possibility of meeting such a gruesome end was the certainty when off-duty of safety and comforts beyond the hopes of ground troops. In the air too, there was great danger but men preferred to face it in a corps which offered the promise of independence and glamour, as well as a degree of comfort unknown to the men in the trenches. Those who served in the Middle East, although spared the worst miseries of the Western Front, shared a similar desire to escape their own discomforts: sand, dust and flies. But the transition

Freepost Plus RTKE-RGRJ-KTTX
Pen & Sword Books Ltd
47 Church Street
BARNSLEY
S70 2AS

DISCOVER MORE ABOUT MILITARY HISTORY

Pen & Sword Books have over 4000 books currently available, our imprints include; Aviation, Naval, Military, Archaeology, Transport, Frontline, Seaforth and the Battleground series, and we cover all periods of history on land, sea and air.

Keep up to date with our new releases by completing and returning the form below (no stamp required if posting in the UK).

Alternatively, if you have access to the internet, please complete your details online via our website at **www.pen-and-sword.co.uk.**

All those subscribing to our mailing list via our website will receive a free e-book, *Mosquito Missions* by Martin W Bowman. Please enter code number ACC1 when subscribing to receive your free e-book.

Mr/Mrs/Ms ....

Address...

....

Postcode.......................... Email address...

Website: www.pen-and-sword.co.uk Email: enquiries@pen-and-sword.co.uk
Telephone: 01226 734555   Fax: 01226 734438
Stay in touch: facebook.com/penandswordbooks or follow us on Twitter @penswordbooks

from moments of extreme danger to hours of peaceful existence, sometimes several times a day, kept men in a constant state of exhaustion.

Men who had already served in the ground forces reasoned that if they survived the day's flying they would at least have the chance to sleep in a comfortable bed. Not everyone, of course, survived the day's flying.

Perhaps it was seeing the Royal Naval Air Service (RNAS) machines over Gallipoli or just a desire to escape the trenches that impelled Sergeant Lancelot Lytton Richardson in the 6th Light Horse to learn to fly. Born to grazier William Richardson and his wife Elizabeth Greedy Richardson in Bogolong, Grenfell, NSW on 18 October 1895, the youngest of five children, he volunteered on the outbreak of the war at the age of 18, just after leaving the North Shore Church of England Grammar School, where he was captain of the football team, stroke of the eight and captain of boxing. After being invalided to Malta, thence to England he transferred into the RFC and went to the Western front and to 25 Squadron AFC. Here, after shooting down seven German machines, he was severely wounded in both arms and thigh. After recovering in England he returned to France, having been gazetted captain. In May 1917 he gained the Military Cross, 'For conspicuous gallantry and devotion to duty. He attacked a formation of five hostile scouts and brought two of them down. On another occasion, although wounded, he destroyed two hostile machines and drove down, damaged at least two others.' Richardson would be out of action for seven months, only to meet his death at the hands of Leutnant der Reserve Hans Klein of Royal Prussian Jagdstaffel 4 on Friday the 13th, 1917 while raiding the German lines and communications during the Battle of Arras. [1]

Owen Gower Lewis, a former dux of Melbourne's Wesley College before becoming an observer in 3 Squadron and one of twenty Australian R.E.8 crewmen sent to France for experience with an RFC squadron during August 1917 wrote poignantly: 'It was the fear of the unforeseen, the inescapable, the imminent hand of death which might… be ruthlessly laid upon me. I realised… why pilots cracked up… nobody could stand the strain indefinitely, ultimately it reduced you to a dithering state, near to imbecility… always you had to fight it down, you had to go out and do the job'. Owen was involved in five combats in six days before being shot in the legs and chest on the seventh on 14 August 1917. Lewis and Norman Sharples, his pilot, were sent on a counter battery shoot at 0745 and were just crossing the lines when three German fighters attacked them 'most aggressively' and fired 'a perfect storm of bullets'. Lewis was hit badly in the foot. He carried on however, but his gun was hit and rendered unworkable. Sharples 'dodged about like fury at 120 mph' but Lewis got hit badly again in the right breast. He was bleeding profusely as Sharples made for home as fast as possible. After landing, Sharples took his badly wounded observer to the hospital. Most of the toes on his left foot had been shot away; there were three gunshot wounds in his chest and another one in each of his thighs. Their machine was riddled with bullet holes and had to be written off. Although his injuries were serious, Lewis' doctor told Norman Sharples that he 'had great hopes of him pulling through'. As he made a slow recovery, Sharples was killed in action.

On 17 August 1917, South African General Jan Smuts presented a report to the War Council on the future of air power. Because of its potential for the 'devastation of enemy lands and the destruction of industrial and populous centres on a vast scale', he recommended a new air service be formed that would be on a level with the Army and Royal Navy. The formation of the new service would, moreover, make the underutilised men and machines of the RNAS available for action across the Western Front, as well as ending the inter service rivalries that at times had adversely affected aircraft procurement.'

In April 1918 the British took the pioneer step of uniting all their air units - the fighters and seaplanes of the RNAS and the fighters, bombers and reconnaissance aircraft of the RFC - into a Royal Air Force. Its first commander was Major General Sir Hugh Trenchard. Vice Admiral Sir Arthur Hezlet KBE CB DSO DSC wrote in *Aircraft and Sea Power:* 'On 1 April 1918 the Royal Air Force had been formed. At first this made very little difference and co-operation went on as before. The Admiralty still controlled operations and there was no change of policy in areas which were purely maritime. Nevertheless all operations were now jointly between the Royal Navy and the Royal Air Force to which latter service all aircraft now belonged.'

Endnotes Preface

1   Hans Klein claimed 22 aerial victories and received the Pour le Mérite (the famous 'Blue Max') and the Knight's Cross to the Hohenzollern House Order. Klein joined the Luftwaffe in 1935 as a Major, retiring in 1943 as a Major General. He died in 1944.

Chapter 1

Zeppelin Raid

I saw the people climbing up the street
Maddened with war and strength and thoughts to kill;
And after followed Death, who held with skill
His torn rags royally and stamped his feet.

The fires flamed up and burnt the serried town,
Most where the sadder, poorer houses were;
Death followed with proud feet and smiling stare,
And the mad crowds ran madly up and down.

And many died and hid in unfounded places
In the black ruins of the frenzied night;
And death still followed in his surplice, white
And streaked in imitation of their faces.

But in the morning men began again
To mock Death following in bitter pain.

Zeppelins, a poem written during the bombings of London, is the mourning voice of a young soldier on the Home Front during the First World War by Nancy Clara Cunard (10 March 1896-17 March 1965) who in 1914 was an 18 year-old heiress to the Cunard Shipping firm. As the Zeppelins flew over London, she witnessed the bombing of the city. Late at night during the air raids, searchlights would light up the sky and the crump of bombs could be heard across the town. Policemen would ride around on bicycles, ringing their bells in warning. Londoners would stay in their homes, or if caught out, flee to the tube stops and safety underground. Anti-aircraft guns fired at the Zeppelins overhead as the bombs and incendiaries fell. Some Londoners died of fright: no-one had experienced war this close to home. Nancy Cunard was born into privilege but rejected convention. During the war she married an injured army officer, but this relationship ended after two years. She would go on to live in Paris, helping to support writers and artists with her fortune. Later she would become an anti-fascist campaigner involved in the French Resistance; later still she became a civil liberties protester in the US.

The weekend had been unbearably hot, but towards evening on Sunday 6 June 1915, a brisk cold front advanced from the Atlantic and caused a rapid condensation in the heavy, humid atmosphere. By evening the whole of southern England shivered in a sudden cold snap and, as night fell, mist shrouded the Channel and brought shipping to a halt. No light shone along

the east coast of England for fear of aiding the German Zeppelins. A black-out
had been in force since the first raid over Norfolk on 19 January when the
Norfolk coast was bombarded. Count Ferdinand von Zeppelin, by this time
76-years-old, had been the driving force in the development of the rigid airship
which bore his name. As early as 1908 one of his craft made a twelve hour
flight over Switzerland, which greatly impressed the Count's fellow
countrymen. A year later, he formed the first passenger air-travel company in
the world, which in five years flew 100,000 miles with not a single casualty.

These achievements had not gone unnoticed by the British. The potential
of the Zeppelin to carry troops and bombs to attack the country was evident
and countering technology and tactics were uncertain. It flew high, by the
standards of the day; it had much greater range than heavier-than-air
machines; its payload was substantial. Military planners therefore saw the
Zeppelin as a major threat, a dagger at the throat of a virtually unprotected
Britain.

Germany entered the war with thirty of these monstrous machines - from
five to eight hundred feet long, filled with up to two million cubic feet of highly
combustible hydrogen. In theory they should have been easy targets for
contemporary fighter aircraft, rudimentary though they were. In practice, their
ability to fly at high altitudes and the inadequacies of fighter gun ammunition
proved to offer them a degree of invulnerability in the early stages of the war.

On 14 April 1915, a more serious attack by a Zeppelin was made in
Northumberland, the airship proceeding over Blyth, Wallsend and South
Shields and dropping several bombs without, however, doing much damage.
The following night a Zeppelin visited Essex and Suffolk and dropped bombs
on Maldon and Lowestoft. On 16 April a biplane dropped bombs at Faversham
and Sittingbourne in Kent. Later in the month a Zeppelin attempted to visit
Northumberland again but failed and early on 30 April another airship
dropped bombs at Ipswich and Bury St. Edmunds. On 10 May the Zeppelins
began a new serious succession of raids. On 31 May the Zeppelin raiders
approached their principal goal, the outlying district on one side of London,
and bombs were dropped at places in Essex and Kent. Gun crews shivered in
the isolated emplacements that were dotted about eastern England and since
the raid on London, only a week before, the ground defences around the
capital had been increased. A few second-grade corvettes and light cruisers,
armed with anti-aircraft guns, stood in the Thames to guard the eastern
approaches.

At 10pm on 6 June in a small upstairs room of a house on the Norfolk coast,
an amateur radio enthusiast named Russell Clarke picked up some halting
Morse signals on his home-made short-wave receiver. Clarke, a barrister,
adjusted his earphones and fine-tuned the frequency. The dots and dashes
went on for a time and then stopped. Then, after a time, there came more -
from somewhere closer. He took off his earphones and hurried downstairs to
the telephone. He rang the Admiralty and gave them the frequency. Clarke's
message was received almost thirty minutes before one from the Navy's own
listening station at Hunstanton, by which time the controller at Whitehall was
already plotting the movement of an enemy Zeppelin force, assisted by stations

and ships on the other side of the Channel. (Two naval Zeppelins, L-9 commanded by Kapitänleutnant Heinrich Mathy[1] and probably L-10, under Kapitänleutnant Klaus Hirsch, left their sheds in northern Germany to bomb England. The army airships, LZ-37, LZ-38 and LZ-39, also rose from their sheds in Belgium. Only LZ-37 and LZ-39 came over the sea.[2]

Shortly after 11pm, Whitehall signalled the information to Commander Arthur Longmore, the Officer Commanding the RNAS at Dunkirk, and instructed him to alert his crews for possible action. The course taken by the Zeppelins was carefully plotted and at 12.45am on Monday 7 June, Longmore took action both to intercept the Zeppelins and to shadow them back over the enemy lines and destroy their bases. A few minutes later, Flight Lieutenant Reginald Alexander John Warneford and Sub-Lieutenant John Rose of 1 Squadron RNAS hurried across the mist-shrouded field to two Morane-Saulnier Parasols.[3] As soon as they were in the cockpits, the ground crewmen swung the propellers and the engines spluttered into life and then settled down to a blasting roar. Presently, the two sturdy little monoplanes were jolting across the field. They turned into wind, throttled up to full boost and sped through the grey-black darkness, climbing towards Ghent. Two minutes later, Flight Lieutenant John P. Wilson and Sub-Lieutenant John S. Mills climbed into their larger Henri Farman bombers and took off in the wake of the fighters.

The three Zeppelins moved slowly across the Straits of Dover at 12,000 feet - three huge, grey pencil-like forms nosing above the swirling mist which shrouded the whole of the coastline west of Flanders.

Each of the monsters was an army airship 536 feet in length; its cotton fabric envelope was painted a metallic grey and marked with a large black cross beneath its sharply pointed nose. Powered by four heavy-duty Maybach engines, it was slow in level flight, but, by discharging its water-ballast, it could out-climb any aeroplane, nosing upwards vertically at over 1,200 feet a minute to a height of 23,000 feet. It was armed with five machine-guns - two in each gondola and one in the turret on top of the hull - and it had a bomb-load capacity of almost 1,000lb. Tonight, each of the three Zeppelins were carrying five 110lb bombs and fifty 7lb incendiaries originally intended for London.

The flight was commanded by Germany's newest hero, Hauptmann Erich Linnartz, the veteran Zeppelin commander who, only a week before, had bombed London, inspiring German newspapers to declaim: 'England is no longer an island! At last, the long-yearned-for punishment has befallen England, this people of liars, cynics and hypocrites, a punishment for its countless sins of the past. It is neither blind hatred nor raging anger that inspires our airship heroes, but a religious humility at being chosen the instrument of God's wrath...'

Hauptmann Linnartz's Zeppelin LZ-38, with a crew of three officers and sixteen men, had lifted off from the new Zeppelin base near Brussels late that afternoon. Shortly before dusk over Bruges it had rendezvoused with LZ-37 commanded by Oberleutnant Otto van der Haegen and LZ-39 commanded by Hauptmann Konrad W. Hans Masius. After dark they had crossed the Belgian coast between the lighthouses of Ostend and Zeebrugge. Linnartz knew from experience that a westerly course from here would take them to the outer mouth of the Thames.

The full moon was due to reach its zenith at midnight, when he had planned to arrive over London. But tonight, as they flew seaward, the mist thickened over the Channel and closed right in, bringing visibility to zero. They cut engines and drifted for a time, hoping to find the bottom lip of the Thames estuary, from whence they would turn due west past Herne Bay.

As they drifted over the Straits of Dover, anxiously working out their position, a Morse message came from base: Terminal weather unsuitable. Cancel mission.

They turned east towards France and a further message came through: 'At your discretion, strike alternative target.'

The Zeppelin strike force altered course slightly towards Calais, while Linnartz studied his maps to locate the position of the secondary target - an important rail junction in the Calais area behind the British front.

Warneford and Rose kept in visual contact for a time, their two little monoplanes flying wing to wing south-west towards Calais. Warneford's sleek red and grey Morane-Saulnier was brand new, straight from the French factory a week before. He had fitted a rack beneath the fuselage to hold his bombs and an improvised bomb-release, worked by pulling a cable that had been threaded through a hole in the cockpit floor. While he was waiting for take-off, his mechanic had loaded six 20lb bombs into the rack.

Suddenly, Rose was wobbling his wings to draw his colleague's attention. Warneford saw him give the distress signal and immediately tilt over and disappear into darkness. The lamp on Rose's instrument panel had gone out and he found himself flying blind by sense of touch. He knew that as soon as he lost visual contact with Warneford he would be in trouble, so he tried to make it back to base alone. There was thick fog covering the flax fields near Cassel and Rose's aeroplane hit the earth hard and turned over on its back.

The pilot climbed out unhurt.

Alone now, Warneford flew on, peering through the foggy darkness for a sight of the grey wraith-like shape of a Zeppelin. The Morane-Saulnier's engine was so noisy that there was no hope of hearing the airship's Maybachs. He circled, throttling back... Suddenly, guns opened up below him, a little to the right. He guessed that they were two particular German anti-aircraft guns his fellow pilots had warned him about. They were called 'Archibald' and 'Cuthbert' - high-velocity cannons which could hurl their shells to a height of 22,000 feet. They were firing at the sound of his engine. He cut the power and glided away and the noise of the gun-blasts faded behind him. He flew on, hopefully anticipating the sight of the enemy, though he knew that his chances of seeing anything in this grey-black wall of mist were practically nil. He was now a few miles west of Ostend.

Separated from Rose, Warneford flew on unsure of his whereabouts and utterly alone until he picked out tiny blue exhaust flames beneath a curious elongated cloud. It was some time before he realised that the 'cloud' was in fact an airship, so impressive was its size. Warneford could not believe his eyes. A great grey ghostly shape slid past his windshield and was nosing downwards ahead of him to port. He throttled back, keeping the long, glistening envelope in view, just following, not noting where he was being led. It seemed to go on interminably. He stalked the eerie shape for almost an hour, staying as far behind as possible without losing him. A gusty head-wind had sprung up and he had trouble keeping up with the Zeppelin's four engines. The eastern sky was lit with an early pre-dawn glow and lightening with every minute. He had to stay out of gun-range as the LZ-37 began to lose height and nosed towards the distant Zeppelin base of Gontrode. Suddenly a machine-gun chattered and shells and tracer ripped past the Morane-Saulnier's wings. The gunner in the turret on the topside of the Zeppelin was blasting away at him to frighten him off. Oberleutenant Otto van der Haegen, grabbed the intercom phone.

'What are you shooting at?' he demanded.

'An aeroplane,' the gunner said, 'Three hundred metres astern.'

Haegen alerted the four gondola gun-crews and two of them opened up on the monoplane.

Warneford banked and climbed, keeping his distance, getting out of sight of the gondola gun crews. He made a wide climbing circuit, content to bide his time, to watch for any sudden move, very aware of the Zeppelin's capacity to out-climb him. He let the minutes go by, content to stalk the monster, exhilarated at the chance of bagging such a prize with his pathetic bomb-load attached to the rudimentary undercarriage rack. His chance came when Haegen suddenly put down the LZ-37's bow and headed for Gontrode, his four Maybach engines at full-throttle. Warneford watched, bringing the Morane-Saulnier into position where he could turn and fly straight and level above the path of the diving airship. He advanced the throttle to bring his aircraft almost 900 feet directly above and then cut his power and dived in a tight spin to within 150 feet before giving a pull on the bomb release, dropping his bombs and flattening away. As he fled, frantically turning on full throttle to escape the blast, an enormous, jarring explosion rent the air and Warneford's midget monoplane was thrown up two hundred feet, whipping violently over on its back - the great Zeppelin had become a blinding ball of flame.

Obersteuerman Alfred Mühler, the LZ-37's helmsman, felt the giant ship lurch and the helm was ripped from his hands. He was skidding, almost flying across the sharply tilted deck, four other crew members with him. His head struck a metal upright and stunned him. He grasped it and held on. There was no-one else on the deck. They had all gone overboard. Above him, the whole ship was a hissing, twisting, roaring inferno. He lay flat on the deck, the flames licking down on him, roasting him alive, as the forward gondola fell and kept on falling.

Warneford recovered and then circled, dazed, elated and trembling with shock and relief, as he watched the giant airship's dying minutes. There was a hissing roar as it threw off great ragged pieces of flaming debris. The huge envelope fell slowly to earth, twisting, contracting, writhing and shooting out bursts of coloured flame - red, blue, orange - lighting as bright as day the countryside around the Mont-Sint-Amand area of Ghent.

LZ-37's flaming forward section crashed through the roof of a dormitory at the Convent of St. Elisabeth, setting fire to the building and killing two nuns and two orphan children and injuring many others. Mühler, still alive, though terribly burned, felt himself somersaulting through the air, and then he blacked out. He was saved by a fall through the roof into a bed! He was the only survivor of the crew of ten.

Warneford was in trouble. The violent blast had knocked his fuel-line loose and he knew he would have to make a forced landing behind enemy lines.

Thirty miles away, Wilson and Mills saw the glow as they were arriving over the big Zeppelin shed at Évère, where they had followed the LZ-38. As their labouring Farmans roared across the target, the Zeppelin was already on the ground and being handled into its hangar. Wilson banked in a wide turn to position his aeroplane for a bombing run. Searchlights picked him up as he began his approach. On a sudden inspiration he seized his flashlight and blinked it on and off through the wind-shield. The Germans held their fire. In the confusion, Wilson and Mills made perfect runs over the hangar and dropped their bombs, which exploded through the iron roof with a clatter of sound and set the Zeppelin on fire. Linnartz and his crew escaped unhurt.

Meanwhile, Warneford had set his monoplane down safely in a clear patch of field. He quickly fixed his fuel-line with a piece of wire and took off again. But his engine was spluttering now and missing badly. In trying to urge some power out of it, he strayed off course in the deceptive half-light and lost his bearings. After flying on for a time, trying to find his way, he turned north and headed for the coast, meeting the sea at Cap Griz Nez. Realizing that he was thirty-five miles too far west, he banked and set course for Dunkirk. Then the engine cut out and he began to lose height quickly. He came down on a wide, flat stretch of wet sand left visible by the ebbing tide. He soon located the source of the problem; a severed fuel line. He successfully managed to effect a repair with a piece of rag and a cigarette holder before swinging the Morane propeller, diving into the cockpit as the machine rolled and taking off into the night.

After landing at Cape Gris Nez for refuelling, Warneford eventually returned safely to Furnes, arriving at noon, and was welcomed by the cheers of his fellow pilots for news of LZ-37's destruction had preceded him. Their adulation was swiftly followed by the award of the Victoria Cross on 11 June 1915. Six days later he was further decorated with the French Legion d'Honneur and after the presentation he went on to Buc in order to pick up a replacement Henri Farman pusher biplane for the squadron. At the airfield he was introduced to Henry Beach Needham, an American reporter who pleaded to occupy the spare seat in Warneford's machine so that he could visit the Flight at Furnes and write a feature on the action. Warneford offered no objections and they set off to the airfield on the coast. Soon after the aircraft had taken off, however, it appeared to become uncontrollable and with wings folding, it spun to the ground, tossing its unbelted occupants out in the process; both were killed. Legend has it that Warneford was still suffering the after-effects of a wild party thrown the night before, but this was never conclusively proven. The body of Warneford was taken to England and buried at Brompton Cemetery in London on 22 June.

In Germany, a shattered High Command analysed the disaster. So shocked were they by the loss of the two Zeppelins that they temporarily halted the army's airship raids. It was left to Führer der Luftschiffer (Leader of airships) Kapitän Peter Strasser's naval Zeppelins to make Germany's yearned-for, but abortive attempt to destroy London the following September.

By the standards of the day, the German airship raids on Britain were terrifying and effective. In the course of the war, more than 200 Zeppelin flights unloaded nearly 6,000 bombs on the country, killing 522 people. British strategy had been rightly focused on elimination of this weapon as a high priority. It was only the speed of the German advance that thwarted the attempt. Three years elapsed before the end of the airship bombardment. In 1917, strong air defence and bad weather broke up a mass raid over London. All the Zeppelins taking part were destroyed. The Germans attempted no more airship attacks on Britain.

Endnotes Chapter 1

1   Kapitänleutnant Heinrich Mathy, born 4 April 1883 at Mannheim, was a household name in Britain. During the 'Zeppelin Scourge' 1915-1916 he was feared as the most daring and audacious of all the Zeppelin raiders. During his two summers at the 'Marine Akademie' in 1913 and 1914 he flew in Count Fedinand von Zeppelin's dirigible airships. At the beginning of 1915 Mathy was transferred to airships at the insistence of Peter Strasser and took part in his first raid on England on 13 January, being forced to turn back on this occasion because of bad weather. Later, he flew on several raids, usually over Northern England. On 8 September 1915, Mathy's L-13 caused great damage by fire to the central area of London and again on the night of 13/14 October. On 24/25 August 1916, in command of L-31, Mathy attacked London once more, again causing considerable damage. While the L-31 was grounded for repairs, news came in that the British had, for the first time, shot down an airship by using incendiary bullets. Attacking London again on 1/2 October 1916, L-31 was shot down in flames by 2nd Lieutenant W. J. Tempest, the ship falling just outside Potters Bar. Mathy's body was found some way from the wreckage of the ship, half-embedded in the corner of a field. His last act had been to leap clear of the falling inferno rather than wait for the crash. According to some accounts, he lived for a few minutes after striking the earth.

2   LZ-38 descended almost immediately. (LZ-37 and LZ-39 were unable to find the English coast, probably owing to fog). LZ-39 returned safely to her shed but LZ-38 was destroyed in an aeroplane attack on her shed at Évère, near Brussels at 0230 on 7 June. Both L-9 and L-10 reached the Norfolk coast at about 1930, when L-10 had to abandon the raid and turn back after suffering engine trouble. Mathy, in L-9, which was clearly identified 12 miles north-east of Mundesley on the Norfolk coast at 2015, went on to bomb Hull and other towns. *Zeppelin Blitz: The German Air Raids on Great Britain During The First World War* by Neil R. Storey (The History Press, 2015).

3   Born in Darjeeling, India on 15 October 1891 Warneford was initially educated at Simla and then England where he ended the Stratford-upon-Avon Grammar School. The Warneford family later moved to Canada, where he soon showed a mechanical flair and he joined the Indian Steam Navigation Company on the outbreak of war. Fearful that the war might end before he got a chance to participate, Warneford returned to England to join up. Headstrong and impetuous, he quickly tired of the Army and in 1915 successfully gained his wings after pilot training in the RNAS and was subsequently posted to 2 Squadron RNAS at Eastchurch on the Thames estuary. On 7 May 1915 he joined 1 Squadron at Dunkirk under Squadron Commander (later Air Chief Marshal, Sir) Arthur Longmore. Warneford soon made a name for himself after several hectic sorties over enemy lines. As Dunkirk seemed an obvious target for the Germans, the Motley collection of squadron aircraft was dispersed and Warneford soon found himself at Furnes, along with Lieutenant J. P. Wilson, Sub-Lieutenant J. S. Mills and Squadron Commander Spenser Grey.

Chapter 2

Home Defence Hero

In view of the fact that the year 1916 saw the height of the German airship campaign, it is desirable to give some account of the activities of the air station on the night of a raid. The following description was written about this time by one of the officers of the station: 'Our actual sleeping quarters are about one and a half miles from the actual sheds and the aerodrome. On about five successive nights now, just as we were sitting down to dinner, a Zeppelin would be reported approaching the coast somewhere on our beat. Result - a general 'hoo-doo'. All the pilots jump into cars and dash down to the sheds, closely followed by all the mechanics in lorries. As our way is right along the front, several cars and two 4-ton lorries loaded with men hustling down to the air station frighten the whole of Yarmouth. On arriving down there our machines are put on the Denes and engines tested - perhaps some unlucky fellow is sent up to do a patrol, the night being as black as pitch... We all sit round the fire in the Officers' quarters down there, waiting for news. Suddenly the telephone rings - an officer is wanted immediately on the 'phone - the others try to read the message by the look on his face. Then he announces that the Zeppelin is travelling north, east, south or west, anywhere but towards us - rather a relief.

Or the other thing may happen - the roar of engines, everyone getting rattled - and then up go the machines, racing backward and forward along the coast, searching the sky or the depths beneath them for any signs of enemy activity. Having stayed up their appointed periods, the sky above the aerodrome is suddenly lit up by the firing of a Very light - the sign that the machine is about to come down. Almost instantaneous with the firing of the light, the inky sky is illuminated by countless flares placed in two long lines the length of the Denes, about 150 yards separating the lines of blazing petrol. There is a roar and a whistling of wind and a machine glides and bumps to the earth between the two rows of fire and almost before the machine comes to a standstill it is swallowed up in the night, the flares being dowsed with a surprising rapidity lest a Zeppelin should be attracted to the spot by the glare.

This is a fairly detailed account of what happens when Zeppelins are near and machines go up. On occasions when they do not actually come near we sit down there waiting and waiting sometimes till dawn breaks for the telephone to blurt out its unwelcome message. I only wish I could give some of those blighters, who wrote to the papers asking what the RNAS is doing and if machines are up at night in full force, one short trip at night... The feeling of absolute loneliness - no passenger being carried - is almost unbearable. Nothing to see save a thin gleam of silver where the waves break on the shore and give off a phosphorescent glint. If it was not for the compass it would be impossible to tell which was land and which was sea. Then the beastly descent, knowing that there is enough explosive beneath one, in the bombs, to blow up the air station. This, mercifully, has been changed, as now all bombs are to be dropped into the sea before landing. One such ride, even if it only lasted for ten minutes instead of two hours, would make these busybodies sit up and think twice before they asked questions on subjects they know nothing about! Still, after all, what we have to put up with is infinitesimal, when compared with what the poor devils in the trenches go through - and we try to remember this.'

Great Yarmouth Air Station by C. F. Snowden Gamble.

In 1916 William Leefe Robinson became the first recipient of the Victoria Cross awarded for action over the British Isles. This award was to remain unique until World War II when Flight Lieutenant James Nicolson was a recipient of the award during action in the Battle of Britain. Leefe Robinson, the youngest of a family of seven, was born in Tollidetta, South Coorg, India on 14 July 1895, the youngest son of Horace Robinson and Elizabeth Leefe. Raised on his parents' coffee estate, Kaima Betta Estate, at Pollibetta, in Coorg, Leefe attended Bishop Cotton Boys' School, Bangalore and when the family moved back to England, the Dragon School, Oxford, before following his elder brother Harold to St. Bees School, Cumberland in September 1909. While there he succeeded his brother as Head of Eaglesfield House in 1913, played in the Rugby 1st XV and became a sergeant in the school Officer Training Corps. In August 1914 he entered the Royal Military College, Sandhurst and was gazetted into the Worcestershire Regiment in December. In March 1915 he went to France as an observer with the RFC, to which he had transferred. After having been wounded over Lille he underwent pilot training in Britain, before being attached to 39 (Home Defence) Squadron, a night-flying squadron at Sutton's Farm airfield near Hornchurch in Essex.

Wounded and sent back to Britain. Leefe Robinson took up pilot training and was eventually posted to 39 (Home Defence) Squadron at Suttons Farm, Essex. The unit was one of several squadrons hastily-formed to help combat the ever-growing threat of the Zeppelin airships which frequently raided London. The Squadron was equipped with converted B.E.2c aircraft with upward-firing machine guns and, although they were vulnerable on the Western Front, they proved to be ideal for attacking Zeppelins. However, for many months the failure of the gun crews stationed around London and the seeming invulnerability of the Zeppelins weighed heavily.

On the evening of 2/3 September 1916 the German army and navy airship divisions joined forces to mount a mammoth raid on London involving sixteen dirigibles for the largest airship raid of the war over England. It was 2308 hours when Suttons Farm learned that Zeppelins had been sighted and Leefe Robinson and other Home Defence pilots were soon in the air to meet the enemy.

The first airship Leefe Robinson sighted was Kapitän Ernst August Lehmann's LZ-98, an army ship. However, the German lost his pursuer in heavy cloud and after fifteen minutes the British pilot gave up the chase. Flying towards sweeping searchlights Leefe Robinson found another airship. It was the German Army's recently-commissioned wooden-framed Schütte-Lanz SL-11, commanded by Hauptmann Wilhelm Schramm, which had arrived over northern London at St. Albans. Schramm had been born at Old Charlton, Kent and lived in England until the age of 15 when, on the death of his father, the

London representative of the Siemens electrical firm, he returned to Germany and joined the army. He was given his first command in December 1915. As SL-11 bombed the northern suburbs, the airship was picked up by searchlights at Finsbury and Victoria Parks. Turning back to the north, the SL-11 was spotted by Second Lieutenant Robinson. Although two other pilots dived on the vessel, he was first to the action. Despite having anti-aircraft fire bracketing the ship, Robinson pressed home his attack, diving underneath and emptying a whole drum of ammunition into the hull. When this had no effect, he made a second run with another drum of ammunition, meeting with a similar result. Changing to his final drum of ammunition the British pilot tried another tactic and poured the entire contents into one area beneath the huge tail fins. The trail of tracer bullets disappeared into the airship's fabric and the Lewis gun fell silent. Suddenly a dull pinkish glow appeared deep inside the airship and in seconds the whole tail was ablaze with flames which towered a hundred feet high.

The L-16, commanded by Kapitänleutnant Erich Sommerfeld was less than a mile away from SL-11 when she burst into flames and she attracted the attention of one of the British pilots chasing SL-11. Sommerfeld however, sped off to the north, escaping the glare before the British planes could arrive at his position. Of all the airships, Oberleutnant zur See Kurt Frankenberg in the L-21 correctly deduced the cause of SL-11's loss. He and his crew thirty miles to the north could plainly see two aircraft around the Army airship and after she caught fire, one was seen to drop red and green flares (which Robinson did). The rest of the airships completed their bombing runs all across eastern England and safely returned to their bases, having dropped a total of 17 tons of explosives on English soil. The bombing caused £21,000 worth of damage, at the cost of sixteen airshipmen dead and one £93,000 airship lost. The doomed airship was seen by Londoners as a ball of fire which grew bigger and exploded with a brilliant flare. The civilians watched the blazing hulk 11,500 feet above hang motionless for several seconds before it finally slid out of the sky to fall and crash in a field behind the 'Plough Inn' at Cufley in Hertfordshire where it burned for over two hours. After a flight of over three hours Leefe Robinson had very little petrol left and, following his return to Suttons Farm, he scribbled a report and collapsed into a sleep which remained unbroken until his fellow pilots woke him on Sunday morning and drove him over to the wreck.

In his combat report to his Commanding Officer, Leefe Robinson wrote:
Sir:
I have the honour to make the following report on night patrol made by me on the night of the 2-3 instant. I went up at about 11.08 pm on the night of the second with instructions to patrol between Sutton's Farm and Joyce Green.
I climbed to 10,000 feet in fifty-three minutes. I counted what I thought were ten sets of flares - there were a few clouds below me, but on the whole it was a beautifully clear night. I saw nothing until 1.10 am, when two searchlights picked up a Zeppelin SE of Woolwich. The clouds had collected in this quarter and the searchlights had some difficulty in keeping on the airship.
By this time I had managed to climb to 12,000 feet and I made in the direction of

the Zeppelin - which was being fired on by a few anti-aircraft guns - hoping to cut it off on its way eastward. I very slowly gained on it for about ten minutes.

I judged it to be about 800 feet below me and I sacrificed some speed in order to keep the height. It went behind some clouds, avoiding the searchlight and I lost sight of it. After fifteen minutes of fruitless search I returned to my patrol.

I managed to pick up and distinguish my flares again. At about 1.50 a.m. I noticed a red glow in the N.E. of London. Taking it to be an outbreak of fire, I went in that direction. At 2.05 a Zeppelin was picked up by the searchlights over NNE London (as far as I could judge).

Remembering my last failure, I sacrificed height (I was at about 12,900 feet) for speed and nosed down in the direction of the Zeppelin. I saw shells bursting and night tracers flying around it.

When I drew closer I noticed that the anti-aircraft aim was too high or too low; also a good many shells burst about 800 feet behind - a few tracers went right over. I could hear the bursts when about 3,000 feet from the Zeppelin.

I flew about 800 feet below it from bow to stem and distributed one drum among it (alternate New Brock and Pomeroy). It seemed to have no effect; I therefore moved to one side and gave them another drum along the side - also without effect. I then got behind it and by this time I was very close - 500 feet or less below and concentrated one drum on one part (underneath rear). I was then at a height of 11,500 feet when attacking the Zeppelin.

I had hardly finished the drum before I saw the part fired at, glow. In a few seconds the whole rear part was blazing. When the third drum was fired, there were no searchlights on the Zeppelin and no anti-aircraft was firing.

I quickly got out of the way of the falling, blazing Zeppelin and, being very excited, fired off a few red Very lights and dropped a parachute flare.

Having little oil or petrol left, I returned to Sutton's Farm, landing at 2.45 am. On landing, I found the Zeppelin gunners had shot away the machine-gun wire guard, the rear part of my centre section and had pierced the main spar several times.

I have the honour to be, sir,
Your obedient servant,
(Signed)
W. Leefe Robinson, Lieutenant
No. 39 Squadron RFC.

Already the area was seething with police, army personnel and civilians: all the pilots could see was a high tangle of wire, charred fragments of the wooden hull and four burned-out engines strewn over a wide area. These pathetic remnants were all that remained of the SL-11: the first airship to fall over England (though at the time and for many years after, it was misidentified as Zeppelin L-21). In a corner of the field a green tarpaulin covered the charred bodies of thirty-year-old Hauptmann Wilhelm Schramm and his crew of fifteen who were later buried with full military honours at Potters Bar.

As a result of his victory, Lieutenant William Leefe Robinson received the Victoria Cross, an award of £3,500 in prize money and a silver cup donated by the people of Hornchurch and the adoration of thousands. On 16 September Robinson crashed his aircraft when attempting to take off for a night patrol. It was a total wreck and he escaped just before it was consumed by fire. This incident led to his being grounded, as he was too valuable a national figure, with a long string of official engagements, to run these risks. However, after continual pestering of the authorities to allow him to return to active service, in April 1917 Robinson was posted to France as a Flight Commander with 48 Squadron at La Bellevue, flying the then new Bristol F.2a, which evolved into the famous F.2b Fighter. On the first patrol over the lines, on 5 April, Robinson led five F.2a aircraft on their first operational sortie over the lines with the fixed plan that, if attacked, the group was to adopt a tight circle, each gunner protecting the aircraft behind it with his field of fire. These were fine tactics for lumbering F.E.2b pushers but not for such a new fighting machine. Thus the stage was set for disaster. They encountered five Albatros D.III fighters of Jasta 11, led by Manfred von Richthofen and in a battle which lasted barely ten minutes four F.2a's were shot down. Robinson was wounded and captured. He was posted as dead, until two months later when a letter arrived from him in a PoW camp.

Zeppelin, Zeppelin, burning bright
Over Dover in the night;
Sometimes over Folkestone too,
What is there 'twixt me and you?

Zeppelin, Zeppelin, how I wish
You were but a silver fish;
Swimming like a submarine,
Underneath the ocean green.

Zeppelin, Zeppelin, your delight
Is in dropping bombs at night;
How I wish that you and I
Were dropping bombs on Germany!
Maurice Baring, 14 June 1916

Chapter 3

Night Flying

A.R. Kingsford

Alfred Reginald Bellingham-Kingsford was born on 4 May 1891, at Maidstone, Kent. He was the only son of dairy farmer Alfred Kingsford who died whilst 'Reg' was still a child. He was apprenticed to a photographer during his early teens and then emigrated to Australia at the age of 19, to take up a photographic appointment in Sydney. He later moved to Moree to join a friend working there as a stockman, before sailing to New Zealand to take up an offer of employment in a photographic studio in Nelson. This was where the outbreak of the First World War found him. Reg volunteered and sailed to Egypt shortly after war was declared, enlisting in the Medical Corps - the 6th Reinforcements of the 2nd NZ Division, NZEF. Surviving the torpedoing of HMT Marquette he served as a corporal from 1914 to 1917, the year in which he married. In 1917 whilst in France, he transferred to the RFC. Second Lieutenants Alfred Kingsford, 'Brooky', 'Inky' and 'Waty' Watson, having completed aerial fighting and gunnery school training at Turnberry in Scotland, were posted to 33 Squadron as Home Defence Operation pilots, much to their disgust.[1]

33 Squadron had formed from part of 12 Squadron at Filton on 12 January 1916, as part of an initiative to counter the Zeppelin raids. Until then, the responsibility for Britain's air defence lay with the RNAS and the Admiralty. A new organisation, the Home Defence, was formed which became the responsibility of the War Office and who introduced a spread of defence airfields from Kent to the Firth of Forth. 33 Squadron based its HQ in Gainsborough (including a small landing ground) and set up three airfields at Elsham, Kirton Lindsey and Brattleby. Gainsborough included the Squadron workshops. First equipped with B.E.2s, these were supplemented with F.E.2s. The latter were replaced by Bristol Fighters in June 1918, which were in turn replaced by dedicated night fighter Avro 504 in August. The squadron did not destroy any enemy airships, despite a number of interceptions. 33 Squadron was disbanded in June 1919. In addition to Home Defence air defence patrols, 33 Squadron trained pilots and observers in night flying. C Flight, at Elsham Wolds, co-operated with the artillery batteries located at Spurn Head and Kilnsea.

'Our new aerodrome was a good one and a decided change after Hounslow. It was about three-quarters of a mile long, with a good width. In addition to the Home Defence Flight, there were two training squadrons flying Avros, B.Es and an odd 'Spad'[2] or two. There was plenty of activity.

Our machines were F.E.2b's, equipped with 160hp Beardmore engine. A machine gun was fixed to the front seat, to be used by the observer. There were three machines, with the same number of pilots and observers for operation. Emergency landing flares, which could be ignited by pressing a button in the cockpit, were fixed under each of the lower planes. A parachute flare could also be dropped from the back seat. This would hang in the air and light up the ground for about three minutes. There were also three other machines, used for training purposes.

'Ours was 'A' Flight, while 'B' and 'C' were thirty miles north and west. Our patrol was north to the Humber and ten miles south of Lincoln.

'After a few flights, we realised that these buses were totally unfit for the job. They were not capable of climbing higher than about twelve thousand feet, while the Zepps seldom came over at less than eighteen to twenty thousand. We expressed our views and were granted permission to do anything with the machines to enable them to get higher. This caused tremendous competition between the three of us. Ceiling tests were frequent, without producing anything startling until the engine was taken out of my bus and a three hundred Rolls Royce put in. With this extra power, we expected something great, but even then, old 1884 would not go higher than sixteen thousand and it took nearly an hour to get there. I did away with the observer, put the machine gun on to a mounting to enable the pilot to use it, placed a cowling over the front seat and streamlined it and then re-rigged her. But I only got another hundred feet, so we took the cowling off again. It seemed hopeless trying to get Zepps in these antiquated machines.

'England's aerial defence at this time was pretty rotten and the Hun could have done what he liked with us had he known. That's what makes me think that his secret service couldn't have been what it was cracked up to be, or he would have known just how weak our defence was. However, we did our best in the circumstances. I think Robinson, Brandon, Tempest[3] and those chaps must have got their Zepps at lower altitudes, probably when they came down to do their bombing. They were in B.E.'s and perhaps got a bit more out of them than we did out of our old 'Fees'.

'The Huns' Zepp Base was at Heligoland, due east of Spurn Head. His course was due west until he struck Spurn Head, where he would pick up the lights of Hull, invariably turning south and passing right over our aerodrome, then picking up Lincoln and apparently following the Northern Railway down to London. He always came in what we called the dark period, when there was no moon and during this time we were not allowed to leave the aerodrome after dark, operation pilots standing by the whole time, with machines ready and ears pricked up every time the telephone bell rang. We always hoped it would be orders to take the air, our first intimation usually being from the Navy. 'Zepps sighted forty miles east Spurn Head, proceeding west,' later, 'Zepps still proceeding west, now twenty miles from coast.' At this stage, the first operation pilot would be ordered up with certain instructions, the remaining two at ten-minute intervals. Our patrol was for three hours and we took our turn in being first.

'Owing chiefly to the fog, England was not the best of countries for flying, particularly at night. The fog was our worst foe and, being near the coast, we had to be extra careful not to go wandering out over the sea, a matter very easily accomplished at night in a fog. Two or three of our chaps went west that way and we never heard of them again. We could only conclude that the North Sea claimed them as victims.

'On 21 August 1917 I took the air in quest of Zepps for the first time. We received our first news of them at ten-thirty pm and at eleven o'clock, Robiers and I taxied out, having been given a great send-off. All the pupils from the training squadrons used to turn out to see our show and would hang about all night for our return.

'We circled the aerodrome for some time to gain height and then turned north, registering 5,000. The night was beautifully clear and starlit, but cold and we tootled along past the blast furnaces at Scunthorpe, where the reflection could be seen for miles. No doubt the Hun knew the position of this furnace and it would help him to get his bearings. Why they didn't try to lessen the flare we could never understand and it was some considerable time before they thought to do so.

'By the time we reached the Humber, our height was 10,000 and again we circled round and round to get higher, both piercing the darkness with bulging eyes in the endeavour to glimpse a target. Seeing a searchlight pop up over Hull, we set our nose in that direction and soon there were about half a dozen, lighting up the sky. This show promised well. We were now over the Humber, just about where the ZR.2 broke her back some time later. We were hoping to break the back of a Zepp before long.

'I don't know what Robie's eyes were like, but mine seemed to be nearly out of my head by this time. Shells were bursting all over the place, although there was no sign of the Zepp as far as I could see. Our altimeter showed twelve thousand. Gee! This old bus was slow, but I had a feeling that our luck was going to be in. We were now off our patrol, but what did that matter so long as there was something doing. The gun-fire stopped and the searchlights were scanning to and fro, an almost certain sign that they'd lost him. Our hopes went down correspondingly, as one by one the searchlights lowered, until all was darkness again and the Zepp went gaily on her errand of destruction.

'We groped around for another two hours, realising that we'd been pretty near and still not wishing to give up all hope, saw the remaining hour out and then, benzine being low, were obliged to land. We longed for the next raid and began to feel that after all there was a certain amount of fun in Zepp hunting, never knowing when you might spot one, even if he was 5,000 feet above you.

'Brooky and Watson were both down when we arrived. Like us, they had seen the gun-fire and sat with bulging eyes. No one got a Zepp that night, but poor old Joe, one of 'B' Flight's pilots, crashed on landing and was killed.

'The next dark period was a disappointing one; the Huns left us alone and we were very peeved. All kinds of new gadgets had been invented and adorned the cockpits. Reid, my new observer, was itching to hunt the skies and we did a good deal of night flying without incident or crashes, save for one fatality, for which I was responsible.

'We were carrying out forced landings one night and I pushed the parachute flare through the tube, but it failed to ignite. A few days later, a bill for twenty-five pounds was presented to me by a farmer, who called at the aerodrome with the complaint that the flare had hit his pet horse on the head. The following morning, Tony did not answer the roll call.

'About this time, the Americans sent over two hundred of their picked men for the Flying Corps. The heads didn't know what to do with them, as the training squadrons were all going hard with our own pupils. Eventually they sent a few to each Home Defence Flight and in our spare time we were told we could teach them something.

'Eight of them turned up at our Flight, good chaps too and we enjoyed their company. Big Jeff was full of good humour, stood six feet odd and weighed about fifteen stone. I pictured him trying to get into the cockpit of a 'Spad' or Sopwith Pup, but anyway, our Jeff turned out a good flyer and flew in the Dole Race.

'Ned was a great boy, too, full of Yankee stories and he used to have competitions with Sid to see who could yarn the most. They introduced all sorts of new drinks into the mess, port flips, egg flips, all sorts of flips. One of their number would get up and act as shaker, mixing the concoction, then shaking at considerable length in a metal tumbler arrangement with a lid. After it was shaken into what appeared to be all froth, he would triumphantly hand you the mixture and if you blew the froth off, you blew the drink away. Nevertheless, the port flip was quite a decent thirst quencher.

'These chaps were the keenest mob for flying I ever struck. They were willing to go up any time, in any weather and with anyone, irrespective of their ability as a pilot. Jeff loved speed and I used to take him up in the F.E.2d which I used for operations. The machine did about ninety full out, which in those days wasn't bad.

'On one occasion we were up about five hundred feet, when he yelled over from the front seat.

'Won't she go any faster?'

'Yes,' I called back, 'you watch her.' I accordingly stuck her nose down, with the engine full on and lowered to about fifty feet off the ground and one hundred and forty miles per hour holding her there until I thought the wings might buckle and watching Jeff all the time. He never grabbed hold of the sides until he thought I'd gone mad and was going to fly straight into the earth and then I pulled her up in a great zoom, finishing up in a climbing turn. He turned round as I flattened out again and at first his face was a blank, then it suddenly lit up and he yelled:

'Gee! Boy; that was great.' He'd had his first real thrill in the air, he said. The next time I took him up, we reached twelve thousand and his nose started to bleed all over the show. He was in some pickle by the time we got down and I told him it was due to too many port flips. Jeff was annoyed and asked me not to let any of the boys know. He was afraid it might be looked upon as a physical defect and be the result of his getting chucked out. I believe that would have sent him potty, he was so keen.

We did lots of bombing practice and machine gunning for these chaps and now and then a little visiting to the other Flights. 'C' Flight over at Kelstern was a favourite flip for Jeff and myself.

'Our next Zepp raid did not take place until October eighteen. Something must have gone wrong that night. We had a warning and were up at the Hangars, machines ready and flares alight, with the usual crowd to see the fun. We were standing by our machines and I was booked to take the air first, when, without any warning, there was a terrific explosion on the far side of the landing ground, followed by another at not half a minute's interval.

'Even then we did not realise what it was until Reid, my observer, who was standing by, grabbed my arm and said:

'Listen, can't you hear it?' There was no doubt about it now, a Zepp was right overhead and there were we, still on the ground, waiting for orders to go up. The

Zepp had seen our landing lights. We waited no longer for orders, Reid swung the prop, kicked the chocks away, hopped in and off we went, realising that it was a golden opportunity lost. A Zepp and right over our aerodrome; how on earth it had got so far without our receiving orders, puzzled us. Someone had been lax of course and by the time we reached any height worth mentioning, the Zepp was probably fifty to a hundred miles away.

'We patrolled to and from the Humber to south of Lincoln and two hours passed. Having nothing to do, we were frozen and I gazed overboard, to see the landing lights of an aerodrome burning. We turned north again, noticing the beauty of the starlit night, although, as we neared the river once more, things appeared rather hazy and by the time we had reached our most northerly point and turned south, nothing could be seen at all. The familiar ground lights had disappeared and we seemed to have run into a cloud, so we continued south for a bit, thinking we were somewhere near our own aerodrome. We came lower to see what it was like - at 14,000 everything was thick, fog everywhere. Pulling the throttle back, we dived down a couple of thousand feet, but it was still so thick that I couldn't see Reid's head in the front seat. I was obliged to fly by the bubble to keep her on an even keel and came down to three thousand. Trying a few miles in every direction in hopes of finding a clear patch, proved without avail, dense fog enveloped everything. We couldn't even find our way down at a few hundred feet, our three hours was up and I knew that our benzine supply must be pretty low. Anyhow, we had to land somewhere, but where? We were in a rotten hole. Reid called over:

'What are you going to do?'

'Land as soon as I can see where to,' I replied, then turned her north and decided to give it another ten minutes. My altitude was showing three hundred feet. Fortunately it was flat country and I knew we were pretty safe, my only fear being that we might get out to sea, as the coast was only twenty miles from our aerodrome and in such a dense fog it was easily done.

'After proceeding north for a short time, Reid yelled excitedly:

'Lights, slightly to the port side.'

'We made for them right away, came down to one hundred feet and flew round a few times.

'What do you make of them?' I yelled to Reid.

'Looks like an emergency landing,' he said.

'It certainly did too, for there was the long and short arm of the letter 'L' dimly discernible through the fog. The parachute flare lit all right when I pushed it through, but it seemed to make matters worse and increase the haze near the ground. Waiting for it to burn out, I decided I'd have to land without lights. We couldn't have been fifty feet up now and I turned round into position and, throttling back in the fog, misjudged the distance. Before either of us knew anything, we had hit the ground. Reid was thrown clear, turning a complete somersault as he left the bus, while I managed to knock out some teeth on the dashboard. The machine presented a good picture, with crushed under-carriage and tail up in the air.

'Two mechanics who were posted at these emergency stations came rushing out.

'All right, Sir?' one inquired.

'Yes and damned glad to get down,' said Reid. 'Give us a cigarette.'

'Gosh, you weren't half lucky, Sir,' the mechanic said, 'we heard you for some time up in that fog, wonder you didn't knock the top off something flying around here.'

'Next morning, we realised just how true his words were. We had landed at an emergency ground just south of the Humber and our OC had rung up, hoping to get news of us. They had tried to recall us with rockets owing to the bad weather coming.

'With the aid of these rockets, Brooky and Watson got down all right and we wished we had done the same. Still, we were safe, although I felt annoyed that the old bus was damaged.

'We arrived back at our aerodrome the following afternoon and found them relieved beyond measure to know of our safety. One of C Flight's had forced landed the same as ourselves and one of B Flight's had not been heard of. The worst was feared and our suspicions were verified a few days later when some wreckage of an aeroplane was found by a trawler in the North Sea.

This Zepp strafing job wasn't much good, so Brooky and I decided to put in a request to be transferred overseas.

'That night, the Zepps had a bad spin too, five being brought down one way and another. One surprised a sector in the southern part of the line in France, by looming out of the fog just over their heads in the early hours of the morning, giving them good target practice.

'A week after this incident, Brooky and I were sent down to Lympne, near Folkestone, to ferry two new buses back to Scampton. We left Lympne about three o'clock in the afternoon of a winter's day and reckoned on reaching Hounslow in order to spend the night there. On arriving at dusk the OC seemed like a bear with a sore head, must have had a night out, we thought. At any rate, he told us we couldn't stay there, his hangars were full up.

'And you can't leave new machines out all night' he said, 'you'll have to go on to Hendon.' There was a bit of mist about too and we knew we had valuable aeroplanes with us. It had been impressed on us before leaving that we could not, on any account, take risks with them. We were keen to land the machines safely at Scampton, so there was nothing for it but to push on, more especially as the OC ordered us to leave. We arranged to keep together, both knowing the country pretty well and providing we could pick up the Welsh Harp, we would be all right. It was quite near Hendon aerodrome, but the landing ground in those days was not good, just a three-cornered place, with the railway running along one side.

'Immediately we got up, we lost sight of one another and the increasing darkness gave us no time to look round. Luckier than Brooky, I picked up the Welsh Harp and was set. Landing in the dark, however, I very narrowly escaped disaster, for my wheels touched ground not two yards away from a large hole in the middle of the aerodrome, made by the Huns in their last raid. I could just see a flag sticking up as I passed over and wondered why the dickens it hadn't been filled in before. I went and had a look at it and realised how near a smash I'd been.

'Brooky and I had previously arranged, in the event of being parted, to meet at the Strand Palace and I waited about for him, but he failed to put in an appearance until just after nine o'clock. He had landed down at Northolt and was obliged to wait for a train to town.

'The following three or four days proved impossible for flying, thick fog predominating everywhere. We went to our respective aerodromes each morning, hanging around all day for nearly a week, until one morning I rang our OC at Scampton, to learn that the weather was all right there and received orders to try and get through. By ringing aerodromes on the way north, we found that the fog was only in a fifteen mile radius, so I decided to give it a go and rang Brooky at Northolt to that effect. He was agreeable, so I left Hendon and stuck to the Great Northern Railway track, flying no higher than one hundred feet, until, a little north of Hatfield, the fog disappeared and we ran into perfect weather conditions. We eventually landed at Scampton just after lunch, with everything OK. The new buses were the centre of great attraction, being absolutely the latest and we handed them over with feelings of relief.

'Less than eight hours after our return, we were in the air again looking for Zepps. Our disappointment was great when we discovered that the new machines were not equipped for operations, for we had hoped to have accomplished something with them. Our chances with the old machines were pretty remote and nothing happened worth recording.

'There was one more fatality, Solomon, a New Zealander, went west.

'Christmas was approaching and the days were spent mostly in flying our American pupils, practising bomb dropping and machine gunnery. At night it was the same thing, with a bit of search-light dodging thrown in. There was another casualty too, Livingstone, another New Zealander, side-slipped coming in and crashed, the machine catching fire. Livingstone was a live wire, great on the ivories and we missed him very much.

'C' Flight had a nasty accident the same night, a machine landing at one of the emergency grounds and when taking off, flew straight into a farmhouse, knocking half of it down and giving the poor old farmer and his wife, who were in bed, a rude awakening, in addition to having to dig their way out of the debris in the dark. Fortunately, nothing caught fire, although the pilot was injured beyond recognition.

'There was an occasional raid, but our luck was out and we got disheartened, more and more anxious to be off overseas. Christmas passed and still nothing exciting beyond the fact that everyone was blotto and suffered with heads for days afterwards. Boxing night, things were pretty willing, Brooky and Pad announcing just after midnight that they wanted to fly. We all went up to the hangars and got the machines out into the moonlit night without needing the flares. Why someone didn't break his neck is hard to say, for we did all sorts of mad things and in the end lost Brooky and Pad. We thought they must have forced landed somewhere and carried on until four in the morning. They hadn't turned up then, so we returned to the mess and saw the break of day whilst sipping cocktails.

'About eleven o'clock in the morning, when we were all peacefully sleeping, the telephone bell went mad. Brooky and Pad had just awakened and found themselves at Retford aerodrome, where they had gone to see the boys and have a spot. They had been put to bed and knew no more until the morning saw them in fresh surroundings and they thought they'd better let us know. The OC was away when they left, but had a few words to say on their return and told Brooky, when he did turn up, that the sooner he went overseas the better, to which Brooky heartily agreed.

'The funny part of it was that the following morning, orders came through for Brooky and I to report at Adastral House at once. Just what we wanted and we couldn't pack quickly enough, for we knew it meant overseas for us. This loafing on Home Defence was no good at all; all very well for chaps who had been flying overseas, but not for us. A tender was ordered and with several rounds of drinks, we said 'Cheerio' to 33 Squadron.

'At Adastral House, we were given our tickets and told to embark on the seven o'clock train from Victoria the following morning.

'We set to and enjoyed our last night in dear old London and it was some night too. I went over to Portland Place and rounded up some of my nurse friends, Brooky dropped into Selfridge's and picked up a couple of his pals and we all met back at the Strand Palace, where we fell in with three more chaps we'd been through Oxford with. They were also for overseas duty, so we persuaded them to join our party and bring their lady friends. In the end, we mustered fourteen.

'A table was set for us in the grill room and after a couple of rounds of appetisers, we adjourned for the feed. At dinner, someone discovered that it was Jerry's birthday, so he was obliged to shout some fizz and we promoted him to the top of the table, calling for a speech. On rising to oblige us, he knocked his drink over and as the bottle was empty, shouted another and this time he drank it before he rose.

'He started off, 'On behalf of the widows and orphans' and suddenly got an inspiration, changing the subject to the declining birth rate. Then he got hiccoughs badly, sat down and everyone agreed that it was the right way to finish up a birthday speech.

'Three hours later, we were on the platform at Victoria, no farewells to make, we'd had them all the night before. We staggered into seats aboard the train, made ourselves as comfortable as possible and as the train pulled out on its way to Folkestone, tried to secure some of the sleep we'd lost the night before.

'No one spoke, but we all wondered when, if ever, we'd see dear old London again.'

Endnotes Chapter 3

1   A. R. Kingsford, *Night Raiders of the Air*, first published in 1930.
2   Société Pour L'Aviation et ses Dérivés, also Société Provisoire des Aéroplanes Deperdussin and Blériot-SPAD, French aircraft manufacturer (1912–1921).
3   While on patrol from Hainault to Sutton's Farm at 12.45 am on 23/24 September 1916, Second Lieutenant Alfred de Bath Brandon attacked L-33 north of Chelmsford and after jettisoning cargo went out to sea. Rather than risk drowning, Kapitänleutnant Alois Böcker preferred to land and he ordered the crew to make a forced landing. It came down 3 miles inland, north-east of Mersea and the crew were taken prisoner. *Zeppelin Blitz* by Neil R. Storey.
4   Tempest became firm friends with his fellow pilots, William Leefe Robinson and Frederick Sowery. On 22/23 September 1916, flying B.E.2c 4112 of 39 Squadron, Second Lieutenant Frederick Sowrey shot down German Navy Zeppelin airship L32, commanded by Oberleutnant zur See Werner Petersen. Sowrey was awarded the DSO. Major Fred Sowrey DSO MC ended WW1 as CO of 143 (Home Defence) Squadron. He remained in the RAF until after WW2 and died in 1968.

Chapter 4

'Reggie'

John Lea

17 August 1889. Cromwell Road, in west London. James and Amy Marix become the proud parents of Reginald Lennox George. A great time to be born. Queen Victoria, full of years and glory, although still grieving for her beloved Albert, is entering the final decade of her reign. Her country revels in being the most powerful on earth. The officers of the Royal Navy know that their fleet is the strongest afloat. Great splashes of red colour the maps of the globe. God's in His heaven, all's right with the world. James Marix came from an old Huguenot family. Reginald was educated at Upton School in 1904 and he went on to Radley College, where he boxed at bantam weight and was a rowing cox. Other than that and the fact that shortly before the outbreak of the First World War he landed an aircraft on Radley playing field, little information exists. Reginald was enrolled in the Royal Naval Volunteer Reserve and was discharged as Leading Seaman on appointment to a commission on 1 November 1912. On 17 January 1913, with the winds of war gathering force, he was posted to the Central Flying School at Upavon. Here he found himself on Course No 2, one among nearly forty RFC pilots under training. The course Adjutant was an over-age Major by the name of Trenchard, who had been a trainee on Course No. 1.[1] On graduating from the Central Flying School, Sub Lieutenant Reggie Marix returned on 17 April 1913 to Eastchurch where he was cast in the role of instructor, with the rank of Flying Officer, RFC, Naval Wing. Or rather, a dual rank: he also carried the rank of Lieutenant RNR. Officers in the Naval Wing of the RFC before 1 July 1914, when the RFC and the RNAS officially became separate entities and in the RNAS after that date, were distinguished by having two ranks. In July 1914 he thus became a Flight Lieutenant, RNAS, while retaining his two stripes as a Lieutenant, RNR. After the war had started, the 'Reserve' part of his rank seemed to fade away, perhaps because, unlike most RNAS officers who had temporary rank, he enjoyed a permanent commission in the RN Air Service.

On 4 August 1914 Reggie Marix was at Eastchurch but six days later he was transferred to Scapa Flow on Fleet reconnaissance work. Not for long; the record reveals that on 1 September 1914 his posting was 'Antwerp, Bomb dropping Squadron.' This was the Eastchurch (Mobile) Squadron, which had separated from the RFC, naming it No.3 Squadron RNAS by September 1914. Its commander was the legendary Commander Charles Rumney Samson, born in Crumpsall, Manchester on 8 July 1883, the son of Charles Leopold Samson, a solicitor and his wife Margaret Alice. In 1911 Samson was selected as one of the first four Royal Navy officers to receive pilot training and obtained his Royal Aero Club certificate on 25 April 1911 after only 71 minutes flying time. He completed flying training at Eastchurch before being appointed Officer Commanding of Naval Air Station

Eastchurch in October 1911. In January 1912 he was promoted to acting Commander. The following April he was appointed Officer Commanding the Naval Flying School at Eastchurch. When the RFC was formed from the Air Battalion on 13 May 1912, Samson took command of its Naval Wing and led the development of aerial wireless communications, bomb and torpedo-dropping, navigational techniques and night flying.

Samson took part in several early naval aviation experiments, including the development of navigation lights and bomb sights. He was the first British pilot to take off from a ship, on 10 January 1912, flying a Short S.27 from a ramp mounted on the foredeck of the battleship HMS *Africa*, which was at anchor in the river Medway. On 9 May he became the first pilot to take off from a moving ship, using the same ramp and aircraft, now fitted to the battleship HMS *Hibernia* during the 1912 Naval Review in Weymouth Bay. He repeated the feat on 4 July, this time from HMS *London* while the battleship was under way.

Antwerp was strategically placed to challenge the potential Zeppelin menace. The bomber aircraft was still only a concept, but at least the Belgian city put the machines of the day almost in range of the airship bases at Cologne and Düsseldorf. Early assessments were that the Zeppelins would be at their most vulnerable on the ground and it became a priority objective to destroy them there. It had to be done quickly if this menace to Britain were to be averted. There was a sense of urgency to attack the enemy's airships in their sheds while there was yet time, before the invading German tide could sweep away the machines which could do the job. The Schlieffen Plan meant that Antwerp would be scheduled for capture early in the war. But Antwerp was one of the very few places, perhaps the only place, from which the Zeppelin sheds at Cologne and Düsseldorf could be attacked by aircraft. The machines of the day were of course slow (90 mph was a good speed) and of very short range, so the inevitable loss of the city would ensure the safety of the German airships in their sheds.

Samson's handful of keen-as-mustard flyers with their motley collection of ill-assorted machines had their work cut out to destroy those airships in the little time left to them. To attack the Zeppelin bases while Antwerp was still tenable became their overriding goal. In August 1914 the first naval air unit to be dispatched abroad was Samson's Eastchurch Squadron, which moved to Ostend on 27 August, with ten aircraft, an airship and a variety of mechanical transport. Initially responsible for air reconnaissance, Samson's formation was quickly ordered to seek means of preventing German airships from operating. By mid-September he had acquired additional motor vehicles, which were then armoured and fitted with machine guns. Leading this tiny 'armoured car' force. Samson then proceeded to harass the German forces in Belgium, attacking cavalry and infantry formations wherever they were encountered. In the air Samson's men undertook many bombing raids against German forces and communications posts, but the gradual retreat of the British Expeditionary Force meant that the Squadron was eventually forced to move to Dunkirk, from where it was withdrawn to England in February 1915. On his return, Samson was immediately given orders to prepare his squadron for service in the Dardanelles.

The first assignment was to cover the exposed left flank of the Allied armies against the German thrust, using their aircraft and armoured cars. Among

Samson's ten pilots were Bell Davies, Bigsworth, Collet, Spenser Grey and 'Reggie' Marix. They 'brought a tremendous zest and a completely unorthodox, but most historical, appetite for private adventure', wrote Henry Robert Moore Brooke-Popham.[2] 'They were like privateers operating under Letters of Marque.'

Within a few weeks this covering operation gave way to the more urgent task of countering the Zeppelins. At first the squadron didn't have much luck. The machines were so slow, so short ranged, so lacking in instrumentation that the slightest worsening in the weather could abort an operation. In *Fights and Flights,* Samson describes one such: 'On 22 September the long-expected attack was made on the Zeppelin sheds. Four aeroplanes started out from Antwerp, flown by Major Eugene Louis Gerrard, Royal Marines, Lieutenant Charles Herbert Collet RMLI, Lieutenant Marix and Lieutenant Spenser Douglas Adair Grey, the latter carrying Flight Sub-Lieutenant Walter Shackfield Newton-Clare RNAS as passenger. They started soon after daylight. The weather was very suitable at first but they ran into a fog at the River Boer, which extended as far as the Rhine. Collet was the only one who located his objective and he made a splendidly determined attack on the Zeppelin sheds at Düsseldorf. Unfortunately, he was too low for his bombs to function, as at his low altitude combined with the height of the shed sufficient time was not permitted for the safety fan of the bombs to unwind, thus preventing the explosion of the bomb when it hit. One of the three bombs that missed the shed exploded just outside the door and killed two or three soldiers.'

Although the four aircraft returned safely from this mission, it could not be termed a howling success. It would be another couple of weeks before Reggie Marix would be able to claim a victory, the first successful bombing raid of the war on German territory. During those two weeks the German advance made the fall of Antwerp imminent - and with its fall would go the last chance of having a crack at the Düsseldorf and Cologne bases. The decision to evacuate the city was made, but Samson left two aircraft and a handful of mechanics to take this last chance. The two pilots were Squadron Commander Spenser Grey, in command of the tiny force and Flight Lieutenant Marix. 8 October found the city within easy range of German artillery. On the previous night, the two pilots left their machines out in the middle of the aerodrome, where they felt that there was less chance of their being damaged by shellfire.

Samson tells the bare bones of the story that followed: '...Spenser Grey and Marix set off in their 'Tabloids'. Spenser Grey got to Cologne, but found it obscured by mist and he could not locate the Zeppelin sheds; he therefore dropped his bombs at the railway station. He got back to Antwerp at 4.45 pm. At 8.30 pm the enemy commenced shelling the aerodrome and the two aeroplanes, his own and Flight Lieutenant Sydney Vincent Sippe's, were both put out of action by shells.[3] It was therefore useless to remain any longer and he started off with the mechanics in a motor-car for Ostend. Marix, who had Düsseldorf for his objective, achieved a great success. He let go of his bombs from 600 feet and scored direct hits with both of them; he had the gratification of seeing the roof fall in and flames shoot up into the sky, proving that he had destroyed the Zeppelin. He encountered a very heavy fire from machine guns and his aeroplane was hit in numerous places; twenty miles short of Antwerp, close to the Dutch frontier, he was forced to alight owing to running out of petrol. Abandoning his aeroplane, he got into Antwerp after a most adventurous journey, going some of the way by bicycle and some by a railway engine. He got away from Antwerp in the motor-car. We were all very pleased at Marix's success and he and Spenser Grey richly deserved the DSOs they were awarded. Thus the Squadron now possessed four DSOs after six weeks' fighting. Not bad going for a small unit.'

'Reggie' Marix had an unusual talent for recounting a story. In later life, he would use his writing skills in musical criticism, in humour, in playwriting. Fortunately, he took the time to set down on paper the definitive version of what led up to the Düsseldorf raid and what happened in those autumnal skies over Germany. Most importantly, he gave an insight into the urgency placed at the highest level on containing the Zeppelin menace. It was one of those rare occasions when those concerned with national decision making in time of war bring the front line soldier (or - in this case - aviator) into their confidence.

'As far as I was concerned it started with a telephone call from the Admiralty. I had recently returned from Scapa Flow where I had been flying reconnaissances for the Fleet and on this particular morning late in August 1914 I was in one of the hangars at Eastchurch helping to dismantle a Gnome engine. I was told that I was wanted on the telephone. It was Squadron Commander Spenser Grey who had been Winston Churchill's pilot before the war and who had given him flying lessons. He said he was with Churchill (then First Lord) and that I was to come to Admiralty House (part of the Admiralty which is the First Lord's residence) as soon as possible. I remember that my hands were black with oil - and castor oil at that - but the station staff cars were open ones and the old road from Eastchurch to London was very dusty in the summer, so that in any case I would need a good wash on arrival. I decided not to waste time and left as I was.

'On arrival I was obviously expected and in my even dirtier condition was shown straight into a small dining room where at a round table three men had just finished lunch. They were Churchill, whom I had met a few times at Eastchurch before the war, Spenser Grey and an old man with grizzled white hair, dressed in an old fashioned black frock coat but wearing what looked like a petty officer's India rubber or celluloid collar and a narrow bright red tie.

'Churchill greeted me, 'Ah, Marix, just in time for coffee and a brandy, sit down.' (A fourth place had been laid). Of course I had no lunch and incidentally that was the first time I had ever drunk liqueur brandy from a balloon glass.

After the servant had left the room I found out the reason for my summons. Churchill was keen to have a crack at the Zeppelin sheds at Düsseldorf and Cologne, operating from Antwerp, but how was it to be done with the naval aircraft then available? He then told us about two little aeroplanes going begging at Farnborough. They were land adaptations of the Sopwith Schneider Trophy seaplane which had won the last race at Monaco, but having wheels instead of floats they were even faster. They had been sent to Farnborough for trial by the RFC but had been turned down as unsafe. Would Spenser Grey and I like to try them? If we liked them we could have them. Both Spenser Grey and I were fans of the Sopwith products and we could not believe that the firm would turn out something which was radically wrong. We said that we would like to try them.

'We then discussed how the raids could be carried out and now and then the mysterious old man made some remark to which, I am afraid, I paid scant attention until Churchill to some rejoinder of mine said, 'Are you sure about that? Because as the First Sea Lord has just remarked...' With a shock I realized that a Flight Lieutenant had more or less ignored the great Lord Fisher and decided it was high time to put a 'Sir' into my answers.

'After we had finished talking Churchill took us into the drawing room to meet Mrs Churchill, where I became even more conscious of my dirty hand when she offered me hers. The next day Spenser Grey and I went to Farnborough, where we were introduced to the little biplanes. We were solemnly warned (1) not to fly in level flight as they were unstable at top speed (having 80hp Gnôme rotary engines, these could not be throttled back) but to climb or glide; (2) not to leave the vicinity of the aerodrome as in the event of an engine failure they were impossible to land in a field. Spenser Grey and I had previously arranged that if we were satisfied with the aircraft we would crack right off to Eastchurch. We were to wave to each other after a few circuits. As far as I could make out there was nothing although certainly the machine was very light on the controls compared with any other aircraft I had ever flown. We waved and that was the last Farnborough saw of the two 'Tabloids'.

'A 'Bomb dropping Squadron' was then formed for Antwerp (to which I was posted on 1 September 1914) under the command of Major Gerrard. The Squadron finally included Captain Charles Collet with an old Sopwith, Flight Lieutenant Newton-Clare with another old Sopwith, Sippe with a B.E. (Gerrard also had a B.E.)

'Lord Carbery with a two-seater Sopwith Tabloid joined us, but not long after his arrival he crashed with the Prince de Lignes as his observer. He stalled coming in to land and I think this machine was overloaded with a passenger. Carbery damaged a knee and had to be invalided home and de Lignes broke an ankle. The aeroplane was a write-off. Spenser Grey and I with our two new Tabloids completed the party.

'As I have mentioned, these single seater Tabloids were Schneider racers with wheels and fitted with an 80hp Gnome. They did 90 mph on the level and had warping wings (not ailerons). The range was about 200 miles. At Eastchurch they were fitted with a simple bomb dropping gear, a rack under the fuselage to hold two 20lb Hale bombs. The bombs were released by pulling on two toggles connected by wires to the pins holding the bombs on the rack. There was no bomb sight. As soon as they were ready, Spenser Grey had flown them to Wilryck (the aerodrome just outside Antwerp), refuelling at Dunkirk on the way. At Wilryck the officers were quartered in a mansion almost on the edge of the aerodrome and a small party of mechanics and ratings were billeted in the vicinity. We gathered as much intelligence as we could about the Zepp sheds, made plans and in the meantime carried out reconnaissance for the Belgian Army, to which we were attached.

'Düsseldorf is about 110 miles from Antwerp and Cologne about 120. It was clear that none of us could get to either place and back to Wilryck with the amount of fuel we carried. We had become chummy with the Belgian armoured car officers; their famous leader was Baron de Caters, who was a real fire eater. He hardly ever came back from raids into the open country without Uhlans' lances, swords and helmets as trophies.

'We arranged with him that when all was ready and the weather favourable he would take some armoured cars well to the west, I think about 50 or 60 miles, fix up a landing field and have with him supplies of petrol and oil so that we could refuel on our way back. He would also have with him some of our mechanics. We carefully marked the chosen spot on our maps and ground signals were arranged. The first attempt was made on 23 September. I do not remember who was detailed for where, but I was found for Cologne. All went well as far as the Meuse, but after crossing the river the weather began to thicken and soon the ground was covered with 100% cloud. At 2,500 feet I was well above it.

'When I calculated that I was nearing the Rhine, I came down to try and get under the cloud, but the first things I saw were tree-tops sticking out of thick mist and I pulled out just in time. I made a second attempt a little later but according to my altimeter the cloud or fog must have been down to the ground. The only thing to do was to turn back. The weather was still clear west of the Meuse and I found the landing ground to which we all got back.

'The only pilot to score any success was Captain Collet, whose target was Düsseldorf. Here the weather was clearer. He found a gap in the clouds, got down, found the airship shed but unfortunately missed it, his bombs exploding nearby. (One version was that he hit the shed, but that it was empty). De Cater had done a grand job in establishing the landing ground, quite a hazardous undertaking since Germans were all over the place in those parts. However, all went well and all the aircraft and cars got back to Antwerp.

'For the next week the weather was unfavourable and there were various delays. By the end of September the whole situation had deteriorated and there seemed little likelihood that Antwerp could hold out. Also, with the general German advance, it was now impracticable for de Caters to provide an advance landing ground - without it, our aircraft could not get to the Rhine and back. So Spenser Grey and I induced some Belgian mechanics to construct and fit an extra petrol tank into our aircraft. With it we should be able to do the job. But there was a maddening delay in getting the specially shaped tanks made and fitted. By the time all was ready and the weather was right, Antwerp was on its last legs. This was on 8 October. Churchill had come to Antwerp and was at British HQ in the Hotel Sint Antoine. On that morning, Spenser Grey went to HQ and told Churchill that we were ready to start. Churchill replied that it was now too late, Antwerp was to be evacuated that day and the Germans might be in that night. We were all to get out of Wilryck as best we could and that was that.

'W.C. then retired to the w.c, but Spenser Grey followed him and through the closed door went on pleading, explaining that we would get back in time to get out. It seems that to get rid of him, Churchill gave his consent.

'What with one thing and another, it was afternoon before we were airborne, Spenser Grey bound for Cologne and I for Düsseldorf. I had a good trip and got to my destination without incident. But the shed was not where I had expected to find it and my map had been wrongly marked.

'So I had to fly around a bit, which excited some interest. I was at 3,000 feet and some AA opened up, but well wide of the mark. I found the shed further away from the town than expected.

'I closed and as soon as I was sure of my target I put my nose down and dived with my engine still on. One would not normally do this as it puts an awful strain on the rotary Gnome as the revs go up. One usually switched off to come down, but then it took a certain amount of time for the engine to pick up again. I wanted no loitering near the ground.

'The Gnome stood up and when I was at about 500 feet I released the two bombs, one after the other and began to pull out of the dive. I had kept my eyes fixed on the shed but I vividly remember the rapid points of flame as the ground machine guns opened up. I had been robbed of surprise by having to fly around looking for the shed.

'Having got into a climb, I tried to turn away, but to my momentary consternation found that I could not move the rudder. The rudder bar was quite solid and I was heading further into Germany. But I quickly appreciated that one can turn, although more slowly, on warp alone. This I did and set course for Antwerp.

'As I pulled out of my dive I looked over my shoulder and was rewarded with the sight of enormous sheets of flame pouring out of the shed. It was a magnificent sight.

'The wind must have shifted, as I got five to ten miles north of my track. When I realized this, the light was beginning to fail and I knew I would have a job to get back to Wilryck before dark. Also I was getting worried about my petrol and I simply dared not risk a forced landing with no rudder control. It was high time I got down. I then had some difficulty locating a field big enough, as I needed more room without a rudder than with one. (By the way, I should have mentioned that the rudder was fortunately jammed dead fore and aft). I picked my field and got down. Soon some gendarmes arrived and confirmed that I was north of Antwerp. I explained the situation and the gendarmes helpfully said that shortly a railway engine would try to get into Antwerp to bring out a trainload of refugees and that I could have a ride on the footplate.

'We were near the station and while waiting I examined the Tabloid. I had been lucky. The rudder bar was connected to the rudder by duplicate wires on either side running through tubular metal guides fixed to the uprights of the fuselage. On the port side a bullet had cut one wire, while another had hit one of the guides, welding the other wire to it. The elevator was operated by a pair of wires on either side to the control column. A bullet had cut one of these.

'I was wearing a leather skull cap, but had taken my uniform cap with me by letting it hang against my back suspended by a string round my neck (so as to have it if I had to land and get out in a hurry - or even if taken prisoner). There was a bullet hole through the peak.

'In all, there were about thirty bullet holes in the wings and fuselage. No serious damage, so I arranged for the gendarmes to mount a guard until I returned in the morning with mechanics and petrol. I did not know that I was to be escaping west long before daylight.

'I boarded the engine, but it could only get to within about five miles of Antwerp. With some difficulty I commandeered a bicycle and pedalled off. It was not quite dark. I found that I could not ride into the city because a bridge I had to cross was strongly blocked with barbed wire. With the help of a sentry I got on the outside of the bridge rail and hung the bicycle on my back. (Difficult, but can be done with a man's bike). I manoeuvred myself across by putting my feet between the rail supports and hanging on to the rail.

'Antwerp presented a strange sight. It seemed to be quite deserted, with houses on fire here and there. I pedalled to the Hotel St Antoine, which was also deserted except for an old caretaker. That morning it had been a hive of activity. By now I was rather tired, so before going any further I persuaded the old caretaker to produce some wine and something to eat. Refreshed, I pedalled off and in one of the big squares came across some Belgian soldiers who had a couple of cars. I prevailed upon them to drive me out to the aerodrome, which was deserted, so we went to the house alongside where we British officers were quartered. Here, as I discovered later, I might have ended my career, louring my absence much had happened. The few serviceable British and Belgian aeroplanes had been got away. Spenser Grey had returned safely from Cologne where, unable to locate the Zepp hangar, he had dropped his two 20lb bombs on the railway station. Only he and Sippe (whose aircraft was unserviceable) were left in the house with half a dozen marines.

'When we arrived at the house in complete darkness, the [two] Belgians who had accompanied me began talking to each other in Flemish. Sippe was at a window in a darkened room and was just about to open fire on whom he took for three Germans when I fortunately called out something in English. It seems that I had returned just in time, as the small party were on the point of leaving before any real Germans arrived.

'I eventually got away in a small lorry with a naval mechanic and a couple of Marines. The road west was a nightmare, crowded with refugees carrying or pushing in wheelbarrows, etc, such possessions as they had room for. There were old men and women, children, all sorts of animals and the pace was a crawl. Broken down vehicles had to be ditched. As we got further west, the traffic thinned and we got to Ghent an hour or so after daylight. There I managed to obtain a welcome breakfast and later went on to Ostend where I joined Commander Samson who was there with No.3 Squadron and some armoured cars. I never heard what happened to my little Tabloid.

'The impact of the successful raid on the Zeppelin base and the destruction of one of the latest German airships was dramatic. Europe had only been at war for a short time; the British public were surprised and elated to learn of this astounding feat in the air. In Germany, the idea of the Fatherland being attacked on its home turf was a difficult one to take in.'

The concept of powered heavier-than-air flight was new. Even newer was its skilful and intrepid use against the enemy. The exploits of the Naval Wing of the RFC were splashed across all the popular journals. No aviator was more publicised than Reggie Marix.

Official recognition came quickly. *The London Gazette* of 23 October 1914:

'Flight Lieutenant Marix, acting under the orders of Squadron Commander Spenser Grey, carried out a successful attack on the Düsseldorf airship shed during the afternoon of the 8 October. From a height of 600 feet he dropped two bombs on the shed and flames 500 feet high were seen within 30 seconds. The roof of the shed was also observed to collapse. Lieutenant Marix's machine was under heavy fire from rifles and mitrailleuses and was five times hit while making the attack.'

In *The VC and the DSO,* Creagh and Humphries quote the *Gazette* and go on to add 'for his services on this occasion, he was created a Companion of the Distinguished Service Order.'

The Daily Sketch of 10 October 1914 featured a big photograph of THE MAN WHO WRECKED THE ZEPPELIN seated in the cockpit of his aircraft.

On the same day the more restrained *Daily Chronicle* ran multiple headlines for its story, in the manner of the time: AIR WAR was the top line, followed by SECOND VISIT TO THE RHINE. It went on: ZEPPELIN SHIP DESTROYED; NEUTRAL POWER'S VIEW OF CAMPAIGN. The paper's description of the raid was an abbreviated version of Reggie Marix's own. It added the comment 'the feat would appear to be in every respect remarkable having regard to the distance (over 100 miles) penetrated into country held by the enemy and to the fact that a previous attack had put the enemy on their guard and enabled them to mount anti-aircraft guns.'

The Call on 12 October featured a studio picture of Marix under the heading DESTROYER OF KAISER'S ZEPPELIN AT DÜSSELDORF. But it was the *Sportsman* of that date which perhaps best caught public reaction. Under the headline OUR HEROIC AIRMEN, it ran:

'On Saturday the question in every mouth was, 'Who is Lieutenant Marix?' Of Commander Spenser Grey the public had already heard, for he was the airman who on occasions had piloted Mr. Winston Churchill in aerial trips . . . but of Lieutenant Marix not even the initials were known . . . The fact that the outstanding achievements of the Flying Arm have so far been accomplished by comparatively unknown men clearly indicates that the Naval Air Service contains talent such as the public never imagined.'

The Times took a different tack, as one would expect from the 'Thunderer', then very much the newspaper of record. Under the headline THE DÜSSELDORF AIR RAID, the sub-heading was GERMAN ADMIRATION OF BRITISH DARING. The story came from the paper's own correspondent in Copenhagen and is worth quoting for its perspective from the other side.

'The latest British air raid into Germany appears to have caused some surprise in Germany... The Rheinische Westfalische Zeitung describes the successful attack on the airship shed at Düsseldorf. The flier was exposed to heavy shrapnel and rifle fire. Near the new shed he suddenly dived so that the spectators thought he was hit. But he obviously dived to avoid the shrapnel and make more certain of his aim. With one shot he hit the shed about the middle of the roof. A gigantic burst of flame followed and there was great smoke for about ten minutes. Externally nothing was to be seen but a large hole. It is supposed that the flier must have learned through treachery that this Zeppelin had only been transferred three days previously from the old shed.'

Many other newspapers carried the story, either as a piece of instant reportage or after the lapse of a few days as more in-depth analysis. *The Star, The Queen,* the *Daily Express,* the *Daily Mail* all covered the feat in their own ways. Interestingly, the *New York Times* ran the story on 12 October, having received the news by cable. GERMANS AT ANTWERP NEARLY POTTED MARIX was the headline. It was sub-headed BRITISH AVIATOR WHO DESTROYED DÜSSELDORF ZEPPELIN ESCAPED WITH THE LOSS OF HIS MACHINE. Reggie Marix's fame had quickly spread to the United States.

More deeply researched articles followed in popular and specialized magazines. *The Aeroplane* of 14 October contented itself with the brief story put out by the Admiralty's Official Press Bureau, but added a biographical sidelight on the pilot, illustrated with his photograph: 'Flight Lieutenant Marix was formerly in the Royal Naval Volunteer Reserve and was appointed to the RNAS in its early days. He soon established a Service reputation as a skilful flier and did excellent work on a Caudron biplane with the Naval detachment in the Army Manoeuvres of 1913. Early this year he looped the loop on the same machine. He has flown every make of aeroplane owned by the Navy and seems equally skilful on all of them. He was educated at Radley and his school may well be proud of him as the first British pilot to destroy an airship.'

Flight magazine of 16 October covered the story fairly briefly. The writer differed from Reggie Marix's own account by saying that he had been picked up by a naval armoured car after abandoning his aircraft on the return trip. It added one other interesting titbit, a quote from the *North German Gazette* which represents an early attempt at disinformation:

'The airman's undertaking was only successful to a very slight extent. The Düsseldorf shed, which was constructed in the year 1910 and belongs to the town, is one of the most modern airship sheds and was protected as far as is possible against attacks from the air. In the construction of airship sheds it was naturally necessary to take bombardment into account. Measures of precaution therefore were taken which cannot be discussed, but which, as the present case shows, are nevertheless efficient enough to prevent the airships lying in the sheds from sustaining very serious damage. The airship which has just been damaged and which had already gained some brilliant successes in the war, should be ready for active service again in a very short time.'

The Sphere came out on 24 October with a magnificent double page illustration showing the attacking dive of the Tabloid and the effect of the bomb on the airship shed. THE BURNING OF THE NEW ZEPPELIN SHED AT DÜSSELDORF was the caption. The story was a shortened version, but contained an interesting observation: 'Since the visit of the aeroplane the nerves of Düsseldorf have been so badly shaken that the general in command has had to issue a communiqué rebuking the inhabitants and advising them not to become so agitated when the enemy score.'

Flight Lieutenant Marix's destruction of the new Z-IX in its shed brought a new dimension to aerial warfare. His slow machine, short ranged and primitively equipped, had proved capable in the hands of a determined aviator of pressing home an attack on enemy territory. His 20lb bombs were enough to ignite the huge volume of hydrogen filling the airship, even though he had no bombsight and only the most elementary bomb release gear. The tiny Sopwith had shown itself capable of absorbing all sorts of punishment.

Reggie Marix's flying skill, coolness under intense fire and tenacity in reaching his target brought him immediately into the public eye. Even though the destruction of Z-IX had demonstrated the power of aerial bombing, in the short term it was not able to halt the German programme to use the airship as a weapon of strategic bombardment. The storming success of the Schlieffen Plan, the fall of

Antwerp and the disappearance of any British aircraft within range of Germany put paid to repeat performances.

On 28 October *The Illustrated War News* came out with a full page picture captioned THE HERO OF THE AIR RAID ON DÜSSELDORF ZEPPELINS: FLIGHT-LIEUTENANT R L G MARIX AT OSTEND. The photograph features what the text describes as an armoured car. It looks rather like an ordinary car with some plating awkwardly welded to it. That is probably what it was: Samson's team, forced out of Antwerp and bereft of aircraft, saw their role as continuing to help the left wing of the allied armies by forming armoured car units. The sailors trained as aviators were about to become soldiers.

In *Fights and Flights,* Samson describes this phase of the war for his Squadron. Officers and men became adept at harassing the German units who were swarming through Belgium by this time. Many a successful ambush was carried out using armoured cars often hastily improvised from civilian vehicles and fitted with any weapons available. Tactics, too, were improvised. With the spur of combat they rapidly developed into highly effective manoeuvres.

Within a few days of his escape from capitulating Antwerp, Marix was in the thick of this new sort of fighting. These early days of the war saw cavalry used by both sides. The static horrors of trench warfare, the murderous defences of massed machine guns, the advent of the tank, were in the future. The Squadron operated in Flanders in mixed melees between its Heath Robinson armoured cars and German Uhlans with their horses and lances, ranging over miles of countryside not yet bogged down in the trenches.

Reggie Marix again showed his initiative and his ability to function under unorthodox conditions. Samson graphically describes an engagement:

'On 19 October we had some very tough fighting and the 3-pounder proved its worth. Reporting to General Byng, he sent me on to General Kavanagh, one of the Brigadier's 3rd Cavalry Division and from him I received orders to split up my party. One section, consisting of two armoured cars, was to attack Ledeghem in support of some cavalry, whilst the other section, which comprised two armoured cars and the 3-pounder lorry, was to support a Squadron of the 2nd Life Guards, who were to deal with some Uhlans at Rolleghemcappelle. I sent Osmond in Command of the first section and went myself with the second, taking Marix, Warner and Lathbury. Staff-Surgeon Wells, with an ambulance and a touring car, was in attendance on both parties.

'...Marix, with his car, moved about twenty yards farther up the road, where he got a good enfilade fire to bear on another big body of Germans debouching from a wood on our side of the village. This fire stopped them from advancing and they fell back.

'Marix arrived back at Poperinghe late that night, having had a most interesting time. He had, after leaving me at the windmill, gone back to Moorslede and got into Roulers, where he found the French Cavalry about to retire. On the way back from there he found the Duke of Roxburghe, who was severely wounded, lying in a farmhouse with his servant standing by him. Marix got him into the car and thus saved him from certain capture. Coming along to Moorslede via Passchendaele, he arrived at the former place, where he found some Cavalry outposts outside the village. I had just left, he was told; at the request of a staff officer he did some covering work with his Maxim on the Germans, who were apparently about to advance through the town. In this work he was assisted by a Belgian armoured car driven by Monsieur Charbon, a most gallant gentleman, who well earned a reputation for his armoured-car work.'

These actions were the last of the mobile war. October/November 1914 saw von Falkenhayn and the Franco-British forces locked in the bloody battle of First Ypres. The carnage became known as the 'graveyard of the old British Army.' It also resulted in the long drawn out trench stalemate which dominated almost the entire war.

Reggie Marix himself was involved in the fighting which led up to First Ypres, probably in the armoured car skirmishes which preceded the set piece infantry battles. Later, he was stationed in Dunkirk, from where the Wing raided targets on the Belgian coast.

On 31 October 1914 he was promoted to Flight Commander, RNAS. If he ever had the time or the inclination to look back over the previous eight years, he must have pictured them as some sort of a whirlwind. Radley - the Sorbonne - the City of London - Royal Reserve - flying training - the Düsseldorf Zeppelin attack and his well-earned DSO - armoured car and infantry fighting in the Flanders countryside - flying from the Dunkirk base.

But Reggie Marix thrived on excitement and challenge. He had no way of knowing what developments would call upon his fine-honed skills of combat flying. Whatever they were, he would welcome them.

As the winter of 1914-1915 dragged on and the fighting men bogged down in the mud and blood of the trenches, the Allied leadership was searching for ways to break the deadlock. For Flight Commander Marix DSO there was more action to come. Skirmishes against the rapidly advancing German units - many of them cavalry - kept Marix and all the other aviators of the Eastchurch Wing busy for the rest of that first year of war. Armoured car and infantry units intercepted the wide-ranging enemy patrols as they moved further into France and Belgium. These units bolstered the efforts of the allied armies to halt the Schlieffen Plan swing from the north-east.

In mid-October, Wing Commander Samson left Marix with a small group of troops guarding an aeroplane which had crash-landed near Ypres and which risked capture by German patrols. This task was rather tedious to an officer of 'Reggie' Marix's active disposition, so he set off in search of any Germans who might be around. Taking with him eight soldiers and marines on this scouting expedition, he found quite a lot of them. German Uhlans were reported to be lurking in a nearby chateau; Marix surrounded it with his men. When they were all in place, he took two of them and advanced stealthily towards the old building. With two hundred yards to go, more than twenty Germans dashed out of the chateau, some on foot, others mounted. Reggie Marix and his team of two opened fire on the escapers. Their headlong rush indicated that they believed themselves to be opposed by a much bigger force.

The Germans who were already on horseback got clean away. But those cavalrymen who were on foot were not so lucky: their horses were behind a haystack and the fire-fight turned into a running chase to see who would get there first. The British group won. One German was killed. The officer in command of the Uhlans and a trooper got to their horses, but too late. Their horses shot from beneath them, the German captain decided that discretion was the better part of valour. He saw that Marix was taking aim at him, so he threw down his pistol and handed over his sword as a sign of surrender. Reggie realised that the officer's horse was mortally wounded and was about to shoot it, when he thought that the captain might prefer to perform that sad task himself. He handed back the pistol on the German's word of honour that he would use it only to shoot the horse, the animal was put out of its misery and the gun returned to Marix.

While this was going on, the German trooper accompanying his captain had been lying beside his horse - unhurt. Only after repeated orders from his officer did he get up and surrender his weapons - lance, sword, rifle and pistol. Surrender completed, it dawned on the German officer that his party had been tricked into surrendering with so little fight. He found it hard to believe that the British force was one third the size of his... 'We thought you were the British army,' he complained angrily.

In *Fights and Flights* Samson describes Marix's delivery of the two prisoners, the Captain of Uhlans and the trooper, back to base and into the hands of the Provost-Marshal. The officer was still angry, but in Samson's words, 'very punctilious.' His name turned out to be impressively fitting for a cavalry officer: Baron Wilhelm Freiherr von Lersner.

So ended a remarkable example of the chivalric afterglow that still hung over the mobile battlefields of 1914. Light forces, skirmishes between probing patrols, semi-improvised armoured cars versus brilliantly-uniformed cavalry: from our nuclear and electronic perspective the picture is akin to Arthurian legend. Not maudlin and sentimental, but civilised, gentlemanly and humanitarian. Not quite the end of the affair, however. Through the rest of the war and long after it, Reggie Marix had the Baron's sword in his keeping. He didn't look upon it as a prize of war, some emblem to reflect British versus German martial prowess. To him it was another's property to be held in trust until it was possible to return it.

The opportunity did not arise until December 1931, seventeen years after the event. By now a Wing Commander, Marix had spent time and effort trying to locate his old opponent among the chaos of post-war Germany. Not until all those years had elapsed did the Air Attaché at the British Embassy in Berlin finally pin down the Baron, by that stage working in a Berlin bank. The sword was sent to the Attaché, who arranged a small ceremony to hand back the sword. This RAF officer then wrote to Marix to describe the occasion, as which in his own words 'all manner of pious sentiments for the friendship of the two nations were expressed.'

He went on to write: 'Von Lersner was a prisoner in France until very nearly the end of the War when he managed to get back to Germany by shamming lunacy. He is perfectly fit and well and an exceptionally nice man... he was really delighted to get (the sword) back.'

A postscript was added by von Lersner himself in a letter of thanks for the return of the sword.

'I should like now to tell you personally how very much your magnanimous gesture has delighted me. Neither of us in October 1914 thought that the war would have lasted so long; and neither of us thought then that after the war so much distress would have pervaded the whole world and both our countries as a result of a misguided peace.

'The return of the sword just as this moment has not merely brought me personal joy, but I regard it also as a sign that the soldierly, chivalrous feeling, shown towards the opponents at the Front in the fight for existence, is purer and loftier than we otherwise experience in daily life or even in the political struggles among the nations. I should like to think that from those who fought in the war, irrespective of country, a new attitude of mind might develop which would lead to appreciation of the feelings and rights of others.'

The Baron went on to conclude, 'I should be delighted to shake hands and thank you personally for your gracious gesture.'

Flowery words perhaps, but sincere and well-meant. Less than eight years after they were written, however, Europe was again engulfed in desperate conflict in which Reggie Marix was again to serve, this time at a much more senior level of command. For the moment, he was happy to have played the gentleman, even among the confused inhumanity of total war.

By April 1915 the war had reached stalemate in the trenches. Attempts by both sides to break the deadlock - General Haig's at Neuve Chapelle, von Falkenhayn's response which led to Second Ypres - were destined to produce appallingly long casualty lists, but no breakthroughs. The Germans used gas for the first time during the months, but again to no avail.

The frustrated British leadership was in a mood to try anything, any change in strategy, to break through the ring of steel which the Central Powers had built around themselves. When beleaguered Russia pleaded to the western allies for a diversion to relieve the pressure on her from Turkey, she found willing supporters. The First Lord of the Admiralty, Winston Churchill, seconded by the First Sea Lord, Admiral Sir John Fisher (both of whom Marix had met during the discussion about the Düsseldorf raid) were already persuading the government that it would be feasible to force the Dardanelles and knock Turkey out of the war. The enemy, Churchill predicted, might well come tumbling down like a house of cards if this could be achieved. The impasse in France would be broken and the war would be over.

The main assault on the Dardanelles took place on 25 April 1915, but naval landings had been ineffectually attempted in the preceding two months. Flight Commander Marix went out to this new war theatre with Commander Samson's No. 3 Wing and was in the thick of the aerial operations during the landings at Cape Hellas, Anzac and Suvla Bay.[4]

The flavour of Reggie Marix's part in this early example of ground support is best experienced through the eyes of Samson himself, in *Fights and Flights*:

'On May 2nd we had our first successful air flight, as an enemy seaplane came towards Tenedos. Marix set off in chase of him and caught him up near Kephrez Point; he forced the seaplane to land on the water and killed the observer. Marix came down to about 50 feet to do this and of course got a hot time, as he ended up only about 300 yards from Chanak.

'On May 17th Marix had his big Breguet ready for action. As our principal objective with this aeroplane was an attack on Constantinople, we had to test it out well before allowing the attempt to be made, so in order to see what it could do I made one of my infrequent trips as passenger. We carried no less than one 100lb and fourteen 20lb bombs and also a Lewis gun, a pretty formidable amount for those days. Off we set with the idea of giving Ak Bashi Liman a look-over. Arriving there, we found the place a scene of great activity. We let go of all our bombs and created complete panic and also did a lot of damage.

'I have since talked with Turks who were actually on the spot at the time and they all said that we put a complete stop to work for two days, as the labourers fled to the hills. The loss of life was severe, thirteen killed and forty-four wounded.

'Marix and I came back delighted with the Breguet; but rather doubtful if the engine was reliable enough, as it was missing fire most of the time. However, we both had great faith in Dessoussois, who said he would get it right.

'During the first fortnight in June Marix was hard at work with the Breguet, making frequent flights to get it ready for the Constantinople trip. I went up three times with him and on one occasion we got the bag of our life, as we found about 400 Turks in a gulley behind Anzac. They were in a dense mass, being paid or drawing rations or something like that. We dropped a 100 lb bomb at them and, following its flight the whole way with our eyes, saw it burst immediately in the centre of them. We could see that the loss of life was tremendous.

'On June 21st Reggie Marix, with myself as passenger, set off at 1.30 am for Constantinople. The engine started to misfire as soon as we left; but Reggie, a most persistent fellow, carried on. We got as far as Anafarta Saghir, which is beyond Anzac, when we both decided that it was hopeless to go on, so reluctantly we turned for home. On the way back we bombed every campfire we could see and, I hope, disturbed the Turks a bit with the fourteen bombs we gave them. We neither of us thought we would reach Tenedos, as the engine went weaker and weaker and we came down gradually towards the water; we succeeded, however. Immediately we landed, Dessoussois rushed up and started taking the plugs out. He got three out, then flung down his tools and said, 'Commandant, what this pig of an engine wants is not a mechanician but one 'ammer.' He then burst into tears and had to be led away. Pour soul, he had worked like a slave on the engine, although suffering from dysentery. Marix was terribly disappointed, as there was little doubt that the engine was a bad one; certainly if Dessoussois couldn't make it go nobody else could. 'Constantinople had to be given up. None of my other aeroplanes could carry sufficient fuel as well as bombs for this long journey.'

Such were the trials, tribulations and successes of ground support operations in those technically primitive days. The aircraft were liable to all sorts of breakdown and failure, but the men flying them were a different breed. Samson again:

'Reggie Marix once bet me he could run to Tenedos, if I gave him five minutes' start, faster than I could ride on *Nigger*, the horse I had captured in France. Unknown to Marix I sent off one of my most expert Marines to clear away some of the principal obstacles and to mark out the best bits of going, by whitewashed stones; then I accepted Reggie's challenge. He never had a dog's chance; I came close up to him before halfway. Pretending I was in difficulties, he was deceived into making fresh efforts; after a bit I had compassion and passed him and we called the bet off. I am certain he would have broken a blood-vessel if I hadn't stopped him, as he was a most determined fellow.

'Marix was recalled to England in October. His departure was a great loss to the Squadron. Not only was he one of the finest pilots that there ever was; but he combined this skill with the most conspicuous gallantry and grim determination.

'If I told him off for a job, I knew the work would be done like clockwork. He never failed me once. I always considered Davies and Marix as the two most skilful pilots Eastchurch ever turned out. Reggie's departure made me feel that the old Squadron was beginning to break up . . .'

Reggie's part in the campaign did not go unrecognised. The Supplement to the *London Gazette* of Tuesday, 14 March, 1916:

Admiralty

The undermentioned Officers have been commended for service in action in despatches received from the Vice-Admiral Commanding the Eastern Mediterranean Squadron covering operations between the time of the landing on the Gallipoli Peninsula in April, 1915 and the evacuation in December, 1915 - January 1916.

The name of Flight Commander Reginald Lennox George Marix DSO RNAS is in the list which follows.

The Dardanelles campaign was a failure - glorious, but a failure none the less. Names like Anzac and Gallipoli are woven into the history of the British Empire. Anzac Day is still one of the most nationally important days of the year in Australia and New Zealand, whose troops proved themselves in those terrible months to rank among the toughest fighters in the world.

Air support was insufficient to turn the tables in what turned out to be a wild throw of the military dice. But Samson's team in No. 3 Wing fought and flew to the limit of men and machines. Reggie Marix was on the cutting edge.

Samson felt that 'the old Squadron' was beginning to break up but Reggie's[5] next appointment when he got back to England from the Dardanelles was to create a phoenix from the ashes. Following a brief spell at Eastchurch, he went to Detling to form the new No. 3 Wing. By April, he was commanding the Wing at Manston, in Kent.

Reggie's success over Düsseldorf had played a major part in convincing the country's military leadership that aircraft could be highly effective in the bombing role. Major Christopher Draper DSC in his book *The Mad Major,* sheds some interesting light on how this innovative thinking led to Marix's new job: 'The earlier RNAS attacks on Friedrichshafen and Düsseldorf had evidently turned the Admiralty towards the idea of forming what must be regarded as the first strategic air force in the world. It might be as well to explain that the RNAS at this time did not have Squadrons in the same way that the RFC had. The service consisted of Naval Air Stations and Seaplane bases, each of which might have anything from one to fifty aircraft. Right from the outbreak of war, however, smaller formations had been formed at these stations and bases and were known as Wings.

'The beginnings of this strategic air force were to be found at Manston, near Margate, where 3 Wing RNAS was formed. It consisted at first of a miscellaneous collection of aircraft, which included a couple of Renault-engined B.E.2c's, an American Curtiss R2, a Short Bomber, three each of single and two-seater 1½-Strutters and a machine described as a 'Sopwith School Bus.' A number of the Sopwiths which supplemented and eventually replaced these machines were erected at Detling and flown to Manston, then a virgin field with its personnel housed under canvas.[6]

'The unit was commanded by Captain W. L. Elder CMG RN who left for France with an advance party in May 1916, leaving Lieutenant Commander R L Marix, my friend from Eastchurch, in command at Manston.'[7]

In *Sailor in the Air,* Vice Admiral Richard Bell-Davies describes how he took over command of the newly-formed Wing from Reggie Marix, soon to be assigned the task of taking a squadron out to France: 'I... was appointed wing commander of No. 3 Wing about the middle of June. The squadrons were forming at Manston in Kent, where land had been taken over by the Admiralty and a few tents erected. The wing was to operate from Luxeuil, near the French frontier fortress of Belfort, where a large repair base was also to be set up, the whole organization under the command of Captain Elder. At Manston I found Reggie Marix training the first flight which had just been formed. The pilots were nearly all Canadians and were a first-rate lot. The aircraft were to be Sopwith 1½-Strutters, which were just coming into production and it was hoped that they would be followed by some twin-engined Handley Pages. The 1½-Strutters were a great advance on anything we had had before. The bomber and fighter versions were in essentials identical aircraft... their operational range was excellent and to test it Reggie had flown one from Manston to Mevagissey, in Cornwall and back without landing.

'There was nothing much for me to do at Manston as Reggie had the training well in hand.'

By this time Squadron Commander Marix was a highly skilled pilot, capable of flying many of the types then in existence. He had as much combat experience as anyone then in the air and had been decorated for his exploits. No officer was more suited to head up a fighting wing committed to using the new air weapon in support of the ground troops. Reggie's future was alive with promise. If he survived the hazards of the Western Front, he would be in the very forefront of military aviation. It was not to be.

In October 1916, Reggie was severely injured in a flying accident. The French Nieuport he was piloting crashed shortly after take-off. Both his legs were pinioned under the engine; the surgeons managed to save one (at the insistence of his sister who rushed out to join him) but the other had to be amputated.

There are two or three differing accounts of just how the accident happened. Draper: 'We flew out via Paris, landing at Villacoublay, but a ghastly accident spoiled my first visit to this enchanting city. Reggie Marix and I were motoring out to Villacoublay and as we passed the aerodrome at Issy les Moulineaux we stopped to watch a Frenchman spinning a Nieuport biplane. It was the first time we had seen a spin and we had quite a discussion as to how it was done.

'When we got to Villacoublay I said I would like to try a spin and Reggie, who knew the local French aviators, borrowed a Nieuport for me. I found the spin quite thrilling but not difficult and managed both right and left-hand varieties. I don't know if my success tempted him or not, but off went Reggie in another Nieuport. When I landed I was surrounded by a number of French mechanics, gesticulating and shouting such a gabble of French that I could not grasp a single word. It transpired eventually that poor Reggie had spun into the ground and broken both legs. I felt partly responsible and was very sad.'

Bell-Davies: 'In July the first squadron of 1½-Strutters set out from Manston, led by Reggie. At Paris where they landed he was invited to try a new French machine in which he had a very bad crash and as a result one leg had to be amputated. The surgeons fortunately managed to save the other so that he lived to have a long career in the RAF; his loss was a grave blow to No 3. Wing.'

Bell-Davies had the date wrong by about three months.

Another version is that he had gone to Paris to collect a Nieuport with which to augment the number of machines in his Wing - at that time, the French were the biggest aircraft builders in Europe and supplied many to the British services. He may have been using the fact that the RNAS had more 'pull' with the suppliers than the RFC had to get hold of a new machine!

When he arrived at the airfield, the Nieuport was there, but the French test pilot was nowhere to be seen. It should have been his responsibility to check the new aircraft thoroughly; the industry was still in its infancy and the stringent manufacturing controls which characterized later times had not yet been introduced. The checking routines included a short test flight.

Reggie asked the airfield staff where he could find the tea pilot. The rather sheepish answer was that, the hour being after eleven in the morning, M. I'aviateur had already departed for the local estaminet where he habitually took a few glasses of lunch-time wine. It was unlikely, M'sieu, that he would be back again before the next morning.

Reggie was not one to let grass grow under his wheels. 'Very well,' he said, 'I will test it myself.' And off he went into the October sky.

At about 200 feet altitude, one wing detached itself from the fuselage. The Nieuport, totally out of control, spun down like wounded bird and Marix was trapped underneath.

It is hard to be sure which description is closest to the truth after the lapse of so many years. For a pilot of his great experience and flair, it seems unlikely that he would put an aircraft into a situation from which it could not recover. On the other hand, for a defective machine to be delivered from the factory which was producing under the pressures of war is by no means inconceivable. It happened; and Britain lost the operational contributions of one of its finest airmen.

The press in Britain quickly picked up the news of Reggie's injury and linked it with his earlier exploits. The *Daily Express*, for example:

'Squadron Commander Reginald L. G. Marix DSO RN who is officially reported to have been severely injured, destroyed a Zeppelin in its shed at Düsseldorf in October 1914.'

There was great concern that an airman of his stature and success had effectively terminated his aviation career. But those expressing this concern had not taken into account Reggie's bulldog tenacity, which would not only enable him to continue his career, but to rise to Air rank nearly a quarter of a century later, in the Second World War.

The price he paid in life-long suffering will never be known. It could well have been a crushing blow to a lesser man, but for Reggie Marix it served to reinforce the core of steel which lay below the affable exterior. It would give him an ability to communicate with people, as though he used the interplay of personalities as a way of sublimating his own pain.

Handicapped? Obviously. Out of operational flying? Of course. No longer effectively in the war? Certainly.

Crushed? Defeated? Never.

After his accident, Reggie knew that he would not fly again during the war. He began working on the painful hard work of once more becoming mobile. His right leg had been amputated leaving only just enough stump to enable the fitting of an artificial limb and the left leg was severely damaged. But he was determined to continue his Service career, even though it would be a long time - if ever! - before he would again function as a pilot. He was inactive during the rest of the war, but by the time peace came on 11 November 1918 he was a permanent commissioned officer in the new Royal Air Force, which had been created only a few months earlier.

On 10 September 1917 he was awarded the *Croix de Chevalier de I'Ordre de la Couronne,* by King Albert of Belgium - a foreign order of knighthood. This was in recognition of his gallantry in the air and on land in the defence of the little country which had suffered so much.

Endnotes Chapter 4

1   Trenchard was promoted in 1915 to Major General and became head of the RFC. Sir Hugh Trenchard was instrumental in creating the RAF and the Royal Naval Air Service in April 1918, thus earning the sobriquet 'Father of the Royal Air Force.'

2   The first OC of 3 Squadron, Brooke-Popham went to France as the Deputy Assistant Adjutant and Quartermaster-General in the HQ of the RFC where he was responsible for the administrative and technical support to the squadrons deployed in the field. His understanding of the importance of air power and its support to land forces led him to criticize the lack of adequate air support to the B.E.F. On 20 November 1914 Lieutenant Colonel Brooke-Popham was appointed OC No.3 Wing. During the Battle of Neuve Chapelle he directed his Wing's operations and was later awarded the DSO. By 1915 Brooke-Popham was too senior an officer to take part in much operational flying and he also had limited experience of air combat. In May 1915 he was appointed Chief Staff Officer and in March 1916 he was granted the temporary rank of brigadier-general. In April 1918 he was transferred to the newly created Air Ministry in London, serving as the Controller of Aircraft Production. Brooke-Popham was C-in-C British Far East Command only months before Singapore fell to Japanese troops on 15 February 1942. ACM Sir Henry Robert Moore Brooke-Popham GCVO KCB CMG DSO AFC died on 20 October 1953.

3   The youngest of nine children, Sydney Sippe was born in 1889 in Brixton, London, where his parents lived. He was educated at Dulwich College from May 1903 to December 1905. Sippe was named after Sydney, Australia, where both his parents had lived.

4   On 23 March 1915 Samson arrived at Imbros with his unit. For the remainder of the year 'Samson's Pirates' - a soubriquet acquired during their service in Belgium and enhanced by their leader's stocky, bearded appearance-carried out a continual bombing assault on Turkish forces, interspersed with reconnaissance sorties. During this period, on 19 November, a pilot of No 3 Wing (as Samson's unit had become) Squadron Commander Richard Bell Davies DSO earned the Victoria Cross for deliberately landing near Turkish forces and retrieving another pilot of No. 3 Wing who had crashed. The Allied evacuation of Suvla and Anzac in December meant the withdrawal of Samson's unit to England, while

Samson himself was taken ill and spent several months convalescing in England. In May 1916 Samson was ordered to take command of HMS *Ben-my-Chree* with its attendant 'squadron' of two cargo steamers HMS *Anne* and HMS *Raven II* all based in Port Said, Egypt. In co-operation with both the Army and the Royal Navy, Samson's new command included reconnaissance of Turkish communication lines and general operations in the Red Sea. The *Ben-my-Chree* had been converted to carry floatplanes in a hangar, these being hoisted over the side when needed for operations and flown from the sea. Samson and his crews pursued an air and sea offensive against German and Turkish opponents from May 1916 to January 1917, creating a minor legend for their courage and daring. However, on 9 January, while harboured at Castelorizo the *Ben-my-Chree* was fatally hit by a Turkish land battery and Samson was forced to abandon ship with the crew. Finally on 13 January the ship sank in the shallow waters.

5   Arriving in Britain at the end of May 1917, Samson spent six months on staff duties with the Admiralty Air Department, then in November 1917 returned to more active duties when he was appointed commander of the naval air station at Great Yarmouth, home of several operational flying boat units. Here he remained until the formation of the Royal Air Force on 1 April 1918, although his heavy administrative responsibilities as station commander did not prevent him participating in many operational sorties in the Felixstowe flying boats and Sopwith Camels of his command.

With the reorganisation of the (now) single air service in April 1918, Samson left Yarmouth on transfer to Felixstowe, where he was given command of an RAF Group, comprising Felixstowe, Yarmouth, Westgate, Manston and a number of smaller units at Covehithe, Bacton, Holt, Brouah Castle, Lowestoft and Shotley. On 30 May 1918, Samson flew the first trial take-off in a Sopwith Camel from a 30 feet wooden platform being towed at sea and nearly drowned when the Camel toppled into the water. Undeterred, Samson had the platform modified and his labours came to fruition on 31 July when Lieutenant Stuart D. Culley successfully took off from the platform. On 11 August Culley rose from a similar towed 'runway' in a Camel and an hour later destroyed the airship L53 in flames. Continuing the energetic command of his Group until the Armistice, Samson decided to remain in the RAF at the end of the war, rather than return to the Royal Navy. Awarded the DSO and AFC, Samson was shortly afterwards promoted to air commodore and given command of RAF Near East.

6   The Sopwith two-seater, colloquially known as the 1½-Strutter due to its unusual wing strut arrangement, was the Company's first true fighting aircraft. It was armed with a Vickers gun firing through the propeller arc by means of the Kauper-Sopwith gun gear operated by the pilot, while the observer in the rear cockpit wielded a Lewis gun on a universal mounting. After reaching the RNAS in April 1916 the RFC pressed for similar aircraft required for the coming Battle of the Somme. Teething troubles with engine and gun stoppages were gradually overcome. A single-seat bomber version was produced and these became some of the first strategic bombers with the Royal Navy's No. 3 Wing in eastern France, carrying four 65lb bombs each to targets in the Ruhr. Impressed by both versions and influenced by the use of a French 130hp Clerget engine, the French air service equipped 70 escadrilles in 1917-18 with licence-manufactured aircraft. In all, over 4,200 were built in France for the French and Americans, while the Sopwith factory at Kingston built 246 and other British contractors 900. In 1918, after numbers had been relegated for training in Britain, some were converted as naval spotter aircraft for shipborne use.

7   It is interesting that Draper uses the rank 'Lieutenant Commander.' Reggie's Record of Service shows him as having been promoted to Squadron Commander, RNAS on 1 January 1916. There was always some difficulty in disentangling the RFC from the RNAS; not completely resolved until the formation of the RAF in 1918.

Chapter 5

Beating the Fokker
Captain Norman Macmillan

Returning from my morning fly
I met a Fokker in the sky,
And judging from its swift descent,
It had a nasty accident.
On thinking further of the same
I rather fear I was to blame.

Aon RFC

Norman Macmillan was born in Glasgow, Scotland, the son of John Campbell Macmillan and Jeanie and was educated at Allan Glen's School and the Royal Technical College. On the outbreak of the First World War, Macmillan enlisted as a private in the 9th (Glasgow Highland) Battalion of the Highland Light Infantry and served in Belgium and France, spending 16½ months in the trenches. He then transferred to the RFC, being commissioned as a temporary second lieutenant (on probation) on 26 September 1916 and was appointed a flying officer on 27 February 1917. Posted to 45 Squadron RFC, flying the Sopwith 1½ Strutter and Sopwith Camel aircraft, he became an ace, being credited with nine aerial victories between 5 June and 20 October 1917. He was also appointed a flight commander with the temporary rank of captain on 1 September 1917. Macmillan was removed from front line service after a flying accident on 6 January 1918 and returned to England where he served as a flying instructor. He received the Military Cross 'for conspicuous gallantry and devotion to duty' in February 1918 and also the Air Force Cross.

In addition to flying, Macmillan wrote numerous magazine articles, as well as books on aviation, including a series detailing the history of the Royal Air Force during the Second World War. Despite being partly written during the war they are remarkably detailed and accurate. He served in the Royal Air Force during World War II as a war correspondent, rising to the rank of acting wing commander.

'In the first few months of World War I', he wrote, 'most of our aeroplanes had certainly had the best of the German types in climb and speed. The Germans had probably realised before the war that this would be the case and when mobilisation was ordered they had several new types nearing completion. During 1914 the Germans usually kept out of our way; the design of our machines made forward shooting difficult and so rendered the pursuit of hostile aircraft a somewhat futile enterprise. We had two or three very high speed Sopwith Bullets with the original Expeditionary Force, but they were reported difficult to fly and were soon crashed. They had no satisfactory form of armament, though endeavours had been made to fix a rifle to fire outside the propeller and it had even been suggested that they should fly over their adversary and attack him with a grappling iron. The output of Lewis guns was only just beginning and the first guns of this type had so far proved very unreliable.

'Meanwhile the new German types had progressed and in the early summer of 1915 the first Fokker appeared on our front. This was a monoplane with a machine-gun firing through the propeller, a device which was turned down by the War Office in 1913 as being impracticable; its tactics were to hang about high up and then dive suddenly on the tail of some unsuspecting machine busily engaged in artillery reconnaissance, firing a heavy burst as it passed. The Fokker seldom persisted after two or three unsuccessful attacks and rarely manoeuvred or put up a fight if counter-attacked, but it took us by surprise and caused a certain number of casualties among our artillery machines, the B.E.2C.

'Unfortunately, the politician and the Press at home took up the Fokker and proclaimed its superiority to anything we possessed with great vehemence... The Germans must have rejoiced, for when we captured a Fokker a little later on, we found it to be a machine of very mediocre performance; its real strong point lay in the fact that its machine gun fired through the propeller. However, our best pilots soon took its measure and, with the advent of our single-seater fighters the De Havilland 2 and F.E.8, the Fokker of that type finally vanished from the scene.

'The appearance of this German gear for firing through the propeller and which came to be known as the 'interrupter gear,' caused a great flutter among our designers. Our efforts to introduce a similar device into our own Service were at first a little pathetic. We used guns firing over the top plane; we cased our propellers in bullet-proof steel and fired through them regardless of hitting the blades. Sopwith produced a mechanical interrupter gear which worked fairly well; finally a Rumanian named Constantinesco gave us his hydraulic gear which became our standard interrupter. I look upon this as the cleverest invention I saw throughout the war. It was far superior to anything the Germans had and was absolutely reliable if properly looked after.'[1]

Macmillan relinquished his RAF commission 'on ceasing to be employed' on 10 June 1919 though this was later cancelled. He was re-employed by the RAF and granted a temporary commission as a flight lieutenant on 15 April 1921. He served as a flying instructor to the Spanish Navy and Army Air Forces, seeing action in the Spanish front lines during the Rif War in Morocco.

In 1922 the *Daily News* sponsored round the world flight from England via Paris, Marseilles, Athens, Aboukir, Baghdad, Karachi, Calcutta, Rangoon, Hong-Kong, Japan, Vancouver and then across America and the Atlantic. On 24 April Major W. T. Blake, Lieutenant Colonel Browne and Captain Norman Macmillan left Croydon on the first stage to Calcutta in a modified De Havilland D.H.9 (G-EBDE). Quite early they experienced trouble and put their machine out of gear in a forced landing at Marseilles, where Geoffrey Malins took the place of Lieutenant Colonel Browne. After a long wait for a new machine (G-EBDL) the journey was resumed; Brindisi was reached on 27 June and Athens on 4 July. After making a fine flight of 464 miles across the sea in the land machine, they drained their petrol tanks and came down in the Arabian Desert. Machines from Baghdad went out in search of the airmen with petrol supplies. At length the dogged aviators reached India, where they met with much stormy weather and continual engine troubles and at Calcutta Major Blake was ill and had to be left behind in hospital. Macmillan and Malins continued the second stage of the flight from Calcutta to Vancouver on a Fairey IIIC floatplane (G-EBDI) but after fresh engine troubles they were forced to descend in a rough sea in the Bay of Bengal. For three days and two nights they were on their overturned seaplane without food or water. By sheer good fortune they were then rescued and further flight was abandoned. Macmillan would subsequently write of the attempt in his 1937 book, *Freelance Pilot*. During the early 1920s, Macmillan worked as a free-lance test pilot, unattached to any particular company. He flew Fairey aircraft from 1921 and also took five Parnall aircraft on their first flights, taking part in the 1923 Lympne light aircraft trials, demonstrating the Parnall Pixie aircraft. Macmillan eventually joined Fairey full-time in early 1925 as chief test pilot and stayed with them until the end of 1930. He then became chief consultant test pilot to Armstrong Whitworth Aircraft. In 1925 he was the first to land (an emergency landing) at Heathrow, which was then a row of cottages in land used for market gardening.[2]

Endnotes Chapter 5

1   George 'Gogu' Constantinescu was a Romanian scientist, engineer and inventor. During his career, he registered over 130 inventions. He settled in England in 1912. His hydraulic machine gun synchronization gear allowed aircraft-mounted guns to shoot between the spinning blades of the propeller. The Constantinesco synchronization gear was first used operationally on the D.H.4s of 55 Squadron RFC from March 1917 and rapidly became standard equipment, replacing a variety of mechanical gears. It continued to be used by the RAF until World War II - the Gloster Gladiator being the last British fighter to be equipped with 'CC' gear.

2   Wing Commander Norman Macmillan OBE MC DFC DL died on 5 August 1976.

Chapter 6

Flying Circus, Knights
Under The Black Cross

There they came, gaining height over No Man's Land in a wide climbing sweep, the throaty roar of their primitive Mercedes-160 engines ripping the morning air. They were sleek-lined, V-strutted Albatros D.IIIs - twenty of them - drawn from Germany's four crack hunting squadrons, led by Manfred von Richthofen.

There was something menacing in the sight of them. The Red Baron's machine was scarlet. The others in his legendary Jasta 11 were also red, but with individual markings: Allmenröder, a white tail; Schaefer, black tail and black elevators; Richthofen's brother Lothar, yellow strips. The rest of the aeroplanes in the awesome flying wedge had been painted in the whole spectrum of vivid colours, in every garish combination the Teutonic brain could conjure up.

Far beneath Richthofen's flight lay a section of the Western Front. They could see the lines of the great battle that had been raging since Easter Monday. Ragged puffs of white smoke told them where the enemy's barrage shells were bursting. The ground on both sides of the zigzag lines of trenches was dark brown where it had been churned up by the heavy shelling of the past few weeks.

There was plenty of activity this morning. The British artillery was blasting a barrage all along the front, the greatest fire being concentrated near Arras and Vimy Ridge. Allied aeroplanes were operating with the guns, ranging them on the German lines. There were Martinsydes, 'Spads', Bristols, Sopwiths, Nieuports, R.E.8s, F.E.2s...

Schaefer saw them first. He pointed below. The leader looked down and saw a flight of British aeroplanes. They were F.E.2s of 57 Squadron and Sopwith Pups of 3 (Naval) Squadron. Richthofen gave the signal to attack and the formation dived to intercept.

As they dived their minds were blank of everything but the action to come. Certainly they did not think that this attack was to herald a new concept in aerial warfare. For this was the first encounter by history's first Jagdgruppe - a fearsome flying Armada with enormous fire-power, against which no enemy machine operating singly could hope to survive. It was the last day of Bloody April 1917.

Manfred von Richthofen, the war's highest-scoring ace with eighty victories, well known for his all-red fighter aircraft and 'Flying Circus' Jagdstaffel (fighter squadron), came from a distinguished family, long prominent in eastern German government and economic affairs, which in 1741 was elevated to baronial status in the Kingdom of Prussia. It was not until the 19th Century, however, that the family produced its first career military officer, Major Albrecht Freiherr von Richthofen. In turn, he became the father of two of the most prominent German fighter aces of World War I. Manfred and Lothar von Richthofen, whose combined combat score totalled 120 enemy aircraft. Both sons were born in Breslau, Germany before the era of powered flight began. Manfred on 2 May 1892 and Lothar on 27 September 1894. Their father's military career was cut short when he developed an ear infection after plunging into a stream to rescue a member of his dragoon regiment. The elder von Richthofen could no longer serve on active duty and was granted a disability pension. Although a Freiherr - the lineal title of the von Richthofen's - he was just half a step below a baron in the German nobility, it generally carried with it a sizeable estate. It was to this estate in Schweidnitz, in the province of Silesia (now part of Poland) that Major von Richthofen and his family retired. There, young Manfred and Lothar spent their formative years, learning the duties and obligations of their station in life. Manfred, a natural horseman and athlete, wanted only to spend his days on the playing fields of Schweidnitz. His father had other ideas, however and at the age of 11 Manfred was sent to the Cadet Academy at Wahlstatt. He spent six years in the Cadet Corps and two years in the military School in Lichterfelde before taking and passing his army officer's examination in 1911.

Manfred was commissioned in the autumn of 1912 and was deployed with the Uhlan Regiment No 1 in eastern Germany when World War I began on 1 August 1914. Encamped along the Russian border, the Uhlans were among the first German troops to march into Czarist territory. The main concern of German military planners at this time was the Western Front, so before the war was a month old Manfred von Richthofen's unit was heading for France. There, the long and dismal prospects of protracted ground warfare became immediately clear to von Richthofen. His early interest in cavalry activities grew out of the knowledge that those mounted troops were always assigned the exciting missions of reconnoitring enemy lines through a series of fast dashes past bewildered infantrymen. However, the growing network of trench fortifications was particularly frustrating to cavalry elements on both sides of the lines.

To circumvent the long line of trenches and obtain badly-needed intelligence information, military planners designated their military aircraft the 'cavalry of the clouds'. Sensing this development was the way to end the boredom of life behind the lines, Manfred von Richthofen applied for transfer to the German Fliegertruppe, as the flying service was then known.

On 10 June 1915 Leutnant Manfred von Richthofen reported to Fliegerersatzabteilung 6 at Grossenhain in Saxony to begin his training as an aviation observer. At the time it was customary to train enlisted men as pilots - making them literally aerial chauffeurs - and placing officer observers in charge of the aircraft. Hence, it was in keeping with von Richthofen's status to train him initially as an observer. Accepting all of this, von Richthofen was quite surprised when he was quickly posted to Feldfliegerabteilung 69 and assigned a pilot senior in rank to him; Oberleutnant Georg Zeumer. The two men fast became friends, but Manfred von Richthofen was to serve for less than two months with Feldfliegerabteilung 69 on the Eastern Front. In the third week of August 1915 he headed west again for an assignment with a unit in Flanders, where he would see aerial combat.

Leutnant von Richthofen was assigned to a squadron with the curious name of Brieftauben Abteilung Ostende (Carrier Pigeon Unit, Ostend), this being a codename to conceal the unit's mission. This posting introduced von Richthofen to the first generation of large, multi-engined German bombers. Reunited with his friend Oberleutnant Georg Zeumer, Manfred von Richthofen was in one of the unit's AEG GI bombers when he shed his first drop of blood for the fatherland. Assigned to drop bombs over the side of the fuselage, von Richthofen leaned too far on one occasion and nicked a finger on one of the propellers moving the twin-engined pusher aircraft. He subsequently wore his blood-stained glove like a badge of honour. Zeumer and von Richthofen were flying a morning reconnaissance patrol on 1 September 1915 when they spotted a Farman biplane performing a similar mission. A quick nod of agreement between pilot and observer was all that was needed for them to abandon their patrol and undertake their first aerial combat. The two slow and awkward aircraft went around and around, each trying to gain the advantage. When the battle appeared elusive, the Farman pilot slipped away, leaving Zeumer and von Richthofen frustrated at the lack of a conclusion to what they had imagined to be a glorious event.

During the Battle of the Champagne in the autumn of 1915, Manfred von Richthofen chanced to meet the celebrated ace Oberleutnant Oswald Böelcke. Born on 19 May 1891 in Giebichenstein, the son of a schoolmaster, Böelcke was one of the most influential patrol leaders and tacticians of the early years of air combat. Böelcke's family moved to Dessau, the capital of the Duchy of Anhalt when he was young. As a youth he caught whooping cough; in order to build up his stamina, he became increasingly involved in playing sports but retained a tendency towards asthma throughout his life. Among his athletic pursuits were swimming, tennis, rowing and gymnastics. Oswald Böelcke was studious as well as athletic, excelling at mathematics and physics. His father was a nationalist and a militarist. Under his influence, the 13-year-old Böelcke had the audacity to write a personal letter to the Kaiser requesting an appointment to military school. His wish was granted, but his parents objected and he did not attend Cadet School. Instead he attended Herzog Friedrichs-Gymnasium, graduating Easter 1911. After leaving school he joined Telegraphen-Bataillon Nr.3 in Koblenz as a Fahnenjunker (cadet officer) on 15 March 1911. After attending Kriegsschule in Metz, Alsace-Lorraine where he took his lieutenant's exam, he received an officer commission in the Prussian Army a year later. Since Böelcke had Abitur, his commission was pre-dated 23 August 1910, making him senior to the other new lieutenants in his battalion.

Böelcke is considered the father of the German fighter air force, as well as the 'Father of Air Fighting Tactics'. He was the first to formalize rules of air fighting, which he presented as the 'Dicta Böelcke'. While he promulgated rules for the individual pilot, his main concern was the use of formation fighting rather than single effort.

Eager to learn the secrets of successful aerial combat, Richthofen blurted out: 'Tell me honestly, how do you really do it?' Böelcke laughed at the directness of the question and then answered: 'It is really quite simple. I fly in as close as I can, take good aim, open fire... and my opponent falls.'

Böelcke's simple piece of advice was enough to convince Manfred von Richthofen that he could never make a significant contribution to the war effort sitting in the back seat of a bomber or reconnaissance aircraft. To correct that situation he prevailed upon Zeumer to teach him how to fly. Less than a week later, on 10 October 1915, von Richthofen made his first solo flight, which would have been perfect if his over-eagerness had not caused the aircraft to turn over on landing. Zeumer later flew with Jasta 2 in 1917, by which time he was suffering from tuberculosis. He was killed in action on 17 June 1917, a quicker end to his suffering.[1]

After further, more formal training at Döberitz and a visit to the Fokker aircraft factory at Schwerin, Manfred von Richthofen was assigned to Kampfstaffel 2, a unit which used a variety of aircraft. He became involved in an aerial combat south-west of Douaumont on 26 April 1916 and, although the German Army official report mentioned his actions, he did not receive full credit for a Nieuport fighter which he brought down that day. To add to von Richthofen's frustration, his unit was sent back to the Russian Front, where there would be even less opportunity for aerial combat.

A second chance meeting with Hauptmann Oswald Böelcke, who was charged with assembling one of the first fighter squadrons and was on a tour of various units to select the best pilots changed that. Meeting von Richthofen, the great ace remembered the zealous young nobleman and subsequently added his name to the list of candidates for the new squadron, officially known as Jagdstaffel 2. Manfred von Richthofen was so pleased to have finally joined a fighter squadron that he urged his younger brother Lothar to apply for aviation duties. Like his older brother, Lothar had attended the Cadet School and then the Military School. When, in the autumn of 1916, he received Manfred's letter extolling the virtues of the air service, he was already a veteran of cavalry service with Dragoon Regiment No. 4 and had learned the frustration of cavalry unable to fulfil its proper role. Lothar was further encouraged when he learned that on 17 September Manfred had scored his first official aerial victory, an F.E.2b of 11 Squadron, which he attacked over Villers-Plouich. By the year's end, Manfred would be one of the leading lights of the Imperial German Air Service with fifteen victories.

While Manfred von Richthofen was adding to his score, Lothar was undergoing observer's training which culminated in a posting to Kampfstaffel 23 on the Somme in December. He would not remain long in an obscure combat unit. On 28 October 1916, less than four months after the death of Max Immelmann, Oswald Böelcke rushed to get ready for his sixth sortie of the day with his two best pilots, Manfred von Richthofen and Erwin Böhme and three others. The patrol eventually led them into a dogfight with single-seater D.H.2 fighters of 24 Squadron RFC. In the ensuing dogfight, Böelcke and Böhme, unaware of each other's presence, closed in on the same aircraft, flown by Captain Arthur Gerald Knight. Born in July 1895 in Bedford, the younger Knight was a student of Applied Science at Upper Canada College when he joined the RFC in 1915. His first victory was on 22 June 1916, flying an Airco D.H.2 of 24 Squadron to destroy an LVG C reconnaissance aircraft over Courcelette. His next two kills were of the 'driven down out of control' variety, but for his fourth victory, on 14 September, he helped Captain Stanley Cockerell flame a Fokker fighter. The following day, he singlehandedly flamed another German fighter. A month later, he drove a Roland C.II down out of control. On 9 November 1916 he shared the destruction of an enemy fighter with Lieutenant Alfred Edwin McKay and Lieutenant Eric Clowes Pashley. In May 1913 Eric had opened a Flying School at Shoreham with his brother Cecil under the name Pashley Brothers and trained many pilots who would later join the RFC. 'Eddie' McKay was born on 27 December 1892 at

Brussels, Ontario and attended the University of Western Ontario.

Von Richthofen dived in on the flightpath of McKay's D.H.2. McKay, pursued by Richthofen, cut across between Knight and his assailants. In the resultant dodges and swerves, Böhme's landing gear wheels damaged Böelcke's upper wing and Böelcke swerved to avoid a collision with the interceding aircraft. As the fabric peeled off the upper wing of his aircraft, Böelcke struggled for control. He and his aircraft fell out of sight into a cloud. When it emerged, the top wing was gone. However, Böelcke made a relatively soft crash-landing. The impact seemed survivable. However, in his haste to get airborne Böelcke had failed to strap on his safety belt properly and his lap belt did not restrain him; and he never wore a helmet when he flew. Minutes later, his lifeless body was pulled from his smashed Albatros D.II. Böelcke, victor of forty aerial engagements, was dead at age of 25.

Captain Knight transferred to 29 Squadron as the flight commander, 'B' Flight, still flying a D.H.2. He was awarded the Military Cross on 14 November and a DSO followed on 11 December. He scored his eighth victory five days later, destroying an enemy fighter northeast of Arras, continuing his attack on a second despite a broken machine gun extractor. On 20 December Knight led his final patrol before ten days' leave. He did not return. His patrol of four made it back, but badly battered by combat. Knight had become the Red Baron's thirteenth victim. The British pilot was just 21 years old. The only known description of Knight's demise comes from the victor's combat report: '...I attacked him at closest range.... I saw immediately that I had hit the enemy. First he went down in curves and then he crashed to the ground. I pursued him until 100 metres above the ground.'

Eric Pashley was killed in a flying accident on 17 March 1917. He had eight victories. 'Eddie' McKay would score ten victories before his death in combat on 28 December 1917 when his 'Spad' was shot down by a German two-seater between Gheluvelt and Dadizeele.

With the loss of Max Immelmann and Oswald Böelcke the Imperial German air service's need for a hero figure was met by Manfred von Richthofen. By the middle of November 1916 his score stood at thirteen and there it nearly ended for on 23 November Richthofen fought what he later described as the toughest air battle of his whole career. His opponent was the leading RFC ace of the day, Major Lanoe George Hawker VC DSO, officer commanding 24 Squadron, who was flying an Airco D.H.2 single-seat scout.

Son of a distinguished military family, Hawker was born on 30 December 1890 at Longparish, Hampshire. Lanoe was sent to Stubbington House School and at the age of 11 to the Royal Navy College in Dartmouth, but although highly intelligent and an enthusiastic sportsman, his grades were disappointing. As a naval career became more unlikely, he entered The Royal Military Academy in Woolwich before joining the Royal Engineers, as an officer cadet. A clever inventor, Hawker developed a keen interest in all mechanical and engineering developments and his innovative ideas throughout his flying career would greatly benefit the still fledgling RFC. On 1 August 1914 his request for attachment to the RFC was granted and he reported to the Central Flying School at Upavon.

Hawker was posted to France in October 1914, as a captain with 6 Squadron, flying Henri Farmans. The squadron converted to the B.E.2c and he undertook numerous reconnaissance flights into 1915, being wounded once by ground fire. On 22 April he was awarded the DSO for attacking a Zeppelin shed at Gontrode by dropping hand grenades below 200 feet from his B.E.2c.

During the Second Battle of Ypres, Hawker was wounded in the foot by ground fire. For the remainder of the battle he had to be carried to and from his aircraft, but refused to be grounded until the fight was over. Returning to 6 Squadron after hospitalisation, the squadron now received several single seat scouts and some early F.E.2 'pushers'. His first aerial victory was in June 1915. Then, on 25 July when on patrol over Passchendaele, Captain Hawker attacked three German aircraft in succession. He shot the first one down by emptying a complete drum of bullets from his single Lewis machine gun into it; the second was driven to the ground damaged and the third, an Albatros C.I which he attacked at a height of about 10,000 feet, burst into flames and crashed. (Oberleutnant Uebelacker and his observer Hauptmann Roser were both killed.) For this feat he was awarded the Victoria Cross.

Hawker claimed at least three more victories in August 1915, either in the Scout or flying an F.E.2 before being posted back to England in late 1915 with seven victory claims making him the first British flying ace. Hawker flew before Britain had any workable synchroniser gear to enable the pilot shooting through the propeller arc, so his Bristol Scout had its machine gun mounted on the left side of the cockpit, firing forwards and sideways at a 45 degree angle to avoid the propeller. The only direction from which he could attack an enemy was from its right rear quarter - precisely in a direction from which it was easy for the observer to fire at him. Thus, in each of the three attacks, Hawker was directly exposed to the fire of an enemy machine gun.

Early in 1916 Hawker was promoted to major and given command of 24 Squadron at Hounslow Heath aerodrome. This, the RFC's first (single seater) fighter squadron, flew the Airco D.H.2 'pusher'. After two fatalities in recent flying accidents, the new fighter, which featured a rear mounted rotary engine and was armed with a forward-mounted Lewis machine gun, soon earned a reputation for spinning, due in part to its sensitive controls which made it very responsive. Hawker flew a D.H.2 over Hounslow Heath and in front of the squadron pilots, put the aircraft through a series of spins, each time recovering safely. After landing, he carefully described to all pilots the correct procedures to recover from a spin. Once the pilots became used to the D.H.2's characteristics, confidence in the aircraft rose quickly, as they came to appreciate its manoeuvrability.

Major Hawker then led the squadron back to Bertangles, north of the Somme in February 1916, where the squadron quickly helped counter the Fokker Eindecker monoplanes of the Fliegertruppe which were dominant over the Western Front in the run up to the Somme offensive in July 1916. Hawker's aggressive personal philosophy of 'Attack Everything' formed the entire text of his tactical order of 30 June and 24 Squadron claimed seventy victories by November for the loss of twelve aircraft and 21 pilots killed, wounded or missing. Around this time, Hawker developed a ring gunsight and created a clamp and spring-clip device to hold the Lewis in place on the D.H.2. He also designed sheepskin boots that reached to the upper thigh, known as 'fug-boots,' which became standard issue to combat the risk of frostbite at high altitude. By mid 1916 RFC policy was to ban squadron commanders from operational flying but Hawker continued to fly frequent offensive patrols and reconnaissance flights, particularly over the Somme battlefields. As the year wore on, the Germans introduced far more potent fighters to the front, starting with the Luftstreitkräfte's first biplane fighter, the single-gun armed Halberstadt D.II and shortly thereafter the even more advanced, twin-gunned Albatros D.I, rapidly making the D.H.2 obsolete.

On 23 November 1916, while flying an Airco D.H.2 (5964), Hawker left Bertangles aerodrome at 1300 hours as part of 'A' Flight, led by Captain John Oliver Andrews and including Lieutenant Robert Henry Magnus Spencer Saundby, the son of Professor Robert Saundby, born in Birmingham born on 26 April 1896. Andrews, a Manchester brewer's son born on 20 July that same year, led the flight in an attack on two German aircraft over Achiet. Spotting a larger flight of German aircraft above Andrews was about to break off the attack, but spotted Hawker diving to attack. Andrews and Saundby followed him to back him up in his fight; Andrews drove off one of the Germans attacking Hawker and then took bullets in his engine and glided out of the fight under Saundby's covering fire.[2]

Losing contact with the other D.H.2s, Hawker began a lengthy dogfight with an Albatros D.II flown by Manfred von Richthofen. The Albatros was faster than the D.H.2, more powerful and, with a pair of IMG 08 machine guns, more heavily armed. Richthofen fired 900 rounds during the running battle. Running low on fuel, Hawker eventually broke away from the combat and attempted to return to Allied lines. The Red Baron's guns jammed fifty yards from the lines, but a bullet from his last burst struck Hawker in the back of his head, killing him instantly. His D.H.2 spun from 1,000 feet and crashed 220 yards east of Luisenhof Farm, just south of Bapaume on the Flers Road, becoming the Red Baron's eleventh victim.

Von Richthofen described the battle between Bapaume and Albert with supreme arrogance in his diary: 'The Englishman tried to catch me up in the rear while I tried to get round behind him. So we circled round and round like madmen after one another at an altitude of about 10,000 feet. First we circled twenty times to the left and then thirty times to the right. Each tried to get behind and above the other.

'When we had got down to about 6,000 feet without having achieved anything particular, my opponent ought to have discovered that it was time for him to take his leave. The wind was favourable for me, for it drove us more and more towards the German positions. At last we were above Bapaume, about half a mile behind the German front. The gallant fellow was full of pluck and when we had got down to about 3,000 feet he merrily waved at me as if to say, 'Well, how do you do?'

'The circles which we made around one another were so narrow that their diameter was probably no more than 250 or 300 feet. I had time to take a good look at my opponent. I looked down into his cockpit and could see every movement of his head. If he had not had his helmet on I would have seen what kind of face he was making.

'My Englishman was a good sportsman, but by and by the thing became a little too hot for him. He had to decide whether he would land on German ground or whether he would fly back to the English lines. Of course he tried the latter, after having endeavoured in vain to escape me by loopings and such tricks. At that time his first bullets were flying around me, for so far neither of us had been able to do any shooting. When he had come down to about 300 feet he tried to escape by flying a zigzag course, which makes it difficult for an observer on the ground to shoot. That was my most favourable moment. I followed him at an altitude of from 250 to 150 feet, firing all the time. The Englishman could not help falling. But the jamming of my gun had robbed me of success.

'My opponent fell, shot through the head 150 feet behind our lines. His machine gun was dug out of the ground and it ornaments the entrance of my dwelling...' German Grenadiers reported burying Hawker 250 yards east of Luisenhof Farm along the roadside.

Manfred von Richthofen scored his 16th victory on 4 January 1917. Twelve days later he was awarded the coveted 'Pour le Mérite', the strikingly attractive gold and blue enamel Maltese cross with black and white neck ribbon referred to as the 'Blue Max', the highest Prussian bravery award. Manfred was given command of his own fighter squadron, Jagdstaffel 11 and, like Böelcke before him, was allowed to select many of the members. An early choice was his brother Lothar. When Manfred von Richthofen was proposed for the special distinction of golden oak leaves for his 'Pour le Mérite', some members of the German General Staff protested that such an honour should be reserved for a higher-ranking officer who had won a battle. To that the German Army Chief of Staff, General Erich Ludendorff, replied that Manfred von Richthofen, then a rittmeister or cavalry captain, 'had done more than win a battle'. Manfred von Richthofen had certainly paid a certain price for his success. He had suffered a slight head wound during a fight in July 1917 and the cumulative effect of it was to cause headaches of increasing intensity. Shortly before his death, he wrote: 'I am in wretched spirits after every aerial battle. But that no doubt is an after-effect of my head wound. When I set foot on the ground again at my airfield after a flight I go to my quarters and do not want to see anyone or hear anything.'

Within two weeks of his arrival at Jagdstaffel 11, Lothar von Richthofen proved his worth by scoring his first aerial victory. On the afternoon of 28 March he shot down an F.E.2b of 25 Squadron RFC near Vimy. The following month - made infamous as 'Bloody April' due to the high level of casualties suffered by the Allies - both von Richthofen brothers added significantly to their scores. Manfred shot down another 21 British aircraft, bringing his total to 52, while Lothar shot down fifteen British aircraft to raise his score to sixteen.

Rittmeister Manfred Freiherr von Richthofen described his 33rd victory on 2 April 1917 in *My First Double Event*. 'The second of April 1917 was a very warm day for my Jasta. From my quarters I could clearly hear the drumfire of the guns which was again particularly violent.

'I was still in bed when my orderly rushed into the room and exclaimed: 'Sir, the English are here!' Sleepy as I was, I looked out of the window and, really, there were my dear friends circling over the flying ground. I jumped out of my bed and into my clothes in a jiffy. My Red Bird had been pulled out and was ready for starting. My mechanics knew that I should probably not allow such a favourable moment to go by unused. Everything was ready. I snatched up my furs and then went off.

'I was the last to start. My comrades were much nearer to the enemy. I feared that my prey would escape me, that I should have to look on from a distance while the others were fighting. Suddenly one of the impertinent fellows tried to drop down upon me. I allowed him to come near and then we started a merry quadrille. Sometimes my opponent flew on his back and sometimes he did other tricks. He had a double-seated chaser. I was his master and very soon I recognized that he could not escape me.

'During an interval in the fighting I convinced myself that we were alone. It followed that the victory would accrue to him who was calmest, who shot best and who had the clearest brain in a moment of danger. After a short time I got him beneath me without seriously hurting him with my gun. We were at least two kilometres from the front. I thought he intended to land but there I had made a mistake. Suddenly, when he was only a few yards above the ground, he once more went off on a straight course. He tried to escape me. That was too bad. I attacked him again and I went so low that I feared I should touch the roofs of the houses of the village beneath me. The Englishman defended himself up to the last moment. At the very end I felt that my engine had been hit. Still I did not let go. He had to fall. He rushed at full speed right into a block of houses.

'There was little left to be done. This was once more a case of splendid daring. He defended himself to the last. However, in my opinion he showed more foolhardiness than courage. This was one of the cases where one must differentiate between energy and idiocy.

'He had to come down in any case but he paid for his stupidity with his life.

'I was delighted with the performance of my red machine during its morning work and return to our quarters. My comrades were still in the air and they were very surprised, when, as we met at breakfast, I told them that I had scored my thirty-second machine.

'A very young Leutnant had 'bagged' his first airplane. We were all very merry and prepared everything for further battles.

'I then went and groomed myself. I had not had time to do it previously. I was visited by a dear friend, Leutnant Voss of Böelcke's Jasta. We chatted. Voss had destroyed his twenty-third machine the day before. He was next to me on the list and is at present my most redoubtable competitor.'

Werner Voss, a dyer's son from Krefeld, born 13 April 1897, began his military career in November 1914 as a 17-year-old Hussar. After turning to aviation, he proved to be a natural pilot. After flight school and six months in a bomber unit, he joined the newly formed Jagdstaffel 2 on 21 November 1916. There he became friends with Manfred von Richthofen. By 6 April 1917 Voss had scored 24 victories and awarded Germany's highest award, the 'Pour le Mérite'. The medal's mandatory month's leave removed Voss from the battlefield during 'Bloody April'; in his absence, Richthofen scored thirteen victories. Nevertheless, Richthofen regarded Voss as his only possible rival as top scoring ace of the war. Soon after Voss returned from leave, he was at odds with his squadron commander. He was detailed from his squadron to evaluate new fighter aircraft and was enthused by the Fokker Triplane. After transferring through three temporary squadron commands in two months, Voss was given command of Jagdstaffel 10 on 30 July 1917 at Richthofen's request. By now, his victory total was 34.

Voss was brought down on the evening of 23 September, just hours after his

48th victory, by 56 Squadron S.E.5a's. For at least eight minutes Voss fought his attackers but was eventually defeated by 2nd Lieutenant Rhys-Davids,[3] Captain James McCudden, Captain Geoffrey Hilton 'Beery' Bowman DSO MC* DFC CdeG,[4] Captain Richard 'Dick' Aveline Maybery MC*,[5] 2nd Lieutenant Keith Knox Muspratt MC[6] and Lieutenant Verschoyle 'Versh' Philip Cronyn MC. Voss, who made no attempt to escape, fired on and hit McCudden in the wing and forced Muspratt and Cronyn, a Canadian, born 20 September 1895, out of the battle with hits to their engines.

'C' Flight arrived led by Captain Reginald Theodore Carlos 'Georgie' Hoidge MC* as another German fighter, a red-nosed Albatros, arrived to assist the besieged Triplane. Born in Toronto, Ontario, Canada, Hoidge originally served with the Canadian Royal Garrison Artillery before transferring to the British Army, taking a commission in the Royal Garrison Artillery (Special Reserve) and was attached to the RFC as a second lieutenant on 15 November 1916. He was posted to 56 Squadron to fly the S.E.5 in 1917. He flew this aircraft for all his 28 victories. He and Maybery attempted to attack the Triplane but were unsuccessful, as was a counter-move by the Germans which was broken up by McCudden and Rhys-Davids. Arthur Percival Foley Rhys-Davids DSO MC* was born on 26 September 1897 to an affluent family. His father was a professional academic and his mother a prolific author which afforded the young Rhys-Davids thorough schooling. He showed considerable potential in all subjects and was an excellent student. A fine athlete and classical scholar, at the age of 14 he attended Eton College where he was head boy and gained his School Certificate in July 1913 with higher marks than any other student. In mid-1916 he applied for a commission in the RFC. On 28 August 1916 he reported for training and was assigned to 56 Squadron on 7 March 1917. Rhys-Davids gained his first victory on 23 May and began a steady run of success.

His first victory on 23 September is claimed to have been Oberleutnant Carl Menckhoff, who had 39 victories, who is said to have come to the aid of Werner Voss. Rhys Davids reportedly turned from engaging Voss and damaged Menckhoff's Albatros so badly that he had to crash land it. However, Menckhoff made no mention of this engagement in his later memoirs and his involvement has been questioned. As Rhys-Davids attacked the Fokker, the Albatros engaged him from astern. Maybery forced it to disengage. The Triplane was now alone in the fight. Voss, wearing a colourful civilian silk dress shirt beneath his unbuttoned knee-length brown leather coat, his polished brown boots shining from below the coat's hem, his 'Pour le Mérite' at his throat, repeatedly evaded 56 Squadron's fighter attacks. Eventually he made a flat turn enabling Rhys-Davids to get onto his tail. Bowman believed the German was momentarily distracted intent on attacking himself, otherwise doubting Rhys-Davids' ability to get onto the Fokker's tail so easily. With his propeller 'boss almost on the rudder' Rhys-Davids fired.

With the exception of Muspratt, who had landed at the 1 Squadron aerodrome with a seized engine, the rest of 56 Squadron landed back at Estrée-Blanche. Combat reports by the pilots were written and submitted.

'When we heard the news at luncheon', continues Maurice Baring, 'the General sent me to 56 Squadron, where the pilots had brought him down, to get details. This was Rhys-Davids' account of the fight as he told it to me himself:

'I saw three Huns attacking one S.E.; one triplane, light grey and brown, with slight extensions, one red-nosed V-Strutter, one green-nosed Scout. I never saw the green Scout again after the first dive. I then saw four S.E.'s fighting the triplane and the red-nosed V-Strutter. The triplane's top-plane was larger than the middle-plane. The engine was not a Mercedes, but I thought it was stationary. I wasn't sure. It had four guns. I thought the pilot was wearing a black leather flying-cap. Fired six or seven times and then went off to change my drum. The Hun either had armoured plates or else he was very lucky.

'Last dive but one. I went for him. He came from the east. Not quite straight behind, fired from a hundred yards to seventy and emptied a whole drum. The triplane only turned when twenty yards away. I turned to the right, so did he. Thought situation impossible and that there would be a collision. I turned left and avoided him. I next saw the triplane at 1,500 feet below gliding west. Dived again, opened fire at about 100. Got one shot out of the Vickers (my Lewis drum was empty) without taking sights off. Reloaded my Vickers. Fired another twenty or thirty rounds. He overshot and zoomed away. Changed drum, then made for the red-nosed V-Strutter and started firing at about 100 yards. The V-Strutter was flying at an angle of about 45 degrees across the front and I came at him slightly above. We both fired at each other. He stopped firing. I dived underneath him and zoomed up the other side. I saw the V-Strutter about 600 feet below spiralling North-West. I then lost sight of him and kept a good look-out low East, but saw no signs of him. During the whole scrap there were eleven to fourteen enemy aircraft higher east who made no attempt to fight.'

'If I could only have brought him down alive...' Arthur Rhys Davids to Captain James McCudden.

McCudden said he saw a crash NNW of Zonnebeck. On the evening of the 23rd he had just attacked and destroyed an enemy two-seater aeroplane when he saw another S.E.5 pilot in combat with a Fokker triplane. With other members of his squadron he joined in the fight and it soon became apparent that the German pilot had exceptional skill and courage. He fought seven opponents for some time, single-handed, but was later joined by a red-nosed Albatros fighter. Later still, formations of other Albatros fighters arrived, with a group of British 'Spads' close behind them. For some time the fight was waged fiercely, with the Fokker triplane dazzlingly elusive. Then at last Second Lieutenant Rhys-Davids got into a favourable firing position. What happened next is told in an extract from his combat report: '...The red-nosed Albatros and the triplane fought magnificently. I got in several good bursts at the triplane, without apparent effect and twice placed a new Lewis drum on my gun. Eventually I got east and slightly above the triplane and made for it, getting in a whole Lewis drum and a corresponding number of Vickers into him. He made no attempt to turn, until I was so close to him I was certain we would collide. He passed my right-hand wing by inches and went down. I zoomed. I saw him next with his engine apparently off, gliding west. I dived again and got one shot out of my Vickers; however, I reloaded and kept in the dive. I got in another good burst and the triplane did a slight right-hand turn, still going down. I had now overshot him (this was at 1,000 feet), zoomed, but never saw him again. Immediately afterwards I met the red-nosed scout, who was a very short way south-east of me. I started firing at 100 yards. The enemy aircraft then turned and fired at me. At thirty yards range I finished a Lewis drum and my Vickers stopped, so I dived underneath him and zoomed. When I looked again, I saw the enemy aircraft spiralling down steeply out of control.'

Captain McCudden watched the triplane, still being engaged by Rhys-Davids. 'I noticed the triplane's movements were very erratic... I saw him go into a steep dive into the ground on the British side of the lines where it seemed to disappear into a thousand fragments for it seemed to me that it literally went into powder.'

When the remains of the German pilot were examined, he was identified as Fliegerleutnant Werner Voss, who was at the time of his death, second on the list of successful German fighting pilots with forty-nine Allied aeroplanes to his credit... In his career and in his character he had much in common with McCudden, who wrote: 'As long as I live I shall never forget my admiration for that German pilot, who, single handed, fought seven of us for ten minutes and also put some bullets through all of our machines. His flying was wonderful, his courage magnificent and, in my opinion, he was the bravest German airman whom it has been my privilege to see fight.'

Maybery said: 'I saw the triplane and went down after it. It was grey with slight extensions as far as I can remember. It was followed by a green Scout. Someone came and shunted the green Scout. After that I saw Rhys-Davids dive on the triplane, followed by the red-nosed Scout. I attacked the red-nosed Scout. I zoomed up over him and couldn't see anything of them. I saw a triplane going east, but this one seemed to be different and green.'

Hoidge said: 'I saw the bright green Hun going down on Maybery's tail at about 3,000 feet and I fired with Vickers and Lewis at about 100 yards in order to frighten him. When about thirty yards away, the Hun turned south and was flying directly in the line of fire. I finished a full drum of Lewis gun at about ten yards from him. He turned right over and went down in a short dive and turned over again. The last I saw of him was going straight down in a dive about 800-1,000 feet. I stopped following him because the triplane was right up above him and I had an empty drum. I flew to the line climbing and put on a full drum and came back and attacked the triplane from the side as it was flying nose on to McCudden. I attacked him four or five times, but I didn't see what happened after this. I never saw the red-nosed Scout at all. The green man didn't get a chance to 'scrap'.'

'When he started to fly home I offered to accompany him part of the way. We went on a roundabout way over the Fronts. The weather had turned so bad that we could not hope to find any more game.

'Beneath us there were dense clouds. Voss did not know the country and he began to feel uncomfortable. When we passed above Arras I met my brother who also is in my squadron and who had lost his way. He joined us. Of course he recognized me at once by the colour of my machine.

'Suddenly we saw a squadron approaching from the other side. Immediately the thought occurred to me: 'Now comes number thirty-three.' Although there were nine Englishmen and although they were on their own territory they preferred to avoid battle. I thought that perhaps it would be better for me to repaint my machine. Nevertheless we caught them up. The important thing in airplanes is that they are speedy.

'I was nearest to the enemy and attacked the man to the rear. To my greatest delight I noticed that he accepted battle and my pleasure was increased when I discovered that his comrades deserted him. So I had once more a single fight.

'It was a fight similar to the one which I had had in the morning. My opponent did not make matters easy for me. He knew the fighting business and it was particularly awkward for me that he was a good shot. To my great regret that was quite clear to me.

'A favourable wind came to my aid. It drove both of us into the German lines. My opponent discovered that the matter was not so simple as he had imagined. So he plunged and disappeared in a cloud. He had nearly saved himself.

'I plunged after him and dropped out of the cloud and, as luck would have it, found myself close behind him. I fired and he fired without any tangible result. At last I hit him. I noticed a ribbon of white benzine vapour. He had to land for his engine had come to a stop.

'He was a stubborn fellow. He was bound to recognize that he had lost the game. If he continued shooting I could kill him, for meanwhile we had dropped to an altitude of about nine hundred feet. However, the Englishman defended himself exactly as did his countryman in the morning. He fought until he landed. When he had come to the ground I flew over him at an altitude of about thirty feet in order to ascertain whether I had killed him or not. What did the rascal do? He took his machine-gun and shot holes into my machine.

'Afterwards Voss told me if that had happened to him he would have shot the airman on the ground. I ought to have done so for he had not surrendered. He was one of the few fortunate fellows who escaped with their lives.

'I felt very merry, flew home and celebrated my thirty-third aircraft.'

'Bloody April', the April of 1917, was what the RFC called the battle for aerial supremacy over Northern France. It was the second time in the war when the Germans gained the upper hand. The previous occasion had been with the introduction of the first Fokkers two years earlier. From the autumn of 1915 to the spring of 1916 the Fokker Eindekkers ruled the skies over the front. Up until now British machines had proved scandalously inadequate and no match for Richthofen's Albatroses, with their raked wings, oval tail-plane and shark-like bodies. At least fifty of the Red Baron's personal score of 80 victories had been two-seater 'crocks', most of which were obsolescent and suicidal to fly. Had there been more twin-gun S.E.5s or French Nieuport 17s in service, the alarming ratio of German victories - over four to one - would have been considerably less.

By April 1917 the RFC's turnover of pilots and aeroplanes had reached the point where 18-year-old pilots, with only ten hours solo experience, were sent into battle against German flying machines which could out-fly them and out-gun them. Yet there seemed no end to the reservoir of British pilots, nor to the RFC's B.E.2s, F.E.2s and R.E.8s. With the Allies and Huns locked in the bloody Battle of Arras, with appalling casualties in the trenches, Field Marshal Haig was calling on the RFC for a still greater effort. For its aeroplanes were needed now more than ever - for artillery spotting, bombing, photography and reconnaissance. The obsolete B.E.2s and R.E.8s were crossing the lines in increasing numbers, despite the appalling losses.

Spring was traditionally a time for new offensives and the Allied commanders had planned a huge 'push' with the French attacking on the Aisne and the British at Arras. In the end the French attack failed, because the Germans had captured documents that gave away the French plans and in time to move up reinforcements to resist it. The British offensive at Arras, an action on the model of the Somme battle, was eventually a limited victory. The air campaign associated with it was, however, a disaster.

The British air offensive began on 4 April, which was five days before the land battle was to start. The aim was to drive German aircraft away from the battle area, leaving the skies clear for the Allied photographic and gunnery spotting aeroplanes. The air offensive was not helped by bad weather at its start, with low clouds and rain. In the first five days the British lost no fewer than 75 aircraft in combat and a further 56 in ordinary flying accidents, making a total of 131 machines down. Flying crews lost in action totalled 105; nineteen were killed, 73 missing and thirteen wounded. The RFC had been trying to introduce large numbers of new aircrew to service on the Western Front and to do this had been cutting back dangerously on their training. The average flying experience of new pilots going into action was just 25 hours.

The British were also introducing a new type of aircraft, the Bristol Fighter. There had been many training accidents with 'Brisfits' in England and the type had gained a reputation as a killer, with structural weaknesses that made it unsafe for it to be thrown about as was needed in combat. There were some small problems of the sort common with new military aircraft; little defects of the guns and engine, rather poor visibility from the pilot's cockpit and so on; but these were quite quickly remedied. Much of its reputation was just gossip among young and inexperienced pilots. The 'Brisfit' crews also made a major mistake in tactics - probably the result of poor training. This was to assume that the observer's gun, mounted so it could be swivelled on a ring around his cockpit, but generally a rearward-firing defensive gun, was the important firing unit. They tended to neglect the pilot's fixed forward firing gun, perhaps because it was necessary to aim the whole aircraft at the enemy and not just the gun. The Germans had new aircraft too; they had re-equipped with Albatros and Halberstadt aircraft earlier in the year, but by April had got used to them and flew them without the hesitancy they had shown earlier. Such was the new German confidence that there were occasions in April when a single German scout attacked an entire Allied formation. The new German types were superb fighting machines. Before April the old Allied pushers such as the D.H.2 had often been able to give a good account of themselves when attacked, but this was no longer the case. 'The hostile scouts with their superior speed and good handling were able throughout the fight to prevent the pilot from getting a single shot at any one of them,' reported one D.H pilot in his combat report. 57 Squadron, flying the powerful 250 hp F.E.2d suffered very heavy casualties. On 5 April they lost five aeroplanes on a single patrol to a formation of German two-seaters. That same day four out of a patrol of six of the new Bristol F.2a' from 48 Squadron, led by Captain William Leefe-Robinson VC were shot down and one of the two survivors returned having been badly shot up. This had been a dogfight with von Richthofen, no less, who personally got two of the Bristols. The Baron said that he thought his own aeroplane to be unquestionably superior to the new Bristols; this news got around among the German pilots and helped elevate their morale still further. In fact von Richthofen was misled; the Bristols, once their pilots had become accustomed to them and built up confidence in them, were fine machines.

One F.E. squadron, on almost its first sortie in France, was sent up as bait to lure von Richthofen and his pilots down to where they could be attacked by waiting British fighters. These fighters, however, never arrived. The bombers found that when the 'Red Baron' attacked, over Douai, they were on their own. The pushers were led by Lieutenant Tim Morice, who led his men into a defensive circle. This forced von Richthofen to fly around the British pushers just out of range, shaking his fist at them and making rude gestures while he waited for a chance to attack. It came when a German two-seater droned past just underneath and one of the RFC pilots left the circle and set off after it. Quick as a flash, von Richthofen was into the gap in the circle and the battle was on. Two F.E.s went quickly down, though Morice's observer managed to damage two German aircraft. Then the Baron appeared as if from nowhere, firing head-on and the pusher's instrument panel was blown to bits. Morice and his observer were both unhurt and managed to crash-land in the middle of a British gun emplacement.

In the earlier period of German air supremacy the effect had been a huge shrinkage in the RFC's operational strength. A similar phenomenon occurred in 'Bloody April'. Reconnaissance formations could only be sent up with large fighter escorts; thus one single mission could involve more than a dozen aeroplanes. It was not unusual to see fifteen fighters escorting three observation aircraft. Bombing sorties had to be curtailed; twelve fighters - six two-seaters in close escort and six single-seaters above and behind - were needed to accompany just six B.E. bombers. The German pilots, because of their lower losses resulting from careful and economical employment of the German air strength, were more experienced than the average British pilot, as well as more confident and better-mounted. The Germans also had the tactical initiative; they could dive in and dive out of combat at will, whereas the British had to stand and fight whatever the odds and in the prevailing westerly wind that tended to blow them over the German lines the longer they fought. Many damaged British aeroplanes that might otherwise have crawled back to British territory were in fact lost because they could not fight the headwinds to get back to the Allied side of the lines.

'Bloody April' was vividly described by a Royal Navy Sopwith Pup pilot of 3 (Naval) Squadron, flying one day with some S.P.A.Ds of 23 Squadron as escort to a formation of B.E.s on a bombing raid. Over Cambrai they were attacked by German Halberstadts and Albatroses. 'I attacked an Albatros head on at about 8,000 feet. I saw many tracers go into his engine as we closed on one another. I half-looped to one side of him and then the Albatros dived with a large trail of blue smoke. I dived down after him to about 4,000 feet and fired about fifty rounds when he went down absolutely out of control. I watched him spinning down to about 1,000 feet, the trail of smoke increasing. I was immediately attacked by three more Albatroses which drove me down to about 200 feet. We were firing at one another whenever possible, when at last I got into a good position and I attacked one from above and from the right. I closed on him, turning in behind him and got so close to him that the pilot's head filled the small ring in the Aldis sight. I saw three tracers actually go into the pilot's head; the German then simply heeled over and spun into the ground. The other two machines cleared off. I saw two other German aeroplanes spinning down out of control and while fighting saw two BEs being attacked by German aircraft. Having lost sight of the other machines and being so low I decided to fly home at about that height, 200 feet. After about five minutes I was again attacked by a Halberstadt single-seater and as he closed on me I rocked my machine until he was within about fifty yards. I side-looped over him and fired a short burst at him. He seemed to clear off and then attacked me again; these operations were repeated several times with a slight variation in the way I looped over him, until within about five minutes of crossing the lines (flying against a strong wind), when he was about 150 yards behind me, I looped straight over him and coming out of the loop I dived at him and fired a good long burst. I saw nearly all the tracers go into the pilot's back, just on the edge of the cockpit. He immediately dived straight into the ground. I then went over German trenches filled with soldiers and I was fired on by machine guns, rifles and small field guns, in and out of range... I landed at the first Allied aerodrome I saw. My machine was badly shot about.'

In contrast to the mass fighting, two of the greatest fighter pilots of all time, Captain Albert Ball of 56 Squadron and Captain 'Billy' Bishop of 60 Squadron, flew alone on 'roving commissions', going their own way, seeking combat where they found it. Ball's tactics against the German two-seaters were to dive from the half-rear, rather obviously, so that the observer swivelled his gun into position in that direction.[7] Then Ball would dodge underneath the two-seater and fire at close range from below on the other side, before the enemy observer had time to reposition his gun. It was a most effective approach.

In *My Record Day* Rittmeister Manfred von Richthofen, described the events of 13 April 1917. 'The weather was glorious. We were ready for starting. I had as a visitor a gentleman who had never seen a fight in the air or anything resembling it and he had just assured me that it would tremendously interest him to witness an aerial battle. We climbed into our machines and laughed heartily at our visitor's eagerness. Friend Schäfer thought that we might give him some fun. We placed him before a telescope and off we went. The day began well. We had scarcely flown to an altitude of 6,000 feet when an English squadron of five machines was seen coming our way. We attacked them by a rush as if we were cavalry and the hostile squadron lay destroyed on the ground. None of our men was even wounded. Of our enemies three had plunged to the ground and two had come down in flames.

'The good fellow down below was not a little surprised. He had imagined that the affair would look quite different, that it would be far more dramatic. He thought the whole encounter had looked quite harmless until suddenly some machines came falling down looking like rockets. I have gradually become accustomed to seeing machines falling down, but I must say it impressed me very deeply when I saw the first Englishman fall and I have often seen the event again in my dreams.

'As the day had begun so propitiously we sat down and had a decent breakfast. All of us were as hungry as wolves. In the meantime our machines were again made ready for starting. Fresh cartridges were got and then we went off again.

'In the evening we could send off the proud report: 'Six German machines have destroyed thirteen hostile aircraft.'

'Böelcke's Jasta had only once been able to make a similar report. At that time we had shot down eight machines. My brother Lothar had destroyed two, Schafer two, Festner two and I three. [Another] one of us had brought low four of his opponents. The hero was a Leutnant Wolff, a delicate-looking little fellow in whom nobody could have suspected a redoubtable hero.'

Kurt Wolff's youthful looks and frail physical stature masked his deadly skills as a combat pilot. Born in Greifswald, Pomerania, he was orphaned as a child and was raised by relatives in Memel, East Prussia. He enlisted in the army in 1912 at the age of 17, joining a transport unit, Railway Regiment Nr.4. Receiving a commission on 17 April 1915, he transferred to the air service in July. Wolff's first flight was almost his last. The aeroplane crashed, dislocating Wolff's shoulder and killing his pilot instructor. Nevertheless, Wolff received his pilot's badge in late 1915 and was assigned to two-seater unit Kasta 26 of Kagohl 5, followed by service with Kagohl 7 and KG 40. On 12 October 1916 he was posted to the then undistinguished Jasta 11. For months, Wolff, like most of his Jasta comrades, had no success in the air. That changed when command was given to Manfred von Richthofen. Under the 'Red Baron's leadership, Jasta 11 thrived and Wolff became an excellent scout pilot. Like his commanding officer, Wolff soon became an avid collector of souvenirs from the aircraft he shot down. His room at his airfield soon became decorated with serial numbers, parts and guns from his victims. He first claimed on 6 March 1917, a B.E.2d of 16 Squadron RFC. Four more followed during March and he scored 22 victories during 'Bloody April'. Like the rest of the Jasta, Wolff's Albatros D.III was painted red, though he added individual markings by painting his elevators and tailplane green.

'We went to bed in the evening tremendously proud but also terribly tired' wrote von Richthofen. 'On the following day we read with noisy approval about our deeds of the previous day in the official communiqué. On the next day we downed eight hostile machines.

'A very amusing thing occurred. One of the Englishmen whom we had shot down and whom we had made a prisoner was talking with us. Of course he inquired after the Red aeroplane. It is not unknown even among the troops in the trenches and is called by them le diable rouge. In the Squadron to which he belonged there was a rumour that the 'Red Machine' was occupied by a girl, by a kind of Jeanne d'Arc. He was intensely surprised when I assured him that the supposed girl was standing in front of him. He did not intend to make a joke. He was actually convinced that only a girl could sit in the extravagantly painted machine.'

Leutnant Kurt Wolff followed his four victories on 13 April with three victories on 29 April, including Major Hubert Dunsterville 'Bay' Harvey-Kelly DSO commanding 19 Squadron.[8] Harvey-Kelly was not due to fly on 29 April. Partly due to a rule that Squadron commanders did not fly (although many did) and partly due to a last minute switch, he was instead due to meet with Hugh Trenchard and Captain Maurice Baring. However, because Richthofen was operating in the area he went up. In the attack Harvey-Kelly, with Lieutenants Hamilton and Applin, spotted eight Albatros D.IIIs. Although outnumbered the attack was pressed when Harvey-Kelly spotted six Sopwith Triplanes of 1 Squadron RNAS. However, there are conflicting reports of whether these engaged or sheered away. During the dog fight Harvey-Kelly was shot down and he and 2nd Lieutenant Richard Applin were reported as KIA but the major died of head wounds in a German hospital three days later.[9]

Wolff was awarded the coveted 'Pour Le Mérite' on 4 May and on 6 May was assigned to command Jasta 29, replacing Leutnant von Dornheim who had recently been killed. Wolff shot down a French SPAD on 13 May and a 60 Squadron Nieuport 17 on 27 June before he returned to command Jasta 11 in July 1917, replacing Leutnant Karl Allmenröder, who had fallen in combat. Wolff shot down a R.E.8 of 4 Squadron and a Sopwith Triplane of 1 Naval Squadron in early July. However, on 11 July Wolff was shot in both his left hand and left shoulder by gunfire from a Sopwith Triplane flown by future nine-victory ace Flight Sub-Lieutenant Herbert Victor Rowley of 1 Naval Squadron RNAS, born in Crich, Derbyshire on 24 October 1897, the second son of the Reverend Arthur Rowley and his wife Agnes. Wolff crash landed his aircraft on the Courtrai railway line. The crash ripped off the undercarriage and flipped the aircraft over. He then spent significant time in a Field Hospital in Courtrai with his injured commander, Manfred von Richthofen.[10]

Despite their superiority in the air during 'Bloody April', the German high command wanted complete domination of the skies and to this end had conceived a new strategy. Now the time had come to put it into effect. They planned to introduce a new offensive element into aerial warfare - the Jagdgruppe. This was a powerful formation of bombers and fighters which, because of its assembled firepower, would be able to destroy any opposition the Allies could offer. Thus, with complete control of the skies, it would be able to sweep unhindered behind the enemy lines and bomb airfields, installations and grounded aircraft. Such a strategy, they reasoned, would result in crippling the Allied air strength once and for all. Thus it was on 30 April, with the RFC reeling from the month's calamitous losses, the Luftstreitkräfte assembled twenty Albatros D.IIIs of Jastas 11, 10, 6 and 4 (later to become known as Jagdgeschwader I or 'Richthofen's Circus') and sent them up from Douai aerodrome to clear the skies over Arras. The seven British machines should have been cut down in the opening seconds by the formation's forty Spandau machine guns. But the technique of holding tight formation while bringing to bear a withering cross-fire had not yet been developed. The German formation wavered awkwardly, some machines crowding their neighbours.

The British pilots saw them coming and split up to make individual attacks but not before three F.E.2s had taken hits, one by Lothar von Richthofen. The Sopwiths came in, their Lewis guns spitting fire. The German flight floundered. Some of the aeroplanes stalled. Others dived out of danger. Two of the F.E.2s spiralled down out of control. The other was limping back across the lines with a wounded pilot and a dying navigator. It took the Germans several minutes to regroup and form up again. East of Douai nine Halberstadts joined them and with this greatly increased fire-power the formation continued its patrol. Richthofen saw a ragged group of five British triplanes and six Bristol fighters reconnoitring the new trench positions. He signalled the attack. This time the British pilots had time to manoeuvre. As the Jagdgruppe bore down on them, the Bristols scattered and came at the flight from all directions, their frontal guns chattering. Once again the Germans broke and scattered and it was every man for himself, with machines whirling, spinning, rolling all over the sky. It went on for minutes. Then three S.E.5s of 56 Squadron joined the battle. A few seconds later one of the Halberstadts fell out of the melee, turning over and over like a dead leaf. Then another stood on its tail, stalled and fell away. One of the S.E.5s dived out of control, pouring black smoke. In those two short encounters the whole theory of the Jagdgruppe was cast into doubt. Perhaps it was because the German pilots had learned too well that the name of the game was 'kill or be killed'. In those early days of aerial warfare, every man was a lone wolf, with ambitions to become another Richthofen. The personal tally was the thing. At any rate, from this point on, the battle reverted to the old-style dog-fight, with individual duels happening all over the sky.

During 'Bloody April' 316 British aviators were killed or posted missing. This amounted to one third of the flying strength of the RFC's fifty squadrons facing the Germans on the mainland of Europe but in May and June, 757 British machines reached France and the picture changed. British losses dropped by 61 and the Germans' rose by 73 for the month of June. By the end of June, the Allies were able to claim 1,401 hostile aircraft and 52 kite balloons destroyed, compared with the enemy's claim of 955 aircraft and 45 kite balloons destroyed. Yet, despite the lessons of 30 April, the German high command persisted with its Jagdgruppe obsession, using larger formations led by Manfred von Richthofen. But the Circus's inexperience in mass manoeuvre continued to invite disaster and the concept of fighter support for bombers found no unanimity. Certainly, an escort was vital. But how close to the bombers should it fly?

Much of the credit for the German successes in 'Bloody April' must be due to their reorganisation into independent jagdstaffeln, fighter squadrons which were further grouped into jagdgeschwadern, wing-sized units. These wings could be moved as entire units, aircraft, equipment and all, in special trains. The Germans had always made exceptional use of their fine railway system in their war plans. Jasta 11 was commanded by von Richthofen; he had recently been awarded the 'Pour le Mérite', which was famous not only in the German press but in the British and French newspapers as well. Such prestige had military value; it inspired the pilots and men who served under him and helped terrify the inexperienced British pilots he came up against. To aid the process he chose to have his aeroplane painted in an instantly recognisable blood red. He was not the first to try the idea of having a wildly distinctive machine; Oswald Böelcke, Richthofen's teacher in fighter tactics, had flown unusual all-white and all-black machines and the French pilot Jean Marie Dominique Navarre, who was credited with twelve confirmed aerial victories and fifteen unconfirmed ones, had flown a striking all-red Nieuport 11 over Verdun in the spring of 1916 when von Richthofen had been operating in that area as a two-seater pilot. Now von Richthofen adopted the idea of colour-coding aircraft to the limit, until not only he but his entire jasta flew gaudily-painted and patterned machines; in this way one pilot could recognise another in combat. The idea quickly spread to the rest of the German fighter service, but was never generally adopted by the Allies.

In pre-war times travelling circuses had sometimes moved around by train and the German jastas on the move in this way, with their brightly-painted aircraft dismantled to fit on the railway wagons, much resembled a circus travelling from one engagement to the next. Hence, the 'circus' nickname for the jagdgeschwadern.

The adoption of bright colour schemes helped ground observers' spaced at regular intervals along the German lines with field glasses and telephones to confirm the combat claims of individual pilots. Indeed, von Richthofen shot down no fewer than twenty Allied aircraft, a quarter of his total score at his death, during 'Bloody April'. With his total score now 43, he was for the first time the world's top-scoring fighter pilot.

Lothar shot down eight more aircraft in May 1917, giving the German propagandists an opportunity to enhance his stature even further. It was subsequently claimed that Captain Albert Ball VC DSO** MC who crashed to his death in a field in France on 7 May 1917, sparking a wave of national mourning and posthumous recognition, was the 20th victim of Leutnant Lothar von Richthofen. Ball's death remains a mystery. Captain Ball, flying his S.E.5, had dived into dense cloud while chasing a German single-seater near Lens. He emerged upside down from low lying cloud and crashed apparently without prior injury in the air. His back was broken, his chest crushed and he suffered numerous broken bones on impact. He died shortly afterwards at the scene. Ball's body bore no wound and what caused his aircraft to crash has never been established. The enemy later discovered his wrecked aircraft and his body. While it is possible that the younger von Richthofen was involved in a fight with a British triplane, which he claimed to have shot down, it is unlikely that he shot down Ball's S.E.5. Manfred von Richthofen remarked upon hearing of Ball's death that he was 'by far the best English flying man'.

At the time of his death Ball, 20 years and nine months old, was the United Kingdom's leading flying ace and he remained its fourth-highest scorer behind Edward Mannock, James McCudden and George McElroy. He had taken part in 100 air combats and had 44 victories. His Victoria Cross was gazetted on 3 June 1917.

Lothar von Richthofen scored his 24th aerial victory late on the morning of 13 May when he brought down a B.E.2c near Arleux. In the same fight, however, his red Albatros fighter suffered a number of hits and Lothar barely managed to return to his own airfield. The following day Lothar was awarded the coveted 'Pour le Mérite', which was presented to him in the hospital bed which he was to occupy for the next few months. Legend has it that the first time the medal rested at the base of his neck, the reflection of the blue enamel was so strong on his otherwise pale complexion that he was kingly referred to as 'Blue Max'.

Manfred von Richthofen had been on leave when Lothar was wounded. When he returned to the Front in June, he attacked his adversaries with a vengeful fury, shooting down four enemy aircraft within the space of a week. With 56 kills to his credit, Manfred von Richthofen was the undisputed aerial ace of World War I. The handsome young nobleman - erroneously referred to as a 'baron' - had a darker side to his nature. Not content merely to shoot down his adversaries, the elder von Richthofen brother often followed his hapless quarry for a distance, watching the crew burn to death or, in the absence of parachutes, leap hopelessly from their burning aircraft. At night, in the quiet of his comfortable quarters, he would write to his mother, telling her how they died.

When the famed Dutch-born aircraft constructor Anthony Fokker produced the first of the successful Dr. I triplanes, he made sure that they met with von

Richthofen's approval. The great ace went on to score more than twenty of his final victories in Fokker triplanes, his aircraft bearing the overall red finish which won him the soubriquet of 'Red Baron'.

On 1 May 1917 von Richthofen returned to Germany on leave and his departure coincided with a slackening in the German effort in the air, which they had been sustaining to the limits of human endurance. In no other month of the war was the RFC so hard-pressed, or were its casualties so heavy. From the beginning of May, however, things began to improve for the British. They had learned much in April. They had gained confidence and experience in handling their machines. Their morale improved and they had old scores to settle. The squadron mechanics had come to understand their new equipment and technical problems had been sorted out. It also became apparent that there were disadvantages to the new German tactics of grouping their fighters; it localised their efforts in limited areas, leaving the sky clearer elsewhere. The jastas were also seen to lack cohesion, being more loose collections of fighting individuals who tended to split up in combat rather than a cohesive and centrally-led unit.

With new equipment, fresh pilots and renewed confidence, the RFC squadrons began to exploit the flaws in the German operational procedures and with each successive week their victories mounted and their losses dropped. They had registered the most disastrous month in the history of the service and the air war over France.

A British six-victory ace who would be Manfred von Richthofen's penultimate victim in April 1918, Richard Raymond-Barker was the third son, one of nine children, born on 6 May 1894 to Edward Raymond-Barker and his wife Rose Mary in Forest Gate, London. Educated at Wimbledon College, he was commissioned as a second lieutenant on 30 November 1914, serving in the 12th Battalion, Northumberland Fusiliers. In mid-1915 he learned to fly at the Hall Flying School at Hendon aerodrome and was granted Royal Aero Club Aviators' Certificate No. 1460 on 18 July. He transferred to the RFC on 6 August 1915, completing his pilot training and being appointed a flying officer on 19 October. He was posted to France on 22 November. On 1 April 1916 he was appointed a lieutenant in the RFC and on 17 June was appointed a flight commander, with the temporary rank of captain. During this time, he served with Nos. 6 and 16 Squadrons, transferring on 29 December 1916. On 12 May 1917, Raymond-Barker was posted to 48 Squadron as a flight commander, flying the Bristol F.2b. He gained his first victories on 20 May, driving down a pair of Albatros D.IIIs out of control over Brebières. On 26 May he destroyed another D.III and on 5 June drove down an enemy reconnaissance aircraft near Bullecourt. On 1 July 1917 he was promoted to the substantive rank of lieutenant. He scored his final two triumphs soon after, on the 8th (with Sergeant Jack Mason as his observer) and 17th, bringing his total to two Albatros D.IIIs destroyed and four enemy aircraft driven down out of control. He was subsequently awarded the Military Cross, which was gazetted on 14 September. Three days later Raymond-Barker was appointed a squadron commander, with the temporary rank of major. He took command of 3 Squadron, flying Sopwith Camels.

On 20 April 1918, 3 Squadron ran into a patrol of Fokker Triplanes of the Flying Circus and Raymond-Barker was shot down and killed by Manfred von

Richthofen. As Richthofen reported it: 'With six aeroplanes of Jasta 11, I attacked a large enemy squadron. During the fight I observed that a Triplane was attacked and shot at from below by a Camel. I put myself behind the adversary and brought him down, burning, with only a few shots. The enemy plane crashed down near the forest of Hamel where it burned further on the ground. 'Three minutes later Richthofen attacked the Sopwith Camel of 2nd Lieutenant David Lewis, forcing it down northeast of Villers-Bretonneux, only fifty yards from the first Camel. Lewis was able to escape with only minor burns and bruises. Richthofen made a pass, waved at Lewis and then continued over the infantrymen in the trenches and column of men on the road.[11] These were Richthofen's 79th and 80th aerial victories.

Next day, 21 April 1918, Rittmeister Manfred Freiherr von Richthofen was dead. The pilot who was officially credited with shooting down World War I's highest scoring fighter ace was a 24-year old Canadian named Captain Arthur Roy Brown.

Brown, born in Caleton Place, Ontario, on 23 December 1893 had joined the RNAS in 1915, qualifying as a pilot on 24 November. In England the following May, he was badly injured in a crash and spent three months in hospital with back injuries. After he recovered he was kept from completing his training through illness, but eventually went to France in April 1917, posted to 9 Naval Squadron flying Sopwith Triplanes. He remained with the unit only a short time and then served briefly with 11 and then 4 Naval, before returning to 11 Squadron RNAS, where he gained his first victories on 16 July, downing three German aircraft in one day. The following day he shot down an Albatros Scout. His next claim was made on 9 September and six days later, having rejoined 9 Naval Squadron, he drove down an Aviatik two-seater. On the 16th he damaged another two-seater and on the 20th shared an Albatros Scout shot down 'out of control'.

Flying over Ostend in October he gained two victories, a DFW two-seater in flames on the 13th and a single-seater scout on the 28th. The award of the DSC was gazetted on 2 November 1917 when Brown was sent back to England for a rest: 9 Naval Squadron was also pulled out of France for a rest and re-equipped with the Sopwith Camel. In February 1918, Brown was made a Flight Commander with 9 Naval, returning to France with the squadron on 20 March 1918, the day before the German March offensive began. The squadron was based at Bray Dunes near Dunkirk, but the field was shelled by German artillery, forcing them to move to Teteghem. On 22 March Brown led an offensive patrol and while escorting a French observation aeroplane, he spotted a German two-seater and shot it down in flames. On 12 April Brown shared the destruction of a Fokker Dr.I Triplane which fell in flames - the Canadian's twelfth victory. On 1 April with the amalgamation of the RNAS and the RFC to form the Royal Air Force, 9 Naval became 209 Squadron. When the RAF was seven days old, 209 Squadron moved to Bertangles, just north of Amiens.

On 9 April, Second Lieutenant Wilfrid 'Wop' May, an old school friend of Roy Brown, was transferred to 209 Squadron and was no doubt cheered by the fact that his mentor had never lost a subordinate pilot in action. Born in Carberry, Manitoba, the son of a carriage maker, Wilfrid's family had moved to Edmonton in 1902. On the way, they stayed with family and friends; his two-year-old cousin,

Mary Lumsden, could not pronounce Wilfrid and called him 'Woppie'. This gave him his nickname 'Wop'. He attended Victoria School while in Edmonton. In February 1916, May joined the Army. He rose through the enlisted ranks to sergeant and spent most of 1916 as a gunnery instructor. In 1917, his battalion, the 202nd battalion C. E. F. (Edmonton Sportsmen), was shipped to England, where he and his friend Ray Ross applied to join the RFC. His first flight resulted in the destruction of both his and another aircraft; nevertheless, the RFC accepted his application and May resigned from the Canadian Army. After initial training in London in October, he was moved to a fighter training squadron and graduated in February 1918.

The inexperienced new arrival spent most of April getting used to his Sopwith Camel and Roy Brown told him to 'stay out of the fights and simply keep an eye out' but on his second patrol on 20 April, 'Wop' May fought his first aerial combat with 209 Squadron and the Fokker Triplane he attacked crashed of its own accord during the brief fight. The following day saw 209 Squadron again on patrol. Before they took off Brown once again instructed May to sit out any dog-fight and watch from above. At around 1000 hours the squadron attacked a group of triplanes. During the dog-fighting, May circled above as instructed but when he spotted another aircraft doing the same thing, he decided to launch an attack. He chased the aircraft which fled into the middle of the dogfight but when his machine guns jammed, May quickly dived out of combat. Unknown to anyone, May's target was Wolfram von Richthofen, cousin of Rittmeister Manfred Freiherr von Richthofen. Shortly before his nineteenth birthday, in 1914, Wolfram was commissioned into a Prussian cavalry regiment, the 4th Silesian Hussars. He led a platoon into combat in August 1914, where his cool display of leadership under fire in the war's first battles earned him an Iron Cross. In the autumn, his cavalry regiment moved to the Eastern Front, where he saw considerable action throughout 1915. But as the war settled into the trenches, there was little for the cavalry to do. For an ambitious officer hoping to make his mark, it was an unbearable situation. Manfred von Richthofen and his brother Lothar had abandoned the cavalry by this time, transferring to the Imperial German Air Service in 1915. In 1917 Wolfram followed his cousins' example, showing enough aptitude to be selected for the fighter arm. He arrived at his famous cousin's wing in early April 1918.

Like May, Wolfram had also been given orders to sit out above the fight and watch because he was a novice flyer too. On seeing his cousin being attacked, Manfred started to chase May as he turned to pull out of the dogfight. Roy Brown, who was flying above, also noticed the Red Baron peeling off to attack May. Diving in from behind, Brown intercepted von Richthofen's red Fokker Dr.I. The fight that followed remains one of the most well documented air actions of that war and many students of military aviation have long argued about the results of that battle.

Brown, never a strong man, was now living almost entirely on his nerves and was close to both physical and mental collapse after constant action, but he continued to lead his men across the enemy front lines, as he did on the morning of 21 April. From Cappy aerodrome, opposite Bertangles on the German side of the lines, Baron von Richthofen was also leading his pilots towards the front. Both patrols had brief encounters before engaging each other in combat, the Camels with two Albatros two-seaters and the Germans with R.E.8s (or 'Harry Tates'' as they were known colloquially[12]) of 3 Squadron AFC. As the battle developed, von Richthofen attacked 'Wop' May, who was flying on the edge of the dog-fight. May rapidly turned towards the lines but von Richthofen followed him. May said later: 'Just near Corbie, von Richthofen beat me to it and came over the hill. At that point I was a sitting duck; I was too low down between the banks to make a turn away from him. I felt that he had me cold and I was in such a state of mind at this time that I had to restrain myself from pushing the stick forward and diving into the river, as I knew that I had had it.'

Brown saw the danger and he dived down in pursuit of the Fokker Triplane. The three machines flew low down the Somme valley, over Morlancourt Ridge, in the 4th Division's sector and the result of the combat has been a constant source of controversy ever since. Brown shot the Fokker from the tail of the Camel and saw it go down. Other members of the British patrol confirmed this. From the ground claims by several Australian ground gunners, it was their fire that brought down the Red Baron. Near Corbie, two Australians of the 24th Machine Gun Company - Sergeant Cedric Bassett Popkin and Gunner R. F. Weston - had loosed off a long burst at the Triplane as it flew low past them in pursuit of May. A few seconds later, two anti-aircraft Lewis guns of the 53rd Battery, 14th Australian Field Artillery Brigade, manned by Gunners William John 'Snowy' Evans and R. Buie, had also fired on it. Later, all these men were to claim the credit for shooting down von Richthofen. When the Australian soldiers reached the wrecked Triplane, Richthofen was still alive but died moments later. Another eye witness, Sergeant Ted Smout, reported that Richthofen's last word was 'kaput' ('finished') immediately before he died. Whatever the truth, von Richthofen died that April morning, crash-landing inside the British lines.

May noted in his combat report: 21/4/18 Camel D3326 90 minutes Engaged 15 to 20 triplanes - claimed one. Blue one. Several on my tail, came out with red triplane on my tail which followed me down to the ground and over the line on my tail all the time got several bursts into me but didn't hit me. When we got across the lines he was shot down by Captain Brown. I saw him crash into side of hill. Came back with Captain. We afterwards found out that the triplane (red) was the famous German airman Baron Richthofen. He was killed.'

Brown was awarded a bar to his DSC for this action, May survived to become an ace himself and receive the DFC. Brown had however, flown his last war patrol. Now totally exhausted, he returned to England to instruct and was sent to No. 2 School of Aerial Fighting. On 15 July he fainted in the air and in the resultant crash sustained a fractured skull, neck and back and punctured lungs and was thought to be dead. He recovered, however and left the RAF in 1919. He died of a heart attack at Stouffville, Ontario on 9 March 1944. May continued flying with 209 Squadron until the end of the war and eventually claimed one destroyed and one shared aircraft captured, six destroyed with one shared and three destroyed and one shared 'out of control'. He was awarded the DFC in 1918. He relinquished his RAF commission on 8 May 1919, with the rank of captain.

On the day Manfred von Richthofen died, the first aircraft he attacked on his last patrol was a pair of 3 Squadron AFC R.E.8s. The two R.E.8s saw a formation of nine German Scouts and were attacked by a pair of red nosed Fokker Triplanes, one being fully red. After exchanging shots, the red Triplane dived away, the second Triplane was seen with splinters flying off its wings due to fire from the R.E.8s. Major D. V. J Blake after discovering the combat and putting two and two together thought 3 Squadron may have been responsible for the death of Manfred von Richthofen, though when it was realised the fatal shots which brought Richthofen down were later in the day, the Combat Report was withdrawn. Richthofen was brought down in 3 Squadron's area and the squadron salvaged his aircraft and were to later give the 'Red Baron' a full military burial. The last surviving member of the Australian Flying Corps, Howard Edwards, who passed away in 1998, was a guard at Richthofen's funeral.

The next day, a British aircraft flew over the German airfield at Cappy and dropped a message. It read: 'To the German Flying Corps. Rittmeister Baron von Richthofen was killed in aerial combat on 21 April 1918. He was buried with full military honours. From the British Royal Air Force'. Richthofen was only 25 years old.

Lothar von Richthofen was absent from Jagdstaffel 11 when his brother was killed. Lothar had been wounded in a fight on 13 March and was convalescing at the time of Manfred's death. That was the second time the number thirteen had proven unlucky for Lothar von Richthofen. Then on 13 August 1918, the day after he scored his 40th aerial victory, his wartime career was ended when he was shot down again. With the return of peace, Lothar von Richthofen worked briefly on a farm before accepting an industrial position. He married Countess Doris von Keyserlingk in Cammerau in June 1919, fathering a son, Wolf-Manfred (1922-2010) and a daughter, Carmen Viola (1920-1971), before the marriage was dissolved. He then became a commercial pilot, carrying passengers and mail between Berlin and Hamburg. On 4 July 1922, Richthofen died in a crash of his LVG C.VI at Fuhlsbüttel due to an engine failure. Lothar von Richthofen was interred next to his father at the Garrison Cemetery in Schweidnitz, but the cemetery was levelled by the Poles when the city was transferred to Poland after World War II. Lothar is buried next to his brother Manfred von Richthofen on the Südfriedhof in Wiesbaden.

Many toasts were drunk to Richthofen by men who would have gladly killed him, given the chance. When he was killed, Australian airmen placed wreaths on his grave. In the Middle East, Oberleutnant Gerhard Felmy, the leading German pilot facing 1 Squadron, earned the admiration of his adversaries. It was not uncommon for him to drop messages and photographs of recently captured Australian airmen on their home field. The Australians did the same for the Germans and drank toasts to Felmy in their mess. On the Western Front captured enemy pilots were treated with respect by their allied counterparts and vice-versa.

Lucky to survive the dogfight that killed Manfred, Wolfram von Richthofen went on to demonstrate the Richthofen killer instinct by shooting down eight Allied aeroplanes. He hoped to remain in the air force after the end of the war but the Treaty of Versailles abolished it and reduced the army to a small, 100,000-man force. So he left the army and earned a degree in aeronautical engineering at the Technical University of Hanover, one of Germany's top engineering schools. In 1924 the former flier, qualified engineer and decorated combat veteran was invited to rejoin the army after completing his studies. As a Luftwaffe commander Wolfram von Richthofen was a brilliant master of the tactical and operational air war and one of the key catalysts in the resurrection of Germany's air force. Long overshadowed in history by his cousin, von Richthofen served in seven major air campaigns from 1936 to 1944 and as senior air commander he was always at the centre of the action. In late 1944 Wolfram von Richthofen was diagnosed with a brain tumour. After two unsuccessful operations, he was relieved of command in November and sent to the Luftwaffe hospital in Bad Ischl, Austria. He died there as an American prisoner in July 1945 at the age of forty-nine, a few weeks after General Patton's Third Army occupied the area.

Endnotes Chapter 6

1   *The Red Baron: A History in Pictures* by Norman Franks.

2   Andrews (later AVM Andrews CB DSO MC*) was credited with twelve aerial victories. His most significant victory was over German double ace Stefan Kirmaier, Staffelführer of Jasta 2. Saundby, (later Air Marshal Sir Robert Henry Magnus Spencer Saundby KCB KBE MC DFC AFC) distinguished himself gaining five victories in World War I and he is chiefly remembered for his role as Deputy AOC in C Bomber Command under Sir Arthur 'Bomber' Harris during the latter part of World War II.

3   By 11 October 1917, Rhys-Davids had an official total of 27 aerial victories - 23 of them individual kills. Rhys-Davids had earned a reputation as a 'fighter' and pursued enemy aircraft wherever and whenever he spotted them. On 27 October Rhys-Davids was promoted to lieutenant. That same day he took off on a routine patrol and was last seen flying east of Roeselare, Belgium chasing a group of Albatros fighters. The Luftstreitkräfte (Imperial German Air Service) credited Karl Gallwitz with shooting him down. It was not until the 29 December that a report came through that a German aircraft had dropped a note to inform the RFC of Rhys-Davids' death. Despite disappearing less than five miles from the crash site of Werner Voss, shot down by Rhys-Davids one month earlier, his remains have never been found. William Orpen, the artist who painted Davids' portrait, said that he 'hated fighting, hated flying, loved books and was terribly anxious for the war to be over, so that he could get to Oxford'

4   Geoffrey Hilton 'Beery' Bowman DSO MC* DFC, so called because of his florid complexion, was born in Manchester on 2 May 1891, the son of Dr. George Bowman, a physician and his wife Mary. He was educated at Haileybury College and Trinity College, Cambridge. Having served in the Officers' Training Corps, Bowman was commissioned as a probationary second lieutenant in the 3rd Battalion, Royal Warwickshire Regiment on 15 August 1914. After serving with his regiment in France, on 20 March 1916 Bowman was seconded to the RFC. He joined 29 Squadron on 7 July 1916, at Abeele, flying the Airco D.H.2. His first victory was against a Roland C.II two seater, with which he unintentionally collided on 3 September; he turned into its attack, firing away and the German machine tore away his aileron kingpost. Bowman 'babied' his crippled craft home despite its lack of lateral control. His second victory on 27 September was a run-away German observation balloon but he crashed while trying to land alongside the wreckage on Mount Kemmel. On 1 January 1917 he was appointed a flight commander with the temporary rank of captain, receiving promotion to the permanent rank of captain on 1 April. On 11 May he was posted to 56 Squadron as a flight commander, flying the S.E.5. By July he had claimed another five victories. On 23 September Bowman was one of the eight British aces who fought and shot down German ace Werner Voss. Bowman was awarded the MC on 14 September and a bar on 26 October. On 9 February 1918 he was posted to command of 41 Squadron. Awarded the DSO in March 1918, his final tally at the end of the war in November was one aircraft shared captured, one balloon destroyed, 15 aircraft destroyed and 15 driven 'out of control'. He was awarded the DFC on 30 May 1919 and the Croix de guerre from Belgium in July 1919.

5   Richard 'Dick' Aveline Maybery MC* was born in Brecon, Wales, in January 1895, the only son of Aveline Maybery, a solicitor and his wife Lucy. He was educated locally and at Wellington College, Berkshire, before going on to the Royal Military College at Sandhurst. After his graduation he joined the 21st (Empress of India's) Lancers. At the outbreak of war he served in the North West Frontier province until he was injured in a riding accident. Bored during his rehabilitation and unable to sit on a horse he became involved in observing for a unit of the RFC who were based nearby. Later he travelled to Egypt where he trained to be a pilot, before he was posted to France with 56 Squadron. Aggressive and headstrong, Maybery accounted for 21 enemy aircraft ; 14 and two shared destroyed and five 'driven down 'out of control between 7 July and 19 December 1917. He was awarded the Military Cross on 26 September and on 18 November was appointed a flight commander with the temporary rank of captain. His second MC was awarded on 17 December. Maybery scored his 21st and final victory on 19 December 1917 when he shot down an Albatros DV over Bourlon Wood. Maybery's S.E.5a was then either hit by anti aircraft fire from a mobile AA battery, (credited to K-Flakbatterie 108 commanded by Leutnant Thiel) or shot down by Vizefeldwebel Artur Weber of Jasta 5 and crashed near the village of Haynecourt.

6   Keith Knox Muspratt, born in Bournemouth, Hampshire on 22 December 1897, erstwhile instructor and future test pilot had learnt to fly at 16 in his holidays from Sherborne School; one of his pupils had been Arthur Rhys Davids...Two of McCudden's original flight in 56 Squadron, Keith Muspratt, who was killed on 16 March 1918 and Leonard Monteagle Barlow, born 5 June 1898 in Islington, London who on 25 September 1917 attacked four German aircraft over the Houthulst Forest and shot down three of them in three minutes (killed on 5 February 1918 testing a Sopwith Dolphin); both died while test-flying at Martlesham Heath. See *The Royal Flying Corps In France; From Bloody April 1917 to Final Victory* by Ralph Barker (Constable 1995).

7   Captain William Avery 'Billy' Bishop shot down a total of 72 air victories, including two balloons, 52 and two shared 'destroyed' with 16 'out of control' and was thus one of the top-scoring aces on both sides in the First World War.

8   Harvey-Kelly, born 1891 was credited with being the first RFC pilot to land in France in the war and of being the first RFC pilot to shoot down an enemy aircraft.

9   Harvey-Kelly is buried in the Browns Copse Cemetery, Roeux. His cigarette case and other personal belongs were sent by the Germans back to his unit and remain with the Harvey-Kelly family to this day.

10   On 11 September 1917 Wolff returned to Jasta 11 from leave to recuperate from his injuries. On his return, Wolff was eager to fly one of the first two Fokker Triplane prototypes that had been allocated to Jagdgeschwader 1 in Richthofen's absence. On 15 September he found his opportunity. Despite heavily overcast skies, he took off in Fokker Triplane #102/17, accompanied by Leutnant Carl von Schoenebeck flying an Albatros D.V. Meanwhile, eight Camels of 10 Squadron RNAS led by Flight Lieutenant Fitzgibbon, were escorting a number of D.H.4 bombers back to Allied lines. In the vicinity of Moorslede, Belgium, Fitzgibbon spotted a flight of Albatrosses below them and led half of his men to attack. The remaining Camels stayed with the bombers and were attacked by Wolff and Schoenebeck. The dog fight was intense though brief and in the confusion the British pilots mistakenly thought that five Albatrosses and four triplanes were involved. As Wolff singled out a Camel, he was suddenly fired on from behind within 25 yards by Flight Sub-Lieutenant Norman MacGregor who then had to zoom to avoid colliding with the Fokker. MacGregor saw his tracers entering his machine. Next he saw the Fokker going down in a vertical dive, apparently out of control. MacGregor would eventually claim seven kills and be awarded the DSC. It seems probable that Wolff was already dead when his Fokker Dr.I crashed and burst into flames north of Wervik at 1730 hours. His remains were taken back to Memel for burial.

11   *Attack Out of the Sun: Lessons from the Red Baron for Our Business and Personal Lives* by Durwood J. Heinrich Ph.D. (2010).

12   After Harry Tate, an English comedian (4 July 1872-4 February 1940) who performed both in the music halls and in films. Tate (real name, Ronald Macdonald Hutchison) worked for Henry Tate & Sons, Sugar Refiners before going on the stage and took his stage name from them.

Chapter 7

The Eagle of Lille

It was 9 in the evening, when the rat-tat of aerial machine guns lured me out of my quarters and I saw at a height of several thousand yards five aeroplanes in a hot fight; two Fokkers and three English and French biplanes.

Max Immelmann was the first German World War I flying ace. He was a pioneer in fighter aviation and is often mistakenly credited with the first aerial victory using a synchronized gun. He was the first aviator to be awarded the Pour le Mérite and was awarded it at the same time as Oswald Böelcke. His name has become attached to a common flying tactic, the Immelmann turn and remains a byword in aviation. He is credited with fifteen aerial victories.

Max Immelmann was born on 21 September 1890, the oldest of three children, in Dresden, Saxony to an industrialist father who died when Max was young. Although Max was not strong as a child, at the age of 15 he was enrolled in the Dresden Cadet School in 1905. While he was a gifted engineer, his behaviour was unacceptable; he and the army parted ways eight years later. Fascinated with mechanical devices and engines, he chose to join the Eisenbahnregiment (Railway Regiment) Nr.2 in 1912 as a fahnrich (ensign), in pursuit of a commission. He left the army in March 1912 to study mechanical engineering in Dresden. He was promoted to Leutnant des Reserves in July 1914. He returned to service on the outbreak of war, as a reserve officer candidate. He was assigned to Eisenbahnregiment Nr.1, but by that time he had been influenced by German aviation developments taking place at the Johannisthal airfield near Berlin and was determined to make his mark as a member of the Fliegertruppe (military air service). When World War I began, Immelmann was called to active service. Early in World War I the German high command regarded aviation as adjunct to the cavalry, which traditionally provided intelligence by reconnaissance. Hence, the emphasis was on two-seater aircraft in which the officer observer took charge of the mission. Since the pilot in this arrangement was little more than an aerial chauffeur, he was usually selected from the enlisted ranks. Nonetheless, Max Immelmann persisted in his efforts to join the Luftstreitkräfte as an officer and was finally accepted for pilot training at Johannisthal airfield on 12 November 1914. His brother Franz was accepted a short time afterwards.

His record as a pilot trainee is unclear. Some sources say he was a poor student. Others describe him as a natural. He learned on the Rumpler Taube, the Albatros and the L.V.G. His letters home described a fairly easy syllabus. He exceeded the requirements of his certification tests by wide margins: reaching 2,600 metres instead of 2000; gliding 2200 metres instead of eighty; and staying aloft for ninety instead of thirty minutes. He was an introvert; his closest friends seemed to be his mother and his dog, 'Tyras' who often slept in or on his bed. Immelmann never married, did not smoke or drink and wrote daily to his mother who regularly sent him chocolates. When he flew he wore old velvet trousers but on the ground dressed at his best. He loved having his photo taken whenever he had a new medal.

Max was initially stationed in northern France, serving as a pilot with Feldflieger Abteilung (Field Flier Detachment) 10 from February to April 1915 and then in FFA 62 by early May 1915. Initially he flew the mail and supplies to the German airdromes. He moved up to the Douai airfield. On several occasions he engaged in combat while flying the unarmed LVG B.I two-seat reconnaissance biplane designed by Luft-Verkehrs-Gesellschaft for the Luftstreitkräfte, with which his units were equipped, but never with any success. On 3 June 1915 while flying a photographic sortie, a French Farman shot him down. He landed safely within his own lines and surprisingly was decorated with the Iron Cross, Second Class for preserving his aircraft. Not long afterward, a young Dutch airplane designer, Anthony Fokker, arrived at Douai with two of his new monoplanes, each equipped with a potent innovation, a machine gun with interrupter gear that allowed it to fire forward through the propeller arc. Immelmann and Oswald Böelcke familiarized themselves with the Fokker E-I 'Eindekkers' and their revolutionary new weapons.

Max Immelmann applied his innate sense of discipline to flying and became one of the most successful students at the Adlershof training facility. It was customary at that time for squadron commanders to visit the training centres and, on the basis of their own observations, select prospective members of their units. Immelmann was therefore eager to prove his worth in February 1915, when Generalleutnant Günther Ludwig Feodor von Pannewitz arrived at the base to make his choice. A veteran of 130 perfect flights, this time Immelmann landed on a part of the airfield adjacent to a cow pasture. As he taxied across the field he failed to notice a manure pile that the neighbouring farmer had forgotten to remove. Von Pannewitz and several other officers witnessed Immelmann's aircraft hit the obstruction and flip over on its back. Consequently, several other pilots drew coveted front-line assignments that day - but not Fähnrich Immelmann.

Before the creation of specialised aviation units, the German Fliegertruppe was largely composed of feldflieger-ibteilungen (field flying sections). Hence, when Max Immelmann finally received a front-line posting on 12 April 1915, it was to Feldffiegerabteilung 10, an artillery-spotting squadron based at Vrizy. Within two weeks, however, he received a reprieve from such dull duty and was sent back to Germany, where Feldffiegerabteilung 62 was being formed at Döberitz.

On 13 May the veteran combat flier Hauptmann Hermann Kastner led Feldfliegerabteilung 62 to the airfield at Douai in the Arras sector of the Western Front. While Fahnrich Max Immelmann undertook routine reconnaissance patrols with Leutnant von Teubern, an old comrade from the cadet academy as observer. Oberleutnant Oswald Böelcke, also flying with Feldfliegerabteilung 62, was beginning to make a name for himself.

Immelmann, who had been flying the LVG B. I. subsequently 'inherited' Böelcke's LVG B.II, which was fitted with a captured French machine gun, making it one of the very few armed B-types. When Böelcke moved on to the unit's first

Fokker E.III monoplane fighter, Immelmann received his Albatros C.I. two-seater. It was the single-seat Fokker fighter however that caught Immelmann's imagination. Nobody had yet used the type in aerial combat, as there was some question about its structural integrity and a real danger that the torque of the rotary engine would tear the power plant from its mounting. Two very early examples of the Fokker Eindeckers were delivered to the unit, one Fokker M.5K/MG production prototype numbered E.3/15 for Böelcke's use, with Immelmann later in July receiving E.13/15 as a production Fokker E.I for his own use before the end of July. It was with the IMG 08 machine gun-armed E.13/15 aircraft that he gained his first confirmed air victory of the war on 1 August 1915, a fortnight after Leutnant Kurt Wintgens obtained the very first confirmed German aerial victory on 15 July with his own Fokker M.5K/MG production prototype E.5/15 Eindecker, one of five built, following two unconfirmed victories on 1 and 4 July, all before Immelmann.

After finishing a reconnaissance flight with von Teubern on 1 August, Immelmann went up in Böelcke's Fokker Eindecker after ten B.E.2c's bombed their aerodrome. Böelcke and Immelmann went after the departing RFC fighters, but Böelcke's gun jammed after he had fired a few rounds. He landed to fix it and saw Immelmann attack the B.E.2s. Immelmann dived and fired, first at one enemy aeroplane and then another. 'Like a hawk, I dived... and fired my machine gun. For a moment, I believed I would fly right into him. I had fired about sixty shots when my gun jammed. That was awkward, for to clear the jam I needed both hands - I had to fly completely without hands...' One started into a steep glide and Immelmann tailed it all the way to the ground. Lieutenant William Reid, originally of the 6th Battalion, King's (Liverpool) Regiment before he transferred to the RFC and to 2 Squadron, fought back valiantly, flying with his left hand and apparently firing about sixty shots with a pistol with his right before his gun jammed. Nonetheless, the 450 bullets fired at him took their effect. Reid suffered four wounds in his left arm and lost his engine, causing a crash landing. The unarmed Immelmann landed nearby. He and Reid shook hands and Immelmann informed the Englishman that he was a prisoner and rendered first aid.

While medical personnel treated the wounds of Immelmann's opponent, the Saxon officer was reporting to his commander the events concerning the squadron's first victory with the Eindecker. For this exploit, Max Immelmann received the Iron Cross, First Class. A member of Reid's squadron recorded on 2 August that 'Reid, Leather and I ascended at 5.0 am with six bombs each to drop on Vitry aerodrome... At the time of writing Lieutenant Reid has not returned. The Germans dropped a message last night over the French lines saying that Lieutenant William Reid is a prisoner and wounded in two places in the left arm but not seriously'. Reid was interned both in PoW camps and Switzerland, having been deemed by the Germans to be unfit to be of any use in further active service. He married his Swiss-Italian nurse whilst in Switzerland and was repatriated to England in March 1918. He then taught the Queen's father to fly, at RAF Cranwell.

Max Immelmann soon had his own Fokker monoplane fighter and he and Böelcke became engaged in friendly rivalry to see who could shoot down the most enemy aircraft. In all cases, the early German fighter pilots went up alone, climbing to maximum altitude about 10,000 feet from which they could pounce upon their prey. As additional Fokker Eindeckers were assigned to Feldegerabteilung 62, other pilots were instructed in the tactics of the Hawk. Although Max Immelmann may not have been the first pilot to use such tactics, he certainly did much to refine the turn that bears his name. The so-called 'Immelmann Turn' combines the first half of a loop with slow roll at the top of the loop - a manoeuvre which enables the pilot to effect a complete change of direction and gain altitude at the same time. Max Immelmann used the manoeuvre with great success. Immelmann wrote, 'I do not employ tricks when I attack.' In none of his writings does he refer to the half-loop, half-roll that bears his name. One source even suggested that Allied pilots used this manoeuvre to get away from Immelmann.[1]

Immelmann became one of the first German fighter pilots, quickly building an impressive score of air victories. During September, three more victories followed and he became the first German ace. Immelmann scored on 9 September and the 21st. But on the 23rd a French Farman shot up his aeroplane, holing the fuel tank and destroying the landing gear. Somehow Immelmann survived and soon scored his fourth victory, a B.E.2c over Lille. His fifth victory was a RFC biplane over Arras. On 7 November, another B.E.2c followed for his sixth kill and on 5 December, his seventh claim, a Morane. And then in October he became solely responsible for the air defence of the city of Lille. By this time, the German press was idolizing him, Der Adler von Lille (*The Eagle of Lille*).

On a flight over Lille, Captain Arthur Holroyd O'Hara Wood and gunner/observer Ira Jones of 4 Squadron AFC flying a B.E.2c had been warned of Immelmann's presence in that sector. O'Hara Wood was educated at Melbourne Grammar School and attended Trinity College, Melbourne University in 1908. He won the men's singles tennis championship of NSW in 1913 and of Victoria in 1914. That same year he won the Australasian Championships, played in Melbourne, defeating compatriot Gerald Patterson in the final in four sets. In 1915 O'Hara Wood joined the RFC. He saw service in France and did instructional work in England in 1916 before he was temporarily transferred to the Australian Flying Corps in France.

While Jones had a Lewis gun, there were four different mounts for it; he had to lift the machine gun from one to the other when needed. A Fokker monoplane came after them and quickly maneuvered into the B.E.2c's blind spot: low and behind. Desperately, Jones picked his Lewis gun up and fired it while holding it in his hands. The recoil of the heavy weapon and the violent movement of the airplane made him lose his grip and it fell out of the aeroplane. The two British fliers expected the worst, but the Fokker flew off, out of ammunition. Later Captain Wood informed Jones that their opponent had been the famous Max Immelmann, whom he had recognized by his skillful flying.[2]

Immelmann and Oswald Böelcke vied for the position of Germany's leading ace. Having come second to Böelcke for his sixth victory, Immelmann was second to be awarded the Royal House Order of Hohenzollern for this feat. On 15 December Immelmann shot down his seventh British aeroplane and moved into an unchallenged lead in the competition to be Germany's leading ace.

In recognition of his success Immelmann received an array of military orders and decorations. On 26 August, the day after his second victory, his native Saxony honoured him with the 'Albrechts-Orden' (Knight's Cross of the Order of Albert).

A few months later, on 21 October he received one of Saxony's highest awards, the 'Militär-St. Heinrichs-Orden' (Knight's Cross of the Military Order of St. Henry). The latter distinction was rarely outdone, but for Immelmann the grade of Commander 2nd Class was subsequently conferred, even though such an honour usually went to officers of the ink of colonel or above. On 12 January 1916 Immelmann and Böelcke both scored their eighth victories and they were both awarded the Prussian 'Pour le Mérite'. Immelmann's medal was presented by Kaiser Wilhelm II. Böelcke scored again two days later. Immelmann would chase him in the ace race for the next four months, drawing even on 13 March at eleven each, losing the lead on the 19th, regaining it on Easter Sunday (23 April) 14 to 13, losing it again forever on 1 May. It was about this time, on 25 April, that Immelmann received a salutary lesson in the improvement of British aircraft. As the German ace described his attack on two Airco D.H.2s: 'The two worked splendidly together... and put eleven shots into my machine. The petrol tank, the struts on the fuselage, the undercarriage and the propeller were hit... It was not a nice business.'

Success only made Immelmann bolder. As the spring of 1916 drew into summer he added to his victory score, shooting down at least another seven Allied aircraft. On 31 May Immelmann, Max Ritter von Mulzer and another German pilot attacked a formation of seven British aircraft. (One of the most famous Bavarian airmen of WW1, von Mulzer began his flying career at 21 years of age in 1914. Commonly referred to as 'Bavarian Max' he was one of Bavaria's first recipients of the 'Pour le Mérite' as well as the first Bavarian knighted for his achievements). Immelmann was flying a two-gun Fokker E.IV Eindecker and when he opened fire, the synchronizing gear malfunctioned. (Early the previous summer the Feldflieger Abteilung two-seater observation units of the future Luftstreitkräfte had received examples of the Fokker Eindecker monoplane with a fixed, forward-firing machine gun fitted with a 'synchronization gear' that prevented the bullets from striking the propeller. The first claim using this arrangement was by Leutnant Kurt Wintgens on 1 July 1915. Pilots like Wintgens and Leutnant Otto Parschau, another pioneering Eindecker pilot, could employ the simple combat tactic of aiming the whole aircraft and presenting a small target to the enemy while approaching from any angle, preferably from a blind spot where the enemy observer could not return fire.)

A stream of bullets cut off the tip of Immelmann's propeller blade. The thrashing of the unbalanced air screw nearly shook the aircraft's Oberursel engine loose from its mounts before he could cut the ignition and glide to a dead-stick landing. Despite this hair-raising experience Immelmann pressed on with his usual zeal.

In the late afternoon of 18 June, Immelmann led a flight of four Fokker E.III Eindeckers in search of a flight of eight F.E.2b two-seat reconnaissance aircraft of 25 Squadron over Sallaumines in northern France. The RFC flight had just crossed the lines near Arras, with the intent of photographing the German infantry and artillery positions within the area when Immelmann's flight intercepted them. After a long-running fight, scattering the participants over an area of thirty square miles, Immelmann brought down one of the enemy aircraft, wounding both the pilot Lieutenant George Clarence Rogers and observer.[3] This was his 16th victory claim, though it would go unconfirmed. At 2145 hours that same evening, Immelmann in Fokker E.III (246/16) encountered 25 Squadron again, this time near the village of Lentz. Immediately, over Wingles he got off a burst which hit 2nd Lieutenant John Raymond Boscawen Savage the pilot of F.E.2b pusher (6940), killing him instantly. Born at Bradford on 3 August 1898 and educated at a Winchester prep school and Oundle College, Savage joined the RFC on his 17th birthday, gained his pilot's certificate in a Maurice Farman biplane at Brooklands on 18 October 1915, his wings on 3 February 1916 and was sent to the front the following month. Savage was mortally wounded, being forced to land his F.E.2b behind German lines south of Lens, where he succumbed to his injuries and his observer 2nd Airman Robinson was taken prisoner. At the time of his death Savage was still only 17 years of age and his Commanding Officer wrote to his father: 'Your son was a very gallant boy and I wish with all my heart that he was back with us.'

This was Immelmann's 17th victory claim, though Savage and Robinson were finished off by Max Mulzer and this was later credited as his fourth victory though this was eventually overturned. (On 26 September 1916 whilst test flying a new aircraft, Mulzer lost control and was killed. He was only twenty-three years of age).

A contemporary German eyewitness described the fight this way: 'The tiny, swift Fokkers were like swallows compared with the big, lumbering, sure flying double-deckers. There was an increased liveliness aloft as the Fokkers overtook the biplanes and swooped down upon them with frightful speed. Amid a mad rattle of five machine guns our hearts stood still. Now the Fokkers have reached the enemy and they have turned themselves loose again. Then they pounce with fresh strength on the biplanes, which are now flying in confused circles. One of the Fokkers singled out his prey and he doesn't leave him. While the big biplane only seeks to fly lower or higher, the Fokker cuts off the escape each time. Suddenly the big machine reels. 'Hurrah; he's hit!' is roared from a thousand throats.'

The crew of the second aircraft Immelmann closed on was being flown by Second Lieutenant George Reynolds McCubbin aged 18½ with Corporal James Henry Waller as gunner/observer when he suddenly broke away. Born 19 January 1898 in Cape Town, son of David Aitken McCubbin, Chief Architect for South African Railways and Lucy McCubbin, George was educated at King Edward VII School, Johannesburg where he became captain of the 1st XI Football and vice-captain, cricket. Despite his background, his family roots were firmly in Liverpool. The teenage pilot's grandfather, J. T. McCubbin lived in Merton Road, Bootle and his father had been educated at Liverpool College before emigrating to South Africa where he designed railway stations across the country. First George became a member of the East African forces and then he entered the Army on 28 February 1916 before joining the RFC and gaining his aviator's certificate in March that year at the age of 18.

Waller continued firing, but the fight was over for Oberleutnant Max Immelmann. As he plunged downward, for whatever reason, his Fokker broke up and the wings collapsed. His body was subsequently found in the wreckage.

The German publication, *Tägliche Rundschau*, printed an eyewitness letter that

Left: Front cover of *The War Budget* depicting Flight Lieutenant Reginald Alexander John Warneford's epic shoot down of the Zeppelin.

Above: William Leefe Robinson VC

Below: Zeppelin damage to Bolton on 25 September 1916.

Above: A Zeppelin over the Houses of Parliament on 19 January 1915.

Right: Führer der Luftschiffer (Leader of airships) Kapitän Peter Strasser.

Below: Wrecked German Zeppelin brought down by the RFC near the coast of Essex in 1916.

Left: a British airman dropping a bomb.

Below: DFW C.V (Aviatik) 5845/16 banking in early morning sunlight. Note the Aviatik trademark on strut; flares in holder behind observer's cockpit; and fully-armed LMG 14 'Parabellum' machine gun.

irst many aviators
eved the war in the
o be preferable to life
e trenches but scores
housands of pilots
observers lost their
s in aerial combat and
nly a few hundred
, many also died. But
cult of the fighter
t had been born and
norised with stories
hivalry in the clouds
these early airmen
e inspired generations
r since. In reality
th in the air was most
n just as cruel,
alid and
antaneous as it was in
trenches.

Above: Royal Flying Corps of Canada personnel attending a lecture on rigging at the School of Aviation.

Left: Vice Admiral Richard Bell-Davies VC CB DSO AFC who was awarded the Victoria Cross on 1 January 1916 for an action at Ferrijik Junction in Bulgaria near the border with Ottoman-controlled Europe on 19 November 1915. He was 29 years old and in command of 3 Squadron RNAS.

Above: Squadron Commander Reginald Lennox George Marix DSO RN who was severely injured during his destruction of a Zeppelin in its shed at Düsseldorf in October 1914.

Left: The legendary Commander Charles Rumney Samson.

Above left: Captain Stanley Cockerell who later became a test pilot for Vickers.

Above right: 2nd Lieutenant Richard Raymond-Barker.

Left: Werner Voss.

Below: Wreckage of the 'Red Baron's Fokker Triplane being examined by Australian Air Flying Corps officers.

Above left: Erwin Böhme.

Above right: Major Hubert Dunsterville 'Bay' Harvey-Kelly DSO commanding 19 Squadron.

Centre: Kurt Wolff.

Below left: Major Lanoe George Hawker VC DSO, officer commanding 24 Squadron.

Below right: Oswald Böelcke.

Above: Captain Richard 'Dick' Aveline Maybery MC*.

Below: Captain James Byford McCudden VC.

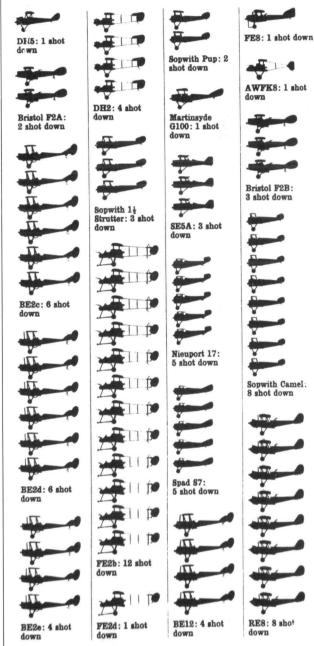

Richthofen's score

Through the chances of war, all but one of the aircraft Richthofen was officially credited with shooting down were British (the exception was a Belgian Spad). As with all aces, most of his victims were reconnaissance, not fighter aircraft. The drawings below illustrate the full tally of 20 types of Allied aircraft that fell to Richthofen.

DH5: 1 shot down

Bristol F2A: 2 shot down

BE2c: 6 shot down

BE2d: 6 shot down

BE2e: 4 shot down

DH2: 4 shot down

Sopwith 1½ Strutter: 3 shot down

FE2b: 12 shot down

FE2d: 1 shot down

Sopwith Pup: 2 shot down

Martinsyde G100: 1 shot down

SE5A: 3 shot down

Nieuport 17: 5 shot down

Spad S7: 5 shot down

BE12: 4 shot down

FE8: 1 shot down

AWFK8: 1 shot down

Bristol F2B: 3 shot down

Sopwith Camel: 8 shot down

RE8: 8 shot down

Right: Australian Flying Corps officers of 3 Squadron AFC pose for the camera with Spandau machine guns from von Richthofen's downed Fokker Triplane.

Left: Manfred von Richthofen otherwise known as 'The Red Baron'.

Below: Fokker DR.VII of Jasta 10.

Left: Max Immelmann, with his dog 'Tyras'. The first German WW I flying ace, Immelmann is often mistakenly credited with the first aerial victory using a synchronized gun. He was the first aviator to be awarded the Pour le Mérite and his name has become attached to a common flying tactic, the Immelmann turn which remains a byword in aviation. He is credited with fifteen aerial victories.

Below: Albatros D.III fighters of Jasta 30.

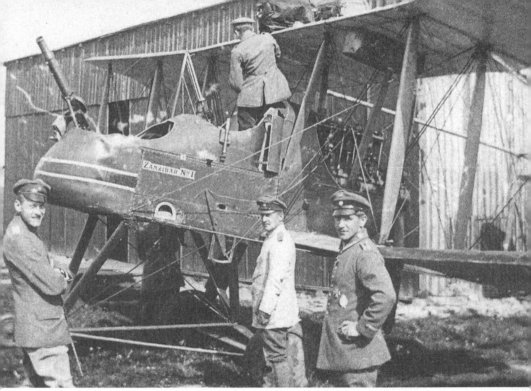

Above: Immelmann with
captured 25 Squadron F.E.2b
63411 *Zanzibar*.

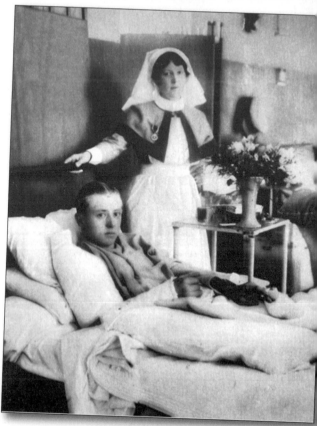

Right: Second Lieutenant
George Reynolds McCubbin
in hospital on 26 July 1916.

Left: Brigadier General Sir David Henderson. Right: Captain Ian Henderson.

Below left: Cecil Arthur Lewis. Below right: Lieutenant Frank Albery DCM of 4 Squadron AFC.

Above: 1 Squadron AFC in Palestine in 1918. (State Library of Victoria)

Left: Eric Rupert Dibbs AFC.

Right: Bert Hinkler.

Below: B.E.2s of 1 Squadron AFC on the flight line in the Sinai in 1917. (AWM)

Above: 2 Squadron AFC D.H.5. Scout
in 1917. (AWM)

Centre: Charles Kingsford Smith.

Below left: Major Wilfred
McCloughry MC DSO DFC.

Below right: RNAS 'Tripehound' ace,
Roderic 'Stan' Dallas DSO DSC*.

Top left: Edgar James McCloughry AFC.

Top right: Elwyn R. King AFC

Centre left: Lieutenant Francis Hubert ('Frank') McNamara VC.

Centre right: James M. Sandy AFC.

Below left: Captain Robert A. 'Rickie' Little DSO** DSC* CdeG of the Australian Flying Corps (AFC).

Below right: Captain F. R. McCall DSO MC AFC at Arras on 22 February 1918 when serving with 16 Squadron RFC.

On the evening of 14/15 April 1916, Squadron Commander Joseph Ruscombe Wadham Smyth-Pigott led a raid on Constantinople by four pilots flying B.E.2Cs, which had been shipped out to Moudros, a small Greek port on the Mediterranean island of Lemnos.

Right: The ex-German battle cruiser *Goeben* which with the SMS *Breslau* were transferred to the Ottoman Empire in August 1914, to entice the Ottomans to join the Central Powers in World War I in port in Constantinople.

Below: Squadron Commander Kenneth Stevens Savory DSO's Handley Page 0400 at Manston on 22 May 1917 shortly before the transcontinental flight to bomb warships at Constantinople on the evening of 9/10 July.

Above: The Magdeburg-class cruiser SMS *Breslau* formerly of the Imperial German Navy.

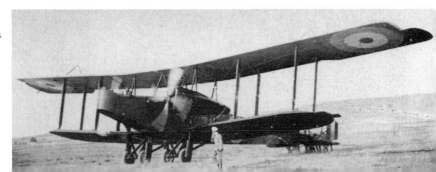

Top left: Lieutenant Colonel William George Barker VC DSO MC**, the most decorated Canadian of the war and the third top Canadian ace with fifty victories.

Top right: Captain Arthur Roy Brown DSC*.

Centre: Raymond Collishaw, the second highest scoring Canadian 'ace' with sixty kills.

Below: William Avery 'Billy' Bishop on 60 Squadron beside his Nieuport 17 Scout. Bishop topped the list of Canadian aces and was second among all Allied aces with 72 kills.

described the scene:

'Immelmann didn't make it easy for his enemies. He had already shot down three enemy fliers and at the time of his death plunge he was engaged in a fight with two enemy machines. While he was pursuing and firing at the one his Fokker was hit by the other. Probably a steel truss was broken, but Immelmann had bitten himself so firmly into his enemy that he didn't notice it. He continued to pursue his victim until suddenly the tail broke off and Immelmann and his rudderless Fokker plunged to his death. His half-annihilated enemy was then brought down by Immelmann's comrades, also in Fokkers.

Another eyewitness's letter was quoted at length in the New York Times. In part it said:

'I was watching closely and noticed that the Fokker, too, was making curious tumbling motions, righting itself like an animal mortally wounded, then fluttering down, first slowly, then faster. A sudden jerk brings the machine again to a horizontal position. Thank God, I think and breathe easier, when suddenly the Fokker overturns completely, the tail falls away, one of the wings flutters off and, with an uncanny whistling sound, the machine precipitates from 6,000 feet earthward and strikes with a dull thud.'

A number of British pilots claimed the victory. The British commanders have decided that they need to have a definitive claimant for morale purposes and scotch the German claims that the celebrated ace shot off his own propeller. RFC Officer Commanding, Hugh Trenchard notified Director of Air Organization Sefton Brancker that he had reviewed the eyewitness evidence and that this was sufficient to award the victory to Second Lieutenant George Reynolds McCubbin and his gunner, Corporal James Henry Waller and he sent out a peremptory order to all RFC squadrons to that effect. On the German side, many had seen Immelmann as invincible and could not conceive the notion that he had fallen to enemy fire. The Imperial German Air Service at the time claimed the loss was due to (friendly) anti-aircraft fire. Others, including Immelmann's brother, believed his aircraft's gun synchronisation (designed to enable his machine gun to fire between the whirling propeller blades without damaging them) had malfunctioned with catastrophic results. This is not in itself unreasonable, as early versions of such gears frequently malfunctioned in this way. Indeed, this had already happened to Immelmann twice before (while testing two- and three-machine gun installations), although on each occasion, he had been able to land safely.

On 12 July 1916 the *Liverpool Echo* revealed the McCubbin had been awarded the DSO for shooting down German ace Max Immelmann the previous month in an aerial battle near Lens. (Waller gained his sergeant's stripes, a DSM and the Russian Medal of St. George, 1st Class). The report added: 'The family in Bootle received news today of the fact that he has been severely wounded in two places, in a contest subsequent to that with Immelmann.' McCubbin's official citation stated: 'Seeing one of our machines about to engage two Fokkers, he at once entered the fight and his observer shot down one Fokker, which crashed to the ground. On another occasion, when returning from a bombing raid, he saw one of our machines being followed by a Fokker. He recrossed the lines to the attack and his observer shot down the Fokker. Although very badly wounded in the arm, he successfully landed his machine well behind our lines.'

McCubbin, in a 1935 interview, claimed that immediately after Immelmann shot down McCubbin's squadron mate, the German ace began an Immelmann turn, McCubbin and Waller swooped down from a greater altitude and opened fire and the pioneer German ace fell out of the sky. Waller also pointed out later that the British bullets could have hit Immelmann's propeller.[4] Damage to the propeller resulting in the loss of one blade could have been the primary cause of the structural failure evident in accounts of the crash of his aircraft. The resultant vibration of an engine at full throttle spinning half a propeller could have shaken the fragile craft to pieces. At 2000 metres, the tail was seen to break away from the rest of Immelmann's Fokker, the wings detached or folded and what remained of the fuselage fell straight down, carrying the 25-year old Oberleutnant to his death. His body was recovered by the German 6 Armee from the twisted wreckage, lying smashed and lifeless over what was left of the surprisingly intact Oberursel engine (sometimes cited as under it), but was only identified because he had his initials embroidered on his handkerchief.

Immelmann was given a state funeral and buried in his home of Dresden. His body was later exhumed, however and cremated in the Dresden-Tolkewitz Crematorium.

While the controversy over Immelmann's death raged, the legend of his exploits and hawk-like tactics grew, inspiring the German fighter pilots who pressed on for another two-and-a-half years of intense aerial combat.

Endnotes Chapter 7

1   In an article published on 20 July 2016, Thomas Van Hare had this to say about the so-called 'Immelmann Turn': 'Whereas many today credit Immelmann with inventing a half-loop manoeuvre with a roll at the top back upright, in actual fact, the original Immelmann Turn was anything but that. Immelmann's actual manoeuvre was a vertical pull-up into an extreme version of a chandelle, but with kicking the rudder hard at the top to pull the nose back around and down, thus allowing the plane to fall nearly vertically back into the enemy formation for a second attack. Immelmann's favoured manoeuvre, if anything, resembles what we now consider a hammerhead stall.'

2   On 17 July 1918, when he celebrated his third anniversary at the war, Arthur O'Hara Wood was appointed to an important post at flying school in England. Major O'Hara Wood was in command of a squadron when, during a patrol over Sainte-Quentin on 4 October 1918, another aircraft flew into his. He died two days later at the 37th Casualty Clearing Station from multiple injuries.

3   Captain George Clarence Rogers of 52 Squadron died of wounds on 30 October 1917 after being fatally wounded on 27 October 1917 while flying an R.E.8. on an artillery observation mission with Lieutenant H. E. Judge as his observer. The crew battled three or four Albatros D.Vs over Nieuport and Judge was also wounded. A victory was credited to Vizefeldwebel (later Leutnant) Franz Hemer of Jasta 6; it was the first of his eventual 18 victories.

4   Promoted to Lieutenant in the RFC in June 1917 McCubbin was made a Staff Captain on 11 April 1918. After the war he briefly played cricket for Transvaal. McCubbin died in Johannesburg in 1944. He was 46.

Chapter 8

Flight of the Black Cat

Allan Burnett

Captain Ian Henderson was born in 1896 into a wealthy Scottish family. His father was a Glaswegian shipbuilder's son called Sir David Henderson. Sir David was a highly decorated soldier and pioneering military pilot who became a founder of the RFC in 1912. Ian Henderson's mother, Henrietta Dundas, belonged to an aristocratic Edinburgh family.

Henderson grew up with a younger sister, Angela. He was given an elite school education in England at Eton College and then the Royal Military College Sandhurst. He graduated from Sandhurst, on 13 January 1915 and was commissioned as a second lieutenant in the Princess Louise's (Argyll and Sutherland Highlanders) - his father's Scottish regiment - rising to the rank of Captain. After war broke out Henderson was sent to fight on the front line but was seconded to the RFC and was appointed a flying officer on 21 August 1915. He was promoted to lieutenant in his regiment on 21 January 1916 but had to wait until 1 June before receiving the same in the RFC. On 1 July he was appointed a flight commander with the acting rank of captain. Henderson was assigned to 19 Squadron, flying the B.E.12, gaining his first two victories in August and was subsequently awarded the Military Cross, which was gazetted in October 1916. His citation read: 2nd Lieutenant (Temporary Captain) Ian Henry David Henderson, Argyll & Sutherland Highlanders. For conspicuous gallantry and skill on several occasions. He drove down a machine out of control and two days later dispersed six enemy machines which were attacking his formation. A few days later again he brought down an enemy biplane, the observer being apparently killed. A week after this he attacked and drove down another machine which had wounded his leader. He has also carried out several excellent contact patrols and attacked retiring artillery and a kite balloon.

Henderson was officially credited with seven aerial-combat victories. He had to wait until November for his third victory, gained while flying a SPAD S.VII. In 1917 he was posted to 56 Squadron, flying the S.E.5a, where in July he shot down four Albatros D.Vs. He was appointed to the General Staff as a 3rd Grade Officer, remaining there until March 1918, when he was re-appointed a flight commander with the acting rank of captain.

Scottish Tales of Adventure by Allan Burnett[1]

Captain Ian Henderson leaned over the side of his open-topped cockpit and craned his neck, scanning the sky above and below him. The wind blasted his cheeks, the noise of the engine and propeller roared in his ears.

Far beneath the wings of his single-seat biplane, through gaps in the ragged, dense blankets of grey cloud, he could see the bomb-blasted fields and shattered buildings of farming villages. Above, cold and mysterious, were the infinite Heavens.

'Where are you hiding, Boche?' Henderson said to himself, cursing his German foe as he sat back down in the relatively quiet cocoon of his cockpit.

He pulled off his leather-bound goggles for a moment. His eyes smarted in the rushing air as he wiped the sweat and engine oil from his brow. He checked the ammunition in his well-worn machine guns and scanned his instruments.

The young pilot was something of a rising star in the RFC, notching up a series of successes against the fighter aircraft of the German Luftstreitkräfte. Now it was time to add to that total. He knew the enemy was out there somewhere, so he throttled up the 200-horsepower engine and got ready for action. It was then that his propeller came off.

At first, just for a moment, it was as though nothing had happened. But the tell-tale change in the tone of the engine made Henderson realise he was in serious trouble. He could also sense it through the controls.

Suddenly he felt his stomach lurch, as the aeroplane began to drop through the air. He gripped the controls tighter and tried to level off, but the aircraft was already nosing into a dive.

The dials on the dashboard span and jerked. The altimeter revealed that he would hit the ground very hard, very soon, unless he could find a way to regain control.

The aeroplane rattled and shook as the descent began taking its toll. Henderson knew of pilots who had met their doom when the stress of a steep dive caused their wings to come off. Having no propeller was deadly enough without that added challenge. He used all his strength to pull, push and lever the controls, desperately trying to find a friendly current of air to ride on.

Still the aircraft kept plunging.

Buildings and hedgerows became sharper and more detailed as the ground loomed closer. Somehow, he just managed to lift the aircraft's nose to make the descent less steep. The aeroplane leapt from side to side as he wrestled with the controls for the rudder and the wing-mounted ailerons, trying to steer to an open patch where he might be able to set down without slamming into a wall or a ditch.

By now he was level with the tops of the trees. In just a few seconds he would strike the ground. His pulse throbbed in his chest and temples. He had to force himself to remain calm, not to allow his tense muscles and sweaty fingers to yank too hard on the controls.

Sensing he was only inches away from the soil, Henderson closed his eyes.

THUD! CRASH! BATTER!

The aeroplane smashed into the ground, wrecking the undercarriage and damaging the propeller-less nose and its huge, square radiator. The fuselage skidded along the ground and the wings shook violently.

Eventually the aircraft jerked to a halt and the engine spluttered, then died. Smoke and steam poured from the wreckage.

A few moments passed. There was no sign of life.

Then a leather-gloved hand emerged and gripped the lip of the cockpit. There was a groan.

Henderson checked his legs and arms, wiggled his fingers and toes. 'Still in one piece,' he reassured himself and leaned his head back, his smile a crescent of ivory white against his smoke-blackened face.

He coughed and came to his senses. There was no time to relax. He had to get out in case the fuel tank caught fire.

Gripping the fuselage he began to haul himself up, then paused for a moment. He grabbed his map and tucked it under his arm, then reached out to an object tied to the dashboard - the toy black cat his sister Angela had given him.

'How many more lives does this leave us with, then?' said Henderson to his mascot as he pulled it free, then climbed out of the wreck and staggered away.

Soon he was back among his friends in the squadron, rested and recovered, with another exciting tale to tell - and ready to fly and fight another day. Yet, returning to earth with a bump was a reminder of how far Henderson had come since the war began. In many ways it was amazing that he had survived this long.

Henderson's wartime adventure had begun quietly and unpromisingly with a miserably cold, long winter in the army reserves, far from the high life of the RFC.

He was given a job guarding the army's big weapons arsenal at Woolwich in London. His accommodation was a stuffy little hole where he and the other men lived on a diet of tinned beef.

Henderson, who had been trained as an officer, was in charge of the sentries who patrolled the premises and he had to check regularly that they were guarding the place properly. It wasn't a job he enjoyed.

One night, while out checking on the men, Henderson and his orderly were caught in a storm. They were walking along a river-bank and a gust of wind sent the orderly reeling, blowing him into the water. Instinctively, Henderson jumped in and managed to drag the man out.

The storm had pulled down trees and it started to snow. Exhausted and frozen, the pair became disoriented and ended up stumbling through a ditch full of dirty water. As they returned to base they were almost shot by one of their own men. It was very late and they were soaked to the skin.

To make matters worse, the stove had gone out in Henderson's room and the window above his bed had blown open - his mattress was sodden.

So when Henderson was finally sent across the English Channel to fight on the front line, it was a relief at first to leave behind such miserable conditions. But he quickly realised there were certain advantages to being on the home front - like not being shot to pieces.

By the late spring of 1915 he was right in the thick of the action with the Argyll and Sutherland Highlanders. The Germans were trying to take the Belgian town of Ypres and the Argylls, together with other British regiments, were trying to stop them.

To get to Ypres, Henderson and his company marched along roads jammed with military and civilian traffic. There were horse-drawn artillery carriages, wounded troops, ambulance wagons, transport wagons, motor cars of all shapes and sizes, dispatch riders on motorcycles, riders on horseback, people on pedal bicycles ringing their bells furiously and a constant chatter of French and English.

As they got nearer the front line the chaos and signs of battle intensified. They had to walk across open fields strewn with the dead bodies of men and horses. When they finally arrived, they found the city of Ypres in ruins.

Henderson was posted to a front-line trench near the ruined city. The network of trenches went on for miles and miles and his was just one tiny part of it. The Germans were dug in nearby on the other side of a small hill and Henderson rarely saw them. But their shells continually blasted and pounded the Argylls and the number of dead and wounded began to mount.

The trench was cramped and freezing cold, especially after dark. When it rained, the muddy floor became a quagmire. Henderson cursed himself for forgetting his coat.

Eventually he found an old coat probably left by a wounded soldier. He found an old sack, too and put that around his shoulders over the coat. They were already sodden but they were better than nothing.

The rain continued. Hour after hour. Henderson's boots became like big mud pies and his legs and kilt were caked with the stuff. At night he huddled in a dugout in the wall of the trench. The dugout was so small that his knees stuck out into the rain.

Days and nights were spent like this and Henderson began to think he might have been better off back at the ammo dump in London after all. To try to stave off madness, he would let his imagination paint a new picture of his surroundings. His smelly dugout became an alcove in a nice restaurant, where he was served a fine meal at a grand table with a white tablecloth, glasses and cutlery.

Letters from home - his parents and wee sister Angela - were what really kept him going. Angela sounded very grown up these days and she gave him advice on how to fend off bombs, which made him smile. Henderson was delighted by the drawings that accompanied her letters.

As a result of the shellfire and snipers' bullets, many of Henderson's comrades were killed. Those who survived did their best to keep their spirits up. It was not uncommon to hear survivors of a shell attack singing or humming the haunting Scottish lament *The Flowers of the Forest* as they went about their business.

Eventually Henderson's company was relieved. The men were sent back from the trenches for a few days' rest at their billet, about a mile or so behind the lines. 'Thank God,' muttered Henderson, stamping the caked-on mud from his boots as he marched along the road.

Early one morning, Henderson woke up with a fright. The relative peace of the billet had been shattered by a terrific sound. German artillery shells were exploding everywhere. He rushed outside and took cover, then looked around, trying to work out what was happening.

The billet was a farm building on the edge of an open field. A road passed through the middle of the field leading toward the woods, from which huge columns of black smoke were rising. After a while the smoke became so dense Henderson could hardly see the trees.

Just beyond the woods and out of sight, Henderson knew there were more front-line trenches containing his fellow soldiers - he presumed they were now the focus of the German shellfire.

Soon rag-tag bunches of wounded men emerged from the woods and began making their way slowly down the road toward the billet, stumbling along and helping each other as best they could. The shells seemed to follow them, blasting craters in the ground with monstrous force. Henderson looked on in horror as two little groups of the retreating men were hit, their bodies torn apart.

A company was ordered to leave the billet and reinforce the trenches. Henderson watched them go, as the shells continued to fall. The men had no choice but to cross the field via the road to reach the cover of the woods. But before they had even gone ten yards they had five casualties - three men blown to bits when a shell slammed into the ground, and two wounded.

When the survivors reached the edge of the woods, they were met by a new wave of terror-stricken men running in the opposite direction, shouting, 'Gas! Everybody has been killed by gas! The trenches are taken! The Germans are in the woods!'

One of the officers took control of the situation and tried to calm everything down. The retreating men were turned around and all the troops marched towards the trenches together, rifles and bayonets at the ready in case the Germans really had advanced as far as the woods.

Then it was Henderson's turn to go.

'I want you to follow them and join the counter-attack,' ordered a senior officer.

'Yes, sir!' replied Henderson.

His company set off and made it through the woods without casualties.

They soon discovered that the Germans had only taken a few trenches, so the counter-attack was called off for the time being. Henderson's platoon rested for the night in a ditch near a chateau - a large French country house.

They were woken up at two in the morning with orders to make a shelter in the kitchen garden of the chateau.

'Why couldn't we have a bit more rest?' said a young soldier about Henderson's age.

'Boche will start shelling us as soon as he's had breakfast,' replied Henderson. 'If we don't get this shelter dug out before then, we'll be done for.'

In response, the soldier began digging frantically in the dark, uprooting the flowers and vegetables.

Just as Henderson had predicted, around nine o'clock in the morning the firing began. A shell came hurtling straight towards the half-finished dugout where he was crouched. It whooshed and rumbled through the air and when it hit the ground it exploded with a deafening BOOM!

Henderson wiped the spattered mud from his face and tried to clear his stinging eyes of the white smoke that had enveloped him. He turned to his left and then his right. The three men next to him were dead. Somehow, by the grace of God, he was untouched.

It was obvious the shellfire wasn't just random luck - the German guns must have located the British troops' position. If Henderson and his comrades stayed there, they would all end up dead. Hastily they made a plan before breaking cover.

While half the men went to try to re-take some trenches, Henderson took charge of the other half, who would wait in reserve until ordered to attack.

'We're going to take cover a few hundred yards up the road that runs past the chateau - follow me!' Henderson commanded his men.

In double time they trooped up the road and hid behind a hedge.

'Corporal!' shouted Henderson. 'Sir!' came the reply.

'Get these men back to the dressing station for first aid.' He nodded in the direction of two soldiers with shrapnel wounds.

'Yes sir!' With the help of two able-bodied men, the corporal quickly went off with the wounded.

'Now, listen up, the rest of you,' continued Henderson. 'We're going to...'

He was cut off by a new sound coming from above. 'Damn it - a Hun aeroplane!' cursed Henderson. 'Keep your heads down!'

The observer in the aircraft must have spotted the kilted soldiers below, as Henderson clearly saw him sending a signal back to his artillery. It wouldn't be long before the German gunners started hammering them again.

'Let's keep moving!' Henderson commanded.

He led his men further down the road to a ditch that gave them a little cover when they lay on their bellies and stretched themselves flat out. As they did so the hedge they'd been sheltering behind was directly hit by four shells and blasted to atoms. Once again, Henderson knew they had to move on.

Next to a stone gateway he found a large shell hole, better shelter for his men than a ditch.

But he soon discovered that the gateway was being used as a target by the German gunners. A light field gun was shooting at it with small shells that made a WHIZZ-BANG sound, like fireworks. They flew past Henderson's head as he clambered down into the hole. He and his men hunkered down and waited for the shelling to stop.

Later, once they were fairly sure the Germans had given up shelling for the time being, they went to re-take a couple of trenches only to find that they had already been taken by the British side during an earlier counter-attack.

After that, things went quiet until early the following morning when Henderson and the others watched German soldiers creeping through the woods in ones and twos. Another British regiment - the Glosters - led a counter-attack and the Argylls joined in. The Germans scarpered.

When Henderson got out of the wood again, he looked up. He kept thinking about the German aeroplane that had spotted him and his men. He was fed up of being on the ground at the mercy of aerial attacks and wished he could fly up there and knock those aeroplanes out of the sky.

Upon his return from the front line, he found a visitor waiting. 'Dad!' he shouted and rushed to his father, who gripped him in a bear hug.

Henderson's father, Sir David Henderson, was a senior figure in the British forces. Like his son, he had served in the Argyll and Sutherland Highlanders and was highly decorated for his part in wars fought long ago.

He was now one of the leaders of the RFC and a skilled pilot himself.

'How are you, laddie?' asked Sir David in his Glaswegian brogue. Soon the pair were deep in conversation, the younger man retelling the exploits of the last few days like the veteran he already was, while the older man nodded his approval. But in spite of the bravado, it was obvious that Ian was troubled.

'I'm desperate to get out, Dad,' admitted Henderson at last.

'Really? A man could get himself shot for deserter's talk like that,' replied his father with mock seriousness.

'You know what I mean,' replied Henderson. 'We were spotted by a flying Hun, who relayed our position to their guns. We were nearly done for. It was beastly.' He sighed. 'I want to be up there,' he continued, nodding at the sky, 'doing something about it.'

'I know,' said his father, his dark eyes glowing as he grinned under his thick moustache. 'That's why I'm here. Get your stuff together - you're about to join the RFC.'

'But...?' Henderson couldn't believe what he was hearing.

'Don't worry, it's all been arranged, laddie,' said his father, holding out his hands in a calming gesture. 'It's what you always wanted, is it not?'

'Yes, but...'

'No more buts,' said Sir David. 'Your company can look after themselves and you'll have plenty of opportunity to catch up with them from time to time. The best thing you can do now is get airborne and help them by taking the fight to the Kaiser's men in the sky.'

For years, Henderson had dreamed of learning to fly like his father and since the start of the war he had yearned to join the ranks of the RFC. Now that it was actually happening and after all he had been through in the trenches of the army's ground war during the past few weeks, it seemed a bit unreal to be suddenly plucked out of the mud and sent into the sky.

He soon forgot his reservations once he put on the RFC uniform and took to the air. Flying was simply wonderful. It was in his blood.

No more muddy trenches, no more shells ringing in his ears or corpses strewn about. The RFC offered freedom from all that. High above the ground, on a clear day, he could see the Earth curving away into the distance.

His career as a pilot began at the Central Flying School near Stonehenge on Salisbury Plain. He flew a Henri Farman, almost identical to the Boxkite aircraft his father had learned to fly on. Indeed the Farman, like the Boxkite, was more like a huge kite than an aeroplane. It had long landing skids sticking out from the front like horns. It was not a great machine, but for Henderson it was a thrill just to be at the controls and learning how to fly up and away. Learning how to land was even more important. After the Henri Farman, Henderson was given a B.E.2a, which was much better to fly, but he found it a beast to land.

Henderson was taught how to drop bombs with the B.E.2a. They were mounted on racks under the wings. When a cable was pulled in the cockpit, the bombs were released. It was important to be very sure the whole lot was dropped. Landing a B.E.2a was bumpy enough without a bomb hanging off the wing. After several weeks' training, the instructors decided Henderson was ready and sent him to France. This was it - active service. As he travelled to join [2 Squadron] at Hesdigneul, near the French port town of Calais and the border with Belgium, from where the Germans were attacking he wondered how long it would be before he faced a Hun - or a Boche, to give the Germans their other wartime nickname - in air-to-air combat.

It was now December 1915 and the weather was hopeless. It rained and rained until the aerodrome was a great mass of mud and water. The aircraft often got bogged down before the pilots could reach take-off speed, especially if there were two men on board. For a good while Henderson didn't get airborne at all.

At least he had a comfortable billet - a room in a huge chateau eleven miles from the front line. They could hardly hear the guns at all from there. And Henderson found the people around him very pleasant.

He spent his time getting to know the mechanics, who did a difficult and dangerous job at all hours of the day and night, often in foul weather, to keep the aircraft in good working order. These men tended to be the unsung heroes of the flying corps, but Henderson quickly realised that the air crews absolutely depended on them.

The waiting was tedious. One evening, a concert was held and, as his contribution to the programme, Henderson sang the tongue-twister Sister Susie's Sewing Shirts for Soldiers. It went down a storm with the other men and the concerts became a regular part of camp life. The squadron set up a cinema projector, too, so they could watch 'movies'.

The New Year came in and the weather remained dreadful. But the aircrews couldn't stay on the ground for ever. Eventually, very early one morning, Henderson managed to take off on a reconnaissance mission.

Accompanied by an observer, Henderson flew over the front lines to see what the Germans were up to and to find out how effective the British manoeuvres had been. Things got even more exciting when the Germans began firing up at his aeroplane. Henderson felt quite proud that the enemy considered him such a threat, going to all that trouble to try to bring him down. But they didn't get near him.

On long winter flights such as this Henderson thanked God for his mother and all the clothes she'd sent him. There was a scarf, gloves, a leather flying cap and big snow boots - all fur-lined to help stave off the deadly high-altitude cold. Henderson's mother had also sent him a long thick coat to replace the filthy secondhand one he'd found in the trenches.

Not only did the new coat help save him from freezing to death in the cockpit, it had other protective powers too.

While flying through German shellfire something pinged sharply against Henderson's arm.

'Was that you?' he shouted to his observer.

'What?' the observer shouted back.

'Did you chuck something at me?'

'No! But don't tempt me - you need to stop mucking about and get us out of here!' The observer laughed and Henderson did too.

It was only when they landed that Henderson realised he had been hit by a piece of shell, about the size of a pea. It had torn a hole in his new coat. Thanks to the thick double-lining, it hadn't pierced his skin.

Soon they were back in the sky, where Henderson engaged with a German aircraft for the first time. It was a Fokker Eindecker. These machines had single wings, so were not biplanes like the RFC aircraft. When Henderson sported the Eindecker, he and his observer were so excited they dived at him and gave chase with great speed.

Henderson couldn't help being impressed by the Eindecker, with its grey fuselage and huge German emblem - the Iron Cross - painted upon its wings and tail. It carried a clever new innovation - a synchronised machine gun up front so its pilot could shoot through his propeller.

The Eindecker was also sprightly. Since Henderson had orders not to follow an enemy aircraft over its lines, he had to let it go. But the thrill of having chased away their first enemy aircraft put the two RFC fliers in high spirits. They began to sing.

Singing soon became part of the routine of flying and Henderson and his observer liked to sing as often as possible during a flight. Even at the top of their voices it was difficult to hear anything over the din of the aeroplane. But when Henderson performed a controlled shut-down of the engine for a brief time, they would keep singing - ecstatic at the sound of their harmonies floating over the clouds.

They had an audience, too - Henderson's Black Cat, his present from Angela. The toy cat was attached above the dashboard at the start of each flight and it appeared to jiggle its arms throughout.

The only time Henderson couldn't see Black Cat was when he needed to get a map out during a reconnaissance mission. The maps were large and filled the cockpit when he rolled them out to check his route. Once they were neatly stowed, Black Cat would be back in view.

Besides maps, there was sophisticated kit on board the RFC aircraft.

A wireless radio was used to direct gunners on the ground to the right targets. On one occasion Henderson saw a flash coming from a big house. After careful thought and a good look at it, he decided it must be a German gun firing.

He wirelessed the enemy position to his own guns on the ground. To his great satisfaction, after a few shots, the house went up in a cloud of brick dust and smoke. Henderson gleefully signalled 'Hit!'

Of course Henderson did his own firing, too. One evening he and his observer were coming back from a reconnaissance flight over the German line when their singing was cut short.

'Three Huns coming our way!' shouted the observer.

'Yes, obviously returning from a mission over our lines!' replied Henderson.

The incoming German aircraft were flying at a higher altitude than Henderson's aeroplane.

'I expect they're going to dive and give it to us hot!' shouted the observer.

However, the Germans appeared to take no notice of them, so concerned were they with making their escape. Henderson did not like being ignored.

'I'm going to increase altitude and then we'll give it to them with both guns' shouted Henderson.

'Righto!' came the reply and the observer began aiming his machine gun.

Once Henderson got as close as he dared, he lined up his own gun. 'Fire!' he shouted.

RAT-TAT-TAT! RAT-TAT-TAT! went the machine guns.

'Wait, what's going on ...!' shouted Henderson, as bullets began ripping at his aeroplane from below. He broke off from firing and directed his goggled eyes down at the ground.

Some French anti-aircraft gunners had spotted the aeroplanes overhead and opened fire.

The French gunners were Henderson's allies and were obviously aiming at the aircraft bearing the Iron Cross. But as rotten luck would have it they hit the very thing they wanted to avoid - Henderson's aeroplane.

The Germans flew away while a frustrated Henderson limped back to the aerodrome with a hole in his tail the size of a football. Not all the crews had been as fortunate.

Later that day, the Germans dropped a note on the aerodrome. It was about some missing men from Henderson's squadron.

The note said they had landed behind German lines with engine trouble. They had been taken prisoner but were all right. This was the civilised, gentlemanly side of war, thought Henderson. Unlike some of his ongoing training with the RFC.

The RFC had devised fiendish and sometimes bizarre ways of toughening men up. After dinner one evening Henderson was strapped to a chair and blindfolded for an 'Archie-ing'. This exercise was meant to improve a pilot's capacity to cope with being hit by shrapnel from an anti-aircraft gun, or Archie'.

'Tangerines' and other 'pieces of fruit' - the shrapnel - were hurled at Henderson's face and body for an extended period of time. Throughout it all he was expected to keep a stiff upper lip. This he did and then went to bed.

Henderson ended up spending a lot more time in bed that spring. A nasty infection got into his lungs and he was struck down with pleurisy. Out of action for weeks, he couldn't wait to get back up in the air.

Luckily he recovered enough to take part in a major confrontation which began that summer between the Allies and the Germans on the ground. It became known as the Battle of the Somme and was a turning point in the First World War.

Henderson escorted a group of five bombers over the German lines. While the other aircraft were dropping their bombs, he found himself under attack by an enemy aeroplane. There was quite a tussle, but eventually he shook the marauder off. When he flew off to rejoin his own group, they had completely disappeared.

Henderson could see a big storm coming in from the direction of the British lines on a strong west wind. He would have to fly through the storm to get home.

On the way he met German aeroplanes coming in the opposite direction, a group of ten or so and he had a brief dogfight with one or two of them. But they scuttled home before the advancing tempest. Henderson wasn't so fortunate.

He was still just inside the German lines when he flew into the thundering cloud. It was pitch black and he couldn't see a thing. He dropped down several hundred feet to try to get under the cloud but flew into a terrific hail shower.

When he tried to stick his head out of the cockpit for a better look, the hailstones cut his skin to pieces. In the end he managed to cross the British lines and land safely. But there was no sign of the five bombers he had been escorting. They must have lost their way in the storm, a sobering reminder of the dangerous conditions in which they were all operating.

But Henderson was determined to carry on. Soon he set off on another bombing raid, this time as the lead bomber, with a big flag on his tail. Their target was about fifteen miles beyond the German lines. They dropped their bombs as planned and everything went beautifully until they were halfway back.

The note said they had landed behind German lines with engine trouble. They had been taken Looking over his shoulder, Henderson saw that one of his group was surrounded by German aircraft, who were all firing at the poor fellow. He was trapped, just circling round and round helplessly - it transpired later that the pilot's gun had jammed. Seeing his comrade in serious trouble, Henderson banked his own aircraft into a sharp turn and went back to give him a bit of help.

He flew towards the attackers. They were all so busy terrorising the isolated British aeroplane that they didn't notice him approaching. He gained height steadily until he was directly above one of them. Then he launched into a terrific dive, firing ferociously.

Down he went; closer and closer. He came so close that he could see the German observer trying to lock his machine gun onto him. But Henderson kept on firing until suddenly the observer slumped lifeless over the side of his machine, his arms dangling.

The pilot must have been hit too, because the aeroplane suddenly dived absolutely vertically. One of Henderson's comrades later said he saw him go into a spinning nosedive, but Henderson didn't stick around to watch.

By now all the other German aircraft were above him and he was afraid they would turn nasty. Luckily they seemed to be so rattled by what had just happened that they flew off, leaving Henderson and the other aeroplanes to return home and land safely.

Returning home in one piece was something that could never be taken for granted. Henderson was reminded of this when his squadron was paid a visit by a battalion of Argylls. It was good to see one or two faces he recognised from his old regiment. But there were many men missing. They had had a bad time of it in the trenches of late, with fourteen officers lost.

The RFC had suffered heavy losses, too. When Henderson's group had come out to the Somme just five weeks earlier, there were twenty pilots. Now only six out of that original twenty were left. The rest were either, wounded, missing or dead.

These missions were the most dangerous so far. Most of their days were spent flying twenty or thirty miles behind German lines. They bombed the enemy's aerodromes, ammunition dumps, railways, troops - everything that might possibly undermine the enemy's military operation. Then they had to try to get home alive.

Airmen needed to look out for each other if they were going to survive. This fact was brought home to Henderson while on a bombing raid led by [Captain William George Bransby 'Sonny' Williams MC], a fellow pilot.[2]

Williams had attached long streamers to his aeroplane to mark him out as the leader. The only trouble with such flags and streamers was that they made an aircraft a lot more visible to the enemy too.

A German spotted Williams early on and went straight in for the kill. Henderson was flying above Williams at a height of more than 3000 metres and could see the dogfight taking place right down in front of him.

Williams seemed to have been wounded by the first shot or so because his aeroplane went down at once, more or less out of control. The German raced after him.

Watching both aeroplanes turn in circles as they descended, Henderson flew after the German, firing when he could, although he was afraid of hitting Williams, who was underneath.

Williams flew into a cloud at just over 1200 metres, followed by his pursuer with guns blazing, who in turn was being followed and fired at by Henderson.

In the cloud Henderson lost them both. He emerged at 1000 metres and couldn't see either Williams or the German aircraft anywhere. Then he spotted five more Huns underneath him. Deciding to attack before he was attacked, he dived on the last one, who dived to avoid him and then flew away.

Henderson was now down to 600 metres, flying above the German trenches. At that level his aeroplane would soon be vulnerable to fire from the ground, so he pulled away as sharply as he could over his own side's trenches to the aerodrome and landed.

Williams' aeroplane had made it home but was smashed and snapped and covered with holes. When Henderson peered inside, he could see the seat and rudder pedals were soaked in blood.

When he found Williams, he was alive and being bandaged up.

'I managed to regain control while in the cloud and shook off the Hun,' said Williams with an exhausted smile. 'You saved my life, Ian,' he continued. 'If you hadn't gone after him, he would have done for me.'

'It was nothing,' said Henderson, feeling a little embarrassed. 'You would have done the same for me.'

There then came a turning point in the whole campaign.

After lunch on 14 September, the squadron was addressed by a colleague of Henderson's father, General Trenchard, Chief of the Air Staff. He told them that the British were going to try to strike a decisive blow against the Germans, to help bring the war to an end once and for all and to do so they were going to unleash a mighty new weapon.

That night British bombers from every aerodrome in the Somme area were sent out with orders to hit anything and everything belonging to the enemy. The aim was to leave the Germans broken and in shock. Then, early the next morning, a big ground assault began.

Henderson was sent up on 'contact patrol'. This meant flying low over the German lines in a single-seat B.E.2 machine to find out how far the British advance was getting.

Henderson found the view fascinating. He could see British soldiers running forward and jumping into the German trenches, then running after the retreating enemy.

His aircraft got shot up by Archies and machine-gunners and he was nearly hit by his own side's shells. But all that training with fruit paid off and he hung on grimly until the job was done.

By the time he got back his face was black with engine oil, but he was bursting with excitement at being able to report on the ground troops' advance.

Later that day he went up again and it was then that he saw the new weapon General Trenchard had told them about. It was the most wonderful invention he had ever seen - the tank!

These huge, diamond-shaped metal beasts were heavily armoured, with toothed caterpillar tracks on their wheels and cannons protruding from either side. They knocked down trees left and right as they went and smashed through enemy trenches.

He was so busy observing the tanks forcing their way behind enemy lines that Henderson and his aeroplane took a battering from the Archies. Wires and struts were shot at and his engine was hit again, but he was determined not to return to base until he'd seen one of the tanks, swiftly followed by a column of British soldiers, capture a village. They cheered and waved at Henderson as he flew over. It was quite amazing to see how an armoured tank was able to lead and shield an advance by a group of soldiers against the enemy artillery. Perhaps the stalemate of both sides being stuck in trenches and endlessly hammered by each other's shells could now be broken. And if the British side had the tanks, then it made victory over the Germans a bit more likely.

But the enemy was very far from being beaten. Henderson was reminded of this while flying over a village - or what had once been a village, it was now in ruins - when terrific machine-gun fire opened on him. His aircraft was hammered so badly the engine nearly stopped. He struggled back to the nearest friendly aerodrome and telephoned in his report.

Henderson flew close to disaster so many times that he felt he must have at least nine lives. Perhaps Angela's Black Cat is looking out for me, he thought.

Many pilots were not so lucky. Henderson was leading a patrol over enemy lines when they were attacked by two big German aeroplanes. They went for Henderson at first, but he shot at them fiercely and they turned their firepower on the two aircraft behind him instead.

Before Henderson had time to turn around and help he saw one of his own patrol catch fire and go down blazing. The pilot in the other RFC aeroplane must have been shot dead because he went down too, in a spin and fell to pieces.

It was a sickening sight. Henderson felt sure his turn would be next, but he must somehow have frightened the Germans. They didn't attack him again and instead flew off.

As winter approached some of the squadron were given new aeroplanes. Henderson was among the lucky ones. The new aircraft was a 'Spad' and Henderson thought it was the most wonderful machine imaginable. Fast, strong and agile, it could even be driven at 130mph along the ground.

Henderson was then moved to the elite 56 Squadron, which spent a lot of time based back across the English Channel defending Britain against enemy air raids. Under cover of darkness the German air force had begun dropping bombs on cities such as Edinburgh and London using Zeppelins - airships whose crew could roam about in large, comfortable cabins slung underneath gigantic cigar-shaped balloons filled with hydrogen and driven by propellers.

As the war went on, the airmen of 56 Squadron faced a foe that was even faster, stronger and more versatile than the Zeppelins. This was the Grosskampfflugzeug - or Gotha - a large and elegant twin-engined bomber aeroplane with a three-man crew, sent in formations of twenty or more to attack British cities during the day.

The Gothas carried up to half a ton - 500kg - of bombs in their fuselage and, propelled by two 260 hp Mercedes engines on their wings, could easily fly at a height of more than 3300 metres. The Gothas brought terror, death and destruction to the home front, while the RFC squadrons did their best to limit the damage.

Henderson's father was in charge of defending the homeland from such attacks and he was heavily criticised for not doing enough. But it was an impossible situation.

There were not enough men and aircraft to prevent all the Gothas and Zeppelins getting through - plus Britain's air defences were too disorganised. Henderson's father began arguing for the creation of a new and improved Royal Air Force. Meanwhile, in their letters and occasional meetings, Henderson comforted his father as best he could.

There was still a war to be won on mainland Europe, however and while he participated in home defence Henderson was never very far from the thick of the action in the skies over France, constantly pushing himself and his aircraft to the limit. His most successful month was July 1917 - but it could easily have been his last.

He was credited with shooting down four Albatros DVs that month. It took his confirmed tally up to seven - but there was evidence he had actually shot down more enemy aeroplanes than that. Henderson felt excited and optimistic. They were really going at the Huns now.

But there were still emergencies to overcome, including the mission during which Henderson's propeller came off in mid-air. The controls jammed and he went into a dive. He managed to crash-land but the machine was wrecked. Somehow he walked away with barely a scratch. The lucky Black Cat was still watching over him and he made sure that he salvaged it from the wreckage.

Henderson held his own in a squadron that was filled with the best of the best - Arthur Rhys-Davids, James McCudden, Albert Ball and Cecil Lewis, to give a few famous names.[3] The friendship between the men was wonderful. Despite the dangers they faced every time they took to the skies, they joked, they sang, there was poetry - and some great concerts, too.

When Henderson was granted leave of absence or posted on home defence, he would join the 'chaps' for some sport or other, or take someone out for a spin on his motorcycle. And then there were the girls, of course.

A dance was organised when the squadron was back in 'Blighty' - a favourite nickname for Britain - for home defence.

They were based at Bekesbourne aerodrome near Canterbury, halfway between London and the English Channel.

The weather was cloudless and perfect for bombing, but there was no sign of any Zeppelins or Gothas so the men kept busy with their dance preparations. They went to Canterbury to round up some eager young ladies and brought them back to the aerodrome, where they had put up a marquee with a dance floor made from some planking a senior officer had scrounged from somewhere.

On the night of the dance the marquee looked wonderful. The tables were beautifully laid with fine china and silver, which twinkled in the candle light. The open ends of the tent flapped in the gentle breeze of the fine summer's night.

Henderson and the others popped champagne corks while the girls, dressed in their evening gowns, were invited to stand in the long grass on the edge of the aerodrome. Henderson and his friend Cecil Lewis then jumped in a couple of aircraft and gave an exhibition of stunt flying.

'That was wonderful, Captain Henderson,' said a pretty young lady after Henderson and Lewis had rejoined the crowd.

'Oh, it was nothing,' Henderson replied, smiling bashfully.

They all ate a beautiful dinner prepared by the squadron cooks and afterwards Henderson led the singing while someone played the fiddle. The evening was full of laughter, talking and dancing.

These were happy times, despite the worries of war. On another happy occasion a photograph was taken showing Henderson, grinning like the Cheshire cat, looking dapper in a blazer with his black hair slicked back and two pretty young ladies standing next to him.

Perhaps one of these girls might have hoped that the dashing young pilot would one day become her husband. Who would this hero of the skies choose as a wife with whom to start a family? He could have taken his pick.

But Henderson's story was to have a rather different ending.

In the spring of 1918 he was sent to Scotland, to the training school at Turnberry on the Ayrshire coast. He wrote to tell his father, who was pleased to know he would be in a part of the country that was home to many of the family's relatives and ancestors.

The training school was an opportunity to test different machines and weapons and to learn new techniques before rejoining the fray. It was a busy but relaxing period for Henderson. When he had some time off, he loved to ride his motorcycle and he and the others sometimes took an old motorboat out along the coast.

His father wrote to tell him that he had resigned from his top job in the air force, as he felt he had done as much as he could do and wanted to try something different. 'I would like to come up to see you, my lad,' he wrote, 'but it is rather a long journey'.

Henderson wrote back to comfort his father, for he knew running and reorganising the air force had been an exhausting job. He described his training at Turnberry and the exciting new aircraft and weapons he was testing. 'I'm looking forward to telling you more about it when I get leave to visit home,' he added. Then his letters suddenly stopped.

Instead, on the afternoon of 21 June 1918, Sir David received a telegram:
DEEPLY REGRET [TO] INFORM YOU CAPTAIN IAN HENRY DAVID HENDERSON KILLED NEAR HERE IN AEROPLANE ACCIDENT THIS FORENOON. CAUSE OF ACCIDENT UNKNOWN. CAPTAIN HENDERSON WAS TESTING GUN AS PASSENGER. PLEASE WIRE WISHES RE: FUNERAL WHETHER BODY TO BE SENT HOME OR BURIAL ARRANGED HERE. ACCIDENTS COMMITTEE ASKED TO INVESTIGATE.

Henderson's flying companion that day had been another experienced pilot and friend called Harold Redler.[4] Henderson had piloted the aeroplane - a de Havilland - when it took off. Then, as they had been trained to do, they carefully swapped places in mid-air, by climbing over the fuselage and holding tight to the wing frames, so that Redler could fly while Henderson tested the Lewis gun. They flew at high speed and very low altitude through the neck of a gulley as it opened out to the sea.

It was then that things went horribly wrong. Just as the aircraft went into a climbing turn, the wind suddenly whipped it viciously and Redler lost control. The De Havilland slammed into the ground, left wing down and both men were killed.

Two young men who had survived for months in the intense heat of battle over the front line in France and in the war-torn skies above Britain had been taken out by a freak gust of wind at home during a straightforward training exercise. In that instant, Captain Ian Henderson joined the ranks of the many young RFC aces - several of them his friends - who would not live to see the end of the First World War.

The luck of Black Cat had finally run out. All that was left for the Henderson family to remember their son was a gravestone in nearby Girvan at Doune Cemetery, some scraps of correspondence, a few photographs and other personal effects. Plus the rich but fading memories of shared conversations, close embraces, gestures and companionable silences - all testimony to a heroic life spent soaring above the clouds. [5]

The loss devastated Sir David, who devoted the rest of his career to humanitarian work, including running the International League of Red Cross Societies in Geneva, Switzerland. He was also a strong supporter of the creation of the Scottish National War Memorial in Edinburgh Castle, which commemorates the nation's war dead. Sir David died in 1921 aged 59.

The Henderson family paid a high price for Sir David and Ian's love of flying. But the two men left behind the legacy of a new and improved Royal Air Force. Plans for it had been drawn up by Sir David and were implemented in 1917. As a result Sir David Henderson was considered by Sir Hugh Trenchard, Chief of the Air Staff, to be the true founding father of the RAF. [6]

Endnotes Chapter 8

1   *World War I: Scottish Tales of Adventure* (Birlinn Ltd (2014).
2   William's father was Bransby William Pharez (14 August 1870-3 December 1961) a British actor, comedian and monologist. He became known as 'The Irving of the music halls.' 'Sonny' Williams was killed on 12 May 1917. His body was never found.
3   Cecil Arthur Lewis MC (29 March 1898-27 January 1997) was educated at Oundle School. Lewis joined the RFC in 1915 after lying about his age and learned to fly at Brooklands. In 1916 he flew the Morane Parasol in combat with 3 Squadron and was awarded the Military Cross for his actions during the Battle of the Somme. He went on to co-found the British Broadcasting Company and enjoy a long career as a writer, notably of the aviation classic *Sagittarius Rising*.
4   Lieutenant Harold Bolton Redler MC born 27 January 1897 in West Monkton, Somerset was credited with ten aerial victories. His most notable triumph was over 27 victory ace, Adolf Ritter von Tutschek, whom he killed in action on 15 March 1918. Redler ran off a string of six more victories by 20 April. The following day, he was wounded in action. He was relieved from his combat posting and returned to England. Redler's Military Cross was gazetted the same day he was killed.
5   His name is inscribed, along with other flying-school members who lost their lives, on a tall granite memorial on Turnberry golf course. He was twenty-one years old when he died.
6   The key sources for *'Flight of the Black Cat', the story of Captain Ian Henderson of the Argyll and Sutherland Highlanders and Royal Flying Corps,* include the private correspondence and papers of Henderson and his immediate family kept at the Archive Collection of the RAF Museum Hendon. In addition, the classic memoir *Sagittarius Rising* by former RFC pilot Cecil Lewis (Frontline, 2009) contains important references to Ian Henderson, as does *Royal Flying Corps Headquarters, 1914-1918* by Maurice Baring (G. Bell, 1920). Other primary sources consulted include the papers and correspondence of Sir David Henderson, kept in the Manuscript Collections of the NLS, as well as copies of the regimental diaries of the Argyll and Sutherland Highlanders held at the Archives and Special Collections of the Mitchell Library in Glasgow. Further sources for the story of the Hendersons and the RFC include *The Royal Flying Corps in World War One* by Ralph Barker (Robinson, 2002); *No Empty Chairs: The Short and Heroic Lives of the Young Aviators Who Fought and Died in the First World War* by Ian Mackersey (Weidenfeld & Nicholson, 2012); and *Fighter Heroes of WWI: The extraordinary story of the pioneering airmen of the Great War.* More generally, the author consulted a number of other texts about the war, including *The Great War* by Corelli Barnett (Park Lane Press, 1979) and various entries in *The Oxford Dictionary of National Biography.*

Chapter 9

100 Squadron

A. R. Kingsford

100 Squadron was established on 23 February 1917 at Hingham in Norfolk as the first RFC squadron formed specifically for night bombing and comprised elements of the Home Defence Wing. The unit was mobilised and crossed from Portsmouth on 21 March 1917 to France and at St. Andre-aux-Bois it received twelve FE2bs aircraft which had been withdrawn from other units where they had operated in daylight, so modifications were required to adapt them for 100 Squadron's operational role. On 1 April 1917 the unit moved to Izel-le-Hameau and acquired a further four B.E.2e's. The squadron began operations on the night of 5/6 April, when eleven F.E.2b's attacked Douai airfield, where Manfred von Richthofen's 'Flying Circus' was based. 128 20lb and four 40lb bombs were dropped; four aircraft hangars were reported as having been set on fire and one of the attacking aircraft was lost. By the end of the 1917 100 Squadron, 55 Squadron and Naval 'A' Squadron were the nucleus of what developed into the Independent Force under Major General Hugh Trenchard for the strategic bombing of Germany. On 4 March 1918 100 Squadron was sent to Ochey, near Nancy. In August the unit converted to Handley Page 0/400 heavy bombers and therefore longer range sorties over industrial sites in Germany became possible. The squadron conducted these raids throughout the rest of the war, moving to Saint Inglevert on 17 November 1918.

Alfred Reginald Bellingham-Kingsford was born on 4 May 1891 at Maidstone in Kent. He was the only son of dairy farmer, Alfred Kingsford who died while 'Reg' was still only a child. He was apprenticed to a photographer in his early teens and then emigrated to Australia at the age of 19 to take up a photographic appointment in Sydney. He later moved to Moree to join a friend working there as a stockman, before sailing to New Zealand to take up an offer of employment in a photographic studio in Nelson. This where the outbreak of WW1 found him. In 1917, in France, he transferred to the RFC from the New Zealand Army where he was a Corporal in the Medical Corps. Serving first in 33 Squadron he then became a Lieutenant serving in 100 Squadron.

'When joining up with a new Squadron, one is naturally curious as to who's in it and that is how I felt while awaiting the arrival of the tender that was to fetch me from Nancy. The same feeling was apparently at the aerodrome too, although not on my account, for the same tender was bringing the mails and who should step out of the orderly room when we arrived but my old operation observer, Reid. He nearly fell on my neck with surprise.

'Jove, Bow, it's good to see you again' he said. 'Come to join the happy family?'
'I suppose so' I muttered. 'How long have you been here?'
'Three months' he told me.
'Anyone else here I know?'
'Sure, there's Lucas, Tatham, Albu, Windsor; he got the MC did you know? Miles is here too, great show this' Reid rambled off.

'Should think so, by the looks of it,' I said, as my eye wandered from one bomb hole to another, then to the remains of a hangar.

'I note you have dug-outs' I remarked.

'Too right and you darn well want 'em too. Let's go and find the rest of the boys' and he dragged me across to the mess.

'It looked comfy. In the middle of the ante-room was a brazier, a big open-work basket of wrought iron, holding a huge, cheery wood fire. On a corner table was a phonograph, apparently suffering badly with asthma, judging by the wheezing noise it made, the walls were adorned with cuttings from illustrated papers, while over in the far corner stood a piano, minus one caster, judging by its tilt.

'Two or three of the fellows were reading round the fire, while at a couple of small tables card games were in progress. It impressed me more favourably than I had expected and everyone looked up as we entered. The next minute, I found myself trying to shake hands with half a dozen at once. This was great; I seemed to know most of them. There was [2nd Lieutenant Walter George] Albu, an old Flight Commander of mine, who had previously had something to do with diamonds in Africa. Tatham, the six-footer, who used to rest his chin on his knees in the front seat of the old Fee - too much leg. Windsor, complete with MC, who still wore the same grin, while poor old Lucas was looking just as worried as he always did in Blighty. He was still the fair-haired boy from Canada, hadn't gone grey yet. Miles hadn't altered a bit, still as mad as ever on poker. He and I had some good goes.

'I was introduced all round. There was Alec Ward, an Aussie with no nerves. He was the bird the Huns said knocked the chimney tops off flying over Thionville one night, got the MC, then went home and was killed in England. Billy Barnes, who went over as many times as anyone and did some great bombing. 'Little Box', who was so tiny that he had to have stilts to reach the rudder bar. His only fault was that he was too keen, got the DFC and then was killed, crashed on our side. Hughie Chambers, he was a quiet one, liked climbing mountains better than flying; it was his pet hobby in New Zealand. Crofts had only just left school, mad as a hatter, didn't mind bombing, but didn't like being bombed. He celebrated his twentieth birthday soon after my arrival. Dear old 'Dad' Crystall was the EO who fathered all the boys. Edwards Evans, who showed me the way first time over, had been in the Infantry, got the MC and was a good man to have in the front seat. Big Bill Rutherford, who tried to train a seven-a-side moustache, I mean it was a horrible failure, made good ballast for any machine. Darby was from the 'Hielands,' the solemn, gloomy one, full of dry wit, pulled off the DFC.

'While the introductions were going forward, the CO entered; the DSO and MC below his wings catching my eye immediately. Reid introduced me - Major Tempest - seemed very young to be CO, certainly not more than 24. I was full of curiosity, so I asked Reid: 'Is he Tempest of the Zeppelin fame?'

'The same fellow' he informed me.[1]

'You've come to some flash Squadron, my boy, but let's have a drink to christen you.' He pressed the tit, as he put it and a corporal appeared. This was Minns, so I was told, came from Oxford, big chief drinks and his tunic certainly looked it, couldn't see the cloth for splashes. I noticed it was also necessary for him to leave the two bottom buttons undone.

'It was Minns who brought the drinks, Minns who waited at table, Minns who brought the breakfast in bed and collected half a franc for bringing it, Minns, who cleaned the boots, made the beds, in fact, Minns did this and Minns did that and there was nothing Minns didn't do. It was also Minns who led the crowd to the dug-out, at the double too, when the alarms went, yet through it all his ruddy face was always beaming.

'There was a happy crowd at dinner that night. The wash-out had been given, no flying, weather too bad. At midnight, poker was still going strong and my new home had certainly impressed me favourably. It was like old times among all the old boys, they were a good mob, mostly youngsters, game for anything, at any time, as it was proved later.

'Ochey aerodrome was situated on a slight rise; the only obstacles were the hangars. Those occupied by a naval squadron and our own three were on one side, while at the top end were several used by a French Squadron. On the far side of the landing ground was Ochey village itself, containing not more than thirty or forty houses. The surrounding country was hilly and thickly wooded in many places, not too good for forced landings at night.

'A little to the north-west was the town of Toul, a military centre, with quaint, cobbled streets and old-fashioned shops, which gave an antique appearance. Its Cathedral was a beautiful building of uncommon design, while the interior was a cause for marvel to the sightseer. This quaint little town stood in the shade of the twin mountains of St. Michel, while the Moselle River ran around the outskirts, both good landmarks for fliers.

'To the NEE was Pont St. Vincent, a fair-sized town on the Moselle River. Like Nancy, this place was a target for many Hun bombs, the steel works being the attraction.

'From the line, our aerodrome was roughly twenty to thirty minutes' flying and lighthouses served as guides at night, signalling letters in Morse. D and C were between the landing ground and the line, whilst others were placed east and west. The idea was good and enabled us to find our way home on many a dark night.

'100 Squadron was the senior night flying squadron in France and was a unit of the Independent Air Force, whose job was reprisals.

'Our authorities decided to give 'Fritz' what he was giving us and for every raid he carried out on England, we did at least six into his territory and as time showed, he didn't like it.

'Our targets were mostly in Alsace Lorraine, Metz, Diedenhofen, Trier, Saarbrücken on the Saar Valley, Kreuzwald, Courcelles and Conflans, enemy troops being in all these towns, as well as anything of military importance and later we gave many of his aerodromes a good smack up.

'The Day Squadron, flying D.H.4s, did as far as Cologne and a darned good show too. The Naval Squadron went a bit farther than we did. They had Handleys, but didn't seem to do a lot of flying.

'Alsace Lorraine was hard country for night fliers and if it hadn't been for the rivers and woods, whose shapes we learnt to know by heart and which could always be discerned in the darkness, we would have been lost many a time. The blast furnaces of the steel works often aided us too, as their reflections could be seen for miles, although, after a time, they managed to keep these completely under control. Targets were hard to find on dark nights, compass courses would have to be followed, although it was difficult to allow for the drift. There were no drift instruments then and coming home was harder than going, until you sighted a lighthouse.

'F.E.2.B. 5564 was allotted to me. I'd hoped for a better type of machine, although these old 'Fees' did some great showing, carrying heavy loads of bombs night after night many miles into Hun territory. A four to five hour show in those days was an accomplishment, but it was done.

'My first overseas flight was to get an idea of the country. I went alone in daylight, travelling eastward until Luneville was sighted. This town was only a matter of eight or ten miles from the line and had already been well shelled. The ruins and debris of many a fine old chateau could be discerned as one flew over. Following the line along, we crossed the Moselle at Pont a Mousson. This town was practically on the line and a mass of ruins, not a house standing. The whole surrounding country was shelled and as far as St. Michel Salient, the chalky lines of the trenches could be picked out quite easily. Just at that time, that particular part of the line was fairly quiet, save for the occasional burst of a shell, throwing clouds of earth into the air.

'One could scarcely distinguish the lakes around Boncouville from the huge shell holes filled with water. Passing these, we flew over the Meuse River and turned our backs on Verdun. On the roads, dotted here and there, troops and transport could be seen making for the line. It was whilst watching some of these troops from an altitude of 4,000 that I received a terrific surprise. A small scout machine flashed past me at an enormous speed. I tried to get a look at him, but he was then above and behind me. The top of my head felt frozen and my hair stuck up so much that it nearly knocked my flying cap off and I felt goosey all over. My first thought was 'It's a Hun' and I expected every second to hear the rat-tat-tat of a machine gun. Swinging the aeroplane round, I tried to get a peep at him and next minute he was alongside, enabling me to see the blue, red and white on his tail. It was just an inquisitive French 'Spad', wanting to have a good look at us. He waved, did a roll and went, but I couldn't help thinking what cold meat I'd have been had it turned out a Hun. The Fees were only night fliers and it was asking for a hurried exit out of this world, buzzing around the line in broad daylight. It was mid-winter and I was beginning to feel frozen. It started to snow a bit, so I stuck her nose down a little and headed for Ochey.

'The snow lasted for a week-end everyone got pretty well fed up. It was as cold as charity everywhere except around the old brazier, where we warmed our knees hour after hour. Someone suggested a wood-cutting parade, anything to relieve the monotony, so we got a tender and went to the Forest de Haye, where axes and saws made the blood circulate once more.

'When we did take the air next time, the whole country was a picture, with its mantle of snow. It seemed to blot out all the destruction of war. There was no show this night; weather too unsettled, but [2nd Lieutenant O. B.] Swart, another new pilot from the same country as Albu and myself, were ordered up to go the round of the lighthouses. It was a perfect starlit night when we left and I enjoyed it... We had been away an hour and not five minutes after our return it commenced to snow again, which stopped the flying for several days.

'Swart and I were keen for the weather to clear, as the CO had told us we could go up on the next show, Edwards Evans being picked for my observer. Each evening the weather report would come through and we would dash off to read it, but always with the same result, 'Dud.' Eventually, however, the weather showed signs of improvement and on the night of February ninth, we had the immense pleasure of unloading four nice large bombs and several drums of ammunition on the enemy. Operation orders read - 'Objective Courcelles Railway Junction - bombs 112 and 230 pounders. 'A' Flight will lead.'

'It is difficult to describe your feelings the first night going over the enemy's lines. I was eaten up with curiosity, anxious to put up a good show, yet not knowing quite what to expect. Old pilots had given advice not to take unnecessary risks, not to come down too low on a first flight to do your bombing, remember to switch off your navigation lights before going on the line and I found their advice useful.

'The night of February ninth was just as dark and cold as it could be and in spite of thigh boots, fur coat and many other accessories, we literally froze.

'At six pm there was activity everywhere at the aerodrome. Flares were out, mechanics dashing here and there, machines lined up and punctually at that hour, Swart and I were strolling with the rest up to our own machines. It was to be our christening, so we shook hands and wished each other 'Good luck.' That was the last time I saw Swart.

'Edwards Evans and I inspected the bombs, parachute flare, wingtip flares and all the rest of the gadgets and then climbed into our seats. The mechanic was ready at the engine.

'Switches off Sir' he shouted.

'Switches off' I replied, 'Suck in' and he swung the propeller round a few times.

'Switch on, Sir' he yelled. I twisted the C.A.V. and away went the prop, at thirteen hundred revolutions to the minute. We let the engine warm up and then tried her full out, OK and waited for the signal to go.

'Our Flight Commander was leading, he taxied out and we were signalled to follow. Swinging her round into the flare path, I pushed the throttle forward and away we went, skimming on what was my first raid of destruction over enemy lines. The aeroplane climbed into the darkness and at three hundred feet we turned. Another machine was just leaving and I watched him as he roared down the flare path, the red-hot exhaust showing clearly in the inky blackness of the night. The first machine to leave was just above us. We circled the aerodrome once and then left at eight hundred feet. The tail light of the first bus showed plainly and I followed it in the direction of D Lighthouse, then turning slightly to the right, headed for C. Looking back, I could still see the lights of the other four machines following. 'B' and 'C' Flights were to leave at ten minute intervals. At C Lighthouse, I switched off our light and set on course NNW. Our target was roughly forty minutes' flying from the line and we crossed this at 3,000 feet.

'We were now over enemy territory.

'Keep your eyes skinned' my observer leant over and yelled to me.

'Can't see a damned thing' I replied and there was not a light to be seen anywhere, just blank, impenetrable darkness, broken only by the red glare of the exhaust and the glow of the dashboard.

'Keeping her nose to the NNW for twenty minutes, I peered over the side to try and distinguish something that might serve to assure us that we were on the right course, but the density of the night gave no sign, except the whistling of the wind as we speeded by. The drone of the engine kept us company, purr, purr, it was running perfectly. We were doing seventy miles an hour at twelve hundred revolutions. We flew on, keeping at three thousand feet; fifteen to twenty minutes more would find us very near our target. In spite of warm clothing and the usual thigh boots, I was getting cold, the bitter stinging of the keen wind making my face tingle. My observer was well hidden in his seat, the only part showing occasionally being his head popping up above the nacelle.

'Suddenly the monotony was broken and I could see my observer leaning over the side, hand on machine gun. Every part of the machine was plainly visible. A searchlight had pierced the darkness and caught us first go. He was directly to the left. Evans stood up, both hands grasping the gun and signalled to swing round. Kicking the rudder and pulling the joy stick over; I throttled back and dived straight down the beam. The machine gun spit forth, a burst of ten or so, but he didn't shut down. I side-slipped and he lost us. We were now at eighteen hundred feet and he was hunting the skies for us, found us for a second and then let us go again. We turned and throttled back once more, taking another dive at him.

'Coming down to one thousand feet, Evans gave two or three good bursts; he immediately switched off and did not light up again. Eventually we picked up our course and proceeded undisturbed. The excitement had warmed us, or else we had forgotten the cold.

'Ten minutes passed and I consulted my map, which showed that we should be within five miles. Evans leant over.

'Can't be far off' he yelled.

'About five miles I reckon. Keep your eyes open for Windsor's phosphorous bomb' I replied. The leader on dark nights carried a phosphorous bomb, which usually set fire to something and lit up the surroundings. Our instructions were to drop our bombs as near this signal as possible.

'Evans had scarcely reseated himself when, over to our right, not more than two miles away, we saw this bomb burst and light up the surroundings. It must have been seen for miles and we immediately swung around and made for it. Approaching and keyed up with excitement as we were, we saw another burst, then three in quick succession and only a few yards apart. It was good bombing and the five made an excellent group. The first had caused a fire and we flew round once to have a look, discerning a group of buildings. Guiding the aeroplane over them, Evans let two go and the bursts were quite visible, close together. We turned back and he let drop the others. Looking down to watch the effect, another searchlight caught us and realising that the place was well protected against aircraft raids, I turned to dodge him and instinctively looking over the side, I noticed a whole string of machine gun fire making directly for us. Like a procession of glow-worms these phosphorous bullets approached and I immediately turned the aeroplane in the opposite direction, dodging one searchlight but running into another line of machine gun fire. We'd dropped all our bombs, so I turned her nose down and beat it. We ended up at eight hundred feet and headed for C Lighthouse. We'd stirred up a hornets' nest and we felt that some of the machines to come after us would have a pretty hot time.

'Looking back, we could see searchlights busy and bombs dropping everywhere. A good strafe was in progress and we pitied the last poor devil, for he'd get it hot and strong. Our chief concern at that moment, however, was to get back and the night was still black. Evans was itching to use his gun, but no more searchlights showed up and nothing could be seen. We flew on through the night, the engine purring away in good style and the excitement of the raid wearing off somewhat, we began to feel the intense cold again. That lighthouse seemed a long way off, no sign of it yet. I looked at the compass and it showed us in the right course; time we picked up the light and we tried to pierce the darkness, but without avail. Surely we must be off our course. There must be a bit of a drift, nothing to take our bearings on and we swung the aeroplane a little to the south. Our eyes were aching with the strain and I closed mine for a second or two, raising my goggles and feeling instant relief.

'Then, away to the left, a tiny speck of light caught my eye, seeming to stand out in the darkness, although no twinkle was visible. At any rate, we swung around in that direction and I yelled out to ask Evans what he could make of it.

'Can't say, but go that way' he called back. We both glued our eyes to the tiny speck, our hearts full of hope and the next moment I could have sworn that it flashed a signal. Evans leant over again and shouted:

'That's it all right - put it here' and we shook hands away up at 3,000 feet. Nothing more was said, but we erealised the other's feelings of relief that we were safely back on our own side of the line. In a short twenty minutes or so, my first raid over Hunland would be over. We'd been lucky though, picking up the lighthouse - a few minutes more and we should have passed it for we were quite fifteen miles out of our course. This verified my suspicions of drift, there must have been a fair wind. A short time after passing the lighthouse, the landing flares could be seen plainly and my whole body seemed to relax its nervous tension. A feeling of complete satisfaction set in and just then a French anti-aircraft battery challenged us, reminding me that I'd completely forgotten to switch on the navigation lights. He challenged us again and I fired a Very light colour of the night and he was satisfied. Throttling back as we neared the aerodrome, I signalled my desire to land. The spotlights were switched on and next minute we swung into view. Our wheels touched earth; we taxied to the hangar, switched off and climbed from our seats. The first thing I did was to grope for my cigarettes, congratulations were extended and I felt very bucked, safely back after my first show.

'Only one other machine had landed, although we could see lights from three others. Evans and I went to the orderly room, made out our report and handed it in to the CO, who seemed very pleased. After all, it wasn't a particularly good night.

'We next made tracks for the mess, to get a spot and celebrate the occasion. Discarding some of our heaviest garments, we strolled back to the hangars to find out how the others had fared. Fourteen out of eighteen machines had landed, groups of men stood here and there, chatting over the events of the trip. They had all found the searchlights troublesome and the machine gun fire hot. Miles got a strut shot through and one of his bombs failed to explode, which annoyed him. He delighted in serving out this destruction. Barnes declared it took a whole damn drum to shut up one searchlight which was particularly troublesome and he seemed to begrudge the ammunition. 'Big Bill's only growl was that he couldn't see a damn thing. Like us, they had all found the drift.

'At this juncture, two machines appeared, only two more to come. A few minutes passed and one more showed up. It turned out to be 'Little Box' and he'd had engine trouble all the way, so much so that he doubted if he'd ever see the aerodrome again.

'Still one more aeroplane to come, who was it? The question went round.

'All 'B' and 'C' Flight are back Sir' a mechanic informed us. Well, who's missing from 'A'? Windsor, Crofts, Miles, Martin, Kingsford, all back. It's Swart [flying F.E.2b B439]. We strained our eyes in the direction of the line, but no machine lights could be seen. I remembered how keen he was and how we had talked of what we hoped to do on our first show. He was determined to put up a good performance and I wondered if he had been tempted to get down too low and so caught some of those tracer bullets. We hung about until we knew his benzine must be exhausted and that he must be down somewhere and not until then did we think of returning to the mess.

'There was no jubilation and one by one we crept to our huts, after a final look to see if the missing machine had turned up.

'At that time, Swart and his observer, [2nd Lieutenant Anthony] Fielding-Clarke, were down in Hunland, groping around in the darkness: their engine having failed them and so forced them to land near the line. They were not sure which side they were on, but received a nasty shock when four of the enemy appeared on the scene. Swart's first show was his last - Karlsruhe prison camp claimed him [both men were later imprisoned at Holzminden].

'The British Official Report of this raid is appended: 'On Saturday night, our night bombing machines carried out a successful raid into Germany, although the weather was by no means good. Nearly a ton of bombs was dropped, with very good results, on the important railway junction and siding at Courcelles-les-Metz (SE of Metz)

'One of our bombing machines is missing.'[2]

Endnotes Chapter 9

1   Wulstan Joseph Tempest of Perdue, Saskatoon, was born in Blackburn, Lancashire and after leaving school joined the Merchant Navy. On the outbreak of WWI he joined up with the King's Own Yorkshire Light Infantry and served with them in Flanders. In October 1914 Tempest was wounded as the Battle of Ypres and was lucky to escape after being buried in a dugout by artillery fire. He returned to England to recover from his injuries and after learning to fly joined the RFC, being posted to 39 Home Defence Squadron at Suttons Farm protecting London from German air raids. On 1/2 October 1916 2nd Lieutenant Tempest left the RFC ground at North Weald in B.E.2c 4577 at 2200 to patrol between Joyce Green and Hainault. Sighting L-31 at 2340 he immediately pursued her. Despite having a broken fuel pump that required him to hand prime his engine at the same time as flying the aircraft and shooting, when at a height of 12,700 feet over Potter's Bar he fired one drum, which was effective. The L-31 fell in flames at 2354. Tempest's aircraft was wrecked on landing at North Weald at 1210 but fortunately he walked away unharmed. Two other aeroplanes were in the locality and one reported that the Zeppelin broke into two parts as she fell, probably owing to the explosion of two or three HE bombs which she had not dropped. Major Tempest DSO MC commanded 100 Squadron until June 1918. He left the RAF in 1921 and died in 1966.

2   Alfred Reginald Bellingham-Kingsford died aged 95 in April 1987.

Chapter 10

Australian Flying Corps

The men of the AFC came down and fairly strafed the Hun, they bombed him and attacked him with machine guns from only fifty feet, flying amongst the tree tops; they were magnificent, they revelled in this work which was great military value to all.
General Hugh Trenchard, Commander Royal Flying Corps, November 1917.

Powered flight did not arrive in Australia until 1910, but less than a year later Harry Hawker, Harry Kauper and Harry Busteed were in England looking for careers in aviation. They would soon be, respectively, Sopwith's Chief Test Pilot, Sopwith's Foreman of Works and Bristol Aeroplane's Chief Test Pilot. In 1911, at the Imperial Conference held in London it was decided that aviation should be developed by the various national armed forces of the British Empire. Australia became the first member of the Empire to follow this policy. By the end of 1911 the Army was advertising for pilots and mechanics. On 30 December 1911 the *Commonwealth Gazette* announced that the Australian military would seek the '...appointment of two competent Mechanics and Aviators', adding that the government would 'accept no liability for accidents'. On 3 July 1912 the first 'flying machines' were ordered: two Royal Aircraft Factory B.E.2 two seat tractor biplanes and two British-built Deperdussin single seat tractor monoplanes. In early August two pilots were appointed: Henry Petre and Eric Harrison. On 22 September 1912 the Minister of Defence, Senator George Pearce, officially approved formation of an independent 'Australian Aviation Corps'; one of the world's first air forces and the only British dominion to set up a flying corps of its own. A Central Flying School was established at Point Cook, near Melbourne on 22 October 1912. Two days later the government authorised the raising of a single squadron. Upon establishment the squadron would be equipped with five flimsy training aircraft and manned by '...four officers, seven warrant officers and sergeants and 32 mechanics' who would be drawn from volunteers already serving in the Citizen Forces. Not everyone was suited to this new field of military operations. Light horsemen or 'bushmen' were thought to be physically fitter and have quicker reflexes and a better 'character' than other men.

In March 1914, a staff officer, Major Edgar H. Reynolds, was officially appointed General Staff Officer in charge of a branch covering 'intelligence, censorship and aviation' within the Army's Department of Military Operations. No.1 Flight of the AFC was raised in the 3rd Military District on 14 July 1914. Following the outbreak of World War I and the expansion of the Army, aviation later became a separate branch commanded by Reynolds but his role was mostly administrative rather than one that involved operational command as AFC operational units were attached and subordinate to Australian ground forces and/or British ground and air commands. The AFC's four line squadrons would usually serve separately under the orders of the Royal Flying Corps. In March

1916 Reynolds would become the first commanding officer of 1 Squadron.

When Britain declared war on Germany on 4 August 1914, most Australians greeted the news with great enthusiasm. Volunteers rushed to enlist for an exciting war which was expected to be over by Christmas.[1] The AFC sent one aircraft, a B.E.2, to assist in capturing the German colonies in northern New Guinea and the Solomon Islands. However, German forces in the Pacific surrendered quickly, before the aeroplane was even unpacked from its shipping crate. Australia's early involvement in the War included the Australian Naval and Military Expeditionary Force taking possession of German New Guinea and the neighbouring islands of the Bismarck Archipelago in October 1914.

Most of the men accepted into the army in August 1914 were sent first to Egypt, not Europe, to meet the threat Turkey posed to British interests in the Middle East and the Suez Canal. After four and a half months of training near Cairo, the Australian and New Zealand Army Corps (ANZAC) departed by ship for the Gallipoli peninsula. The Anzacs landed at what became known as Anzac Cove on 25 April 1915 and established a tenuous foothold on the steep slopes above the beach. During the early days of the campaign, the allies tried to break through Turkish lines, while the Turks tried to drive the allied troops off the peninsula. Attempts on both sides ended in failure and the ensuing stalemate continued for the remainder of 1915. The most successful operation of the campaign was the evacuation of troops on 19 and 20 December, under cover of a comprehensive deception operation. As a result, the Turks were unable to inflict more than a very few casualties on the retreating forces. Following Gallipoli, Australian forces fought campaigns on the Western Front and in the Middle East.

Many pilots of the AFC did not come directly from the Point Cook flying school but arrived from other places and were appointed by direct Commissions. Others came from the AIF after serving as ground troops at Gallipoli, Egypt and France. Major Oswald Watt the Commander of 2 Squadron AFC had, prior to joining, served as an aviator/fighter pilot with the French Foreign Legion Air Corps (L'Aviation militaire française), being awarded the French Legion de'Honneur and the Croix de Guerre. Watt later, as a Lieutenant Colonel, became the Commander of the UK based training squadrons.

Roby Lewis Manuel enlisted in the 43rd Battalion, AIF on 5 April 1916. He swore that he was a natural born British citizen, that he worked as a farmer and that his uncle, Frederick George Jones, was his next of kin. Manuel claimed a year's prior militia experience. He transferred to the AFC on 30 April 1917 and was posted to 2 Squadron AFC in France as a S.E.5a pilot on 6 February 1918. He scored his first aerial victory on 2 April in company with Captain Henry Garnet Forrest; they destroyed a German two-seater reconnaissance machine over Demuin. Two months later, on 2 June, Manuel destroyed two Pfalz D.III fighters and then drove down a third one out of control within the half hour. Ten days later he became an ace by setting another Pfalz D.III afire north of Bussy. His exploits earned him the award of a DFC on 2 July. Manuel was then promoted to captain as he was appointed a Flight Commander. On 22 July he drove down a Pfalz D.III and a Fokker D.VII, both out of control. On the 31st, he drove down an Albatros D.V. The destruction of a D.VII on an evening patrol on 14 August brought Manuel's victory total to nine. On 16 September, Manuel claimed two more D.VIIs in two separate dogfights. When the second Fokker went down near Droglandt, Manuel landed nearby. Unable to aid the German pilot he had wounded, Manuel could only watch him die, then help bury the dead German. This action earned him a Bar to his DFC. British military intelligence later exhumed this German pilot's body to examine the parachute he was wearing.

Manuel's twelfth and final victory came on 24 September. On this occasion the RFC and AFC 'Circus' comprised of Camels of Nos. 2 and 4 Squadrons AFC and Bristol Fighters of 88 Squadron RAF.

'We left the ground at 0900 and completed rendezvous over Merville with Bristol Fighters of 88 Squadron and at 0940, Camels about 9,000 feet, S.Es 11,000 to 14,000 feet and B.Fs 14,000 feet and over. We moved off towards La Bassée at a maximum distance of 1,000 yards behind Camels and crossed lines at 0950 between La Bassée and Lens at slightly higher altitude, 12,000 feet. As we crossed lines I saw several EA in the distance but as we approached they disappeared in the clouds. We continued with the Camels following a course Annoeullin, one mile west of Seclin - Haubourdin - Pérenchies, round North of Armentières. The Bristol Fighters, who were following at a great distance, left us between Seclin and Haubourdin, flying in a southerly direction. This was the last we saw of them. Slightly east of Armentières I sighted a Camel strafing a balloon; taking it to be one of 4 Squadron's I sat around protecting it until machine crossed the lines. We then turned SE and crossed over Sainghin - by this time the Camels were on their way home. No other EA except those first mentioned were seen were seen except doubtful two-seaters high up. On our way home Lieutenant Frank Smith and I shot down an Albatros C two-seater out of control East of La Bassée. At 10.30 this machine was flying west of La Bassée at 10,000 feet. I followed underneath its tail about mid-way between La Bassée and Bethune and pulling down my Lewis Gun; fired a whole drum into it from a range of 200 feet. The machine was turned over and went into a vertical nose dive. I half rolled and dived onto it again twice firing a burst from my Lewis Gun. Lieutenants Smith, Wellwood, Franks and Knight all dived on the EA which dived practically all the way down until it disappeared into the clouds.[2] 'D' AA Battery confirmed this machine out of control.'

Captain Roby Lewis Manuel DFC* would lead the flypast on Anzac Day in London in 1919.

The first operational Australian group dispatched was the half-flight sent to the Mesopotamia. Some excellent reconnaissance work was completed despite poor machines and appalling conditions. Three of the four pilots were killed or captured and a number of ground crew were captured at Kut-el Arama and died in captivity. Units were formed for service overseas with the Australian Imperial Force (AIF). They saw action, initially, in the Mesopotamian Campaign. The AFC later saw action in Palestine and France. In addition, a training wing was established in the United Kingdom.

The first operational flights did not occur until 27 May 1915, when the Mesopotamian Half Flight (MHF), under the command of Captain Henry Petre, was called upon to assist the Indian Army in protecting British oil interests in what is now Iraq. Operating a mixture of aircraft including Caudrons, Maurice Farman Shorthorns, Maurice Farman Longhorns and Martinsydes, the MHF initially undertook unarmed reconnaissance operations, before undertaking light bombing operations later in the year after being attached to 30 Squadron RFC. A Second Half Flight was to be sent to Mesopotamia but the fall of Kut to the Turks, focused the British and Turkish efforts towards the Palestinian Front. In February 1915 the Indian government called on the other dominions to provide trained pilots for service in the Tigris valley during the Mesopotamian campaign. The Indian Army supplied three Maurice Farman aircraft. Captain Henry Aloysius Petre, Lieutenant T. W. White, Lieutenant William Harold Treloar and Lieutenant George Pinnock Merz were the four pilots in the flight who flew the aircraft on operations from Basra. A New Zealander, Lieutenant William Wallace Allison Burn was seconded to the RFC for service as a flying officer, attached to the Indian Expeditionary Force and joined a RFC unit at Basra on 26 May 1915 as one of five pilots. The unit took over three aircraft that had already seen service in Egypt and were in poor shape. The aircraft in the theatre were having serviceability problems due to the harsh environment, adding to the problems the under powered aircraft were having in the thin, hot and often wild air. Operations commenced on 31 May 1915, with a reconnaissance flight over Turkish positions near Kurna. Later two Caudrons arrived to complement the Farmans, on 4 July 1915. They were used for reconnaissance in the battle for An Nāṣirīyah.

Burn flew on a number of these sorties. His parents, Forbes Burn, a station manager and his wife, Isabel Ayers, had emigrated to Melbourne, Australia soon after their marriage at Christchurch in 1885 and their son was born on 17 July 1891. The family moved to Canterbury, New Zealand, where Burn was educated at Christchurch Boys' High School. He showed a keen interest in cadet force training, eventually reaching the rank of cadet captain. In August 1911 Burn joined the New Zealand Staff Corps as a probationary second lieutenant. On 8 August Burn departed, along with three other junior officers, for England for a course of study with the Imperial Forces. He undertook instruction with the military aeronautical directorate and obtained the necessary certificates to qualify as a pilot. Burn returned to New Zealand in September 1914 and was appointed area officer, Auckland, with the rank of lieutenant.

The pair of Caudrons of the Mesopotamian Half Flight proved unreliable, being prone to frequent engine failure. On 30 July they were returning in loose formation from the Nāṣirīyah area to Basra when one suffered an engine failure and landed near a village; the villagers were, fortunately, friendly. The other machine, piloted by Merz with Burn as observer, went missing. According to reports of eyewitnesses, their Caudron landed in the desert about twenty miles from the refilling station at Abu Salibiq. Burn and Merz were immediately attacked by a number of well-armed Arabs and, recognising that they could not defend their machine, they retreated in the direction of Abu Salibiq. Armed only with revolvers, the two airmen carried out a running fight, during which they killed one and wounded five of their adversaries. Then one of them was wounded and his comrade died fighting beside him. Search parties were sent out from Abu Salibiq and Basra, but no trace of the missing airmen was ever found. The aeroplane was found several days later, hacked to matchwood. The loss of Burn and Merz was a severe blow to the unit. Both were capable pilots, Burn being described as 'a laughing and likeable fellow'. Because Burn served with a RFC unit his death is not recorded in the official New Zealand roll of honour. He was the first New Zealand pilot to be killed in action. Missing in action 30 July 1915 in Mesopotamia, Merz was the first AFC casualty in the First World War. In December 1915 after flying supplies to the besieged garrison at Kut, the MHF was disbanded.

The first complete Australian Squadron to form was 1 Squadron. Many of its recruits came from the ranks of the Light Horse; most of these already had years of active service. In early 1916 28 Officers and 195 NCOs and Aircraftsmen of 1 Squadron departed aboard the troopship *Orsorva* for Egypt. The Squadron received 17 Squadron's B.E.2s six weeks after its arrival, as 17 Squadron had been posted to the Macedonian Front at Salonika. The B.E.2s were very slow, lacked both manoeuvrability and climb and were hopeless against the enemy in any form of aerial combat. Their main role was in bombing and strafing of enemy units on the ground. They also lacked forward firing armament, but the squadron and in particular the later Sir Lawrence J. Wackett, devised forward firing mountings for the Lewis machine gun allowing the B.E.2 to operate in the scouting role. Wackett also used one of the squadron's Bristol Scouts to test an interrupter gear he had devised. Allan Betteridge built a hydraulic system similar to and pre-dating the Constantinesco interrupter gear. Betteridge's invention however, fell on deaf ears.

The role of the AFC in Egypt was varied from the time of its arrival on 14 April 1916 as it was placed under the control of the 5th Wing RFC. At Romani in July and August 1916 the AFC supported the ground offensive by both effective strafing and bombing of both Turkish and German airfields and attacking infantry columns. On 22 December the ten aircraft of 1 Squadron supported the Anzac Mounted Division attack on Magdhaba that fell to the Anzac forces. Other support was given in the capturing of Beersheba, Gaza and Jaffa. 1 Squadron's B.E.2s began to be supported by the arrival of Martinsyde G.100 and G.102 Elephants which replaced the unsuccessful attempt to use Bristol Scouts as escorts for the B.E.2s. Up until the Martinsydes arrived the Australians had not possessed an aircraft powerful enough to catch the superior German Rumplers in the theatre. Aerial clashes were few however and the Squadron for the most went about reconnaissance, photographing and bombing. The mapping of the theatre was poor inaccurate and inconsistent. In October 1917, 1 Squadron re-equipped with the R.E.8 and began mapping large areas to give accurate maps for the Armies on the ground. Apart from the danger of facing a German Flieger-Abteilung with faster and more modern aircraft, the other great danger for the squadron came from the aircraft suffering mechanical failures. Finally, in December 1 Squadron began to receive the Bristol F.2b Fighter. The aircraft was long ranged, powerful and when flown aggressively extremely capable as a Scout aircraft. The 'Brisfit' or 'Biff' as it was known in the theatre matched perfectly the multiple roles and long range required of the theatre's operations. Along with complementing the aggressive mentality of the pilots and observers of the squadron, the Bristol Fighter was to sway air superiority to the allied side.

As well as undertaking offensive operations, the Bristol Fighters served in the photo-reconnaissance role. In March 1918, 1 Squadron was completely equipped with Bristol fighters, which were quoted as being the finest aircraft of World War I. During the last week of April, 1 Squadron moved its base forward from Mejdel to a new aerodrome outside Ramleh. Beginning in August, members of the

Squadron, including Captain Ross M. Smith, were attached to the famed Lieutenant Colonel T. E. Lawrence's Arab army (better known as Lawrence of Arabia) to protect it against German bombing. Ross Smith had seen service at Gallipoli for four and a half months from May 1915 but contracted enteric fever and was invalided to England. In October 1916 he returned to the Middle East, shortly afterwards being posted to 1 Squadron in Palestine having qualified as an observer. His service was marked by conspicuous gallantry in action and performed invaluable reconnaissance and photographic work, particularly on long-distance flights. He qualified as a pilot in July 1917 and was the first aviator to overfly Jerusalem. He became the leading ace in the theatre with eleven victories. (No mean feat considering the enemy activity in the theatre never numbered more than one Jasta and four Flieger Abteilungs). The great offensive of September 1917 was led by 1 Squadron AFC and the initial blow was a bombing raid by Captain Ross Smith dropping sixteen 112lb bombs on the telegraph station and railway yards at El Afule, destroying both. The rest of the squadron attacked other key positions completely isolating the Turkish Army further south of the attack.

Colonel Lawrence had called for air assistance for his Arab army that were being constantly attacked by German air forces.' Captain Smith and two others of 1 Squadron in their Bristol fighters went to Lawrence's aid, shooting down several German invaders and order was restored. The New Zealander, Lieutenant Carrick Paul and his observer Lieutenant W. J. Weir were often to be found flying with Smith and Lieutenant Ernest Andrew 'Pard' Mustard, an ace credited with five aerial victories, causing Turkish horses to stampede and chasing German aircraft to the ground where they were strafed.[3] An aircraft forced down in the desert was difficult to recover and make serviceable again. To ensure the enemy aircraft they forced down were wrecked, the Australians would strafe the downed aircraft and aviators. In one case in September 1918, Ross Smith landed next to the DFW he had forced down and burnt the German aircraft with a Very Light.

During operations in support of the Arabs against the Turks Lawrence frequently needed transport. 'Everything' he said 'was being wrecked by 'air-impotence'. After Lawrence conferred with John Maitland Salmond, General Officer Commanding the Royal Flying Corps in the Field and Brigadier General Amyas Eden Borton, Salmond agreed to send Lawrence two Bristol fighters to Umtaiye. Lawrence wrote: 'Had we spares? Petrol? Not a drop? How was it to be got there? Only by air? An air-contained fighting unit? Unheard of! When Colonel Lawrence suggested that heavy bombers were urgently needed in support of General Allenby's operations, a monstrous Handley Page 0/400 bomber was flown out from Cranwell by Brigadier General Borton[4] on 28 May 1918, picking up Major A. S. MacLaren at Manston and finally arriving at Kantara on the Suez Canal on 8 August. The aircraft was then flown to Ramleh on loan to 1 Squadron AFC and Ross Smith was chosen as its pilot. (Smith is mentioned several times in Lawrence's book, *Seven Pillars of Wisdom*). Smith had petrol and ammunition flown into Lawrence's position by the Handley-Page 0/400, the only two engined aircraft in the theatre, which was used for bombing as well as impressing the Arabs, so he could remain with Lawrence's army to protect it. The rest of the offensive went with the RFC and AFC having total air supremacy.

The 'liaison' was so 'complete and informed and quick' wrote Lawrence in *Revolt in the Desert.* 'It was the RAF which had converted the Turkish retreat into rout, which had abolished their telephone and telegraph connections, had blocked their lorry-columns, scattered their infantry units...Tul Keram, Messudieh, Jenin and Afuleh in turn were air-contained so drastically that their use was denied the enemy for hours before any of our ground troops drew near. But the climax of our attack and the holocaust of the miserable Turks fell in the valley by which Esdraelon drained to the Jordan by Beisan.'

Lawrence was referring to The Battle of Nablus which together with the Battle of Sharon was known as the Battle of Megiddo, between 19 and 25 September 1918, in what came to be known as the 'Battle of Armageddon'.[5] On 18 September 5th Corps Wing RAF headquartered at Ramleh was deployed to provide support with 14 Squadron attached to the XX Corps stationed at Junction Station and one flight of 142 Squadron operating from Jerusalem. These aircraft were responsible for cooperation with artillery, contact patrols and tactical reconnaissance up to 10,000 yards in advance of the ground forces. One of the seven squadrons of the Palestine Brigade RAF, the Australian squadron had been allotted the Handley-Page bomber three weeks before the offensive began. This squadron carried out bombing, offensive patrols and strategic reconnaissance's, while the Handley-Page bomber piloted by Ross Smith bombed the central telephone exchange at Afulah, where Lieutenant Colonel Richard Williams' 40th Army Air Wing RFC with a striking force of 1 Squadron AFC, two squadrons of D.H.9As of the RFC and one squadron of S.E.5 fighter scouts of the RFC, led the attack before the artillery bombardment signalled the beginning of battle.[6] Although aircraft flying over the Jisr ed Damieh to Beisan road, the Jisr ed Damieh bridge, Es Salt and Beisan as far as Tubas, reported all quiet at dawn on the morning of 20 September, RAF Bristol Fighters would later attack a convoy of 200 vehicles withdrawing from Nablus, blocking the road, causing many horses to bolt over a precipice on one side of the road while men scattered into the hills on the other side. The last reconnaissance on 20 September reported the whole Ottoman line alarmed, three large fires were burning at Nablus railway station and at the Balata supply dumps, while a brigade of British cavalry was seen entering Beisan. Dawn aerial scouting on 21 September returned reports of the previous day's attacks on roads leading towards the Jordan River, which was only a precursor to the follow up attacks that day. From midday on 22 September and in particular from 15:00 to 18:00, aerial reconnaissance found Ottoman troops at Es Salt and in the surrounding areas withdrawing towards Amman.

On 23 September, the first bombing formation attacked, expending large amounts of munitions on the retreating columns on the Es Salt to Amman road, returning about 0700 when a rout resulted. Amman was attacked from the air during the day and retreating columns from Amman and another column moving from Es Salt to Amman were attacked. An Australian aircraft saw columns retreating from Deraa and Samakh, where trains appeared ready to leave for Damascus. By the afternoon of 24 September, virtually all the area west of Amman was clear of Ottoman soldiers but on 25 September a column moving from Amman was seen at Mafrak. The column was attacked between 6:00 and 08:00 by ten Australian aircraft, with attacks continuing throughout the day expending four tons of bombs and almost 20,000 machine gun rounds.

'The modern motor road, the only way of escape for the Turkish divisions' wrote Lawrence, 'was scalloped between cliff and precipice in a murderous defile. For four hours our aeroplanes replaced one another in series above the doomed columns; nine tons of small bombs or grenades and fifty thousand rounds of S.A.A. were rained upon them. When the smoke had cleared it was seen that the organisation of the enemy had melted away. They were a dispersed horde of trembling individuals, hiding for their lives in every fold of the vast hills. Nor did their commanders ever rally them again. When our cavalry entered the silent valley next day they could count ninety guns, fifty lorries; nearly a thousand carts abandoned with all their belongings. The RAF lost four killed. The Turks lost a corps.' It was the final victory for Britain and France over the Ottoman Empire.

Megiddo was the first known instance where airpower destroyed and demoralised an army's ability to fight. It was a total massacre resulting from attacks from the air, the Australian official history describing it as 'wholesale destruction' on the Turkish Seventh Army'.

By October 1918 the Bristol Fighters had moved forward from Ramleh to Haifa and by the middle of the month were required to patrol and reconnoitre an exceptionally wide area of country, sometimes between 500 and 600 miles, flying over Rayak, Homs, Beirut, Tripoli, Hama, Aleppo, Killis and Alexandretta. They bombed the German aerodromes at Rayak, where 32 German machines had been either abandoned or burnt, on 2 October. On 19 October, the first German aircraft was seen in the air since fighting over Deraa in mid-September, just prior to the Battle of Sharon. Ross Smith and another pilot forced a DFW two-seater to land and destroyed it on the ground by firing a Very light into the aircraft after the German pilot and observer had moved to safety.

On 30 October 1918 Turkey sued for peace. By the time of the Turkish surrender, 1 Squadron had scored over 100 victories and was the only squadron to participate in the campaign from the Suez Canal to Syria. In the wake of the 31 October armistice, 1 Squadron relocated to Ramleh in December and then in February 1919 to Kantara. There its members were personally farewelled by General Sir Edmund Allenby, who congratulated them for achieving 'absolute supremacy of the air ... a factor of paramount importance' to the Allied campaign. The Squadron left behind a proud record for future Australian aviation arms to match in the Middle East.

In January 1916 the British War Office had made a special request to the Australian government. It wanted 200 volunteers from the AIF to be trained and commissioned as pilots and observers in the RFC. 'Exceptionally good work has been done in the RFC by Australian-born officers and the Australian temperament is specially suited to the flying service' the British stated. The Australian military leaders approved the request. Hundreds of Australians rushed to England to earn their wings and spurs with the AFC, RFC, RNAS and RAF. Many left their mark.

Eric Rupert Dibbs was born on a hot, late summer's afternoon at his parents' home in Lytton Street, North Sydney on 9 March 1894. In June 1914, employed as a clerk at the Commercial Banking Company of Sydney, he was commissioned as a 2nd Lieutenant in the 24th Infantry (East Sydney). After service in the Australian Army in France he transferred to the AFC and passed out as an observer. Dibbs sailed for the Western Front on 10 June 1917 and was posted to join 11 Squadron RFC, which had just been equipped with the Bristol F.2B. Dibbs spent just under three months with 11 Squadron. They were, he said, 'my most exciting time at the front.' In Dibbs' time with the squadron they suffered 28 casualties; 12-17 pilots and observers killed or died of wounds, six taken prisoner and five wounded. 'The Bristol Fighter could dive faster than its adversaries, a singular experience for the observer. We usually went out in threes, or sometimes fives, climbed towards the lines and arrived over Hunland at about 10,000 or 12,000 feet.

'As soon as we crossed the lines shell bursts from German batteries would begin bursting round us. Whenever they suddenly stopped, we looked for enemy aircraft and kept our eyes well open. Sooner or later, we would spot them - tiny specks like so many midges in the distance. As we closed, we climbed for height and did our best to get the sun behind us. Of course, they were trying to do exactly the same thing.

'When the leader fired a red Very light, we would put our noses down and dive headlong into the enemy formation. This was sometimes alarming for the observers loose in their cockpits. Only the pilot was strapped in. Those were unforgettable moments – as the pilot dived, the observer was flung on his back with his feet pointing up to the blue sky. He was reassured by the sound of the front gun firing and the smell of the cordite fumes. When the front gun stopped firing, you were in suspense, wondering whether the pilot had been killed, till either he fired again or the machine lurched out of its dive. This went on till the E. A. [Enemy Aircraft] were either destroyed or driven away. Each time the pilot pulled out of a dive, the observer had to clamber to his feet against the centrifugal force, swing both Lewis guns in the direction of the nearest E. A. and let fly. Masses of tracer and hundreds of unseen bullets would be flying in all directions and the opposing aircraft would be wildly dog-fighting in a mad, whirling mass.

'One fight is very like another at this distance of time and I find it difficult to separate them. I can assure you, however, that we were never, never bored. I must admit that I sometimes dozed off in the thin atmosphere on a sunny day when we were not in contact with the enemy. Mauduit would often give me a hard crack on the head to make sure that I was awake… As an observer I often wore a lamb's wool coat with the wool on the outside. Mauduit loved to refer to me as 'his little Canterbury - a lamb led to the slaughter'. Dibbs later gained his pilot's wings and joined 2 Squadron at their aerodrome at Reclinghem on 18 July 1918 where he flew the S.E.5a.

Major Richard G. 'Dickie' Blomfield, born in Sydney in 1890, organised the famous 56th; stood his ground against the Factory over the S.E.5's 'greenhouse' windscreen and wilfully withheld sending his pilots into action during the Arras battle for over two weeks until his pilots were happy with their machines. He left 56 Squadron to take command of the 51st Wing in October 1917 until the end of the war. Then there were those who brought their flying skills home to transform this 'wide brown land'. Horrie Miller co-founded MacRobertson-Miller Airways or MMA, which became Ansett Australia. Norman Brearly bridged the vast distances of Western Australia by starting Australian National Airways - 'the forgotten giant of Australian aviation'. Other pivotal airmen include WW1 Trans-Pacific pioneer Charles Kingsford-Smith and his co-pilot/navigator P. G. 'Gordon'

Taylor, who had came from the RFC and scored five victories; Lieutenant Hudson Fysh and Lieutenant Paul 'Ginty' McGinness who earned their names in the air above Palestine and later took their skills to civil life by starting QANTAS; plus air mail pioneer and 27-victory ace Roy King. Harry Butler joined the RFC and was posted to the Air Gunnery Schools. A gifted instructor, when he returned to Adelaide in 1919 his flying displays attracted crowds that would not be surpassed for fifty years.

Others such Frank Hubert McNamara, Captain 'Rickie' Little and 'Harry' Cobby came from the RNAS and Major Arthur Coningham DSO MC who acquired the nickname 'Mary', a corruption of 'Maori' hailed from New Zealand. Coningham had volunteered for service in the New Zealand Expeditionary Force in August 1914, initially seeing service in the conquest of German Samoa. He then served in Egypt and Somaliland as a trooper in the Canterbury Mounted Rifle Regiment, but developed typhoid fever and was invalided out of service in March 1916. In April Coningham journeyed to Britain at his own expense to join the RFC. Posted to 32 Squadron on 19 December after completing his flying instruction, Coningham flew numerous patrols between 5 January and 30 July 1917, when he was wounded during an aerial combat and invalided back to Britain. During the Battle of Arras, 32 Squadron undertook systematic strafing of German infantry and lines of communication, particularly suited for the Airco D.H.2 machines they operated. He returned to France promoted to the rank of major and in command of 92 Squadron on 1 July 1918 at the age of 23.

On 11 August he was wounded again in a particularly intense air combat, but remained in France and resumed flying almost immediately. To the end of the war, Coningham's S.E.5s conducted bombing and strafing attacks against German aerodromes, troops, gun positions and transport. In eleven months at the front he engaged in 176 patrols over enemy lines, was credited with the personal destruction of nine enemy aircraft and shared in the destruction of three others with Evander Shapard, Frank Billinge and Arthur Randell. He was also credited with seven victories for having driven down an enemy machine out of control. Coningham was decorated with a DSO and a Military Cross, both earned during his time with 32 Squadron. (Coningham was later a senior RAF commander during the Second World War).

Australia would produce several 'aces' but like most of its Great War history their achievements have come second to the Anzac landings at Gallipoli. Numbers 2, 3 and 4 Squadrons AFC, each with eighteen aircraft, flew with the RFC and used many types of aircraft including the famous Camel, Sopwith Pup, 'Spad', Bristol Scout, Bristol F.2b and R.E.8. When the AIF divisions arrived in France, the war on the Western Front had long settled into a stalemate, with the opposing armies facing each other from trench systems that extended across Belgium and north-east France, from the English Channel to the Swiss border. About 3,000 Australian airmen served in the Middle East and France with the Australian Flying Corps, mainly in observation capacities or providing infantry support.

All told eight squadrons were formed. They were; 1 Squadron formed at Point Cook and sent to Egypt in 1916; 2 Squadron formed in Egypt, was a fighter/scout unit and sent to France the same year; 3 Squadron was formed at Point Cook as a reconnaissance unit and deployed to France in 1917; 4 Squadron, a fighter/scout unit, was also formed at Point Cook and arrived in France in December 1917, giving the AFC four combat Squadrons on active service with the remaining 5, 6, 7 and 8 Squadrons being formed in England as training squadrons for the supply of reinforcements for the other four. 3 Squadron continued their role as Corps Reconnaissance for the duration of the war. Their aircraft were mainly R.E.8s; a good reliable two seater, ideal for the task. The squadron had very few combat engagements but did manage to force down two enemy aircraft, one a Halberstadt C.L.II reconnaissance two seater and an Albatros DVa single seater scout.

3 Squadron was the first AFC unit to deploy in France, flying to a staging airfield of Ste-Omer on 9 September 1917 before flying to their aerodrome at Savy the next day. The squadron was equipped with the R.E.8 and was trained as a Corps-reconnaissance and Artillery-spotting Squadron, in support of Army operations. It was at once allotted to the newly formed Australian Corps as 'corps squadron'. In this role it scouted for the Australian Divisions, fought strafing and bombing enemy aircraft and flew close-observation or contact patrols during the AIF's 1918 battles. In November the Squadron moved to Bailleul in support of the Australia Corps in the Messines area. The R.E.8 is undervalued in most histories as an offensive machine, despite its pair of Lewis guns for the observer and the forward firing Vickers on the left hand side of the fuselage. 3 Squadron, like most spotter squadrons not only used their aircraft for army corps duties but also as offensive weapons. The squadron was to be credited with over fifty victories in their fifteen month tour involvement in the Western Front aerial war. One of the aggressive pairs was Lieutenant A. E. Grigson and Lieutenant H. B. James, who destroyed two German aircraft while paired and another each while in other crews. Their first victory while paired was when they watched an Albatros Scout attack the British balloon lines near Tromville. Grigson fired into the aircraft with his Vickers until it jammed and then James fired it into the aircraft with his Lewis guns until the Albatros crashed. 3 Squadron's R.E.8s established an astounding record of service. Flying from ten different aerodromes, they logged 10,000 hours of war flying, fired 500,000 rounds of machine gun ammunition at enemy targets, dropped 6,000 bombs and accounted for 57 enemy aircraft.

Its stability became legend when on 17 December 1917 an R.E.8 piloted by Lieutenant James Lionel Montague Sandy with his observer, Sergeant Henry F. Hughes of 3 Squadron was ranging artillery fire for the 8-inch Howitzers of the 151st Siege Battery. Thirty-five minutes after they'd started, they were attacked by six Albatros D.5a Scouts of Royal Prussian Jasta 29 at Bellincamp. Sandy fought them off and before long, he had shot down Leutnant Rudolf Clausz who was wounded in the thigh and crash landed on ground near the 21st Battalion, 2nd Australian Division AIF and was taken prisoner. His aircraft was recovered and assessed by personnel of 3 Squadron AFC. The aircraft had sustained bullet damage to a fuel tank which caused it to land, largely undamaged, close to Armentières.[7] About then, two other 3 Squadron R.E.8s who happened to be nearby came to Sandy's assistance. Within a few minutes, the remaining enemy aircraft broke off the fight and headed for their own lines. (In itself, this was not unusual because German pilots generally held great respect for the R.E.8 with the pilot's propeller-synchronised Vickers machine gun and the observer's Lewis gun to defend the rear.) After the enemy aircraft had left, both of the other R.E.8s clearly saw that

Sandy's R.E.8 (A3816), with the unmistakable letter 'B' on the fuselage was flying straight and steady, so they waved a farewell and flew off to resume their own assignments. However, Sandy's wireless messages directing the Artillery Battery had ceased transmission. By nightfall, A3816 had not returned to the aerodrome. On the following night, a telegram from No.12 Stationary Hospital at Ste-Pol told of finding the bodies of the two airmen in their grounded R.E.8 in a neighbouring field. A post-mortem of the bodies and an examination of the R.E.8 showed that both pilot and observer had been killed in aerial combat and that the R.E.8 had flown itself around in wide left-hand circles until its petrol ran out. What had happened was that a single enemy armour-piercing bullet had passed through the observer's left lung and thence into the base of the pilot's skull. The R.E.8 came down fifty miles south-west of the battle scene out of skies that hadn't seen any other aerial combat that day. It had crash-landed without further injuring the bodies of the airmen and with the throttle still wide open. The aircraft itself was not badly damaged in spite of its uncontrolled 50 mile flight and this, in itself, was a classic example of the stability and flying qualities of the R.E.8.

2 Squadron crossed the English Channel within two weeks of 3 Squadron and landed at Ste-Omer on 21 September 1917. The complete squadron made the crossing from Harlaxton to Ste-Omer in one day, a record for the Allied flying forces. 2 Squadron was in Warloy the next day ready for operations under the command of the erstwhile Major Oswald Watt, a veteran of the air war including stints with the French Aviation Militaire and 1 Squadron AFC. The squadron was equipped with the Airco D.H.5, unusual for its backward staggered wings and unfortunately underpowered for the war in late 1917 with a significant drop off in performance above 10,000 feet. Many a Combat Report was to claim the German two seater machines just flew away with the D.H.5 unable to catch it. The D.H.5 was excellent however, in the ground attack and Army support roles and 2 Squadron was used heavily during the Cambrai Offensive. Many times, aircraft coming back to land only to be deemed a write off. This was epitomized by Lieutenant Les Holden, a large character in the AFC who earned the nickname, 'Lucky Les, the homing pigeon' due to the number of times his aircraft was written off and the closeness of him receiving bullets.

2 Squadron re-equipped with the S.E.5a in December 1917 and were posted to Savy in mid January where they operated as a Scout unit, flying patrols at 15,000 feet and searching out enemy aircraft to engage them. Oswald Watt while with the French Aviation Militaire had his Farman painted with Advance Australia on the nose. His influence was to show in the insignia of 2 Squadron, a boomerang aft of the roundel, which was adopted by 4 Squadron also. Even wilder schemes and insignia were to grace the aircraft of 1 Wing AFC while under Watt's command. The squadron was also one of the first to exercise the Wing tactics starting to come into use in the British forces, by flying in large staggered groups similar to the manner with which the German Jagdstaffels operated. The Australian squadron discovered though that with large numbers in the air the Germans would shy from combat and in periods of lesser enemy activity 2 Squadron flew in smaller patrol groups.

On 20 June 1918 2 Squadron joined up with 4 Squadron as part of 80 Wing under the command of Lieutenant Colonel Strange, famous for hanging upside down from a jammed Lewis gun of his Martinsyde Scout and kicking out the instrument panel of the aircraft to get his legs back in. With the two Australian Scouting squadrons together a rivalry sprung up between the two to see which squadron could score the greatest amount. Wing tactics were used on attacks to enemy airfields around Harboudin and Lille in August 1918, devastating the aerodromes. As the German Armies began to retreat in September 2 Squadron began taking part on more ground attack operations until there last casualty was Captain Frank Smith, who was shot down two days before the armistice and walked back to his aerodrome. He arrived to discover the Germans had surrendered in his absence. 2 Squadron produced sixteen aces and was victorious over 170 enemy aircraft.

In December of 1917 the last of the operational AFC squadrons came into action when 4 Squadron crossed the Channel to Ste-Omer and Bruay. The squadron was equipped with the Sopwith Camel, an aircraft destined to be the aircraft with which the most enemy aircraft were shot down with. 4 Squadron was in no small way to contribute to this record. The aircraft also had a name for being spectacularly manoeuvrable in the hands of a gifted pilot and potentially dangerous to the novice. 4 Squadron was unfortunate to lose several new pilots to collisions during formation flying. Through the heavy work of the offensive in March 1918 enemy contacts occurred often in the close support operations and the Squadron's aggressive nature began to build a score which was to be the highest averaging per month of any of the Camel squadrons on the Western Front. The squadron was also to build a reputation for aggressiveness epitomized by men such as Captain A. H. Cobby who scored 29 kills and destroyed thirteen balloons between February and September 1918 and Captain Elwyn Roy 'Bo' King.

Captain Arthur Henry Cobby DSC DFC** of 4 Squadron was born on 26 August 1894 in the Melbourne suburb of Prahran, Victoria, the second of four sons of Arthur Edward Stanley Cobby, a tramway conductor and his wife Alice. 'Harry', as he became known, was educated at a state school and completed his senior-level education at University College, Armadale. He gained a commission with the 46th Infantry (Brighton Rifles) a militia unit, in 1912, while working as a clerk with the Commonwealth Bank, Melbourne. He later transferred to the 47th Infantry. When World War I broke out, Cobby attempted to enlist in the Australian Imperial Force but his employer, the Commonwealth Bank, refused to release him as his position of clerk was considered an essential occupation. He eventually managed to join the AFC on 23 December 1916, despite a professed lack of interest in flying and was posted to the Central Flying School at Point Cook where he completed his initial instruction. He embarked for England aboard RMS *Omrah* on 17 January 1917.

Cobby later admitted to being so nervous about the prospect of going into battle that 'if anything could have been done by me to delay that hour, I would have left nothing undone to bring it about'. When he did see combat against the German Luftstreitkräfte for the first time, he had only twelve hours solo flying experience. In 1918 Australian pilots on the Western Front flew regular operations against enemy forces on the ground. 'The job', wrote Cobby, consisted of getting to the 'line' ... as fast and often as one could and letting the enemy on the ground have it as hot and heavy as possible… All this flying was done under 500 feet and our targets were point-blank ones... The air was full of aircraft and, continuously while shooting-up the troops on the ground, we would be attacked by enemy scouts ... The smoke of the battle below mixed with the clouds and mist above rendered flying particularly dangerous ... On top of this there were scores of machine-guns devoting their time to making things as unpleasant for us as they could.' Such flights were both dangerous and exhausting. 'I always emerged from them almost rigid with tension,' commented Cobby.

Many pilots were killed in accidents long before they could join a line squadron. Over a third of the AFC's wartime fatalities occurred in Britain. Pilots who survived training were posted to operational squadrons where the thought of meeting the enemy in the sky was enough to give even the bravest men pause for thought. Harry Cobby admitted his own fear of being posted to the front:

'The nervousness that assailed me during the months of training in England, when I gave thought to the fact that as soon as I was qualified to fly an aeroplane, or perhaps sooner, I would be sent off to the war to do battle with the enemy in the sky and on the ground. I quite freely admit that if anything could have been done by me to delay that hour, I would have left nothing undone to bring it about.

Harry Cobby remembered the strain of continuous operations during the German offensive of 1918, remarking that 'I could not eat, but champagne and brandy with an odd biscuit seemed good enough'

Those like Cobby found that in a dog-fight, which by the end of the war could involve up to 100 aircraft, hitting the enemy was very difficult: 'The air was too crowded, there was little opportunity to settle down and have a steady shot at anything. You would no sooner pick out someone to have a crack at, than there would be the old familiar 'pop-pop-pop-pop' behind you, or you would just glimpse an enemy pilot getting into position to fire on yourself - so hard boot and stick one way to save your skin.'

Most of Cobby's kills appear to have been scored against unsuspecting victims over whom he had the advantage of surprise and speed. Frederick Cutlack considered that 'Cobby was one of the most daring spirits in the Australian air service'. Cobby claimed an early victory, over a DFW reconnaissance aircraft on 3 February 1918 but this was credited only as 'driven down' and not confirmed. Based in the Pas-de-Calais area, 4 Squadron supported Allied forces during the German Spring Offensive that commenced the following month. Cobby's aerial opponents included members of Baron von Richthofen's 'Flying Circus'. On 21 March he shot down two of the formation's Albatros D.Vs, which was confirmed as his first official victories. Having proved himself a talented and aggressive pilot, Cobby's leadership abilities were recognised with his appointment as a flight commander on 14 May 1918 and promotion to captain on 25 May. Described as 'an imp of mischief', he personalised his Sopwith Camel by fitting it with aluminium cut-outs of comic actor Charlie Chaplin. Cobby again scored two kills in one day on 30 May near Estaires, when he destroyed an Albatros and an observation balloon and repeated this feat the next day in the same area. He had been responsible for shooting down 4 Squadron's first balloon at Merville earlier in May; although vulnerable to attack with incendiary bullets, these large observation platforms, nicknamed 'Drachen' ('Dragons'), were generally well protected by enemy fighters and anti-aircraft defences and were thus considered a dangerous but valuable target. Cobby was recommended for the Military Cross on 3 June 1918 in recognition of his combat success and for being a 'bold and skilful patrol leader, who is setting a fine example to his Squadron'. The award was changed to a DFC, appearing in the *London Gazette* on 2 July.

Cobby shot down three German aircraft on 28 June and was recommended for a bar to his DFC. By then he had fifteen victories. On 15 July 1918 he and another pilot dived on five Pfalz scouts near Armentières, Cobby accounting for two of the enemy aircraft and his companion for one. The Australians were then pursued by four Fokker Triplanes but managed to evade their attackers. This action earned Cobby a recommendation for a second bar to his DFC, the citation noting that he had scored 21 kills to date and had 'succeeded in destroying so many machines by hard work and by using his brains, as well as by courage and brilliant flying'. The two bars to his DFC were gazetted on the same day, 21 September. On 16 August, Cobby led a bombing raid against the German airfield at Haubourdin, near Lille, the largest aerial assault by Allied forces up until then, resulting in 37 enemy aircraft being destroyed. The following day he led a similar attack on Lomme airfield and was recommended for the DSO as a result. Gazetted on 2 November, the citation for the award declared that 'The success of these two raids was largely due to the determined and skilful leadership of this officer'.

By the end of his active service, Cobby was in charge of Allied formations numbering up to eighty aircraft. Fellow 4 Squadron ace, George Jones (later Chief of the Air Staff), described him as the unit's 'natural leader in the air and in all off-duty activities'; his exploits made him a national hero. 4 Squadron was recognised as the most successful fighter squadron in France, accounting for as many as 220 victories. In September 1918 Cobby was transferred to a training unit in England, where he found the strain of instructing pupils 'much worse than flying in France'. He continued applying for a return to the front until the war ended in November and was mentioned in despatches by Field Marshal Sir Douglas Haig the same month (gazetted 27 December). Though Cobby's final tally for the war is often given as 29 aircraft and thirteen observation balloons destroyed, claim-by-claim analyses of his victories credit him with 24 aircraft and five balloons, for a grand total of 29, making him the service's only 'balloon-busting' ace. His proudest boast, however was that as a flight commander he never lost a pilot over enemy territory.[8]

Other notables on 4 Squadron included the New Zealander Captain Herbert Gilles Watson as well as Lieutenant Leonard Thomas Eaton Taplin, Captain Garnet Francis Malley and Captain Thomas Charles Richmond Baker.

A clerk when war broke out, Watson enlisted on 28 October 1914, was assigned to 2nd Signal Troop. He embarked with his unit on 22 December 1914 on board HMAT *Borda* and then underwent training in Egypt. He went ashore at Gallipoli at 7am on 25 April 1915. He was evacuated to England in July with scalded feet. By 1918 Watson had transferred to the AFC and was posted to 4 Squadron. He was awarded a DFC on 3 August, the citation for which reads: 'Whilst on offensive patrol he encountered several Pfalz scouts, one of which he shot down. He has also in three weeks shot down four enemy machines and destroyed a balloon, attacking the latter at 6,000 feet, following it down to 1,000 feet, when it burst into flames'. By early October Watson had downed fourteen aircraft, three of these being balloons. He returned to Australia on 21 November on board HT *Suevic*. He died in Brighton Beach in 1942.

An electrical engineer from Sydney, Len Taplin enlisted in the Australian Army Engineers in 1914. Transferring to the AFC, he was posted to Palestine in 1917, serving with 67 Squadron as a reconnaissance pilot. In July 1918 he joined 4 Squadron in France as a Sopwith Camel pilot. Nine days after he scored his first victory, Taplin was very nearly killed in a flying accident on 26 July when his bomb laden Camel crashed during takeoff and he was blown clear, unhurt. On 5 September Taplin's flight of four Camels was overwhelmed and shot down by Fokker D.VIIs of Jasta 26 and 27. Badly wounded, he scored his final victory and was the only Allied pilot to survive the dogfight. Shot down by Christian Mesch, Taplin was captured and remained a prisoner until the end of the war.

Garnet Francis Malley MC AFC was credited with six aerial victories. Born in Sydney, Malley first saw service as an artilleryman with the Australian Imperial Force. He transferred to the Australian Flying Corps in 1917 and the following year flew Sopwith Camels with 4 Squadron on the Western Front. Malley was awarded the Military Cross for his achievements in combat and his subsequent work as a flying instructor in England earned him the Air Force Cross.[9]

Thomas Charles Richmond Baker was born in Smithfield, South Australia, on 2 May 1897, the eldest son of Richmond Baker, a schoolmaster and farmer and his wife Annie Martha. He was educated at St. Peter's College in Adelaide. During his school years Baker was an active sportsman, taking part in rowing, tennis and football, in addition to being a member of the cadet corps. In his youth, he acquired an avid interest in aviation and the construction of model aeroplanes became 'his chief hobby'. Graduating from secondary school in 1914, he gained employment as a clerk with the Adelaide branch of the Bank of New South Wales. During this time, he joined the 11th Royal Australian Engineers of the Citizens Military Force before he enlisted in the Australian Imperial Force in July 1915, for service in World War I. Posted to the 6th Field Artillery Brigade on the Western Front; he was awarded the Military Medal for carrying out numerous repairs on a communications line while subject to severe artillery fire and in June 1917 was awarded a bar to his decoration for his part in quelling a fire in one of the artillery gun pits that was endangering approximately 300 rounds of shrapnel and high explosive. In September 1917 Baker applied for a position as a mechanic in the AFC. He was instead selected for flight training and graduated as a pilot and was commissioned a second lieutenant in March 1918. Posted for active duty in France that June, Baker joined the ranks of 4 Squadron, flying Sopwith Camels. 4 Squadron and 2 Squadron became part of 80 Wing RFC and together they began flying as a group. Over the next four months, Baker rose to the rank of captain and was credited with six victories on Camels. By late 1918 the Camel at higher altitudes was having difficulty in performance with the rapidly increasingly more numerous Fokker DVIIs and 4 Squadron became the first to change to the new Sopwith Snipe, a more powerful, if less manoeuvrable fighter than the Camel. Promoted to flight commander, Baker was credited with six more victories in October 1918.

4 Squadron also began to target enemy balloon installations and a rash of balloon hunting sprung up in the squadron with pilots such as Cobby and Watson,

staking out balloon lines very early in the morning and then attacking them in concert with other flights later in the day. Cobby during his period with the squadron claimed and was credited with the flaming of five balloons, the only balloon ace of the AFC. In the torrid last month of the war, 4 Squadron was to claim 35 victories with the Snipe, including seven by 'Bo' King who was the leading scorer on the type.

All the Australian squadrons were made up of courageous and colourful men who risked their lives in their flimsy machines every moment they were in the air. Several of them were former Anzacs and many had fought in the trenches in France. Thus they always knew and appreciated, that their primary task was to help the embattled infantry below. In all, 460 Officers and 2,234 other ranks served in the AFC during the war. Pilots of the AFC were commissioned officers; the other ranks consisted of mechanics, refuellers, signallers and general ground duty staff. Of the 460 pilots in the AFC, no fewer than 57 Australian pilots became 'Aces' with approximately 100 decorations.

One of the first airmen to be awarded the Victoria Cross, in Palestine in March 1917, was Lieutenant Frank McNamara. Born at Rushworth, Victoria on 4 April 1894, McNamara was the first of eight children to William Francis McNamara, a State Lands Department officer and his wife Rosanna. He began his schooling in Rushworth and completed his secondary education at Shepparton Agricultural High School, which he had entered via a scholarship. The family moved to Melbourne in 1910. McNamara joined the school cadets in 1911 and was commissioned a second lieutenant in the 49th Battalion (Brighton Rifles), a militia unit, in July 1913. He became a teacher after graduating from Melbourne Teachers' Training College in 1914 and taught at various schools in Victoria. He also enrolled in the University of Melbourne, but his studies were interrupted by the outbreak of World War I.

As a militia officer, McNamara was mobilised for service in Australia when war was declared in August 1914. After serving briefly at bases in Queenscliff and Point Nepean, Victoria, McNamara passed through Officers Training School at Broadmeadows in December. He began instructing at the Australian Imperial Force Training Depot, Broadmeadows, in February 1915. Promoted to lieutenant in July, he immediately volunteered for a military aeronautics course at the Central Flying School, Point Cook.

Selected for flying training at Point Cook in August 1915, McNamara made his first solo flight in a Bristol Boxkite on 18 September and graduated as a pilot in October. On 6 January 1916, he was assigned as adjutant to 1 Squadron (also known until 1918 as 67 Squadron RFC). In March, McNamara departed Melbourne for Egypt aboard HMAT *Orsova*, arriving in Suez the following month. He was seconded to 42 Squadron RFC in May to attend the Central Flying School at Upavon, England; his secondment to the RFC was gazetted on 5 July 1916.

Completing his course at Upavon, McNamara was posted back to Egypt in August, but was hospitalised on 8 September with orchitis. Discharged on 6 October, he served briefly as a flying instructor with 22 Squadron RFC, before returning to 1 Squadron. McNamara flew with 'C' Flight, commanded by Captain (later Air Marshal Sir) Richard Williams. On his first sortie, a reconnaissance mission over Sinai, McNamara was unaware that his aeroplane had been hit by anti-aircraft fire; he returned to base with his engine's oil supply almost exhausted. Flying B.E.2s and Martinsydes, he undertook further scouting and bombing missions in the ensuing months.

Potentially leaving a pilot stranded in an inhospitable desert and with hostile Turkish soldiers and Arab tribes in any attempt to reach their front lines. Many successful attempts were made to pick up downed airmen, the most famous of these earned Lieutenant Frank McNamara a Victoria Cross, when he picked up Captain D. W. Rutherford while under Turkish fire. Despite being wounded McNamara flew the seventy miles back to the Squadrons airfield and fainted due to loss of blood as he taxied in.

On 20 March 1917 McNamara, flying a Martinsyde, was one of four 1 Squadron pilots taking part in a raid against a Turkish railway junction near Gaza. Owing to a shortage of bombs, the aircraft were each armed with six specially modified 4.5-inch howitzer shells. McNamara had successfully dropped three of his shells when the fourth exploded prematurely, badly wounded him in the leg with shrapnel, an effect he likened to being 'hit with a sledgehammer'. Having turned to head back to base, he spotted a fellow squadron member from the same mission, Captain David W. Rutherford, on the ground beside his crash-landed B.E.2. Allied airmen had been hacked to death by enemy troops in similar situations and McNamara saw that a company of Turkish cavalry was fast approaching Rutherford's position. Despite the rough terrain and the gash in his leg, McNamara landed near Rutherford in an attempt to rescue him.

As there was no spare cockpit in the single-seat Martinsyde, the downed pilot jumped onto McNamara's wing and held the struts. McNamara crashed while attempting to take off because of the effects of his leg wound and Rutherford's weight overbalancing the aircraft. The two men, who had escaped further injury in the accident, set fire to the Martinsyde and dashed back to Rutherford's B.E.2. Rutherford repaired the engine while McNamara used his revolver against the attacking cavalry, who had opened fire on them. Two other No. 1 Squadron pilots overhead, Lieutenant (later Air Marshal Sir) Roy 'Peter' Drummond and Lieutenant Alfred Ellis, also began strafing the enemy troops. McNamara managed to start the B.E.2's engine and take off, with Rutherford in the observer's cockpit. In severe pain and close to blacking out from loss of blood, McNamara flew the damaged aircraft seventy miles back to base at El Arish.

Having effected what was described in the Australian official history of the war as 'a brilliant escape in the very nick of time and under hot fire', McNamara 'could only emit exhausted expletives' before he lost consciousness shortly after landing. Evacuated to hospital, he almost died following an allergic reaction to a routine tetanus injection. McNamara had to be given artificial respiration and stimulants to keep him alive, but recovered quickly. A contemporary news report declared that he was 'soon sitting up, eating chicken and drinking champagne'. On 26 March McNamara was recommended for the Victoria Cross by Brigadier General Geoffrey Salmond, General Officer Commanding Middle East Brigade RFC. Drummond, Ellis and Rutherford all wrote statements on 3-4 April attesting to their comrade's actions, Rutherford declaring that 'the risk of Lieutenant MacNamara being killed or captured was so great that even had he not been wounded he would have been justified in not attempting my rescue - the fact of his already being wounded makes his action one of outstanding gallantry - his determination and resource and utter disregard of danger throughout the operation was worthy of the highest praise'. The first and only VC awarded to an Australian airman in World War I, McNamara's decoration was promulgated in the *London Gazette* on 8 June 1917. In 1921 McNamara enlisted as a flying officer in the newly formed RAAF, rising to the rank of air vice marshal by 1942. He held senior posts in England and Aden during World War II. Retiring from the Air Force in 1946, McNamara continued to live in Britain until his death from heart failure in 1961.

The most successful Australian pilot in British service was Captain 'Rikki' Little DSO** DSC* CdeG (Croix de Guerre), with 47 kills, which made him the eighth top-scoring British ace and the 15th most successful ace of all nations. Born in Melbourne on 19 July 1895 Robert Alexander Little was educated at Camberwell Grammar School. When the war started he was desperate to join up and see action before it was all over. In August 1914 he discovered that there were already 500 applicants at the Point Cook Military Flying School and believing he had little chance of obtaining an entry without a long wait he decided to sail for England at his own expense. At a cost of £100 he qualified as a pilot and gained his pilot certificate on 27 October 1915 at Hendon. He then immediately enlisted in the RNAS and three months later was commissioned as a probationary Flight Sub-Lieutenant at Eastchurch. He was only 20 at the time.

By June he was at the Naval Air Station at Dunkirk fulfilling the function in France at this time by undertaking reconnaissance along the coast and making attacks on German installations in occupied Belgium. By the autumn of 1916 however the RNAS was being drawn into the land battle further south and had the task of forming the personnel at Dunkirk into fighter squadrons to fight under RFC command. Thus was born the famous 'Naval Eight' - 8 (Naval) Squadron - on 25 October with Flight Sub Lieutenant Little among its first pilots. He was assigned to 'B' Flight under the command of another Australian ace, Stan Goble. Under Squadron Commander Geoffrey R. Bromet they began with three flights of Nieuport 17s, Sopwith 1½ Strutters and Sopwith Pups but by December it was the first all-Pup squadron in action. Little and his fellow naval pilots were delighted with the new aircraft. On 11 November, Little made his first kill, an Aviatik C.1, while flying a Pup (N5182) although most people consider his first kill to have been on the 23rd when he shot down a two seater just north of La Bassée and by December had claimed two Halberstadts.

On 1 February 1917 Naval Eight handed over its Pups to No. 3 (Naval) Squadron who took their place in the line with the RFC while Naval Eight's personnel went back to Dunkirk to reform with a more formidable fighting machine-the Sopwith Triplane. At the end of March the squadron flew south to Auchel, on the Third Army Front near Arras. Opposite them at Douai, once the home of Böelcke and Immelmann was the HQ of Manfred von Richthofen's Albatros D.III-equipped Jasta II. While the RFC squadrons with their obsolete equipment were being bloodily mauled, the naval Triplanes at least cowed the Jasta pilots and Little was by now a master of this highly manoeuvrable machine. Flying with another great Australian naval Triplane exponent, Flight Commander Charles Dawson Booker, who was credited with 29 victories, he got a Jasta II

Albatros over Lens on 7 April.[10] On 24 April he attacked a DFW C.V. German reconnaissance aircraft, put a bullet through its oil tank and then followed its glide down to a field behind the Allied lines. The German made a perfect landing but Little's triplane turned over on landing and the German pilot (who had been a Rhodes scholar at Oxford before the war) had to help his notional captor out of the upturned Sopwith, remarking 'it rather looks as if I shot you down, not me'. In spite of this humiliation, by 26 May Little's victory log totalled twenty-eight and by the end of July he had destroyed thirty-seven enemy aircraft. The DSO and Bar to his DSC were gazetted on 11 August 1917 and the Bar to his DSO on 14 September 1917.

In the summer of 1917 Little was recalled to RNAS Dover for instructional and administrative duties where he tried a new Sopwith Dolphin and a 'Spad'. He could not stay out of the fighting for long, however and was posted back to Naval Three, soon to become 203 Squadron RAF commanded by Raymond Collishaw. His appetite for air fighting was insatiable. When not sharpening his eye on the airfield's rabbits with a .22 rifle, he would lead offensive patrols with scant regard for danger. On one occasion he attacked a particularly effective German ack-ack battery near La Bassée by flying in at 7,000 feet, spiralling earthwards in a controlled 'falling leaf spin and finally flattening out at very near ground level to scatter the amazed gunners with machine-gun fire and then hedge-hop home. On the day Richthofen was killed (21 April 1918) Little, flying a Sopwith Camel picked off the rear-most aircraft in a formation of twelve from Jasta Böelcke. Six avengers turned angrily on Little's Camel and shot his controls away. The aircraft went down to within 100 feet of the ground before flattening out with a jerk. Little, having unstrapped his seat belt against standing orders, was thrown clear as the Camel ploughed into the ground north of the Forest of Nieppe. Two enemy aircraft followed him down to rake the wreck with fire, but Little was out and still fighting, blazing away with his Webley until some British infantry joined in with Lewis guns.

On 28 May Major Charles Booker, now Commanding Officer 201 Squadron RAF was summoned to the scene of a crash in a farm field where a Camel had come down in the French lines. He got a terrible shock. The pilot still at the controls was Little who was shot through both thighs and had bled to death in his cockpit.[11] The previous evening he had taken off in Camel B6318 in an attempt to intercept Gotha bombers making a night raid. It seems that he was mortally wounded by one of the Gothas' defensive gunners while blinded by a searchlight beam and crashed. He was 22 years old. Australia had lost its foremost fighter pilot. Little, who married in 1916 and left behind a young widow and a baby son was buried in Wavans cemetery.

The score of aerial victories RNAS 'Tripehound' ace, Roderic 'Stan' Dallas DSO DSC* is generally regarded as the second-highest by an Australian after Robert Little, but while his official score is commonly given as 39, claim-by-claim analyses list as few as 32 and other research credits him with over fifty, compared to Little's official tally of 47. Born at Mount Stanley a remote property outside Esk, in rural Queensland, to labourer Peter MacArthur Dallas and his wife Honora on 30 July 1891, Dallas showed an early interest in aviation. He travelled to England at his own expense following the outbreak of World War I and became a pilot in the

RNAS in August 1915. At 6 feet 2 inches tall Dallas would later surprise observers with his ability to fit into the cramped cockpits of fighter aeroplanes. Despite his size, he was considered a fine athlete with quick reflexes. Initially seeing action with 1 Naval Wing on the Western Front in Caudrons and Nieuport 11s, he was chosen to test one of the earliest Sopwith Triplanes. This became his favourite type and he achieved many victories with it during 1916-17, earning the DSO and the DSC and Bar.

Dallas became one of the best-known pilots of Sopwith Triplanes in the RNAS. He opened 1917 by setting an altitude record of 26,000 feet in the Triplane while testing a prototype oxygen set; he endured frostbite and oxygen intoxication in the process. By now 1 Wing's fighter squadron had been renumbered as 1 Squadron RNAS and had totally re-equipped with production Triplanes. It also moved airfields from Veurne in Belgium to Chipilly in France, leaving behind RNAS control by transferring to 14 Wing, 4th Brigade of the RFC. Formation flying became the order of the day, as the practice of fighter pilots soloing into combat dwindled. The last three weeks of March were also filled with Dallas's responsibilities for flight and gunnery testing. As British losses in the air began to mount during 'Bloody April', Dallas and his squadron moved airfields once again, to La Bellevue. They were thus positioned to take a prominent part in the subsequent Battle of Arras, where the intense aerial fighting saw Dallas add to his burgeoning score. The combat of 23 April became known as one of the classic air battles of the war. Dallas and his wingman Flight Sub-Lieutenant Thomas Grey Culling, New Zealand's first flying ace credited with six aerial victories, took on a squadron-sized formation of fourteen German aircraft, having gained an altitude edge over their foes. The naval aces exploited this edge by making quick diving attacks from opposite sides, culminating in short bursts of machine-gun fire. Using the Triplane's superior climbing ability, they would then bob back up to position themselves for the next assault. In contrast to the usual hit-and-run tactics of most dogfights, the RNAS duo launched at least twenty gunnery runs over 45 minutes. The Germans were forced progressively lower, into disarray and then chased back over their own lines. While they shot down three of the Germans, Dallas and Culling also achieved a more important outcome by blocking and then breaking up a determined enemy effort against the British ground offensive. The action led to the award of a Bar to the DSC for Dallas and a DSC for Culling, which were gazetted on 29 June.

By June 1917 Dallas had achieved over twenty victories in aerial combat. This experience and his leadership ability led to his appointment as commanding officer of 1 Naval Squadron on 23 June 1917. The unit had been forced to cut back its operational strength from eighteen aircraft to fifteen due to lack of pilot replacements and a shortage of spare parts for the aging Triplanes. It had also moved airfields, to an unprepared site at Bailleul. As a leader, Dallas made a point of shepherding new pilots through their first flights and even setting them up with their first victories by manoeuvring enemy aircraft into a good position for the rookie to take a shot. On the ground he proved to be an efficient organiser, designing and directing construction of the new air base. It was also during this time that he wrote a treatise on air combat tactics, extracts of which have survived. Both the air base layout and the treatise displayed his talent as a sketch artist. On

2 November 1 Squadron moved airfields and reverted to overall RNAS control. The first eight new Sopwith Camels arrived on 9 November as replacements for the Triplanes. Two days later Dallas was again mentioned in despatches, this time by Field Marshal Haig. After gaining its full complement of Camels, 1 Squadron was transferred to England and took up home defence duties at Dover. On 16 February 1918 Dallas led his squadron back to France, where it was based at Téteghem supporting units on operations along the Belgian coast. He commanded it for another six weeks, until 31 March.

On 1 April Dallas was promoted to major and given command of 40 Squadron RAF flying S.E.5s. The squadron boasted several aces in its ranks and its former RFC members were suspicious of Dallas's naval background. He was nevertheless able to overcome their misgivings and established himself as the new CO with his personal demeanour and courage; the nickname of 'Admiral' that they bestowed upon him was an affectionate one. Ten days after taking over, he had adapted well enough to his new mount with its inline engine to score his first victory with his new unit. His men also saw that he would not only look out for his rookie pilots, but would not shirk the dangers of ground attack sorties. His offhand attitude toward two leg wounds he received during a strafing mission on 14 April, after which he made 'a perfect landing', especially impressed his subordinates, as did his appreciation of all ranks for their hard work. He kept notes on his methods of attacking enemy aircraft, which often exploited their structural weaknesses and used them to tutor pilots under his command.

Dallas was briefly hospitalised with the wounds to his thigh and heel on 14 April, but sneaked out four days later to rejoin his squadron. His departure may have been spurred by news of the capture of his friend Richard Minifie. As soon as he was able, Dallas was flying again. By 26 April, he had increased his official score to 37 and been awarded the DSO for operations at Dunkirk. He had also several times been recommended for the Victoria Cross, but it was never approved. His casual attitude towards claiming victories was noted by a member of 40 Squadron, Cecil Usher, who related that Dallas once remarked of an opponent, '...he went down belching a lot of black smoke and after he had gone down someways one of his planes came off, but I didn't see him crash so I shan't claim him.' During a lull in the fighting at Flanders on 2 May Dallas took off in his S.E.5 to taunt his foes. He strafed the German base at La Brayelle to 'attract attention' before dropping a package on the aerodrome with a note reading, 'If you won't come up here and fight, herewith a pair of boots for work on the ground, pilots for the use of'. He then circled in mist until troops came to examine the bundle, whereupon he dropped two bombs and again shot up the base, causing 'general panic'. News of this singular exploit reportedly provoked laughter from Field Marshal Haig and General Sir Hugh Trenchard, two men not known for their sense of humour.

Dallas was raised to lieutenant colonel and appointed to the command of a wing, but would never see the message from headquarters that arrived on 1 June 1918 advising him of the promotion and ordering him to cease flying. He disappeared on a solo flight the same day. It was later learned that he had been killed over Liévin in northern France during combat with three Fokker Triplanes from Jagdstaffel 14, probably by its commander, Leutnant Johannes 'Hans' Werner for the sixth of his seven victories. Dallas was buried in Pernes.

Two leading AFC aces, also from 4 Squadron, were Captain Edgar James Kingston-McCloughry CB CBE DSO DFC* (23 kills) and Captain Elwyn Roy King DSO DFC MiD, who was the fourth highest-scoring Australian pilot of the war (22½ kills). Born Edgar James McCloughry on 10 September 1896, McCloughry joined the Australian Imperial Force in 1914 and served as a military engineer in Egypt and France before transferring to the RFC in December 1916. He graduated from flying training in August 1917 and was posted to 23 Squadron RFC on the Western Front. He was seriously injured in a crash shortly thereafter and, after recovering in hospital, was reassigned as a flight instructor. He was reassigned again in the summer of 1918 to the Australian Flying Corps. He destroyed most of his 21 aircraft and military balloons there in the last few months of the war, making him the 6th highest-scoring Australian ace.[12]

Born on 13 May 1894 at The Grove, near Bathurst, New South Wales, Roy King was the son of English-born Elizabeth Mary (Miller) King and Richard King, an Australian labourer. The youth attended public school and further educated himself in mechanical engineering via correspondence. Having been employed repairing bicycles, automobiles and farming equipment he was living in Forbes and working as a motor mechanic when he joined the Australian Imperial Force under the name Roy King on 20 July 1915. On 5 October King embarked for Egypt aboard HMAT *Themistocles*, as part of the reinforcements for the 12th Regiment of the 4th Light Horse Brigade at Heliopolis which was reassembling following service in the Gallipoli Campaign. The regiment was engaged in the defence of the Suez Canal during May 1916 and subsequently undertook patrols and sorties in the Sinai Desert as a light horseman. He transferred to the Australian Flying Corps on 13 January 1917 and on 18 April was posted to Britain as an air mechanic. He was assigned to a training squadron for flying instruction in August. On 15 October he gained his wings and officer's commission. Allocated to 4 Squadron AFC (also referred to as 71 (Australian) Squadron RFC by the British) in November 1917, King was posted to France for active duty on 21 March 1918.The same day, the Germans launched Operation 'Michael', the opening phase of the Spring Offensive.

4 Squadron was operating its Sopwith Camels in hazardous, low-altitude support of Australian ground troops when King arrived in France and he had little opportunity for air-to-air combat. The burly 6-foot-5-inch King - nicknamed 'Bo', 'Beau' or 'Bow' - also had problems landing the Camel; crammed into its small cockpit, his large frame impeded control stick movement. The resulting rough landings annoyed his commanding officer, Major Wilfred Ashton McCloughry, brother of ace Edgar James McCloughry. King's friend and fellow 4 Squadron pilot, Harry Cobby, recalled that 'there was some speculation that he might go home - but he proved himself an impressive pilot'. Cobby often took King on 'special missions' to make mischief with the Germans; 4 Squadron found that two-man patrols were generally able to lure enemy aircraft into a fight, whereas larger formations tended to deter engagements. On 14 May 1918 King shot down a two-seat German scout that was spotting for artillery between Ypres and Bailleul, but clouds prevented him from confirming its destruction. By 20 May, he had been credited with his first aerial victory, over a Pfalz D.III near Kemmel-Neuve Église.

He was promoted to lieutenant on 1 June. On 20 June he destroyed a German balloon over Estaires; although vulnerable to attack with incendiary bullets, these large observation platforms were generally well protected by fighters and anti-aircraft defences and were thus considered a dangerous but valuable target. Later that month he shot down two more aircraft, a Pfalz and a two-seat LVG, in the Lys region.

King registered his fifth victory, an LVG, after raiding Armentières on 25 July 1918. Four days later, he led a flight of six Camels from 4 Squadron escorting Airco D.H.9 light bombers in another raid on Armentières. In an action that the Australian official history highlighted as an 'example of cool and skilful air fighting', the D.H.9s completed their bombing mission while the Camels drove off an attacking force of at least ten German Fokkers, three of the Australians including King claiming victories, without any Allied losses. He destroyed a German two-seater on 3 August and another the following day, sharing the second with Herbert Watson. 4 Squadron was heavily engaged in the Allies' great offensive on the Western Front, launched with the Battle of Amiens on 8 August. King was credited with two victories - a balloon and an LVG - near Estaires during a bombing raid on 10 August. On 12 and 13 August the Camels of 4 Squadron operated in a massed formation over Flanders with the S.E.5s of 2 Squadron AFC, the former's two flights led by Cobby and King and the latter's by Adrian 'King' Cole and Roy Phillipps.[13] Pickings were scarce and 4 Squadron's only success came on the second day when King and his flight collectively destroyed a two-seat Albatros.

On 16 August 1918 King participated in a major assault against the German airfield at Haubourdin that resulted in thirty-seven enemy aircraft being destroyed on the ground. During the action, described by the official history as a 'riot of destruction', King set on fire a hangar housing four or five German aeroplanes. He also, according to 2 Squadron pilot Charles Copp, flew down Haubourdin's main street, waving as he went, his reason being that 'the girls in that village must have had a heck of a time with all that bombing and must have been terribly scared so I thought I'd cheer them up a bit'. By this time the Lille sector was largely clear of German fighters. The official history recorded that on 25 August, 'King went out alone as far as Don railway station, bombed it, machine-gunned a train and returned among the low clouds - all without seeing any enemy'. The only contact around this time was on 30 August, when King, Thomas Baker and another pilot shot down two DFWs near Laventie. On 1 September, King destroyed an observation balloon over Aubers Ridge. Three days later he shot down an LVG after attacking a train near Lille with Cobby. He was recommended for the DFC) on 8 September. The award, promulgated in The *London Gazette* on 3 December, cited his 'gallant and valuable service in bombing and attacking with machine gun fire enemy billets, trains, troops etc', during which 'he ensured success by descending to low altitudes, disregarding personal danger'. On 16 September, following a lull in aerial combat in the region, King destroyed a Fokker biplane over Lille. Around this time he was promoted to captain and flight commander. He took over 'A' Flight from Cobby, who had been posted to England. By the end of September, King's tally was eighteen. He registered his final victory in a Camel on 2 October, when he used bombs to send down his fourth balloon.

During October 1918 King converted with the rest of 4 Squadron to the upgraded Sopwith Snipe, whose larger cockpit was a better fit for him. He scored with the Snipe on both 28 and 29 October, the latter over Tournai, in what is frequently described as 'one of the greatest air battles of the war'. At Tournai, amid a confrontation involving over seventy-five Allied and German fighters, King evaded five enemy Fokkers that dived on him, before destroying an LVG in a head-on attack. The next day, he downed three Fokker D.VIIs, two without firing a shot. As he zoomed up from shooting one out of control, he cut off another. This second Fokker pulled up to avoid collision and toppled onto a third Fokker. One of the war's last air battles took place near Leuze on 4 November. King's destruction of two D.VIIs in the space of five minutes, the latter in flames, capped his combat career. His tally of seven victories with the Snipe in the closing days of the war made him the highest-scoring pilot in this type.

King's final wartime score of twenty-six included six aircraft driven down out of control, thirteen aircraft and four balloons destroyed and three other aircraft destroyed in victories shared with other airmen. King was recommended for a bar to his DFC, which was upgraded to the DSO and awarded on 3 June 1919. The recommendation noted his victories in the air and described him as having 'proved himself a very brilliant patrol leader' and as 'a magnificent example at all times to all pilots in the Squadron by his keenness on the ground and gallantry in the air which was of the highest possible order'. He was also belatedly mentioned in despatches in July 1919 for his wartime service.[14]

Captain Richard Pearman Minifie DFC** who was only twenty years old at the end of WWI was the AFC's youngest ace with a score of 21 victories. Seventeen of his victories were in 1917 and he was No. 1 (Naval) Squadron's highest-scoring ace on the Triplane. Born in Alphington, Victoria on 2 February 1898 to Englishman James Minifie, a flour miller and his Australian wife Beatrice Kate, he attended Melbourne Church of England Grammar School. Travelling to the United Kingdom, he enlisted in the RNAS in June 1916. Accepted for flight training, he completed his instruction in December and joined No. 1 (Naval) Squadron on the Western Front in January 1917. The unit re-equipped with the Sopwith Camel late in 1917, with Minifie going on to achieve a further four victories on the aircraft. On 17 March 1918 Minifie was forced to crash land in German-held territory near Houthulst Forest, Belgium after a duel with Jasta 47's Friedrich Ehmann. Minifie was captured by German forces at Roulers and taken as a prisoner of war; he spent the remainder of the war at prison camps in Karlsruhe and Clausthal. Roderic Dallas later wrote to Minifie's mother, informing her that Richard had been taken prisoner. In the letter he described Minifie as 'a brilliant pilot and air fighter' and stated that 'his aerial victories were gained by clean, clever fighting and he was always so modest about his great achievements'. Minifie was released at the end of the war and was demobilised as a captain in September 1919. Returning to Australia, he joined the staff of his father's flour milling business. He died in 1969 at the age of seventy-one.

Other Australian aces who served in British units included Alexander Augustus Norman Dudley 'Jerry' Pentland the fifth highest-scoring Australian ace of the war with 23 victories; Edgar Charles Johnston DFC (20 - 7 and 1 shared destroyed, 11 and 1 shared 'out of control') between his entry into the war and the war's end in 1918, making him the fifth highest-scoring Australian pilot of the war; Andrew King Cowper, MC** (19); Cedric 'Spike' Howell DSO MC DFC (19); Fred Parkinson Holliday DSO MC DFC AFC (17) the 11th highest-scoring Australian-born pilot of the war; and Allan Hepburn DFC (16).

Lieutenant Charles E. Kingsford-Smith MC, Australia's most famous aviator, was born in Brisbane on 9 February 1897. He enlisted in the AIF in February 1915 and, after a brief period in the artillery, was posted to the 2nd Division as a signaller. He served on Gallipoli and then in Egypt and France as a dispatch rider. In October 1916 Sergeant Kingsford-Smith transferred to the Australian Flying Corps. In March 1917 he was discharged from the AIF and commissioned as a 2nd lieutenant in the RFC. Having been promoted to flying officer, he was posted to 23 Squadron in France in July 1917. Shot down and wounded a month later, Kingsford-Smith was awarded the Military Cross, having shot down four German aircraft in his first month of operational flying. Kingsford-Smith was promoted to lieutenant in April 1918 and served as an instructor for the rest of the war. In the years after the war, he worked in varying capacities as a pilot, including a brief period as a stunt flyer in California, before joining the fledgling aviation industry in Australia. In 1927 he and his flying partner, Charles Ulm, became the first airmen to fly around Australia. The following year, with the support of wealthy businessmen and government grant money - Kingsford-Smith, Ulm and two Americans, Harry Lyon and Jim Warner, became the first airmen to cross the Pacific. The following August, Kingsford Smith and his crew flew the Southern Cross from Point Cook to Perth and, shortly afterwards, from Sydney to Christchurch, becoming the first airmen to cross the Tasman Sea. His next aerial adventure, a planned flight to England ended in disaster when he made a forced landing in remote north-western Australia. Rescued after more than two weeks in the wilderness, Kingsford-Smith and his crew resumed the journey, eventually breaking the record for a flight between Australia and England.

In England, he and Ulm purchased a fleet of four aircraft with which to open an inter-capital air service in Australia. Australian National Airways, as the company was called, commenced operations in January 1930. Business interests in Australia notwithstanding, Kingsford-Smith made an east-west crossing of the Atlantic, receiving a rousing welcome in New York in June 1930. In October he broke the record for a flight between England and Australia and in November was made an air commodore. In 1932 he received a knighthood for his services to aviation but he was dogged by business failures and periods of ill-health. In May 1935 he began a trans-Tasman airmail service. But for the bravery of his co-pilot who climbed out onto the wing of their aircraft over the Tasman Sea to repair a damaged engine, the inaugural flight would have ended in disaster. On 6 November 1935 he and J. T. Pethybridge, took off from England in an attempt to break yet another aviation record, but the pair were lost when their aircraft crashed into the sea off Burma.

Captain(later Air Vice Marshal) Adrian Lindley Trevor Cole MC DFC was born in Glen Iris, a suburb of Melbourne, to barrister and doctor Robert Cole and his wife Helen. He was educated at Geelong Grammar School and Melbourne Grammar School, where he was a member of the cadet corps. When World War I broke out in August 1914, Cole gained a commission in the Australian Military

Forces, serving with the 55th (Collingwood) Infantry Regiment. He resigned his commission to join the Australian Imperial Force on 28 January 1916, intending to become a pilot in the Australian Flying Corps and flew with 1 Squadron in the Middle East and 2 Squadron on the Western Front.

Posted to 1 Squadron (also known until 1918 as 67 Squadron RFC), 'King' Cole departed Melbourne aboard HMAT *Orsova* on 16 March 1916, bound for Egypt. He was commissioned a second lieutenant in June and began his pilot training in August. By the beginning of 1917, he was flying reconnaissance and scouting missions in Sinai and Palestine. He took part in an early example of Allied air-sea cooperation on 25 February, directing French naval fire against the coastal town of Jaffa by radio from his B.E.2. On 20 April Cole and fellow squadron member Lieutenant Roy Maxwell Drummond attacked six enemy aircraft that were threatening to bomb Allied cavalry, scattering their formation and chasing them back to their own lines. Both airmen were awarded the Military Cross for their actions; Cole's citation was published in a supplement to the *London Gazette* on 16 August 1917: 'For conspicuous gallantry and devotion to duty. With another officer he attacked and disorganised six enemy machines that were about to attack our cavalry with bombs. The engagement was continued until all six machines were forced to return to their lines. His skill and courage on all occasions have been worthy of the greatest praise.'

The day after the action that earned him the Military Cross, Cole was flying a Martinsyde G.100 'Elephant' over Tel el Sheria when he was hit by ground fire and forced to crash land behind enemy lines; after setting his aircraft alight he was picked up and rescued by Captain Richard Williams. On 26 June, following an eight-plane raid on Turkish Fourth Army headquarters in Jerusalem, Cole and another pilot suffered engine seizures while undertaking a similar rescue of a downed comrade; all three airmen were forced to walk through no man's land before being picked up by an Australian Light Horse patrol. Promoted to captain in August 1917, Cole was posted to France as a flight commander with 2 Squadron AFC (also known until 1918 as 68 Squadron RFC). Flying S.E.5 fighters on the Western Front, he was credited with destroying or sending out of control ten enemy aircraft between July and October 1918, making him an ace. In a single sortie over the Lys Valley on 19 August, Cole shot down two German fighters and narrowly avoided being shot down immediately afterwards, when he was attacked by five Fokker Triplanes that were being pursued by Bristol Fighters. On 24 September he led into battle a patrol of fifteen S.E.5s that destroyed or damaged eight German fighters over Haubourdin and Pérenchies, claiming one Pfalz D.III for himself.

Cole was awarded the DFC for his actions on 7 October 1918 when he led 2 Squadron through 'a tornado of anti-aircraft fire' in a major assault on transport infrastructure in Lille. During the raid he successfully bombed a goods engine and a troop train and put several anti-aircraft batteries out of action, before leading his formation back to base at low level. The announcement and accompanying citation for his decoration was gazetted on 8 February 1919: 'On 7th October this officer carried out a most successful flying raid on enemy railway lines and stations. The success of the attack was largely owing to his cool and determined leadership and our freedom from casualties was mainly due to the methodical manner in which he collected and reorganised the machines after the raid. He himself displayed marked initiative and courage in attacking troops and other objectives. Since May Captain Cole has destroyed four hostile machines. He became an ace, credited with ten victories and earned the Military Cross and the DFC. In 1921, he was a founding member of the RAAF.

One of the most amazing stories of the AFC was of Lieutenant Frank Alberry DCM who lost a leg as a member of the infantry prior to becoming a fighter pilot and scoring seven kills. Alberry was born on 29 September 1892 in Hobart, Tasmania, the son of G. F. Alberry. The younger Alberry lived in Port Arthur, Tasmania, when young. He worked his passage to England as a ship's engineer steward when a youth and enlisted in the British Army's Welch Regiment. After a year and a half's service, he deserted to return to Australia. On 24 August 1914, having received a free pardon for his prior desertion, Alberry joined the First Australian Imperial Force's 8th Battalion as an infantryman, at Broadmeadows, Victoria. On 19 October 1914 he embarked on a ship to sail from Australia to Egypt and from there, on 5 April 1915, he took ship for the Dardanelles. He landed in Anzac Cove and served in the Gallipoli Campaign. After being evacuated from Gallipoli, he was promoted to lance corporal on 27 December 1915 at Moudros. He arrived in Alexandria, Egypt on 7 January 1916 aboard the Empress of Britain. On 20 February Alberry was posted to the Machine Gun School at Ismailia, where he was promoted to corporal on the 26th. He gained a distinguished pass with the Lewis Gun at the Machine Gun School and on 15 March was promoted to sergeant in the Lewis Gun Section. On 26 March, he was sent to join the British Expeditionary Force on the Western Front in France, disembarking at Marseille on 31 March. On 25 July, he was commanding a section of four Lewis guns in the Battle of Pozières. When the 8th Battalion's Company 'C' was held up in its attack by the Germans, Alberry led his gunners in a flanking movement that dislodged the defenders. Following that, he took a Lewis gun forward into a shell crater to provide covering fire while the Battalion dug in. The next night, Sergeant Alberry again flanked the Germans with a machine gun while his battalion set up a strongpoint. Alberry then took over the stronghold and held it under fire for two days. He was being relieved from this post on 27 July when a bullet hit his right kneecap. His gallantry in action earned him the Distinguished Conduct Medal, which was gazetted on 20 October 1916.

On 7 August 1916 Alberry was evacuated to England aboard the hospital ship *Asturias* from Le Havre and admitted to the 1st Southern General Hospital in Stirchley, Birmingham where his right leg was amputated above the knee. He remained in hospital until 26 March 1917, when he was discharged. When healed, Alberry still wished to serve, so he resorted to the unusual step of gaining a personal audience with King George V to request a transfer to the RFC. The king assented and on 3 August 1917 Alberry began pilot training at the No. 1 School of Aeronautics in Reading. He was posted to 29 (Training) Squadron RFC at RAF Shawbury as a cadet on 13 September. Having successfully completed training despite his lack of a leg, he was appointed a flying officer on 6 November, with a commission as a second lieutenant in the AIF. He returned to France on 4 April 1918 and was posted to 2 Aeroplane Supply Depot. On 16 June he was posted to 2 Squadron AFC to fly the S.E.5a. On 14 August he was again wounded in action, spending four days at 18 Casualty Clearing Station suffering from a concussion. Alberry returned to his squadron, where between 16 September and 4 November he accounted for seven German first-line fighters - two Fokker Dr.Is and five Fokker D.VIIs. Alberry returned to Australia, leaving England on 20 November 1918. Once home, he was discharged at Melbourne on 6 March 1919. However he remained a member of the Reserve of Officers, gaining promotion to lieutenant on 1 October 1920 and eventually transferring to the retired list on 1 October 1925. He subsequently involved himself in the lumber business. In September 1939, on the outbreak of World War II, Alberry applied to join the Royal Australian Air Force Reserve and served as a recruiting officer from 11 October 1939 to 30 June 1942. Alberry died in 1969.

Captain, later Sir Ross Macpherson Smith KBE MC* DFC** AFC and his brother, Keith were the first pilots to fly from England to Australia, in 1919. Their father migrated to Western Australia from Scotland and became a pastoralist in South Australia. Their mother, the daughter of a pioneer from Scotland, was born near New Norcia, Western Australia. The boys boarded in Adelaide, at Queen's School and for two years, in Scotland. Ross enlisted in 1914 in the 3rd Light Horse Regiment, landing at Gallipoli 13 May 1915. In 1917 he volunteered for the Australian Flying Corps. He was later twice awarded the Military Cross and the DFC three times, becoming an air ace with eleven confirmed aerial victories. On 12 November 1919 he and brother Keith and Sergeant James Mallett ('Jim') Bennett and Sergeant Wally Shiers flew from Hounslow Heath aerodrome in a Vickers Vimy, eventually landing in Darwin on 10 December, taking less than 28 days, with actual flying time of 135 hours. The four men shared the £10,000 prize money put forward by the Australian government. On 13 April 1922 Ross Smith was killed (along with the recently commissioned Lieutenant Bennett) while testing a Vickers Viking amphibian aircraft which crashed in Byfleet soon after taking off from Brooklands. The jury returned a verdict of death by misadventure. The bodies were transported to Australia and Smith was given a state funeral and later buried on 15 June at the North Road Cemetery, Adelaide.

Herbert John Louis Hinkler DSM, better known as Bert Hinkler, was a pioneer Australian aviator (dubbed 'Australian Lone Eagle') and inventor. He designed and built early aircraft before being the first person to fly solo from England to Australia and the first person to fly solo across the Southern Atlantic Ocean. Hinkler was born on 8 December 1892 in Bundaberg, Queensland, the son of John William Hinkler, a Prussian-born stockman and his wife Frances. In his childhood, Hinkler would observe ibis flying near a lake at his school. After gaining an understanding on the principles of flight, he constructed and flew two gliders on beaches near his home town. He later met Arthur Burr Stone at a travelling show in Bundaberg and again at the Brisbane Exhibition where Hinkler worked with Stone to solve a problem with the 'Blériot', the world's first monoplane. In 1913, Hinkler went to England where he worked for the Sopwith Aviation Company, the beginning of his career in aviation. Hinkler served with the RNAS as a gunner/observer in Belgium and France, for which he was awarded the DSM. In 1918 he was posted to 28 Squadron RAF with which he served as a pilot in Italy. Hinkler was an 'exceptional mathematician and inventor' and 'made a lot of aviation instruments which were in use up until the Second World War.' For example, 'one was a gadget to correct drift as airplanes fly a little bit on their side, not straight ahead.' Furthermore, 'in WWI, Hinkler invented a machine gun adaptor for air gunners. Back then, when the biplanes were flying upside down in combat, the hot, ejected shells would fall and burn the chest of the gunners as they fired. Hinkler's invention had the ejected shells all flying off to one side instead.'

After the war, he worked as a test pilot for the aircraft manufacturer A.V. Roe in Southampton. The Australian Government offered £10,000 as a prize for the first flight to Australia; Hinkler entered, but his aeroplane crashed in Europe during a storm. In 1921 Hinkler shipped a tiny Avro Baby to Sydney. It was filled with fuel and flown non-stop to Bundaberg, Queensland a distance of 850 miles. During the 1920s he competed in numerous aviation events and set many records, among which was a non-stop flight from England to Latvia. He was a pilot of the British Schneider Trophy seaplane competitor. Hinkler flew the first solo flight between England and Australia, departing England in Avro Avian G-EBOV on 7 February 1928 and arriving in Darwin on 22 February and back in his home town of Bundaberg five days later. This reduced the England-Australia record from 28 days to just under 15½ days. The flight was little noticed before Hinkler reached India but then media interest intensified. One newspaper nicknamed him 'Hustling Hinkler' and he was the subject of the Tin Pan Alley song Hustling Hinkler Up in the Sky. For the flights in 1920 and 1928 Hinkler had already won two Britannia trophies and the gold medal of the Fédération Aéronautique Internationale. Hinkler is quoted as telling the Australian Prime Minister Stanley Bruce at this time: 'You know, one day, people will fly by night and use the daylight for sightseeing.' He was invited by the Speaker of the House of Representatives to be seated on the floor of the House in recognition of his achievement. After visiting the principal cities of Australia and returning to England, he was awarded the Air Force Cross for the finest aerial exploit of the year.

In 1931 came his most remarkable feat. Hinkler flew in a de Havilland Puss Moth from Canada to New York and then non-stop to Jamaica 1,500 miles, then to Venezuela, Guyana, Brazil and then across the South Atlantic to Africa; this part of the journey was done in extremely bad weather, but despite a tearing gale and practically no visibility for part of the way because of low and heavy clouds, he drifted a comparatively small distance off his course. From West Africa he flew to London. For this he was awarded the Segrave Trophy, the Johnston Memorial Prize and the Britannia Trophy for the most meritorious flying performance of the year. This was the first solo flight across the South Atlantic. He was only the second person to cross the Atlantic solo, after Charles Lindbergh.

Hinkler married in 1932 at the age of 39 and died less than a year later. On 7 January 1933, Hinkler left London Air Park, Hanworth in the Puss Moth in an attempt to break the flying record to Australia held by C. W. A. Scott of eight days twenty hours. Nothing more was heard of him until his body was discovered in remote countryside in the Tuscan Mountains. He was buried with full military honours on Mussolini's orders in the Protestant cemetery at Florence. He is remembered as being thoroughly courageous without being reckless and was successful in his amazing feats because he was practically faultless as a pilot and knew exactly what he and his machines could do.

Sir Peter Roy Maxwell Drummond KCB DSO* OBE MC rose from private soldier in World War I to air marshal in World War II. Born in Perth, Western Australia on 2 June 1894 to merchant John Maxwell Drummond and his wife Caroline, their son was registered as Roy Maxwell Drummond. He acquired the nickname 'Peter' during his schooling at Scotch College and formally adopted it as his first name in 1943. He served in the cadets and worked as a bank clerk before enlisting in the Australian Imperial Force on 10 September 1914. At 5 feet 7 inches in height, Drummond was judged too slight of build for the infantry and was instead assigned to the 2nd Stationary Hospital of the Australian Army Medical Corps as an orderly. In December 1914 Drummond's unit arrived in Egypt. He was sent to Gallipoli in April 1915 and served on a hospital ship, assisting surgeons in candlelit operations on the wounded. Drummond was evacuated later that year, suffering from dysentery. In December he applied for a transfer to the RFC and was discharged from the Australian Army in April 1916.

Following pilot training in the United Kingdom, Drummond received the rank of temporary second lieutenant and was attached to 1 Squadron AFC, which was based in Egypt. During the Sinai and Palestine Campaign, he took part in the air assaults that preceded the Battle of Magdhaba on 23 December 1916. He later wrote, 'The day before the Magdhaba battle, the whole crowd of us with all the bombs we could carry, went out. You couldn't see the place for smoke after we had left ... The Turks were retreating all the time and we had great sport coming down to about 50 feet and peppering them with machine guns ...' On 20 March 1917, Drummond, flying a B.E.2, was one of two pilots who strafed enemy troops threatening Lieutenant Frank McNamara as he rescued a downed Australian airman, the action for which McNamara was awarded his Victoria Cross. Drummond became a flight commander with 1 Squadron (numbered 67 Squadron RFC by the British) in May 1917. He was awarded the Military Cross in August for his 'skill and courage on all occasions' after he and Lieutenant Adrian Cole engaged and drove off six enemy aircraft that were attempting to bomb Allied cavalry. In October 1917 Drummond joined 111 Squadron RFC as a flight commander, with the temporary rank of captain. On 12 December he and observer/gunner John Knowles were escorting two Australian aircraft in his Bristol Fighter near Tul Karem, Palestine when they were spotted by three German Albatros scouts. Drummond attacked and destroyed all three of the enemy aircraft. This achievement earned him the DSO for his 'great skill and daring'.

On 27 March 1918, again near Tul Karem, Drummond and another pilot scrambled to attack a German scout. As his wingman dealt with the intruder, Drummond, flying a Nieuport, single-handedly engaged six other German aircraft that had suddenly appeared. After he had destroyed one and 'sent another down in a spin', Drummond developed engine trouble and had to land behind enemy lines. Finding his engine firing again, he took off before he could be captured by Turkish troops and gained a start over the four still-circling German scouts, 'who had also concluded that the fight was over'. Drummond was forced to land three more times in enemy territory - once in a cavalry camp where he 'carried away a line full of washing' with his undercarriage in his escape - before he shook off all but one of the pursuing fighters and landed safely behind Allied lines. He was awarded a Bar to his DSO for his 'gallant and successful' actions.

Drummond kept the temporary rank of captain when the RFC merged with the RNAS to form the Royal Air Force on 1 April 1918. He was given command of 145 Squadron RAF on 19 July 1918 and made acting major in September. He finished the war with eight victories and was twice mentioned in despatches. Between the wars Drummond served for two years in the Sudan and for four years in Australia on secondment to the RAAF, including a tour as Deputy Chief of the Air Staff. Based in Cairo at the outbreak of World War II, he was Air Marshal Sir Arthur Tedder's Deputy Air Officer Commanding-in-Chief RAF Middle East from 1941 to 1943. Drummond was twice offered command of the RAAF during the war but did not take up the position on either occasion. On 27 March 1945 Drummond was en route to Canada with other dignitaries to attend a ceremony marking the closure of the Empire Air Training Scheme. Their B-24 Liberator called Commando that was formerly the personal transport of Winston Churchill, disappeared near the Azores and all aboard were presumed killed.

Air Chief Marshal Sir William Gore Sutherland Mitchell, KCB CBE DSO MC AFC was also a victim of an air crash. Born in Sydney on 8 March 1888 he was commissioned into the Devonshire Regiment in 1906 and he spent his early military years as an infantry subaltern. He attended the Central Flying School in 1913, being awarded his Royal Aero Club Aviator's Certificate no. 483 on 17 May 1913, before becoming a pilot in the RFC. He saw rapid advancement, serving in turn as Officer Commanding 10 Squadron, 12th (Corps) Wing and 20 Group. Drummond continued to serve in the RAF following World War I. By June 1943 he was a temporary air marshal and appointed a Knight Commander of the Order of the Bath. In 1944 he turned down the position of Air Commander-in-Chief South East Asia Command. Air Marshal Sir Trafford Leigh-Mallory accepted it instead and died in an aircraft accident on his way to take up the post. On 27 March 1945 Drummond was en route to Canada with other dignitaries to attend a ceremony marking the closure of the Empire Air Training Scheme. His B-24 Liberator named *Commando* that was formerly the personal transport of Winston Churchill, disappeared near the Azores and all aboard were presumed killed.

The training squadrons that remained in England were highly praised for their ability to train, not only pilots, but ground staff, to an extremely high standard to keep up with the often urgent need at the front. 5 Squadron and 6 Squadron were stationed at No.1 Station Minchinhampton in Stroud, Gloucestershire and were disbanded in 1919. 7 Squadron and 8 Squadron were stationed at No 2 Station AFC, Leighton and were also disbanded in 1919.The after war report on the AFC showed an outstanding record of enemy casualties credited to the 4 combat squadrons during their time in the Middle East and France. To indicate the effectiveness, the following gives some idea of the total contribution of the AFC. Enemy aircraft destroyed; 517 Balloons destroyed: 33. Late in 1918 Nos. 2 and 4 Squadrons were designated 'Circus' squadrons, that is, offensive action roaming groups to engage and harass the enemy at will. 4 Squadron became the most famous and successful fighter squadron of the front, all told shooting down 199 German aircraft. After the cessation of hostilities, 4 Squadron hopped aerodromes in Belgium before arriving at Bickendorff, Cologne as part of the Allied Occupational Forces. The squadron was demobilised in February of 1919 and staged through England on the way to Australia. 4 Squadron was the highest scoring AFC squadron with a victory score of approximately 220. One of the most aggressive allied squadrons on the front the squadron's scoreboard from 1 July until the end of the war included nineteen enemy aircraft 'flamed', 57 'crashed, 36 OOC, seven driven down and 22 balloons destroyed.

2 Squadron was also successful by downing 185 enemy aircraft, however, the AFC casualties were heavy with the loss of 78 killed, 68 wounded and 33 taken prisoner.

On 21 March 1918 the Germans launched their mighty offensive and swept across the old Somme battlefields around Ste-Quentin. In early April 3 Squadron followed the Australian corps southwards to face the heavy German attacks on the area. They based themselves at Poulainville alongside the Australian Corps Headquarters at Bertangles. There, Owen Lewis, recovering from his wounds and back with 3 Squadron, wrote of going for a walk with George Best. Owen, finding that he and Best got along, agreed to fly together. When a thick winter fog set in, making flying difficult and keeping all but a few aircraft on the ground, it meant rest and another day of life. An entry in Lewis' diary on a day when bad weather prevented flying reveals his feelings about operations: 'This morning I was pleased when the weather was fairly dud - I am afraid I am always pleased when that is so.' His fears were justified. On 12 April, the day after he had teamed up with his new pilot, both men were killed in action on a photographic mission. Their aircraft's engine, which had caught fire on an earlier flight with a different crew, did so again. It is likely that a twisted camshaft caused the fire. Both were incinerated.

At his Melbourne home five days later news of Owen's death prompted scenes all too common in Australia during the war years. His brother Brian recalled that he and older sister Phyllis 'sobbed together … the foundation of our world had melted away.' For five more weeks Owen's letters continued to arrive and long afterwards there came in a thick brown envelope a photograph of the dead boy's grave.

On the ground the German offensive slowed and by May 1918 was defeated. In August the Allies launched what would prove to be their war-winning offensive. In the war's final months German airmen, now in dwindling numbers, were still capable of inflicting disaster on the Allies. On 5 September a 4 Squadron patrol of five aircraft was attacked by three formations of Fokkers, totalling about thirty aircraft at about 10,000 feet. The Australian leader signalled to avoid action and dived away. His four comrades, either not seeing the signal or being unable to escape the Germans, were shot down. Only one survived to become a prisoner.

Following the death in action on 21 April 1918 of Rittmeister Manfred Von Richthofen, Commander of the 'Flying Circus', the Imperial German Air Service went into decline, but their airmen fought on regardless of the lack of equipment, fuel and ammunition. With the German aircraft lacking vital spare parts, many were caught on the ground and on 17 August 1918 Captain Allan Murray-Jones of Caulfield East, Victoria, a 21 year-old pharmacist prior to enlisting on 6 January 1916, led nineteen aircraft of 2 Squadron on a raid of German airfields near Lille in France, resulting in 37 aircraft being destroyed.[15] The next day 2 Squadron again attacked the German airfield near Lomme, destroying a further seventeen aircraft.

By the end of 1918 the AFC, the RFC and the French Air Force dominated the skies of Southern France. In October 4 Squadron replaced its Camels with Sopwith Snipes. In these aircraft the squadron destroyed thirty German machines in the last five days of the month. On one of these late October days the Australians fought in one of the war's largest air battles, when fifteen 4 Squadron Snipes encountered sixteen Fokkers. 'Bo' King shot down a German two-seater that crossed his path as he dived away from five pursuers. George Jones led three Snipes into an attack on ten Fokkers, destroying two. Arthur Palliser shot down three. Other Australians also claimed victories; ten Fokkers in all for the loss of Percy Sims. On 30 October in a similar fight 'Bo' King fought off four Germans. Zooming 'up through their formation' he turned in front of the highest enemy machine, which he had not noticed previously. It fell over on its back to avoid a crash but struck a second Fokker then climbing after King. Both fell to earth. In the same fight Captain Thomas Baker, the 21-year-old, three-year veteran of ground and aerial combat, shot down his twelfth victim.

The AFC kept up the pressure on the Imperial German Air Service until the last days of the war; the last three casualties of the AFC occurring on 4 November 1918 when 4 Squadron's Snipes escorted 2 Squadron on an attack against the German aerodrome at Chapelle-à-Wattines. Leading the formation back across the lines after the raid, the Snipes engaged twelve Fokkers of the famous 'Jasta Böelcke' claiming four, including two victories by King.[16] When the Australians reformed after a few brief, chaotic minutes of battle, four were missing, among them Captain Baker MM* who was last seen diving and firing on a Fokker; Lieutenant Arthur John Palliser, a 28-year old Tasmanian who destroyed a total of six Fokker DR.VIIs and a balloon and Lieutenant P. W. Symons. The German 36-victory ace Karl Bolle claimed all four Sopwith Snipes in the encounter. Baker's death preceded the armistice on the eleventh day of the eleventh month 1918 by seven days. He was one of 175 AFC personnel to have lost their lives during the war. In February 1919, he was posthumously awarded the DFC. In far-away Adelaide, his home town, a pair of stained-glass windows dedicated to his memory flank the baptistery of St. John's Church of England.

As the only Australian unit in the British Army of Occupation, 4 Squadron crossed the German border on 7 December 1918 and spent more than two months at Cologne. 2 Squadron remained near Lille until demobilisation and 3 Squadron ran an aerial postal service between various army and corps headquarters.

By late February 1919, having handed over their machines and stores, the Western Front squadrons went to England before embarking for home in May. 1 Squadron preceded them, leaving Egypt in early March. The AFC would remain part of the Australian Army until 1921, when it was re-established as the independent RAAF.

Endnotes Chapter 10

1 From a population of fewer than five million, 416,809 men enlisted, of which over 60,000 were killed and 156,000 wounded, gassed, or taken prisoner.

2 Lieutenant Francis Ryan 'Frank' Smith was wounded on 8 July. On 10 November he was shot down by ground fire behind German li nes but was not captured. His sixteenth and final aircraft destroyed occurred on 14 October, which earned him the DFC. His citation, in part, said: Leading a patrol of five machines, he saw a formation of twelve Fokker D.VIIs above him. Relying on the co-operation of another higher formation of Bristol machines, he deliberately manoeuvred his formation into a disadvantageous position in order that our higher patrol might be able to attack the enemy while the latter's attention was concentrated upon destroying his formation. The stratagem was entirely successful, with the result that two enemy machines were destroyed and two others were believed to crash. The Fokkers were then reinforced by eight more machines and in the ensuing combat Lieutenant Smith shot down one in flames, his patrol destroying two others for no loss to the Squadron.

3 He returned to service during World War II with the Royal Australian Air Force. Mustard was also responsible for the first aerial survey of Australia's Barrier Reef.

4 Borton, born 20 September 1886 saw active service on the Western Front, in Palestine and in Iraq. On 7 June 1915, while engaged in aerial combat, he received a bullet wound to the head and neck. Although the injury was severe, Borton and his observer Captain Anthony Marshall managed to bandage the wound. Despite severe loss of blood, Borton kept control of his aircraft, completing the reconnaissance sortie and landing safely. He was later awarded the DSO for his actions. Borton's recovery was prolonged. In early July, he was still judged to be 'not yet out of danger' and it was not until late October 1915 that he returned to duty. Air Vice Marshal Amyas Eden Borton CB CMG DSO AFC died on 15 August 1969.

5 Armageddon is the Anglicised version of the Hebrew term Har-Megiddo. Megiddo is a settlement/town in the middle of Israel/Palestine just on the Israeli side of the northwest tip of the West Bank.

6 In later years Williams, the first Australian graduate of the Point Cook Flying School, born in Moonta, South Australia would become Air Marshal Sir Richard Williams RAAF.

7 The Albatros D.5a forced down by Sandy and Hughes is preserved today in the AWM Canberra.

8 Captain Cobby led the AFC fly-past over London on ANZAC Day 1919 before returning to Australia and was discharged from the AIF on 24 July. He married Hilda Maude Urban on 24 April 1920 at Caulfield, Victoria. Acclaimed a national hero, Cobby transferred to the newly formed Royal Australian Air Force in 1921 and rose to the rank of wing commander. Retiring from the Air Force in 1946, Cobby served with the Department of Civil Aviation until his death on Armistice Day in 1955.

9 After a spell in civilian life following the war, Malley joined the RAAF in 1925, serving with 3 Squadron. He became an aviation adviser to China in 1931 and worked closely with Madame Chiang Kai-shek, Soong Mei-ling, from 1937. Malley was able to observe air tactics in the Sino-Japanese War at first hand, though his reports were given little weight in Australia. Returning home in 1940, he served in intelligence roles with the RAAF and later the Commonwealth government. After the war he bought a plantation in Fiji, where he died in 1961.

10 Born in Royal Tunbridge Wells, Kent Booker spent part of his youth in Australia, attending the Grammar School in Melbourne from February 1908 to December 1911.

11 On 11 August 1917, after victory 23, leading German ace, Adolf, Ritter von Tutschek was severely wounded in the shoulder by Flight Lieutenant Booker. If Viktor Schobinger had not intervened and shot Booker down, Tutschek would probably have been killed. (On 15 March 1918 Lieutenant H. B. Redler of 24 Squadron shot down and killed von Tutschek). Booker was KIA near Amiens on 13 August 1918 while leading a novice pilot on an orientation tour of their aerial battlefield. The two Camel pilots ran into a formation of at least six expert pilots from Jagdgeschwader 2. Booker tackled them single-handedly to cover the other pilot's retreat. It was he who verified Booker's final three victories. However, Jasta 12's ace Leutnant Ulrich Neckel finally shot Booker down. Booker had claimed 29 victories; he shared in the capture of two enemy

aeroplanes; destroyed ten, including six victories shared with other pilots; and drove down 17 'out of control', including five shared victories.

12   Edgar James McCloughry left the AFC in August 1919 and pursued a career as an engineer in the United Kingdom before joining the RAF in 1922. He served there in a strategy-planning capacity throughout WWII. In 1940, under the influence of Lord Beaverbrook, he circulated a series of anonymous memos which were highly critical of senior RAF figures; in response, he was posted to South Africa and by the end of the year the Chief of the Air Staff and several other commanders had been replaced. Air Vice Marshal McCloughry retired from the RAF in 1953 and died in 1972 in Edinburgh.

13   Born in New South Wales but raised in Western Australia, Roy Cecil Phillipps MC* DFC (1 March 1892-21 May 1941) joined the Australian Imperial Force as an infantryman in April 1915, seeing action at Gallipoli and on the Western Front. Wounded twice in 1916, he transferred to the AFC and, having falsified his age, was accepted for pilot training in May 1917. He achieved fifteen victories in aerial combat, four of them in a single action on 12 June 1918. A grazier between the wars, he joined the RAAF in 1940 and was killed in a plane crash the following year.

14   Returning to Australia in 1919, King spent some years in civil aviation before co-founding a successful engineering business. He joined the RAAF following the outbreak of World War II and held several training commands, rising to the rank of group captain shortly before his sudden death in November 1941 at the age of forty-seven.

15   By the end of the war, he had been awarded the Military Cross, DFC* and a MiD on three separate occasions. He arrived back in Australia on 16 June 1919.

16   Returning to Australia in 1919, King spent some years in civil aviation before co-founding a successful engineering business. He joined the RAAF following the outbreak of World War II and held several training commands, rising to the rank of group captain shortly before his sudden death in November 1941 at the age of forty-seven.

Chapter 11

The 'Bloody Paralyser'

Handley Page produced a series of heavy bombers for the Royal Navy to bomb the German Zeppelin yards, with the ultimate intent of bombing Berlin in revenge for the Zeppelin attacks on London. Handley Page had been asked by the Admiralty to produce a 'bloody paralyser of an aeroplane'. These aircraft included the O/100 of 1915, the O/400 of 1918 and the four-engined V/1500 with the range to reach Berlin. The V/1500 had only just entered operational service as the war ended in 1918.

The phrase had originated from Commander Charles Rumney Samson (8 July 1883-5 February 1931), one of the first four officers selected for pilot training by the Royal Navy and the first person to fly an aircraft from a moving ship. He also commanded the first British armoured vehicles used in combat. Transferring to the Royal Air Force on its creation in 1918, Air Commodore Charles Rumney Samson CMG DSO & Bar AFC held command of several groups in the immediate post-war period and the 1920s.

On the evening of 14/15 April 1916, 26-year old Squadron Commander Joseph Ruscombe Wadham Smyth-Pigott, the youngest son of the late Mr. Cecil Smyth-Pigott, of Brockley Court, Somerset, led a raid on Constantinople the Turkish capital (now Istanbul), by four pilots flying B.E.2Cs, which had been shipped out to Moudros, a small Greek port on the Mediterranean island of Lemnos, referred to by 'Tommies' as 'Mudros'. Educated at the Oratory School, Joseph Smyth-Pigott served with the RNAS and the RAF, primarily in the Eastern Mediterranean. For his wartime service he would be twice awarded the DSO, four times mentioned in despatches and the French Croix de Guerre. The three other pilots were Squadron Commander Kenneth Stevens Savory, Flight Sub-Lieutenant Richard Sebastian Willoughby Dickinson and Isaac Henry 'Jack' Barnato. 'Jack' was born at 36 Curzon Street in Mayfair on 7 June 1894, the son of financier and rogue, Barney Isaacs who made his first fortune in diamonds in South Africa and returned to England to become king of the market in gold shares ('kaffirs'). 'Jack' Barnato applied to join the military but was initially rejected, with no reason given. It may, however, have been due to him listing himself as head of household with the care of his widowed mother. Undaunted, he tried again and on 15 September 1914 this time was accepted. He earned his Aviator's Certificate at RNAS Eastbourne on 20 August 1915.

The four intrepid pilots started out on their 360-mile flight in fine weather that soon deteriorated into rain and thunderstorms. Savory dropped proclamations and went down to 500 feet in an attempt to locate the Zeitunlik Powder Works, his primary target. These works were seven miles from the entrance to the Bosporus, with the Demirkhan gun foundry one mile to the east, marked by a huge chimney. He was heavily fired upon and his aircraft received two hits. Spotting an airfield he dropped eight incendiary bombs on the hangars, causing a fire and returned to base. Dickinson dropped his eight bombs near the powder works and set off back, meeting strong head winds over the island of Marmara. Exhausted physically and with fuel low, he came down off Cape Xeros near Admiralty Trawler 348 and was rescued, with parts of his aircraft being salved. Smyth-Pigott and Squadron Commander Savory were awarded the DSO.[1]

Now, a year later, on 13 March 1917, having assured the Air Department of his confidence in the new Handley Page 0/100 type, Squadron Commander Savory DSO was recalled from No. 2 Wing RNAS in the Aegean Theatre and placed on the naval Special Service List to test the possibility of ferrying one of the latest and largest of the new British bombers to the Aegean Theatre for strikes on Constantinople, where the ex-German battle cruiser *Goeben* and light cruiser *Breslau* were docked. *Goeben* was the second of two Moltke-class battle cruisers of the Imperial German Navy, launched in 1911 and named after the German Franco-Prussian War veteran General August Karl von Goeben. SMS *Breslau* was a Magdeburg-class cruiser of the Imperial German Navy, built in the early 1910s. Following her commissioning, *Breslau* and the battle cruiser *Goeben* were assigned to the Mittelmeerdivision (Mediterranean Division) in response to the Balkan Wars. After evading British warships in the Mediterranean to reach Constantinople, *Breslau* and *Goeben* were transferred to the Ottoman Empire in August 1914, to entice the Ottomans to join the Central Powers in World War I. The two ships, along with several other Ottoman vessels, raided Russian ports in October 1914, prompting a Russian declaration of war. The ships were renamed *Midilli* and *Yavûz Sultân Selîm*, respectively and saw extensive service with the Ottoman fleet, primarily in the Black Sea against the Russian Black Sea Fleet.

Handley Page had originally been asked to produce a floatplane version for the highly secret mission since the route involved much over-water flying, but the firm did not consider this practicable and instead, the O/100 was selected. The design of the O/100, the forerunner of the much better known O/400, began shortly after the outbreak of war as a result of meetings between the Royal Navy's Director of the Air Department, Captain (later Commodore) Murray F. Sueter and Frederick Handley Page. Sueter requested 'a bloody paralyser of an aircraft' for long-range bombing. The bomber could carry a bomb load comprising sixteen 112lb bombs, was armed with up to five free-mounted Lewis machine guns in nose, amidships and ventral positions and had a top speed approaching 85 mph. The prototype O/100, with an enclosed cabin for the crew, flew for the first time at Hendon on 18 December 1915. Three more prototypes followed and deliveries of the O/100 production aircraft that were built for the RNAS began in September 1916. The first O/100s deployed to France were received by 7A Squadron of the 5th Naval Wing RNAS at Dunkirk in November 1916. The third O/100 for the RNAS was delivered to the enemy intact on 1 January 1917, due to a navigational error.[2] In March 1917 difficulty was being experienced in the cooling of the 266 hp Rolls-Royce Eagle II engines, powering the new Handley Page bombers. Apart from a solitary night raid on a railway junction at Moulins-lès-Metz by an O/100 of the Third Wing on 16/17 March, the O/100s were at first employed in their original intended role of overseas patrols off the Belgian coast, Later they concentrated almost exclusively on night-bombing raids against U-boat bases, rail centres and Gotha aerodromes.

Briefed by the Air Department of the Admiralty, Squadron Commander Savory DSO was told of his appointment to the unique venture and was posted to the O/100 squadron at Manston to assess the feasibility of a 2,000-mile flight. This unnumbered squadron, acting as a depot for the RNAS heavy bomber units based in France, allotted Savory No.3124 for his flight trials. Earmarked for Davis gun trials originally planned to be standard fitting, No. 3124 came straight from the Cricklewood works to RNAS Hendon to be prepared in the utmost secrecy for its flight out east. As well as hammocks and rations for crew comfort at stages along the route, No.3124 was to carry spares including the stripped-down parts of a Rolls-Royce Eagle IV engine and a four-bladed propeller; the latter, too bulky for stowage, had to be strapped on the fuselage top.

Savory's crew had been carefully selected and were: Flight Lieutenant Henry McClelland DSC, 2nd pilot; Lieutenant P. T. Rawlings RNVR, navigator; Chief Petty Officer J. L. Adams, engineer/fitter; Leading Mechanic B. Cromack, rigger/carpenter. Ready on 22 May 1917, their 0/100 was flown to Manston, where Savory collected final intelligence on the airfields en route and was in turn briefed to bring the information up to date. He was to proceed at the earliest possible date and the aircraft was readied that night. With perfect weather next morning, Savory left Manston at 1030 hours and touched down at Villacoublay on the outskirts of Paris three and a half hours later. He was told by the French authorities that in wet weather portions of the field became marshy and these areas were staked out with flags, but it was always prudent to land near to the sheds.

With fair weather holding, Savory and his crew set off next morning on the longer stage to Fort Bron, a large airfield near Lyons suitable for landing on any part. The weather then deteriorated and a day was wasted before the next stage when visibility was poor, particularly along the Rhône Valley. The airfield at Fréjus proved to be very poor and quite unsuitable for heavy aircraft, the soil being soft sand and marsh and which flooded when the wind blew in from the sea. A three-day wait until the 29th was necessary before the leg to Pisa in Italy. Following a coastal route, the Handley Page was subjected first to a beam and then a head wind. At times the aircraft was driven down to 400 feet above the water's surface. At least the landing was easy. Pisa had two airfields, San Giusto and Coltano, the latter being described as having a perfect surface.

Next day the stage to Rome was made in continuous rain. Good visibility was needed for landing at its Centocelle aerodrome as there was a high Marconi transmitting tower sited near the perimeter. Fine weather the following morning led to the flight to Naples and the Campo di Marti aerodrome. Savory reported, 'Has a good surface, but is surrounded by trees and houses. On this day it also had sheep and cattle and hayricks on it.' Mist, typical of Naples, caused a further delay. While there, to Savory's horror, the arrival of the Handley Page was reported in the Italian newspapers and repeated in the British press. It was inevitable that German intelligence would pick up the reports, but at least its final destination was not reported and its importance might not be realised. It was 3 June before the flight across the toe of Italy to Otranto was made. There the RNAS had recently opened an airfield in connection with the naval barrage across the Strait, established to pen the Austrian fleet in the Adriatic. The field was small with a rough stony surface and was shortly afterwards abandoned for another site. On the next stage the mountains of Albania proved higher than charted and the loaded aircraft could not climb over them. The aircraft returned to Otranto where some of the spares were off-loaded for forwarding by ship. The mountains were eventually crossed on 7 June with a landing at Thessalonika before flying on to Marsh aerodrome on Lemnos in the region close to the salt pans on the west of the island, which was reached the next day. In all, 1,955 statute miles had been covered in 31½ hours' flying time, without so much as changing one of the Lodge sparking plugs in the engines. For the bombing of the warships, a torpedo attack had been mooted but discarded in favour of 112lb bombs, the largest in the theatre, as it was thought that while in harbour the ships would be protected by anti-torpedo nets.

In the afternoon of 3 July the 0/100 was bombed up in preparation for an attack that night. Shortly after dark No.3124 took off on its first operational mission but on its flight northward it flew into a hot wind from the south, where during the day the air had shimmered in the heat reflected from sandy desert wastes. The balmy air caused the engines to overheat and the loaded aircraft lost height rapidly. Savory was forced to drop a few of his bombs to prevent hitting the water. He then set a course that would take him over the enemy positions at Bolayir, a town in the Gelibolu district of Çanakkale Province, on the Gallipoli Peninsula in the European part of Turkey, where he dropped the remainder of his bombs.

Savory was taking no chances with his valuable and irreplaceable aircraft. The next night conditions were not quite right and he could afford to wait. So far it was assumed that the enemy were unaware of the presence of the threat. Even if Turkish troops had spotted the aircraft that warm starry night, it is unlikely that they knew a Handley Page. In any case, a number of B.E.2c's and Henri Farmans had been sent out over the Turkish lines that night to confuse the defences. Only if an aircraft had penetrated 100 or more miles into their territory would the Turks be suspicious and the Handley Page had turned back after barely an hour's flight. The airship shed at Moudros was used for the partial hangarage of the O/100. The frames either side of the canvas hangar were also covered canvas and used as wind-breaks when airships were put into or removed from the building.

Weather reports for 5 July were favourable and the aircraft was bombed up. The crew boarded, the engines were revved up, the ground crew dragged away the chocks and the Handley Page rolled forward; then bang went one of the massive tyres and the giant machine slewed round. Savory immediately cut the engines and the flight abandoned. Quickly repaired, it was hoped it would be a case of third time lucky after take-off the following night, but halfway to Constantinople bad weather forced Savory to turn back.

Finally, on the evening of 9/10 July a start was made before nightfall and shortly before midnight, in the light of the moon, Goeben and Breslau were located in Stenia Bay near Constantinople. Savory circled three times before attacking from 800 feet. The first salvo of four 112lb bombs fell among adjacent moored destroyers and submarines, causing a fire and the second salvo of four appeared to hit Goeben just forward of amidships. Turning towards the upper waters of the Golden Horn, Savory dropped two bombs from 1,300 feet at the SS *General,* reputed to be the German liaison Headquarters and the final two bombs were aimed at the Turkish War Ministry. Up to this time the defences had been taken by surprise and not until the aircraft was setting course for base was sporadic anti-aircraft fire sent up by the enemy. Records indicate that the Handley Page landed back at Moudros at 0340 hours. Reports filtering back from Turkish agents reported that a destroyer, the *Yadighiar-i-Milet,* had been sunk (a Bounty of £350 was awarded for the destruction of the Turkish destroyer) and a transport damaged, but that *Goeben* had not been hit. Bombs had fallen near the SS *General* and a bookshop near the Turkish War Office had been destroyed. A total of twenty-nine people were killed and five wounded.[3]

Following this attack the Handley Page was given a complete overhaul. A major problem with the aircraft was its tyres which wore quickly under the great of the fully loaded machine on the stony airfield surface. No further spares were available in the Aegean so the worn tyres were reinforced with fabric. On 4 August it was intended to use the aircraft for attacks on Bandirma in conjunction with a bombing flight of Henri Farmans but three tyres burst on an attempted takeoff. Tyres from a Short bomber were fitted to No.3124 for a second attempt on Bandirma in the early hours of 7 August. Dumps and warehouses around the harbour area were the target and the explosion caused by one bomb rocked the aircraft. The town was blacked out and there was no anti-aircraft gunfire - only rifle fire. For this attack there was a change of crew, the original crew members having been recalled for duty in Handley Page squadrons in France. Local personnel took over. Flight Lieutenant John William Alcock was at the controls with Flight Lieutenant S. H. Gaskell and Sub-Lieutenant A. E. Sole ex-HMS *Ark Royal* based at Lemnos, navigating and observing. The same day enemy aircraft had set out from Suvla Salt Lake airfield on the Aegean coast of the Gallipoli peninsula in European Turkey, south of the Gulf of Saros to bomb the RNAS station on Imbros (at the time under Greek administration and named Imvros). Alcock passed one aircraft in flight on his way back.

Alcock was born on 5 November 1892 at Basford House on Seymour Grove, Firswood, Manchester. He attended St. Thomas's Primary School in Heaton Chapel, Stockport and Heyhouses School in Lytham St. Anne's. He first became interested in flying at the age of 17. His first job was at the Empress Motor Works in Manchester. In 1910 he became an assistant to Works Manager Charles Fletcher, an early Manchester aviator and Norman Crossland, a motor engineer and founder of Manchester Aero Club. It was during this period that Alcock met the Frenchman Maurice Ducrocq who was both a demonstration pilot and UK sales representative for aero engines made by the Italian Spirito Mario Viale. Ducrocq took Alcock on as a mechanic at the Brooklands aerodrome, Surrey where he learned to fly at Ducrocq's flying school, gaining his pilot's licence there in November 1912. Alcock then joined the Sunbeam Motor Car Company as a racing pilot. He took part in the London to Manchester flight competition in 1913 and by summer 1914 he was proficient enough to compete in a Hendon-Birmingham-Manchester and return air race, flying a Farman biplane. He landed at Trafford Park aerodrome and flew back to Hendon the same day. At the outbreak of World War I, Alcock joined the RNAS as a warrant officer instructor at Eastchurch. It was whilst at Eastchurch that Alcock received his commission as a flight sub-lieutenant in December 1915. In 1916 he was transferred to a squadron operating on Lemnos. While stationed at Moudros he conceived and built the Alcock Scout, a fighter aircraft built to his own design round a Benz engine taken from a German twin-engined bomber brought down six months earlier in Macedonia. It was reputed to be 20 mph faster than any other British machine!

On 1 September 1917, again with Alcock and Gaskell, but this time with engineer Warrant Officer S. J. Wise aboard, the Handley Page set out to bomb Adrianople. Off Samothraki a submarine was sighted and two delayed-action bombs were dropped as it submerged. Passing Kuleli Burgas, heavy anti-aircraft fire was met and a bomb was aimed at the battery. At Adrianople a variety of targets was attacked, including the railway bridge over the River Arda, warehouses, the station and railway workshops and a fort. Fires caused by the bombs could still be seen by the crew from sixty miles distant on their homeward leg. Altogether sixteen 6.5lb high-explosive and twenty 16lb Carcass incendiary bombs had been expended.

The Turks, now fully cognisant that their major towns were threatened, had finally latched on to Moudros as the base for the Handley Page. While the bomber was absent on the Adrianople raid, an air attack by seven aircraft was launched on Moudros, spread over 75 minutes. Bombs were dropped on the salt lake, presumably in mistake for Marsh aerodrome. Sixteen bombs also fell on the base depot, damaging two aeroplanes in their cases, pumps and a searchlight engine. There were no casualties.

On 30 September Alcock was taking a bath when the alarm sounded. His 'Alcock Scout' was just tested, the motors running warm and he jumped in and took off! He attacked three enemy aircraft, forcing two to crash into the sea. For this action he was awarded the DSC. After returning to base he then piloted 0/100 No.3124 with Flight Lieutenant Hugh R. Aird of Toronto, commanding 'A' Flight of No.2 Wing at Thasos, as second pilot together with the engineer Wise, to bomb railway stations on both sides, European and Asiatic, of the Bosporus. After ninety minutes' flying an engine failed near Gallipoli and Alcock was forced to jettison his bombs and turn back. After flying on a single engine for more than sixty miles, that engine failed and the aircraft ditched near the coast in the Gulf of Xeros, five miles north of Sulva Bay. For nearly two hours while the aircraft floated, Very signal lights were fired to alert nearby British destroyers, but to no avail and when the aeroplane finally began to sink they swam for an hour to reach the enemy-held shore. All three were taken prisoner next day by the Turkish forces and then, ironically, taken to Constantinople. Alcock remained a prisoner of war until the Armistice and retired from the RAF in March 1919.

Meanwhile at Moudros, where No.3124 was declared overdue at dawn on 1 October, aeroplanes were sent up in different directions, bombed up to combine anti-submarine patrolling with a search for the missing 0/100. All that was found was a strut that was picked up off Imbros by a patrol boat, indicating that the Handley Page was probably not in enemy hands. Then local intelligence picked up from newspapers for 3 October the report: 'In the Gulf of Xeros an English aeroplane was compelled to come down by anti-aircraft fire from our land batteries. The crash which was composed of three men fell into our hands.'

The primary object of disabling *Goeben* and *Breslau* had failed as both ships put to sea later and the RNAS made further attacks on the two vessels with D.H.4s which started to reach the theatre in late 1917. What was achieved was the diverting of German and Turkish aircraft and anti aircraft guns to the protection of Constantinople and other Turkish towns that might otherwise have been used on the Palestinian Front.[4]

On 20 January 1918, *Midilli* and *Yavûz Sultân Selîm* left the Dardanelles under the command of Vice Admiral Hubert von Rebeur-Paschwitz, who had replaced Souchon the previous September. Rebeur-Paschwitz's intention was to draw Allied naval forces away from Palestine in support of Turkish forces there. Outside the straits, in the course of what became known as the Battle of Imbros, the two Ottoman ships surprised and sank the monitors Raglan and M28 which were at anchor and unsupported by the dreadnoughts that should have been guarding them. Rebeur-Paschwitz then decided to proceed to the port of Moudros;[5] there the British pre-dreadnought battleship *Agamemnon* was raising steam to attack the Turkish ships. While en route, *Midilli* struck a total of five mines and sank; *Yavûz* hit three mines as well and was forced to beach to avoid sinking. Three hundred and thirty of *Midilli's* crew were killed in her sinking, 162 survivors were rescued by British destroyers. Only 133 men were rescued from the ship. In 1936 *Yavuz Sultan Selim* she was officially renamed TCG *Yavuz (Ship of the Turkish Republic Yavuz)*; she carried the remains of Mustafa Kemal Atatürk from Istanbul to İzmir in 1938. Yavuz remained the flagship of the Turkish Navy until she was decommissioned in 1950. She was scrapped in 1973, after the West German government declined an invitation to buy her back from Turkey. She was the last surviving ship built by the Imperial German Navy and the longest-serving dreadnought-type ship in any navy.

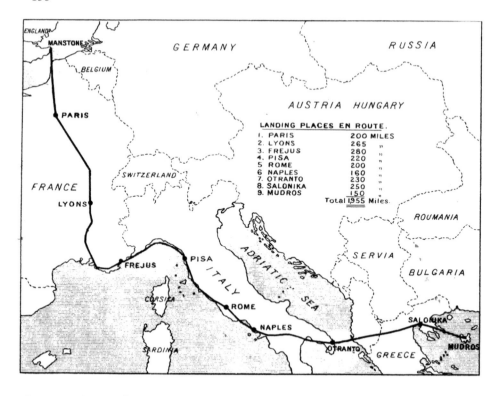

The route taken for the first trans-continental air raid from Manston in England to Mudros in Greece.

Within the map:

ENGLAND · MANSTONE · GERMANY · RUSSIA · BELGIUM · PARIS · AUSTRIA HUNGARY

LANDING PLACES EN ROUTE.

1. PARIS	200 MILES	
2. LYONS	265	"
3. FREJUS	280	"
4. PISA	220	"
5. ROME	200	"
6. NAPLES	160	"
7. OTRANTO	230	"
8. SALONIKA	250	"
9. MUDROS	150	"
	Total 1955 Miles.	

SWITZERLAND · FRANCE · LYONS · ROUMANIA · SERVIA · BULGARIA · FREJUS · PISA · CORSICA · ADRIATIC SEA · ITALY · ROME · SARDINIA · NAPLES · SALONIKA · MUDROS · OTRANTO · GREECE

Endnotes Chapter 11

1   'Jack Barnato died at his residence; 14 Duke Street Mansions in Grosvenor Square, of complications following influenza, on 25 October 1918 aged 24. Group Captain Smyth-Pigott DSO retired in 1934. He returned to duty during WWII and was again mentioned in despatches and made CBE. He died on 8 October 1971.

2   At first the bombers were used for daylight attacks, damaging a German destroyer on 23 April 1917, but the loss of an aircraft to fighter attack two days later resulted in a switch to exclusively night attacks, usually by one aircraft against German-occupied Channel ports, railway targets and airfields. By the end of 1917 the RNAS had four squadrons of O/100s in action, including Naval 'A' Squadron, later 16 (Naval) Squadron, which joined the 41st Wing at Ochey, the nucleus of the Independent Force for strategic raids against targets in southern Germany. These O/100s first operated on the night of 24/25 October 1917 with F.E.2b's of 100 Squadron RFC.

3   Kenneth Stevens Savory was awarded a Bar to his DSO as per *London Gazette* dated 29 August 1917. Henry McClelland and P. T. Rawlings were awarded DSCs.

4   See, *First Inter-Continental Air Strike* by Bruce Robertson (*Air Pictorial*, November 1981) and Graham M. Simons' blog of 2016.

5   Renewed fame arrived in late October 1918 when the armistice between Turkey and the Allies was signed at Moudros.

Chapter 12

The Canadian Contingent

In Flanders fields the poppies blow
Between the crosses, row on row,
That mark our place; and in the sky
The larks, still bravely singing, fly
Scarce heard amid the guns below.

We are the Dead. Short days ago
We lived, felt dawn, saw sunset glow,
Loved and were loved and now we lie
In Flanders fields.

Take up our quarrel with the foe:
To you from failing hands we throw
The torch; be yours to hold it high.
If ye break faith with us who die
We shall not sleep, though poppies grow
In Flanders fields

In Flanders Field by Canadian brigade doctor and artillery commander Major John McCrae. Because the chaplain had been called away, on the evening of 2 May 1915 McCrae was asked to conduct the burial service for his friend, a young Canadian artillery officer, Lieutenant Alexis Helmer, who was killed earlier in the day in the gun positions near Ypres when an exploding German artillery shell landed near him.

Canada has had a proud aviation history dating from 23 February 1909 on Bras-d'Or Lake with J. A. D. McCurdy piloting Alexander Graham Bell's Silver Dart. On 16 September 1914 (while the original Canadian Expeditionary Force was forming up in Valcartier), Colonel Sam Hughes, Minister for the Militia and Defence, authorized the creation of the Canadian Aviation Corps (CAC). This corps was to consist of one mechanic and two officers. Ernest Lloyd Janney of Galt, Ontario, was appointed as the 'Provisional Commander of the CAC' with the rank of Captain. The expenditure of an amount not to exceed five thousand dollars for the purchase of a suitable airplane was approved. The aircraft selected was a float-equipped Burgess-Dunne biplane from the Burgess Aviation Company of Massachusetts. Janney flew the aircraft back to Canada. Upon his arrival in Sorel, Quebec, Canada Customs arrested Janney and the aircraft was impounded. After Canada Customs received notification from the Department of the Militia and Defence, Capt Janney and the aircraft were released. As it turned out, this was to be the only flight of Canada's first military aircraft.

When Great Britain declared war on Germany on 4 August 1914 it automatically brought Canada into the war, because of Canada's legal status as a

British dominion which left foreign policy decisions in the hands of the British parliament. However, the Canadian government had the freedom to determine the country's level of involvement in the war. On 5 August 1914 the Governor General declared a war between Canada and Germany. The British War Office and the British Admiralty viewed Canada only as a potential source of recruits for their respective air services. Initially recruits had to have a valid pilot's licence before the RFC or the RNAS would consider recruiting them. This placed a strain on the small civilian training services available in Canada at that time. These civilian schools were inadequate to handle the increased demand for pilot training. At a cost of $400 for 500 minutes, these intrepid aviators paid for their own training at this time. As the demand for trained aviators increased, the RFC found that there were insufficient training facilities in Britain and they turned to Canada for assistance.

There was no shortage of volunteers for the air war, which initially appeared a glamorous way to fight. Rich Canadians who could afford expensive flying lessons were among the first to join the British flying services. A December 1914 report offered insight into the qualities of recruits: 'an almost ideal combination for an Aviator is that obtaining in a man who has had a British public education, a good all-round engineering training and has outdoor sporting tendencies.' Canadian soldiers sometimes sought transfer to the air forces in order to escape the trenches. Canadians with mechanical experience joined as aircrew to keep the aeroplanes in the air, or to put them back to together when they fell out of it.

As early as 1915 the British Army Council suggested that forces of the Dominions should raise their own air units. The overseas headquarters and the War Council made an attempt in 1916 to create the Royal Canadian Flying Corps but Ottawa would not support this concept and Canada did not have its own air force until the final months of the war. By then the RFC/RAF training establishment had recruited 16,663 personnel and had graduated 3,135 pilots, of whom 2,539 went overseas and 356 remained in Canada as instructors and 137 observers, of whom 85 were sent overseas.

At first the RFC and the RNAS recruited only trained Canadian personnel, mainly pilots. This severely taxed on the training services in Canada. At this time candidates had to pay for their own training (about $400 for 500 minutes of flying) and one prominent Canadian's training school was running at full capacity: John Alexander Douglas McCurdy had a flying school at Toronto Island. However, as the war progressed, the RFC decided to provide pilot training for suitable candidates. The first Canadians to graduate from McCurdy's flying school were F. Homer Smith and Arthur Strachan Ince, both of Toronto. Later, on 14 December 1915 Flight Sub-Lieutenant Arthur Ince shot down a German seaplane off the coast of Belgium for the first Canadian aerial victory in World War 1.

Another Canadian who paid for his own training was John Bernard 'Don' Brophy. Born 4 September 1893 in Ottawa, son of John Byrne Brophy, a civil engineer and Elizabeth (Ella) Hearn. Raised in an Irish Catholic family, 'Don' Brophy attended St. Patrick's School in Ottawa, where he excelled. At Ottawa Collegiate Institute his academic standing dropped as his athletic reputation rose: he scraped through while representing the school in several sports, including football, hockey, baseball and track. In his senior year Don, as he became known, was the champion all-round athlete. Despite his academic weakness, in 1913 he was courted for his talents in football by McGill University and the University of Toronto. He chose McGill and immediately made its varsity team. After failing his first year, he returned to Ottawa, took a menial job with the Department of the Interior and played for Ottawa in the Interprovincial Rugby Football Union. There was talk of his attending the University of Toronto, but the outbreak of World War I in August 1914 presented an attractive alternative. For romantics of his generation, war was sport writ large. War in the air seemed like the ultimate sport and Brophy decided to become a military aviator.

The British government began to recruit potential pilots in the spring of 1915 under a scheme whereby candidates were required to qualify privately before being commissioned in the RNAS or the RFC. Brophy enrolled at the Curtiss Aviation School in Toronto, but his name did not come to the top of the waiting-list until October. Although winter brought flying to a stop, before he could graduate, there was a great demand for pilots. Candidates who had shown sufficient aptitude were commissioned and shipped to England to complete their training. Second Lieutenant Brophy was among them and when he left on 8 December 1915 he began to keep a diary.

Awarded his wings on or about 18 April 1916, Brophy joined 21 Squadron RFC near Hesdin on 6 May. At the time Brophy reached the front, the life expectancy for a pilot was three weeks, but he lasted an incredible five months, flying operational flights from 26 May to 10 November. During this time, he suffered with most of the problems of the day: engine, airframe and propeller failures were common. In addition, during this time, air fighting was in its infancy: rifles and pistols were being carried in cockpits and bombs were strapped to the side of the aircraft... By that time the vital military importance of air forces had been fully recognized. Brophy was credited with bringing down one enemy aircraft, probably destroying two others and forcing down a fourth, successes that earned him a mention in dispatches. During his six months with the squadron, it lost nineteen airmen (killed or wounded) and, by Brophy's count, another six became so neurotic they had to be posted out. Overdue for a rest, in November Lieutenant Brophy was sent back to England to join 33 (Home Defence) Squadron. He died on Christmas Eve in a flying accident when the airframe of his B.E.12 failed during a loop and he spiralled into the ground.

Brophy's diary, which he had kept from 8 December 1915 to 12 November 1916, is one of only two known diaries written by Canadian airmen during the war and the only one relating to the Western Front. Like sport, combat flying was a matter of will-power and hand and eye coordination and life in the RFC was not unlike Brophy's time on the field and in the locker-room. His diary reflects this similarity, but after he had reached squadron service, his tone changes: the deaths of men he must have known are not mentioned and his earlier enthusiasms gave way to both complaints about the number of missions he had to fly and half-acknowledged fears of being posted out for lack of nerve. Occasionally he resorted to bravado and pseudo-biblical language to lift himself over underlying tensions which he may not even have recognized. Brophy's nerves nevertheless held: his brief leaves were enjoyed and until December 1916, his sorties were endured.

In 1917 the RFC decided to establish a training organization in Canada. The original plan called for four training stations with one or more aerodromes at each station and up to five training squadrons per station. After consultation with Canada, the revised plan called for three stations, at Camp Borden, Desoronto and North Toronto and by the end of June 1917 there were three training squadrons operating. With America's entry into the war in April 1917 a reciprocal agreement was established between the RFC and the US Army's Signal Corps. This agreement brought Americans to Canada for training and it allowed the RFC to train in a snow free environment. Fort Worth Texas was selected as the training centre and the school of aerial gunnery and the wings from Camp Borden and Desoronto ceased training in Canada in November 1917 and moved to the Fort Worth area. North Toronto remained open to test the feasibility of training personnel in a Canadian winter. This test was so successful that the training for the winter of 1918-19 was to be in Canada. Meanwhile, the other RFC training units proceeded on their 1600-mile rail-trip to Texas. The winter of 1917-18 was spent in Texas.

Canadian airmen were awarded more than 800 decorations and awards for valour including three Victoria Crosses. The names of such Canadian flyers as William Avery 'Billy' Bishop, William George Barker, Raymond Collishaw and Alan Arnett McLeod vc became household names in Canada and they left a record of daring and devotion that was famous everywhere. There were 171 Canadian air aces during the war, pilots or gunners with five or more enemy aircraft or airships destroyed. William Avery 'Billy' Bishop topped the list of Canadians and was second among all Allied aces with 72 kills. Raymond Collishaw was the second leading Canadian with sixty and William George Barker was third with fifty. Canadian flyers received at least 495 British decorations for gallantry.

Of the twenty-seven allied pilots who had thirty or more combat victories, ten were Canadians. Major William Avery Bishop, the leading 'ace' with 72 victories was born in Owen Sound, Ontario on 8 February 1894. He was the third of four children born to William A. and Margaret Bishop. His father, a lawyer and graduate of Osgoode Hall Law School in Toronto, was the Registrar of Grey County. Attending Owen Sound Collegiate and Vocational Institute, Bishop earned the reputation of a fighter, defending himself and others easily against bullies. He avoided team sports, preferring solitary pursuits such as swimming, horse riding and shooting. Bishop was less successful at his studies; he would abandon any subject he could not easily master and was often absent from class. At 15 Bishop had his first experience with aviation; he built an aircraft out of cardboard, wood crates and string and 'flew' off the roof of his three-story house. He was dug, unharmed, out of the wreckage by his sister. In 1911 'Billy' Bishop entered the Royal Military College of Canada in Kingston, Ontario, where his brother Worth had graduated in 1903. At RMC, Bishop was known as 'Bish' and 'Bill'. Bishop failed his first year at RMC, having been caught cheating. At the termination of a very unsuccessful academic career, 'Billy' Bishop joined the Mississauga Horse and at the outbreak of the war was a cavalry Lieutenant.

Shortly after his arrival in England, Bishop saw his first airplane and at that point he decided that the only way to fight a war is, 'up there above the clouds and in the summer sunshine'. Bishop originally trained as an observer and flew for four months at the front before an injury placed him in the hospital. Upon his release, he discovered he could now apply for pilot training. After completing the course in only fifteen hours, Bishop was posted to a Home Defence unit. Bishop was finally posted to the Western Front in March 1917; reporting to 60 Squadron RFC. It only took him eight days to score his first victory. Bishop quickly established a reputation as a loner and a crack shot and his score of combat victories grew very rapidly.

In *Winged Warfare in WW1* he wrote: 'Dawn was due at 0530 on Easter Monday and that was the exact hour set for the Battle of Arras.[1] We were up and had our machines out of the hangars while it was still night. The beautiful weather of a few hours before had vanished. A strong, chill wind was blowing from the east and dark, menacing clouds were scudding along low overhead.

'The storm had delayed the coming of day by several minutes, but as soon as there was light enough to make our presence worth while we were in the air and braving the untoward elements just as the troops were below us. Lashed by the gale, the wind cut the face as we moved against the enemy. The ground seemed to be one mass of bursting shells. Farther back, where the guns were firing, the hot flames flashing from thousands of muzzles gave the impression of a long ribbon of incandescent light. The air seemed shaken and literally full of shells on their missions of death and destruction. Over and over again one felt a sudden jerk under a wing-tip and the machine would heave quickly. This meant a shell had passed within a few feet of you. As the battle went on the work grew more terrifying, because reports came in that several of our machines had been hit by shells in flight and brought down. There was small wonder of this. The British barrage fire that morning was the most intense the war had ever known. There was a greater concentration of guns than at any time during the Somme.

'The waves of attacking infantry as they came out of their trenches and trudged forward behind the curtain of shells laid down by the artillery were an amazing sight. The men seemed to wander across No Man's Land and into the enemy trenches, as if the battle was a great bore to them. From the air it looked as though they did not realise that they were at war and were taking it all entirely too quietly. That is the way with clockwork warfare. These troops had been drilled to move forward at a given pace. They had been timed over and over again in marching a certain distance and from this timing the 'creeping' or rolling barrage which moved in front of them had been mathematically worked out. And the battle, so calmly entered into, was one of the tensest, bitterest of the entire war.

'On the fourth day of the battle I happened to be flying about 500 feet above the trenches an hour after dawn. It had snowed during the night and the ground was covered with a new layer of white several inches thick. No marks of the battle of the day before were to be seen; the only blemishes in the snow mantle were the marks of shells which had fallen during the last hour. No Man's Land itself, so often a filthy litter, was this morning quite clean and white... It seemed that I was in an entirely different world, looking down from another sphere on this strange, uncanny puppet-show.

'Suddenly I heard the deadly rattle of a nest of machine-guns under me and saw that the line of our troops at one place was growing very thin, with many figures sprawling on the ground. For three or four minutes I could not make out the concealed position of the German gunners. Our men had halted and were lying on the ground, evidently as much puzzled as I was. Then in a corner of a

German trench I saw a group of about five men operating two machine guns. They were slightly to the flank of our line and evidently had been doing a great amount of damage. The sight of these men thoroughly woke me up to the reality of the whole scene beneath me. I dived vertically at them with a burst of rapid fire. The smoking bullets from my gun flashed into the ground and it was an easy matter to get an accurate aim on the German automatics, one of which turned its muzzle towards me.

'But in a fraction of a second I had reached a height of only thirty feet above the Huns, so low I could make out every detail of their frightened faces. With hate in my heart I fired every bullet I could into the groups as I swept over it and then turned my machine away. A few minutes later I had the satisfaction of seeing our line again advancing and before the time had come for me to return from my patrol, our men had occupied all the German positions they had set out to take. It was a wonderful sight and a wonderful experience. Although it had been so difficult to realise that men were dying and being maimed for life beneath me, I felt that at last I had seen something of that dogged determination that has carried British arms so far.'

On 30 April, just before 1000 hours, Bishop took off, leading 'C' Flight of 60 Squadron. In the 53 days since his return from flying school in England, he had shot down 22 hostile aircraft and he and his sleek silver Nieuport 17 were fast becoming a legend over the Western Front. Wedged into the cockpits of their tiny French-built fighters, they climbed at full bore in a wide arc over Lens, to level out at 10,000 feet and get their bearings. Now, far below, they saw two D.H.4s patrolling the German trench system. One of Bishop's men waved frantically, pointing downwards. Bishop looked quickly in that direction and saw four red Albatroses of Richthofen's Jasta bearing down on the D.H.4s. Bishop signalled the attack. Each man picked his target and dived. Bishop pushed down the stick and gave his Le Rhône engine full throttle. The little aeroplane reacted so sharply that the fuselage went beyond the vertical point. He felt himself falling inside the cockpit and the next moment struck his head against the windscreen. There was a blur and panic swept him as he fired his gun then pulled back the stick. The Nieuport gradually righted itself and levelled out.

The Hun had vanished and so had the rest of his patrol. He looked quickly about the sky, banked to cover his tracks and make sure there wasn't a Hun on his tail. Then he swung west and climbed. Altitude, get altitude, was the first rule.

He got up to 8,000 feet and almost immediately saw two enemy bombers making a run over the Allied artillery positions. They were mammoths - the huge three-seater Gothas which soon would be launched against London. He'd never seen them on the Western Front before. He closed in on them from behind, now a little below their flight line. As he drew closer they seemed to grow to monstrous proportions and he felt, as he wrote later, 'like a mosquito chasing a wasp'.

They had seen him.

One of the Gothas banked around in a slow spiral to get at him. Bishop turned with him, under him, as he came around, trying to stay in the German pilot's 'blind spot'. Suddenly there were bullets coming at him. The second Gotha was diving at him from a slight angle, its three machine-guns rattling. Bishop dived, let the giant aeroplane pass overhead, then pulled his nose up under the belly of the first

Gotha and opened fire. His gun had jammed! There was no time to do anything about it. He looped out of trouble, rolled and flattened out. He banged at the gun with the heel of his hand and then tugged at the cocking device. It wouldn't budge. There was no option. He swung west and made for base. He was out of the fight. He flew back, cursing all the way at having to let the two giant Gothas get away. It took only a few minutes for the mechanics to fix the wire cocking device known as 'Nicod's gadget' and Bishop was back in the air south of Lens by 1100 hours. Eight minutes later, he spotted three two-seater German aeroplanes about two miles away and a little below him. They appeared to be spotting for the German artillery. He got the nearest one in his sights and opened fire. But suddenly he was in trouble. He'd begun firing too early, warning the enemy and the three aeroplanes banked to face him, all guns rattling. He found himself in a cross-fire from three Spandaus. Miraculously he flew through the hail of bullets in his first pass. He banked around to find that the three two-seaters had turned away and flew after them. Just in time he saw the trap they had led him into. Five scarlet Albatros D.IIIs led by Richthofen, were waiting to pounce and they swarmed down on him. He banked violently, rolled and levelled out, split-arsing away and pouring on the power to get height.

That had been close and Bishop cursed himself for almost falling for the trap laid by the two-seaters. He continued climbing until he was well above the red Scouts, gradually getting himself into position for an attack. He dived to intercept them, firing at the last second. The Albatros pilots waited for him to pass through their formation so that they could get him in their sights. But just before he reached their level he pulled the Nieuport's nose up and zoomed out of range. He repeated this manoeuvre three times, giving the Germans no chance of returning his fire. They scattered and left him alone. Bishop gained more height in the hope of spotting the two Gothas again, but they were nowhere to be seen. At 1115 hours south of Lens at 8,000 feet he saw two Halberstadts on artillery observation and banked round in a gentle arc to intercept them. Waiting till the last second, he dived on the nearest Hun, giving a burst of twenty rounds. The aeroplane's observer opened fire almost simultaneously and his bullets ripped through the Nieuport's strutting. Bishop pressed home the attack as the second Halberstadt banked round to meet him almost head-on. Bishop passed over him and banked sharply, to see the first machine slip violently to one side, then stand on its nose and go into a spin.

Bishop turned to attack the second machine. The German dived away. Bishop followed, finishing his drum into him. The HA continued diving eastwards and got away. Bishop levelled out and watched the other Halberstadt spiral down to earth and exploded in a ragged stab of flame. He flew south, calmly rearming his frontal guns ready for the next encounter. It came at 1125 hours, east of Monchy, at 6,000 feet. He saw five of Richthofen's fighters chasing two B.E.2s and made one long pass at them, firing twenty rounds without result. Then at 1130, east of Wancourt, at 5,000 feet, he saw two more Halberstadts doing artillery observation and attacked the leading aeroplane head-on. As they closed on each other - at an aggregate speed of something over 200 mph - they each opened fire. The German's bullets ripped through the Nieuport's struts not three feet from Bishop and Bishop's tracers streaked into the HA's engine. At the last instant they pulled away, the Halberstadt diving sharply, Bishop's Nieuport flashing above it.

After banking round and levelling out, Bishop saw the German some distance away, still going down in a long glide, apparently under control. There was no sign of any smoke. Bishop followed, watching him. It had been the Canadian's closest shave in almost a hundred encounters. He wondered how the German was feeling. He turned west. He had very little ammunition left by now. And he was hungry. He took part in two more skirmishes before landing safely back at base in time for lunch.

During the afternoon, Allied bombers pockmarked Epinoy aerodrome, unchallenged except by German anti-aircraft batteries. At Lozingham, enemy bombers which blasted the aerodrome were chased by Naval fighters which later shot down five of twelve Albatroses which they jumped during an attack on two RE8s.

On the day's air-fighting, the odds were about even. But strategically the RFC had won through - by containing the enemy and proving his Jagdgruppe theory to be unworkable.

On 2 June 1917 Major Bishop took off before dawn on a mission he and Albert Ball had discussed; the idea was to attack the enemy before he was prepared for the attack. On that day, Bishop single-handedly attacked a German-held aerodrome and claimed three enemy aircraft shot down that were taking off to attack him and destroyed several more on the ground. For this feat he was awarded the Victoria Cross, the first of three awarded to Canadian airmen during the war, although it has been suggested that he may have embellished his success. His VC was one of two awarded in violation of the warrant requiring witnesses (the other being the Unknown Soldier) and since the German records have been lost and the archived papers relating to the VC were lost also, there is no way of confirming whether there were any witnesses. It seemed to be common practice at this time to allow Bishop to claim victories without requiring confirmation or verification from other witnesses.

Late in 1917 Bishop departed England for Canada for a well-earned rest. Upon his return in early 1918 he was promoted to Major and posted to command 85 Squadron and in his final two weeks in combat he shot down an incredible twenty-five enemy aircraft, twelve coming in the last three days. After this feat, Bishop was posted to a staff job as he was now considered a valuable war symbol. His secondment to the RAF was terminated and he was attached to the Canadian Headquarters Overseas as a temporary Lieutenant Colonel. While in this staff job he pursued the creation of the Canadian Air Force.

Raymond Collishaw, the second highest scoring Canadian 'ace' was born in Nanaimo, British Columbia on 22 November 1893 in an atmosphere of ships, hunting and fishing that gave him a nose for adventure. Up and down the Pacific coast he sailed as a youthful pilot and second officer; then came the opportunity to go with Scott to the Antarctic as navigating officer. Upon his return, he resumed Pacific Coast shipping duties but with the start of the First World War, he sought naval service in England. Just before enlisting, however, aviation caught his imagination and He joined the RNAS in 1914. His first operational sortie over the front was flown in September 1916 with 3 Wing. On 1 February 1917 he was transferred to 3 (Naval) Squadron. Collishaw flew in Robin Mack's flight in Naval

3, the Sopwith Pup aircraft being named *Black Tulip, Black Arrow, Black Bess, Black Prince and Black Maria.* Collishaw received the Croix de Guerre for meeting six German scouts and destroying two of them before the remainder dispersed. In April he was promoted to Flight Commander and posted to 10 (Naval) Squadron. With him he took four other Canadians, Flight Sub-Lieutenants' Ellis Reid of Toronto, John E. Sharman of Oak Lake, Manitoba, Gerald E. Nash of Stoney Creek, Ontario and William M. Alexander of Montreal. With these pilots Collishaw formed the 'Black Flight' (so-named because of their black-painted engine cowlings, wheels and tailfins). Sharman, who did not score any victories whilst with the 'Black Flight', moved to another flight after just a few days. Desmond F. Fitzgibbon who replaced Sharman (who was KIA on 22 July 1917) was also ex-3 Wing and he scored five victories with the 'Black Flight'. As far as is known, he did not have a 'Black' named triplane. He was also not Canadian which probably explains why he has never been regarded as a member of the flight. Eighteen of Collishaw's 33 victories on Tripes were scored in N5492 *Black Maria*, which had only a single MG mount (he scored two victories in N533 also called *Black Maria*): William M. Alexander DSC of Toronto (23 victories) *Black Prince*; Ellis V. Reid DSC (19 victories, KIA 28 July 1917), Black Roger; John Sharman DSC* (8 victories), *Black Death*; and Gerald E. Nash DSC (6 victories), *Black Sheep*.[2]

An intensely egotistical man, Collishaw was a good leader, but regarded as personally reckless - in his own fights Collishaw would simply charge straight in, usually head-on. This resulted in his being shot down twice during his spell with Naval 10. In his memoirs, his CO reported that Collishaw usually returned from each fight with his machine badly shot about. On 6 June 1917, the day before the Allied attack from the Ypres salient, Collishaw fought from dawn till dark; but in one flight before seven in the morning he led his whole squadron into a pitched battle with a German squadron of Albatros scouts. Eighty aeroplanes fought out this duel that ended in a broken German retreat. Collishaw himself engaged the German leader at the outset and sent him down in flames. Two others he destroyed before the fight was over. This and other actions of that time gained him the DSC.

On 15 June he brought down four hostile aircraft, an action chiefly responsible for the award to him of the DSO. In the furious and continued fighting he thrust upon himself, Collishaw came to be known as the 'miracle man'. Twice he had been disabled in the air and only just managed to glide his machine behind his own lines. Once in January he came face to face with the enemy only to find his guns were frozen. But rather than lead his flight into retreat he flew on with them. Once in a heavy fog he landed by mistake on a German aerodrome and only just managed to get into the air again before enemy hands could take him prisoner. Thousands of bullets had passed through his machine - once smashing the goggles from his face. Another time his machine was shot out of control and he crashed to the ground amid its complete wreckage, without even a bruise.

In successive flights, the 'Black Flight' destroyed 66 enemy aeroplanes. On 26 June 1917 Nash was shot down by Leutnant Karl Allmenröder. Nash survived and the next day while lying in a temporary cell Nash heard the tolling of a church bell. It was the funeral of the late Leutnant Allmenröder who had been shot down by Collishaw in a racing, diving, circling, climbing fight that had been carried out within full view of the remainder of the quintet. That was Collishaw's 25th victory and by 27 July his record had reached 37 and he was granted several months leave to return to Canada. Collishaw was virtually unknown to the public at this time and spent his holiday quietly with his family at Nanaimo before returning to the fray in command of 13 Naval Squadron operating from Dunkirk along the coast with the fleet. Submarines became his prey, together with the general assignment of protecting the fleet from attack from the air. Between 30 May and 27 July Collishaw destroyed 29 enemy aircraft - a record still unparalleled.

By January 1918 Collishaw had again been promoted and placed in command of 3 (Naval) Squadron. Naval squadron commanders were not expected to fly, but Collishaw disregarded this rule as much as he could. On 1 April 1918 Collishaw officially transferred to the RAF and was placed in command of 203 Squadron. In his final four months in combat he scored an additional twenty victories. The DFC came to him in August 1918 - with his enemy toll at 47- and in September, he was awarded a bar to the DSO. The Air Ministry said of him on this occasion: 'A brilliant squadron leader of exceptional daring, who has destroyed 51 enemy machines. Early one morning he, with another pilot, attacked an enemy aerodrome. Seeing three machines brought out of a burning hangar he dived five times, firing bursts at these from a very low altitude and dropped bombs on the living quarters. He then saw an enemy aeroplane descending over the aerodrome; he attacked it and drove it down in flames. Later, when returning from a reconnaissance of the damaged hangars, he was attacked by three Albatros Scouts, who pursued him to our lines, when he turned and attacked one, which fell out of control and crashed.'

Collishaw took his total to sixty enemy aeroplanes by a double victory on 26 September in another attack upon a German aerodrome. A few days later he was assigned to England to take part in the organization of the Canadian Air Force and the Armistice caught up with him just after he had been promoted to the rank of Lieutenant Colonel on 1 October. This great airman, who ranked second only to Bishop among British pilots, was headed for a career in commercial aviation after the armistice but the British government offered him command of an RAF squadron to go to the assistance of Denikin in South Russia in the struggle to overthrow the Bolshevik regime. Of 62 flying officers under his command, 53 were Canadians. Here was a colourful war, wild and dramatic and fought under very different circumstances than the long, hard struggle of 1914-1918. But Denikin was forced to retreat at the end of 1919 and Collishaw was sent to Egypt to command a squadron for service against the Bolsheviks in Persia. Here again was war under new conditions. 'We maintain our aerodrome landing field,' he wrote to a friend, 'in decent condition by using 500 camels and 700 horses to trample it down after each snow.'

Just before the outbreak of the Second Great War, Collishaw held one of the RAF's most important commands in the Middle East, with the rank of Air Commodore. The man who was known as the roaring attacker of the Great War had stayed at the controls and become one of the 'master minds' behind the Royal Air Force. Raymond Collishaw retired from the RAF as an Air Vice Marshal in 1943.

3 Squadron was continually over enemy lines artillery spotting and reconnoitring for the Army, their R.E.8s complemented late in the war by 'O'

Flight, a long range flight of Bristol Fighters. Captain John Robertson Duigan, the first Australian to design, build and fly a powered aircraft in Australia, in company with Lieutenant Alec Stewart Paterson discovered the monstrous railway gun firing from Harbonnieres. The gun, whose location was now pinpointed was captured in the offensive of August and taken back to Australia as a war trophy. One of the Squadron's aircraft (A4397/D) was to set a record amongst the British forces on the Western Front for the greatest number of hours in enemy territory by completing 440 hours of service flying in 147 flights across enemy lines.[3] 3 Squadron was to finish its service after the war by flying mail flights through Belgium and France before being demobilised in March of 1919.

In March and October 1918 two more Canadian pilots were awarded the Victoria Cross. Military life had an early appeal for young Alan Arnett McLeod of Stonewall, Manitoba. He was born at Stonewall on 20 April 1899. When he was fourteen, he persuaded the commanding officer of the 34th Fort Garry Horse to accept him as a recruit and went away for summer camp training. He was a big boy for his age and bubbling with enthusiasm. When war broke out he was fifteen, but immediately began his efforts to enlist. The one stumbling block was his youth, but he kept trying and in due course, he had his reward. The big day in the young Manitoba boy's life came on 20 April 1917. He was eighteen at last and his teacher and classmates gave him gifts at a farewell party in the school. The next day he was off to join the RFC. He received preliminary flight training at Long Branch, near Toronto and at Camp Borden before proceeding overseas on 20 August 1917. There was another disappointment in store for the youngster. When he was ready for active service, the officer commanding the training camp in England told McLeod he could not go over to France until he was nineteen. So he was posted to a squadron protecting England from German raiders and had the experience of being shot down over London, luckily without injury.

His eagerness was rewarded, however and he reported to 2 Squadron in France on 29 November 1917. Though he was several years younger than most of his brother officers, he proved popular and developed into a skilful service pilot. He needed this skill on one occasion when he had an inexperienced observer up with him over the lines in a heavy Armstrong Whitworth two-seater machine to spot for the artillery. A German fighter swung onto the tail of McLeod's machine and the observer signalled that his machine gun was jammed. McLeod shook off the German attacker and had a hearty laugh later when he found that the nervous observer had failed to release the safety catch on his gun.

On 14 January 1918 Second Lieutenant Alan McLeod performed a feat which won him mention in dispatches. He dived on a well-protected German observation balloon twelve miles behind the enemy lines, a dangerous attempt for a slow, two-seater machine and destroyed the big bag with a blast from his front gun. Immediately afterwards three Albatros Scouts made a vicious attack. Lieutenant Reginald Key, McLeod's English observer, shot one down and the other two made off. Two days later McLeod took his vengeance upon a German anti-aircraft battery which had troubled him continually while he was spotting for the artillery. He roared down under heavy shell fire and machine gun hail to within fifty feet of the ground and turned his guns upon the battery. When the gunners had crumpled, he turned and bombed the guns themselves, then swung over to disperse a column of troops. Then McLeod peacefully resumed his 'artillery shoot.'

Lieutenant Key was soon parted from McLeod, of whom he wrote: 'He was the finest pilot I have ever flown with, devoid of fear and always merry and bright. Often after getting out of a very tight corner by sheer piloting, with six or seven Huns on our tail, he would turn around to me and laugh out loud.'

Then came his brilliant, selfless act for which McLeod was awarded the Victoria Cross. His action was not against the enemy, but for saving the life of his observer. While on a photo-reconnaissance mission, McLeod's aircraft was attacked by eight enemy triplanes. After a fierce fight, a bullet eventually penetrated the fuel tank and set the aircraft on fire. McLeod continued to fly his aircraft while his gunner/observer, Lieutenant Arthur W. Hammond MC, warded off further attack. The fire became so intense that even with side slipping McLeod had to climb out of the cockpit. From here he continued to fly the aircraft toward a safe arrival with the ground. He was finally able to crash-land the aircraft in no-man's land where, though he was wounded five times and his observer six times, he was able to extract his observer from the wreckage. During this fight, the observer was able to shoot down three of the enemy aircraft.

The citation in the *London Gazette* officially described the action on 27 March 1918 when McLeod and his observer were attacked by eight Fokker triplanes, three of which Hammond's gun accounted for, though he was wounded six times. McLeod, meanwhile, continued to manoeuvre his heavy machine, although he had been wounded five times. Finally, a German incendiary bullet penetrated the gasoline tank and the aircraft caught fire. Fighting the flames and billowing smoke, McLeod's one aim then was to bring his wounded observer safely to earth. He stepped out on the bottom aeroplane, leaning into the cockpit to grasp the control stick. In that position he side slipped the aeroplane from 5,000 feet to the ground, the wind pressure of the sideslip blowing flames and smoke away from the observer, who continued firing until McLeod flattened the aeroplane out and made a crash landing in No Man's Land. McLeod, according to the official citation, 'notwithstanding his own wounds, dragged Hammond away from the burning wreckage at great personal risk from heavy machine gun fire from the enemy's lines. This very gallant pilot was again wounded by a bomb whilst engaged in this act of rescue, but he persevered until he had placed Lieutenant Hammond in comparative safety, before falling himself from exhaustion and loss of blood.'

Leutnant Hans Kirschstein of Jasta 6, holder of the 'Pour le Mérite', Royal House Order of Hohenzollern and the Iron Cross, 1st and 2nd class, with 27 aerial victories, was credited with the kill.[4] British infantry rescued the two badly wounded men from No Man's Land. McLeod was wounded three times in the side and Hammond, who was wounded six times, subsequently lost a leg. He was awarded a bar for his Military Cross. McLeod had a long spell in hospital, which he reached after waiting for hours in the front line trenches constantly under fire. The summer passed slowly with McLeod recovering in Prince of Wales Hospital, London. His father went to England and was constantly at the boy's bedside. When he had sufficiently recovered, McLeod went to Buckingham Palace accompanied by his father and received the Victoria Cross from the hands of His Majesty George V. Much to his regret, a recurring spell of sickness prevented him from accepting an invitation for his father and himself to lunch with the King at

Windsor Castle. Father and son returned to Canada in September and met a warm reception in Winnipeg before proceeding home to Stonewall. Late in October, the virulent form of influenza then sweeping the country struck down Alan McLeod. Smoke and flame of his last fight in the air had weakened his lungs and he died at Winnipeg, 6 November 1918.

William George Barker was born in Dauphin, Manitoba on 3 November 1894 and from his earliest days showed an aptitude for firearms both as a game hunter and as an active member of rifle association's at Dauphin and later at Winnipeg. 'Will' Barker grew up on the frontier of the Great Plains, riding horses, shooting and working as a youngster on his father's farm and sawmill. He was an exceptional shot, using a lever-action Winchester that he had modified with his own peep sight. He was particularly adept at shooting on the move, even while on horseback. One biographer has suggested that he could have been a trick shooter in a circus. He was physically poised, emotionally intense, with wide-ranging interests and had an innate flair for the dramatic act. He was a very good student in school, but had frequent absences due to farm and sawmill life; he was the hunter providing food for the workers in the sawmill, while still a young teenager and missed classes because of this obligation.

Barker fell in love with aviation after watching pioneer aviators flying Curtiss and Wright Flyer aircraft at farm exhibitions between 1910 and 1914. He was a Boy Scout at Russell, Manitoba and a member of the 32nd Light Horse, a Non-Permanent Active Militia unit based at Roblin, Manitoba. He was in Grade 11 at Dauphin Collegiate Institute in the autumn of 1914, just before his enlistment. Life on the farmlands of the prairie seemed to have instilled in him a rugged confidence that remained with him through life.

In December 1914 Barker enlisted as No 106074 Trooper William Barker in the 1st Canadian Mounted Rifles. The regiment went to England in June 1915 and then to France on 22 September that same year. Barker was a Colt machine gunner with the regiment's machine gun section and fought in the Second Battle of Ypres. The mud and monotony of trench life soon turned 'Willy's thoughts skyward and in late February or early March 1916 he transferred as a probationary observer with the rank of Corporal to 9 Squadron RFC, flying in B.E.2 aircraft and operating on the Somme as a mechanic, but he flew several sorties as a machine gunner and fledgling observer. On 2 April he was commissioned as a second lieutenant and given five days leave in London to acquire an officer's uniform and equipment. On his return, he was assigned to 4 Squadron and on 7 July transferred to 15 Squadron, still flying in the B.E.2. On 21 July Barker claimed a Roland scout 'driven down' with his observer's gun and in August claimed a second Roland, this time in flames. He was Mentioned in Despatches around this time. He officially qualified as an Observer on 27 August and on 15 September he worked for the first time with Canadian troops, including his old regiment. On 15 November Barker and his pilot, flying very low over the Ancre River in Picardy, spotted a large concentration of German troops massing for a counter-attack on Beaumont Hamel. The crew sent an emergency Zone Call brought to bear all available artillery fire in the area onto the specified target. The force of some 4,000 German infantry was effectively broken up. He was awarded the Military Cross for this action in the concluding stages of the Battle of the Somme. A long period on the

Somme front followed, during which Barker achieved a brilliant reputation on reconnaissance, artillery observation, photographic and bombing work.

In late 1916 Barker returned to England for pilot training. In January 1917, after spending Christmas on leave in London, he commenced pilot training at Netheravon, flying solo after 55 minutes of dual instruction. On 24 February he returned to serve a second tour on Corps Co-operation machines as a pilot flying B.E.2s and R.E.8s with 15 Squadron. On 25 March Barker claimed another scout 'driven down'. On 25 April 1917 during the Arras Offensive, flying an R.E.8 with observer 2nd Lieutenant Goodfellow, Barker spotted over 1,000 German troops sheltering in support trenches. They directed artillery fire into the positions, thereby avoiding a counter-attack. Barker was awarded the Military Cross on 10 January 1917. A captaincy followed shortly after but in early September he was sent back to England to instruct student pilots. Barker was restless and he applied for a transfer to a scout squadron. In late September he was posted to 28 Squadron flying R.E.8s and not long afterwards was given command of 'A' Flight. In October the squadron proceeded to Belgium and 28 Squadron was moved to northern Italy to bolster the sagging Italian Front. Austrian aircraft had gained command of the Italian sky, but the Austrians had very few aircraft. Therefore the aim was primarily ground support though Barker's personal record jumped from five to fifty aeroplanes destroyed in the air thanks largely to this activity in Italy.

Although Barker was reportedly not a highly skilled pilot - suffering several flying accidents during his career - he more than made up for this deficiency with aggressiveness in action and highly accurate marksmanship. In April Barker led a daring, daylight raid on the Austrian Army Headquarters at San Vito al Tagliamento about fifty miles northwest of Trieste, which took the enemy by surprise. The attackers flew very low, below second storey windows and telegraph wires, shooting out the windows and doors and then swooping up and pulling around to drop their Cooper bombs on the roof.

In May Barker pulled off a series of spy-dropping adventures behind enemy lines with the aid of a specially built Caproni CA.3 bomber and parachute. These covert flights were flown at low level at night without escorts and the approach run over the drop area had to be made with motors idle to avoid detection. On occasion he was assisted on spy-resupply operations by Captain Wedgwood Benn who was then adjutant of Barker's squadron.[5] The high degree of skill required in carrying out this manoeuvre was recognized by the King of Italy who conferred on Barker the 'd'Oro (Gold) Medal of Military Valour' - highest Italian award for any soldiers but her own. It took its place alongside the Croix de Guerre which Barker had previously won from France for services in protecting French flyers from an enemy attack. Another Italian medal for valour came to Barker for his brilliant defensive work in the hard fighting along the Piave River during the desperate offensive campaign of the enemy. Barker's second Italian medal had inscribed on it 'Protector of the Air' and was pinned on his breast by the King of Italy himself.

A first Bar to his MC was awarded on 18 July 1917. Barker was wounded in the head by anti-aircraft fire in August. After a short spell in the UK as an instructor, his continual requests for front line service resulted in him being transferred to become a scout pilot, being offered a post with either 56 Squadron or 28 Squadron. He chose command of 'C' Flight in the newly formed 28 Squadron, flying the Sopwith Camel that he preferred over the S.E.5s of 56 Squadron. 28 Squadron moved to France on 8 October 1917 and Barker shot down an Albatros DV on his first patrol, though he did not claim it as the patrol was unofficial. On 20 October he claimed an Albatros of Jasta 2 flown by Leutnant R. Walter Lange, who had scored seven victories and was killed. Two more, of Jasta 18, followed on 27 October. Leutnant O. Schober was killed flying a red nosed Albatros D.V. West of Roulers and Offstfv J. Klein force landed his D.V. his aeroplane in flames.

On 7 November 28 Squadron was transferred to Istrana airfield in Italy with Barker temporarily in command and most of the unit, including aircraft, travelled by train to Milan. On 29 November he shot down an Austrian Albatros D.III flown by Leutnant Haertl of Jasta 1 near Pieve di Soligo. A Jasta 39 pilot was shot down and killed and a balloon of BK 10 destroyed on 3 December.

Barker seemed to fly with a zest and affection for the task as though it were a sport. Christmas morning in 1917 for instance found him making an unofficial flight from Istrana in pursuit of an Austrian balloon that he had seen while leaving his mess hut. Barker was not supposed to be in the air but he went up to do battle, accompanied by two other machines flown by Lieutenant Harold Hudson and another pilot. The balloon was quickly destroyed, but it was too fine a morning to return home so they carried on into enemy territory and in one of his most successful and also most controversial raids, fictionalized by Ernest Hemingway in the short story *The Snows of Kilimanjaro*, they flew wing-tip to wing-tip across nearby Motta airfield, home to Fliegerabteilung (A) 204 firing their incendiary Buckingham ammunition into the open doors of the hangars. Catching the Germans off guard Barker and Hudson set fire to one hangar and damaged four German aircraft and killed and wounded more than a dozen pilots and mechanics taking cover in their slit trenches before dropping a large piece of cardboard with the message, To the Austrian Flying Corps from the RFC, wishing you a 'Merry X-Mas. Back at Istrana Barker had his mechanics patch up the bullet holes. On Boxing Day the Austrians feebly tried to exact revenge by attacking in a widely scattered formation of thirty or forty machines but only about twenty reached their objective and they were fired on by British AA gunners.

Leutnant Lang of Jasta 1 was killed by Barker on 1 January 1918 and two balloons, two Albatros fighters (one flown by Feldwebel Karl Semmelrock of Flik 51J) and a pair of two-seaters fell to Barker during February. Awarded the DSO on 5 January, he also claimed three more Albatros and an observation balloon. In early February he shot down another Albatros and an Aviatik two-seat reconnaissance aircraft. Captain Mitchell, a fellow pilot, described Barker 'Whilst one could not say he was a good pilot, he certainly made up for this in his shooting. I was his deputy leader and probably knew more about him than anybody else. I have seen enemy machines break up in the air or go down in flames long before I realized they were in range.' Barker was also shot down twice, once landing on Lake Garda when he had to be rescued by rowboat and another time when he had to make a forced landing in the foothills.

On 10 April Barker was made a flight commander but owing to his tendency to ignore orders by flying many unofficial patrols, Barker was passed over when the post of Commanding Officer of 28 Squadron became vacant. Dissatisfied, he applied for a posting and joined 66 Squadron. On 17 April he shot down Oberleutnant Gassner-Norden of Flik 41J, flying an Albatros D.III (Oef), over Vittorio. In May he destroyed eight Austrian machines.

In June there happened the incident for which Barker gained most popular renown. Austrian aeroplanes were doing their work in fits and starts, travelling in search of stray Allied machines but avoiding any pitched battles. Barker, Lieutenant Alfred Birks of Montreal and Lieutenant Clifford MacKay 'Black Mike' McEwen, so-named for his ability to tan easily and darkly,[6] anxious for a show-down, therefore prepared and distributed over enemy aerodromes, thousands of copies of this formal challenge: *Major W. George Barker DSO MC and the officers under his command present their compliments to: Captain Brunmoski, 41 Reconnaissance Portobouffole; Ritter Von Fiala, 51 Pursuit, Gajarine; Captain Navratil, 3rd Company and the pilots under their command and request the pleasure and honour of meeting in the air. In order to save Captain Brunmoski, Ritter Von Fiala and Captain Navratil and gentlemen of his party the inconvenience of searching for them, Major Barker and his Officers will bomb Godigo aerodrome at 1000 daily, weather permitting, for the ensuing fortnight.* Godigo was the largest and most important of the Austrians' aerodromes. Thus, the selection of this site for battle was the last word in open challenge. Barker and his men of 139 Squadron - an 'Imperial' unit of which he had been given command - appeared at Godigo day after day - but the enemy fought shy of open battle and nothing came of 139 Squadron's 'calling card.'

66 Squadron was equipped with Bristol Fighters which proved so effective that a new squadron, 139, was formed almost entirely of F.2bs. On 14 July Barker was promoted major and given command of the new squadron although he continued to retain his Camel. On 18 July Barker in his Camel and a Brisfit and some others of 66 Squadron shot down an entire flight of Austrian machines. Barker destroyed a LVG two-seater, the other Camels destroyed three others and AA gunners claimed the fifth victim. Two days later Barker and two Brisfits destroyed three Austrian machines that attacked Motta airfield. Barker destroyed two Albatros D.IIIs and a Bristol got the other. By now Barker had 33 kills and nine balloons to his name and on 20 July he was awarded a bar to his DSO. On the night of 9 August he flew a Savoia-Pomilio SP.4 bomber to land a spy behind enemy lines. On 16 September he was awarded a second bar to the Military Cross 'for conspicuous gallantry and devotion to duty' and more particularly for attacking eight and then seven hostile aeroplanes, shooting down two the first time and one the second.

Having flown more than 900 combat hours in two and a half years with 33 aircraft (and two shared) aircraft destroyed and five aircraft 'out of control', the highest 'destroyed' ratio for any RAF, RFC or RNAS pilot during the conflict. He also captured one balloon and destroyed two (and seven shared) balloons and nine observation balloons destroyed individually or with other pilots.

Barker was transferred back to the UK in September 1918 to command the school of air fighting at Hounslow Heath aerodrome. But on arrival in England, he convinced the Air Ministry he should be allowed to do two weeks fighting in France to acquaint himself with the latest tactics before he began instructional work. He was granted a ten-day roving commission in France, wherein he selected

Above: Incoming British prisoners.

Left: Captain John Owen Donaldson DSO DFC of the American Air Service who was credited with seven aerial victories and was the first successful Allied escaper of the war.

Below: A captured RFC pilot is taken into captivity.

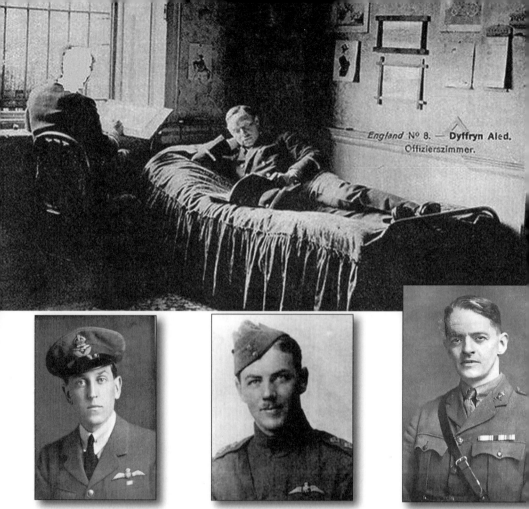

England Nº 8. — Dyffryn Aled. Offizierszimmer.

Top: An officer's bedroom at Dyffryn Aled PoW camp, a late Georgian country house with twenty-five bedrooms near Llansannan in north Wales.

Above left: In 1918 Lieutenant Elias Henry Jones, a Welsh officer in the Indian Army (pictured) and Australian pilot Lieutenant Cedric Waters Hill, captured during the fall of Kut, escaped from the Yozgad prisoner of war camp in Asia Minor. Their epic story was told in Jones' book *The Road to Endor*.

Above, centre: Captain Richard James ('Dick') Tipton who escaped with Captain Edward Herbert Keeling IARO and Lieutenant Harry Coghill Watson Bishop.

Above right: Lieutenant Cedric Waters Hill an Australian officer in the Royal Flying Corps who escaped with Lieutenant Elias Henry Jones.

Right: Pictured with three of their rescuers, Captain Edward Herbert Keeling IARO (back row far left) who could speak Turkish, Captain Richard James ('Dick') Tipton (far right) and Lieutenant Harry Coghill Watson Bishop (the author of *A Kut Prisoner*, (third from right).

Above: German prisoners of war playing football at Donington Hall. (Anton Rippon Coll)

Right: John Bull cartoon lampooning the luxurious conditions afforded German prisoners at Donington Hall.

Below: German prisoners being marched to Donington Hall. (Anton Rippon Coll)

German 'Dining in' night in the canteen at Donington Hall. (Anton Rippon Coll)

Below: Front view of Donington Hall with wire fences and sentry posts. (Anton Rippon Coll)

Above Left: Lieutenant (later Captain) Claude Frank Lethbridge Templer of the 1st Battalion, The Gloucestershire Regiment. Above right: Lieutenant Gerald Featherstone Knight, of 12 Squadron RFC.

Below: Lieutenant Gilbert Stuart Martin Insall RFC receiving the VC for his bravery on 7 November 1915 near Achiet-le-Grand, France.

Above: SM U-38 Type U 31 U-boat which Hermann Tholens (left) hoped to use in his escape plan. It was the third most successful U-boat, sinking 138 ships. Its longest serving captain was Kapitänleutnant Max Valentiner, who was awarded the Pour le Mérite while in command of U-38. Valentiner was in command of U-38 in November and December 1915 when she sank the passenger liners *Ancona* and *Persia;* both were controversial since the ships were sunk by torpedoes without warning, in defiance of the then-current Prize rules, which stated that merchant vessels carrying passengers be given an opportunity to evacuate their passengers before being sunk. In 1917 Valentiner was succeeded as commander of U-38 by Kapitänleutnant Wilhelm Canaris. After World War I ended, U-38 was surrendered to France and broken up in 1919.

Below: Hermann Tholens (wearing cap) being led away to Denbigh jail. (Steve Rogers).

Above: Constable John Rogers in front of Denbigh jail with Hermann Tholens just visible in the courtyard beyond. (Steve Rogers)

Left: Jocelyn Lee Hardy.

Below: Günther Plüschow.

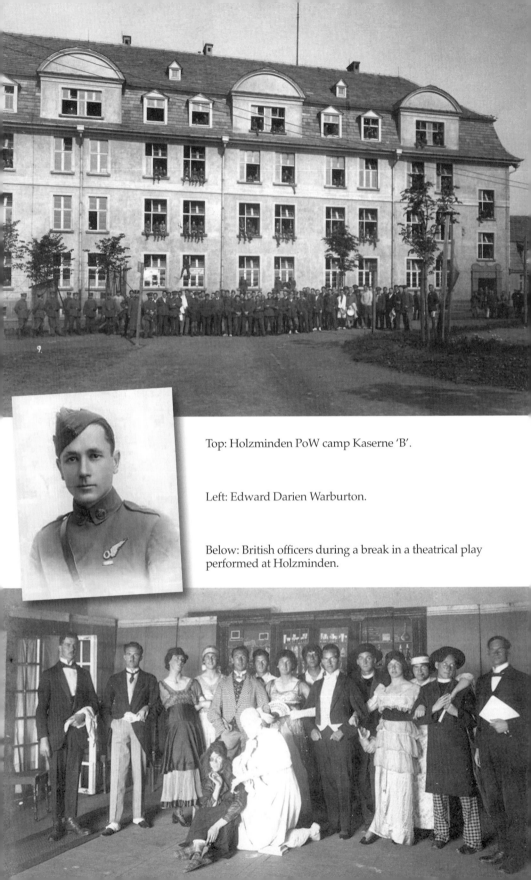

Top: Holzminden PoW camp Kaserne 'B'.

Left: Edward Darien Warburton.

Below: British officers during a break in a theatrical play performed at Holzminden.

Cecil William Blain

2280.   14 Jan. 1916

Top: British officers in front of
Barrack Block at Holzminden in
1918.

Left: 2nd Lieutenant Cecil Blain.

Above: 22-year old Lieutenant Algernon
Frederick Bird, 61st victim of Baron
Manfred von Richthofen (right).

Centre: Colonel Charles Edward Henry
Rathbone DSO RNAS, the senior British
officer of Holzminden PoWcamp.

Above: Lieutenant Thomas Frank Burrill and his comrades at the Holzminden PoW camp where 29 of the PoWs crawled free before the tunnel collapsed. Nineteen of the men were later captured but ten made it to neutral Holland before being welcomed back to Britain as heroes.

Below: Roll call at Holzminden.

HOLZMINDEN TUNNEL. JULY 1918

The 'first Great Escape', at Holzminden.

Left: Heinrich Gontermann.

Below: Allied officers at Holzminden.

Above: Lieutenant Colonel Hesperus Andrias Van Ryneveld known as Pierre van Ryneveld and Captain Brand in February 1920, standing in front of Vickers Vimy, G-UABA, *Silver Queen*, before setting out on an England to South Africa Flight

Below: Arthur Whitten-Brown and John Alcock.

Top left: Lieutenant Christopher Quintin Brand.

Top right: Lieutenant James Mallett Bennett.

Right: Harry Hawker.

Below: Ross and Keith Smith in 1921.

Above: Alcock and Brown leaving Newfoundland in the Vimy at the start of their Trans-Atlantic flight on 14 June 1919.

Below: The catastrophic end on 6 May 1937 of the German passenger airship LZ129 *Hindenburg*, which caught fire and was destroyed during its attempt to dock with its mooring mast at Naval Air Station Lakehurst, New Jersey.

the Sopwith Snipe as his personal machine and attached himself to 201 Squadron RAF whose Squadron commander, Major Cyril Leman, was a friend from his days as a Corps Co-operation airman.

But the time was shortly up and on Sunday, 27 October, he set out again for England. But this was to be no ordinary home-going flight. While returning his Snipe to an aircraft depot, he crossed enemy lines at 21,000 feet above the Forêt de Mormal. He attacked a Rumpler C.VII reconnaissance aircraft, which broke up, its crew escaping by parachute. By his own admission, Barker was careless and while following it down, he was attacked by a formation of Fokker D.VIIs of Jagdgruppe 12 consisting of Jasta 24 and Jasta 44. In a descending battle against fifteen or more enemy machines, Barker was wounded three times in the legs, then his left elbow was blown away, yet he managed to control his Snipe and shoot down or drive down three more enemy aircraft but he also received two more injures (another in the thigh and one in the right elbow). The dogfight took place immediately above the lines of the Canadian Corps. Severely wounded and bleeding profusely, Barker force landed inside Allied lines, his life being saved by the men of an RAF Kite Balloon Section who transported him to a field dressing station.

His actions on 27 October have been regarded as one of the most sensational fights in air history, for which he was awarded the Victoria Cross. At a hospital in Rouen, Barker clung to life until mid-January 1919 and then was transported back to England. He was not fit enough to walk the necessary few paces for the VC investiture at Buckingham Palace until 1 March 1919.

Lieutenant Colonel Barker returned to Canada in May 1919 as the most decorated Canadian of the war, with the Victoria Cross, DSO and Bar; Military Cross and two Bars, two Italian Silver Medals for Military Valour and the French Croix de guerre. He was also mentioned in despatches three times. Only Mick Mannock and James McCudden in the history of the Commonwealth or Empire have received as many British medals for gallantry. Like Barker, both were 'scout pilots'. Barker, Mannock and McCudden each received six British medals, including the Victoria Cross. McCudden was also awarded a French Croix de Guerre. But with his three foreign medals and three Mentions in Despatches, Barker received a total of twelve awards for valour.[7]

On 5 August 1918 the Air Ministry authorized the formation of two Canadian squadrons, one a fighter squadron and the other a bomber squadron. On 22 August a CAF detachment was formed at the school of Technical Training at Halton, England, to train the required ground crew for these two Canadian squadrons. On 19 September the Canadian Privy Council approved the formation of the CAF in England. It comprised two squadrons and a CAF Directorate of Air Services and Lieutenant Colonel William Avery Bishop became the first commander of the CAF in England.

On 5 September the Royal Canadian Naval Air Service (RCNAS) was formed with a main function to carry out anti-submarine operations using flying boat patrol aircraft but three months' later, on 5 December 1918 the RCNAS was disbanded and all the cadets and coxswains were demobilized.

All told, 22,812 Canadians and 13,160 aircrew served with distinction in the RFC, the RNAS (and later the Royal Air Force) as pilots, observers and mechanics, on all the fronts of the war, from the Home Front (England) to the Western Front (France and Belgium) and in Italy and the Dardanelles, the Adriatic and the Mediterranean and Egypt and Palestine. It is difficult to obtain a precise statistical picture of all those who served but 52 percent of fliers were Canadian-born; 13 percent of fliers were non-Canadians; the birthplace of 35 percent of fliers remains unknown; fliers came predominantly from large urban centres, where the rate of enlistment was three times that of fliers who identified themselves as coming from rural areas.[8] By war's end, almost a quarter of all British flyers were Canadian. Of 6,166 British Empire air service fatalities, 1,388 were Canadian also. An additional 1,130 Canadians were wounded or injured and 377 became prisoners of war or were interned. One third of all the fliers died in combat, among them 1,600 Canadians.

By the time the armistice was signed on 11 November 1918, the RAF establishment in Canada had a total strength 11,928 all ranks. It was staffed by 993 officers and 6,158 other ranks and had 4,333 cadet pilots and 444 other officers under training. (In April it was decided to establish several advanced flying training units in Canada). At the time of the armistice, it had an additional 240 pilots and 52 observers that were ready for overseas service. Additionally, there were 130 fatal crashes involving RFC/RAF aircraft in Canada during this same period.

On 20 November, nine days after the signing of the armistice, 1 Squadron (fighter) was formed at Upper Heyford, Oxfordshire; it was followed on 25 November 1918 by 2 Squadron (day bombing) Squadron also at Upper Heyford. To administer these two squadrons, 1 Wing CAF was formed on 25 March 1919. However 1 Wing did not assume their duties until 1 April after the two squadrons had moved south to Shoreham-by-Sea.

The Canadian government decided not to retain a permanent peace-time air force and orders were sent to cease flying and to package up all aircraft and equipment for shipment to Canada. 1 Squadron was disbanded on 28 January 1920 and 2 Squadron and the Wing disbanded on 5 February 1920. The directorate of Air Services was finally disbanded on 5 August 1920.

Endnotes Chapter 12

1   On Monday 9 April 1917 at 5.30 am after an intensive bombardment lasting four days to preclude any retaliation from the enemy, the British 1st Army comprising four Canadian divisions under the command of General Henry Horne set out to conquer Vimy Ridge. Wresting control of this height from the Germans would allow the 3rd Army under General Edmund Allenby to advance on Douai, an important road and rail junction and liberate the coal-mining region. Allenby was also expected to take Monchy-le-Preux, a village lying a few kilometres to the east of Arras which gave a commanding view over the Scarpe Valley and, because of this, could hinder the second arm of the offensive directed at Cambrai, another vital base for the German military apparatus. The 5th Army under General Hubert Gough, placed on the southern wing of the offensive, was given the task of taking the village of Bullecourt, a powerful strategic base of operations for the Germans and part of the Hindenburg Line. The first two days of the Battle of Arras were a clear tactical success for the British who, advancing five kilometres along both banks of the river Scarpe, took the villages of Thélus, Farbus, Sainte-Laurent-

Blangy, Feuchy, Athies, Fampoux, Tilloy-les-Mofflaines and Neuville-Vitasse. The securing of Vimy Ridge enabled the British artillery to drive the enemy from the villages of Givenchy-en-Gohelle, Vimy, Willerval and Bailleul-Sire-Bertoult which, up until that time, had been very effective gun batteries.

2   The other Canadians were W. K. G. Boyd of Toronto; Dissette of Vancouver (KIA 2 June 1917), J. H. Keens (WIA 7 June 1917), P. G. McNeil (KIA 3 June 1917), Q. S. Shirriff of Toronto, J. A. Page of Brockville, Ontario (KIA 22 July 1917), L. H. Parker of Leeds Village, Quebec (KIA 14 June 1917) and C. E. Pattison of Winona, Ontario (WIA 20 May 1917).

3   The aircraft was shipped to Australia after the war and displayed in Melbourne, but its ultimate fate is unknown.

4   On 16 July 1918 Kirschstein flew one of his aeroplanes in for maintenance at the repair depot at Fismes. He was accompanied by a new pilot in his Jasta, Leutnant Johannes Markgraf flying formation in a two-seater Hannover CL. After leaving the Fokker Kirschstein climbed into the rear seat of the Hannover for the return trip. Markgraf, who was unfamiliar with the Hannover, stalled it out at about 50 meters altitude on takeoff. The crash killed both men.

5   Air Commodore William Wedgwood Benn, 1st Viscount Stansgate DSO DFC PC (10 May 1877-17 November 1960) was a British Liberal politician who later joined the Labour Party. Although aged 37 at the time WWI broke out, on 8 December 1914 Benn was commissioned as a second lieutenant in the Middlesex Yeomanry (Duke of Cambridge's Hussars). On 12 May 1916 he was appointed an observer flying officer in the RFC. On 8 July 1916 he was appointed as the commanding officer of a seaplane observer squadron, with the temporary rank of captain. Seeing service at Gallipoli, he was seconded to the RNAS on 17 May 1917. He was awarded the DSO on 4 June 1917. On 12 July 1918 Benn transferred to the RAF and was appointed a temporary staff officer 3rd class, retaining his temporary captaincy. In September 1918 he was awarded the DFC. He was Secretary of State for India between 1929 and 1931 and Secretary of State for Air between 1945 and 1946. He was the father of Tony Benn and the grandfather of Hilary Benn.

6   Born 2 July 1897 at Griswold, Manitoba, he was a graduate of the University of Saskatchewan. McEwen joined the Canadian Army in 1916. In April 1917 he was seconded to the RFC. A founding member of 28 Squadron, he served in Italy as a Camel pilot, scoring 27 victories. In 1919 'Black Mike' returned to Canada where he served as an instructor with the RCAF. From 1932 to 1941 he was commander of air training operations at Camp Borden, Ontario, then at Trenton, Ontario, Toronto, Montreal and Halifax, Nova Scotia. During WWII he assumed command of 6 Group in England in 1944. He attained the rank of Air Vice-Marshal and retired in 1946 but continued working as a consultant to various aircraft manufacturers. He was 69 when he died.

7   In 1920 Barker joined the Canadian Air Force and was sent to England as Liaison Officer at the Air Ministry. From 1924 to 1929 he lived near Simcoe, Ontario actively interested in the tobacco industry of Norfolk County. In 1930 however, he returned to aviation and became president of the Fairchild Aviation Corporation of Canada. But fate worked one of its strangest and cruellest blows when on 12 March 1931 he crashed to death over Rockcliffe Aerodrome near Ottawa while making a trial flight just prior to demonstrating a new type of two-seater aeroplane for the Civil Aviation branch of the Department of National Defence. A stalled engine had done what the combined skill and intent of thousands of enemy pilots in many skies had hitherto been unable to accomplish. His funeral in Toronto was a national tribute to a 'protector of the air' of international renown.

8   Research by the Canadian Forces' Directorate of History and Heritage.

Part Two: Taking Flight

Preface

Only 3,100 of the 13,600 internees held in Britain on 22 September 1914 originated on the battlefields. Most of the remaining 10,500 came from the German civilian community in Britain. The total figure of 13,600 included people captured by the British on the seas, both civilians and naval personnel. The number of captured naval and military personnel remained low throughout the early stages of the war. By 1 February 1915 prisoners consisted of 400 officers (including a small number of Austrians), 6,500 soldiers and naval sailors, together with 19,000-20,000 merchant sailors and civilians (German and Austrian). By November 1915, following the decision in May to intern all enemy aliens of military age, the number of civilian internees had reached 32,440. The number of military prisoners transported to Britain did not begin to increase until 1917 when there was a marked increase in the number of German soldiers captured on the Western Front, even though a significant number had already been interned in France, especially following the Battle of the Somme where they worked as forced labourers. In 1917, 73,131 combatants fell into British hands, followed by another 201,633 in 1918 as the German armies faced defeat.

In WWI 2.4 million Allied soldiers became PoWs in Germany. Of these, 6,778 officers and 168,846 men of the British and Commonwealth forces were captured on the Western Front alone. Nearly 10% of these were held for all four years by the Germans having been captured at the battles of the Marne and Ypres. The Geneva convention did not come into being properly until 1929, hence the 'rules' in place for PoW treatment were made under the Hague convention of 1907. Chapter II of the convention signed in October 1907 is entirely devoted to prisoners of war and begins thus: 'Prisoners of war are in the power of the hostile Government, but not of the individuals or corps who capture them. They must be humanely treated. All their personal belongings, except arms, horses and military papers, remain their property'. The twenty articles comprising this chapter regulate various aspects of life in captivity such as lodging, work, religion, nourishment, dress and mail. This international accord, however, is imbued with 19th-century conceptions of war. Thus, prisoners 'may be set at liberty on parole if the laws of their country allow', for example. The principal nations of the 'Triple Entente' and the 'Triple Alliance' (or central powers) signed the convention, with the exception of the Ottoman Empire, not among the 44 signatories in 1907. The Hague Convention's dispositions entered into force in the German Empire and France on 26 January 1910, but these agreements turned out to be unsuitable in the tumult of World War I. In October 1918 the number of prisoners held in Germany reached 2,415,043 and such a mass of men made it impossible for a country at war to fully respect the conventions in their smallest details. During the conflict, the belligerent parties concluded special accords in order to mitigate these difficulties and in 1929, a new text was produced, amending the applicable regulatory dispositions (The Geneva Convention).

Italy, who fought on the side of the allied nations, had a pact with Germany / Austro-Hungary - a defensive role only: since the other two parties of the Triple Alliance had taken the offensive, this pact was null and void.

Starting in 1915, the German authorities put in place a system of camps, nearly three hundred in all and did not hesitate to resort to near-starvation, various punishments and psychological mobbing; incarceration was also combined with methodical exploitation of the prisoners. This prefigured the systematic use of prison camps on a grand scale during the 20th century. However, the captivity organised by the German military authorities also contributed to creating exchanges among peoples and led a number of prisoners to reflect on their involvement in the war and relation with their homeland.

From the beginning of the war, the German authorities found themselves confronted with an unexpected influx of prisoners. In September 1914,125,050 French and 94,000 Russian soldiers were held captive. Before 1915 conditions of detention in Germany were very harsh and marked by temporary lodging and the absence of infrastructure. The prisoners slept in hangars or tents, where they dug holes to keep warm. The humid forts requisitioned to serve as places of detention led to numerous cases of pulmonary illness. The German authorities also commandeered schools, barns and various other types of shelters. Camps were established in the countryside as well as near the towns, which had consequences when epidemics of cholera or typhus threatened to spread to the civilian population.

Camps were designated: Mannschaftslager - ordinary soldier's camps; Stalag - Stammslager or Mannschaftsstamm-und Straflager. These were the basic camps, made up of wooden barracks 10 metres wide and 50 metres long covered with tar on the outside. Each of these barracks kept around 250 prisoners. On the inside, a central corridor provided access on each side to straw or sawdust beds stacked two high. Furniture was kept to a minimum: a table, chairs or benches and a stove. Camps also featured barracks for guards, a Kantine (cafeteria) where prisoners could sometimes buy little objects and additional food, a barrack for packages, a guardhouse and kitchens. Each camp had its own particular structures, notably sanitary facilities or cultural places like a library, a theatre hall or a worship space. All around the camp, there was barbed wire three metres high; the wires were spaced fifteen centimetres apart, a wooden post every three metres and across other barbed wires every fifty centimetres, forming a mesh.

Not all the camps were situated on German territory; a certain number were built on occupied territories, notably in northern and eastern France. They began to be developed starting in 1915 when the number of prisoners being held captive in Germany reached 652,000. According to official directives, each prisoner had to have use of 2.5 metres^2. The camps mixed a large number of nationalities sharing the same quarters: French, Russian, British, American, Canadian, Belgian, Italian, Romanian, Serbian, Montenegrin, Portuguese and Japanese prisoners were found there, as well as Greeks and Brazilians. Equally, soldiers of various social origins rubbed elbows: workers, peasants, bureaucrats and intellectuals were among those held. The number of prisoners rose very quickly. From February to August 1915 it increased from 652,000 to 1,045,232. In August 1916 it reached 1,625,000, jumping to 2,415,000 by October 1918.

The Geneva Convention ruled that officer PoW's did not have to work but enlisted men were required to do so if asked by their captors. From the parent camp, they were assigned to Arbeitskommandos (Labour detachments) in agriculture or industry. Detachment strength ranged from ten to 2,000 men. Prisoners worked on government-funded projects such as road and bridge construction, railway track maintenance and renewal and land reclamation work. Large industrial companies in Germany hired British and Allied PoWs from the regional Army Corps Commands to work in steel factories, quarries and coalmines. Smaller employers hired them as stevedores, rubbish collectors, foresters and in small groups as farm hands. Prisoners usually lived near the place of their employment.

Those in German camps who did work were paid not with official German currency as it was feared that if they could accumulate large sums of money through working, they could bribe guards to help them escape and then pay their way through Germany to freedom, but in prison lagergeld (camp money). Lagergeld was often specially printed for individual camps and could only be used to purchase goods at the camp store or credited to a prison bank account. Prisoners were paid at a rate, determined by their level of skill and agreement between government or private employer and Army Corps Commands. The lowest paid were farm workers, from 16 to 35 Pfennigs a day. Small industries paid 30 to 50 Pfennigs a day, while those in heavy industry received from 75 Pfennigs to one Mark a day. For the highly skilled and professional PoW the rate was between two and three marks a day. Many PoWs in Germany were pleased to escape the boredom of life behind barbed wire in the parent camp and welcomed the change of scenery and the money they earned at the working camps. The money often supplemented their food rations until food parcels arrived. Although some prisoners complained about working in heavy industry, where cruelty was sometimes inflicted on them, those working on the land and on farms often ate at the same table as their employer and slept in his house and became part of the family. They were often better fed than many city dwelling Germans.

Although British PoWs held in German camps were put to work early in the war, it was not until quite late in the conflict before German PoWs were put to work outside the camps, although calls for them to do so had been made by several prominent people, including Lord Northcliffe, who in 1916 said, 'The authorities in England seem to hide our German prisoners. In France they work and in public ... the sooner German prisoners are put to work and help to shorten the war the better.' By 1917, an increasing food and labour shortage forced the British government to put the men to work. By summer, a PoW labour army of 70,000 men had been formed. Split into gangs of about ten men, 30,000 PoW's travelled from farm to farm helping to bring in the harvest. Others were involved in construction work, quarrying, repairing roads, forestry and re-claiming waste land.

In 1918 an extraordinary document signed by the German Army Chief of Staff,

General Erich Ludendorff, was said to have fallen into British hands. In September of that year it was published in the Morning Post and part of it read, 'Capture at the hands of our inhuman foes, in view of their unexampled brutality of treatment, which is now proved beyond question in so large a number of cases, merely means being slowly tortured to death.' During the German Spring Offensive of 1918, copies of the order had been circulated among 'the German rank and file on the battlefield' and it was, said a British source, intended to 'nerve the German soldier to fight strenuously to the last - to die rather than be taken prisoner. Many German soldiers were found to be in absolute terror as to what would happen to them in captivity.'

The rapid progression of the German offensive in the early part of the war led to a massive influx of Allied prisoners. From 1915, transit camps, the 'Durchgangslager', were built to manage and redirect this wave toward detention camps. There was a special transit camp for Allied prisoners of war at the former Europäischer Hof at 39, Ettlinger Strasse, in Karlsruhe. This was known as 'the Listening Hotel' by the inmates, who recognized that it was a camp devoted to intelligence collection.

Reprisal camps were very often located in regions where the climate or the terrain made life difficult but also near the front, where the prisoners might as likely be taken to rebuild trenches as to cart away bodies. The goal of the reprisals was to put pressure on enemy governments to ameliorate conditions of detention for German prisoners, but also to punish certain ones (for instance following an escape). Life for prisoners sent to reprisal camps was so harsh that many of them died. Robert d'Harcourt describes the arrival of a prisoners' convoy coming from such a camp: 'These men - these soldiers - marched, but they were dead; beneath each blue greatcoat was the head of a dead man: their eyes hollow, their cheekbones jutting out, their emaciated grimaces those of graveyard skulls.' Most often kept in tents resting on mud these prisoners were forced into exhaustive work with their entire diet consisting of soup or perhaps stewed acorns. At certain camps, for instance at Sedan, some prisoners were executed. Reprisal camps for officers existed, too: the fortress at Ingolstadt held Charles de Gaulle, Georges Catroux, Eugène Adrien Roland Georges Garros, the journalist and World War II Resistance member Rémy Roure, the editor Berger-Levrault and the future Soviet Marshal Mikhail Tukhachevsky.

On 18 April 1915, either Garros's fuel line clogged or, by other accounts, his aircraft was shot down by ground fire and he glided to a landing on the German side of the lines. Garros failed to destroy his aircraft completely before being taken prisoner: most significantly, the gun and armoured propeller remained intact. On 14 February1918, after several attempts, Roland Garros finally managed to escape to rejoin the French army. He settled into Escadrille 26 to pilot a Spad and claimed two victories on 2 October, one of which was confirmed. On 5 October he was shot down and killed near Vouziers, Ardennes, a month before the end of the war and one day before his 30th birthday. His adversary was probably German ace Hermann Habich from Jasta 49.

The first successful Allied escape of the war occurred in September 1918 when Captain John Owen Donaldson DSO DFC of the American Air Service who was credited with seven aerial victories and another prisoner escaped, but were recaptured. Donaldson was born in Fort Yates, North Dakota, the son of General Thomas Quinton Donaldson. He left Cornell and joined the RFC in Canada in March 1917. When the US declared war, he transferred to the American Air Service. He was attached to the RAF and posted to 32 Squadron. On 1 September he was shot down by Major Theodor Quandt of Jasta 36; a 15-victory ace.[1] The following day, while being held in a temporary prison camp in the village of Conde, Donaldson and a fellow prisoner escaped. Attempting to steal a two-seater from its hangar at a German aerodrome, they were discovered by a guard. In the struggle that followed, Donaldson received a bayonet wound in the back before the two men overpowered the German soldier and fled into the countryside. On 9 September 1918, the unlucky duo was recaptured while attempting to swim a stream between the Allied and German lines. Three days later, Donaldson, together with his former companion and three other prisoners, escaped again and made his way to safety in the Netherlands in October. He was killed while stunting near Philadelphia, Pennsylvania, on 7 September 1930.

By 5 July 1919 the British held responsibility for no less than 458,392 internees globally. On home soil the figures had declined to 90,276 including 3,373 civilians, 2,899 naval personnel and 84,004 soldiers. While Allied prisoners of war in German camps were released very soon after the Armistice and most were home by Christmas, the same could not be said for prisoners held by the Allies. Many enemy PoWs had to work as forced labour until 1920 on reconstruction and other tasks. And even then, they were only released after 'many approaches by the I.C.R.C. to the Allied Supreme Council.' Some German prisoners of war held in Russia did not gain their freedom until 1922.

Endnotes Part 2 Preface

1   Quandt began his string of victories as a balloon buster, setting a pair of observation balloons on fire on 21 May 1917. His seventh victory was on 17 October 1917 when over Poelcapelle, Belgium he shot down a Bristol Fighter (A7271), piloted by Lieutenant Arthur Gilbert Vivian Taylor. He and his observer, Sergeant William Joseph Benger, who was credited with five aerial victories over German Albatros D.V fighters, were both captured, but died of their injuries shortly afterwards. Benger's award of the Military Medal was gazetted on 17 December 1917, two months after his death. Quandt's eighth victory came on 8 November 1917. There would be almost a ten month lapse before Quandt resumed scoring on 27 August 1918 with a double victory. After his eleventh triumph over John Donaldson, he then scored four more times in the next three days, finishing the war as a leutnant. Quandt was killed in action while flying a Messerschmitt Bf 109 during the fall of France on 6 June 1940.

Chapter 13

Outwitting The Turk

Oh the road to En-dor is the oldest road
And the craziest road of all!
Straight it runs to the Witch's abode,
As it did in the days of Saul,
And nothing has changed of the sorrow in store
For such as go down on the road to En-dor!

Kipling's poem En-Dor, a warning against spiritualism first published in *The Years Between*, which appeared in 1919, while Elias Henry Jones (21 September 1883-22 December 1942) was writing *The Road to En-Dor* (The Bodley Head).

The Siege of Kut Al Amara (7 December 1915-29 April 1916), also known as the First Battle of Kut, was the besieging of the British-Indian garrison in the town of Kut, 100 miles south of Baghdad, by the Ottoman Army. The British finally surrendered on 29 April 1916 after a siege of 147 days. James Morris, a British historian, described the loss of Kut as 'the most abject capitulation in Britain's military history.' Around 13,000 Allied soldiers survived to be made prisoners and they were marched to imprisonment at Aleppo. Half the officers were taken to a town called Kastamuni in the heart of Asia Minor, about 260 miles east of Constantinople 'now Istanbul]. It has been estimated that 70 per cent of British PoWs died in, or on the way to, Turkish camps. Over 3,000 PoWs died on the gruelling marches from Kut Al Amara in 1916 and those that arrived exhausted at the Baghdad railway camps were immediately set to work by the Turks, with little concern for the astronomical casualty rate.[1]

Captain Richard James ('Dick') Tipton of Oxton, Cheshire, born on 25 April 1892, was among those detained for fourteen months with 120 British officers, mostly from the Kut garrison, in private houses cleared for the prisoners. Originally a member of the 3rd West Lancashire Brigade, Royal Field Artillery into which he was commissioned, in May 1915 he transferred to the flying corps and, obtaining his wings on 19 June 1915, went to Egypt as a pilot with 14 Squadron in the autumn of the same year. He was subsequently mentioned in the despatches of Sir John Maxwell and Sir Archibald Murray. On 18 June 1916 he took part in a raid against the German airfield at El Arish as a reprisal for a bombing attack on the camp of the Anzac 1st Light Horse Brigade. Eleven B.E.2cs participated, two of them flying with observers, the rest being flown solo so that more bombs could be carried. Tipton and the rest took off from Qantara and approached El Arish from the sea at 600 feet. There was stiff opposition from the ground and one British aircraft immediately crashed into the sea. Tipton was among those who reached the hostile airfield, where he released his bombs just before being shot down. He crashed outside the airfield but managed to set fire to his machine before Turkish troops arrived to take him prisoner.

During the spring of 1917, Captain Tipton and three others made up their minds to escape. Captain (later Lieutenant Colonel, Sir) Edward Herbert Keeling Indian Army Reserve Officer could speak Turkish. Captain R. T. Sweet DSO had been attached to the 2/7th Ghurka Rifles. Lieutenant Harry Coghill Watson Bishop IARO, attached to the 66th Punjabis later wrote *A Kut Prisoner*. Keeling, born 1888, the youngest son of the Reverend Hulton Keeling, headmaster of Bradford Grammar School, was educated at Bradford and University College, Oxford, graduating with a master's degree in jurisprudence. He was called to the bar at Lincoln's Inn. In 1902 he received employment in the Supply and Accounting Department of the Admiralty. From there he moved to be a member of the Harbour Commission in Burma, then a British colony. With the outbreak of World War I, Keeling received a commission as an officer in the Indian Army Reserve of Officers. He served in the Mesopotamian Campaign and was present at the surrender of Kut by the British at the hands of Ottoman Forces.

The most vital question the would-be escapers faced was what point to make for? The only land frontier was the Russian front line, 400 miles away to the east, across extremely wild and mountainous country and it seemed impossible to escape that way. Their only chance was to get down to the Black Sea, steal a boat and make for a Russian port. If, however, they aimed at the nearest part of the coast they should almost certainly be caught, so they determined to strike for a point much further away, near the mouth of the Kizil River where there was less probability of the beach being watched.

The four compatriots escaped on the night 8 August 1917, each man carrying 30lb of escape kit in homemade rucksacks, as well as a patchwork sail to propel the boat which they hoped to steal on the Black Sea shore. Donning fezes at night and homemade German military headgear by day, they escaped attention of any Turk sufficiently interested to turn them in for two weeks by which time they had walked some 200 miles to reach the Jerse on the Black Sea coast, where, they were suspected of being escaped British officers by the crew of a Government vessel and handed over to the Gendarmerie. They gave German names to the Turkish commandant who asked Tipton to speak German on the telephone to a German officer at Sinope. Tipton who knew only a few words, pretended the phone was 'kaput'.

A guard of nine soldiers was assembled to march them back to Kustamuni. On 27 August, near Sinope, the party was ambushed apparently by bandits. One guard was killed, two others wounded and the rest surrendered. In the meantime Sweet took to his heels as the bullets were flying and despite a thorough search of the roadside was not seen again. His fellow escapers learned after the Armistice that when the outlaws opened fire on the guard he decided that the best thing to do was to get clear away and made no attempt to return to the road on which they waited for him. He pluckily made his way alone to the coast, but was there again recaptured, taken back to Kastamuni with a guard of seventy soldiers, led in procession through the town and kept in the civil jail for six weeks. He was then interned in another prisoners' camp at Yozgad, where he died of influenza just before the war ended.

The outlaws, or 'comrades' as they referred to themselves, proved to be dissidents rather than brigands and were equally anxious to make the Black Sea crossing to Russia. But Turkish troops were drafted into the area and the Gendarmerie reinforced and for over a month Tipton, Keeling and Bishop lived a hazardous life with the 'comrades' in the mountains of Anatolia until a small boat could be secured to carry them across to the Crimea and safety.

'September 21', wrote Keeling in a long account of the escape for *Blackwood's Magazine,* was the most eventful of our whole journey. At dawn we were hurried down to the boat, which was waiting for us close to the shore, about half an hour from our hiding place. It was a fishing boat about 25 feet long and of about two and a half tons, with dipping lug-sail and four oars... By 0615, just after sunrise, everything was ready and we pushed off. There were fourteen of us on board, namely seven Circassians, two Georgians, one Turk proper, one Armenian and three Englishmen. All our friends were Turkish subjects. While embarking, another felucca somewhat bigger than ours had been creeping along the coast from the west and the 'comrades' resolved to board her and thus anticipate any attempt she might make to stop us. Accordingly they rowed alongside and levelled their rifles.'

Thus the voyage proceeded into its second day, with prisoners of their own and two vessels, both of which soon displayed serious defects and it was determined to abandon one of them. After much argument and the transfer of the captured boat's boom to the original vessel the former was left to her fate complete with her cargo of paraffin. On the third day of the voyage the captured skipper shot a dolphin which was cooked on a fire made from the deck.

'At 0530 on the fourth day the voyage of hope became a certainty,' Keeling continues, 'and we were all raised to the seventh heaven of joy by the definite view of the mountains on the north west horizon. The captured crew, who cherished an idea that they would be sent back to Turkey and were quite as eager to land as any of us, began to row vigorously ... Without a wind several hours elapsed before we could reach the [Crimean] shore; but our friends at once began to don their bandoliers and we had some difficulty in persuading them that if they tried to land in Russia with rifles and ammunition misunderstanding might arise.'

Throughout practically the whole course of the escape Tipton had been suffering from some unspecified ailment. A Russian surgeon operated 'not before time' and the arrival of the British officers was communicated to the Commander-in-Chief of the Russian Black Sea fleet who arranged passage to Yalta by car. From Yalta they continued to Sebastopol by sea, then onwards via Odessa, Kieff, Petrograd, Stockholm and Christiana to England. In spite of wholly complimentary remarks, demanded no doubt as an exigency of the time, in the *Blackwood's* article about the Russians, Tipton and the others in fact experienced considerable difficulties as well as co-operation arriving as they did shortly after the Russian Revolution and during the Kerensky regime. It is further known that Keeling for one assisted Russian intelligence and endeavoured to organize a naval expedition to return to Turkey to liberate their comrades at Kastamuni. An unsuccessful attempt was made; after which, during the period of the Bolshevik coup d'état, he returned to Britain after great difficulties and only through the clemency of Trotsky.

On Tipton's return home he was given the honour of a private interview with the King at Buckingham Palace. He turned down the offer of three months' home leave and applied to immediately rejoin the RFC, first going to the CFS at Upavon and then to 40 Squadron (S.E.5a's) in France in early 1918. On 6 March he shot down Leutnant Walter Conderet of Jagdstaffel 52, but was mortally wounded in aerial combat on 9 March by a machine-gun bullet. He nevertheless managed to fly his machine back to British lines and land without mishap. An A.S.C sergeant reported: 'At about 1645 I saw an S.E.5a coming in very low from the direction of Lens. He circled over Calonne Road and made a good landing behind our billet ... Captain Tipton was badly hit in the abdomen but was conscious. He gave me the number of his Squadron and said he didn't mind much, because he got the Hun who hit him and was quite cheerful owing to that fact.' He was removed to a Canadian casualty clearing station but succumbed to his wounds two days later and was buried at Barlin Communal Cemetery, Pas de Calais.

Following his return to England, Keeling served as the head of a special branch (responsible for Turkey and Bulgaria) in the British General Staff for enabling officers to escape. He was awarded the Military Cross in October 1918. His story *Adventures in Turkey and Russia* was published by John Murray in 1924. He entered business and was elected as MP for Twickenham in 1935. From 1945-1946 Keeling served as Mayor of Westminster. In 1952 he was knighted. Keeling held the Twickenham seat until death in 1954, aged 66.

In 1918 two other escapees captured during the fall of Kut, Lieutenant Elias Henry Jones, a Welsh officer in the Indian Army and Australian pilot Lieutenant Cedric Waters Hill, escaped from the Yozgad prisoner of war camp in Asia Minor. Yozgad lies in the heart of the rugged mountains of Anatolia, almost due east from Angora. It is over 4,000 feet above sea level and was probably as inaccessible as any prison camp in the world outside Russia. The nearest railhead (Angora) was 120 miles away. The nearest seaport (Samsun, on the Black Sea) was a little further; about 130 miles. Three hundred miles as the crow flies would have taken them to friendly territory; either to the Crimea or to the Russians at Erzinjan or to Cyprus. Their epic story was told in Jones' book *The Road to En-dor.*

Hill was born on 3 April 1891 at Maryvale station, near Warwick, Queensland, fourth child of Edward Ormond Waters Hill, grazier and his wife Phillis, both native-born. At Brisbane Grammar School, Cedric was 'sluggish at his work, but good natured and honourable'. He learned sheep-farming in New Zealand, took an apprenticeship with a Brisbane engineering firm, completed a course in shearing-machinery maintenance and began working in sheds around Queensland. After seeing the magician Nate Leipzig perform, Hill studied and practised conjuring; his other interest was flying and he built two gliders before World War I broke out. Sailing to England, Hill was commissioned in the RFC on 3 July 1915 and by the end of the year was in Egypt with 14 Squadron. His precision bombing of the reservoir at Bir el Hassana on 27 February 1916 won acclaim and he was mentioned in dispatches that year. On 3 May anti-aircraft fire forced his B.E.2c down, east of Romani. Using his dismounted Lewis Gun, he traded fire with some Arabs for six hours before surrendering and being handed over to the Turks. They took him to the prisoner-of-war camp at Yozgad where he befriended Lieutenant Elias Henry Jones. To entertain their comrades, Hill and Jones communicated with the spirit world by Ouija-board, conjured ghostly 'manifestations' and perfected a telepathy act.

Although forbidden to escape by their own superiors, Hill and Jones decided to exploit the greed and superstition of the camp's commandant in order to get away. In early 1918 they convinced him that their supernatural informant, 'the Spook', could reveal the whereabouts of buried treasure if he were consulted on the Mediterranean coast - whence they planned to abscond to Cyprus. To justify their removal from the camp, they feigned madness, Hill exhibiting symptoms of 'religious melancholia' and Jones general paralysis of the insane. A mishap foiled the plan, but the conspirators decided to persist with the ruse of insanity to gain repatriation on medical grounds.

Having hoodwinked the local doctors, Hill and Jones were sent to Constantinople in May. On the way, a fake, double-suicide attempt almost cost them their lives, but it helped to lend authenticity to their deception. In hospitals and camps, in and around the capital, they underwent psychiatric examinations and overcame ploys to expose them. With his 'forehead puckered, jaw dropped and mouth open', Hill read from the Bible and fasted until he became ill from malnutrition and dysentery. By August he and Jones had been certified insane and approved for an exchange of prisoners with the British. Hill sailed for England on 1 November 1918 and resumed his career in the Royal Air Force.

While again serving in the Middle East, Hill married a fellow Australian, Jane Lisle Mort on 16 March 1921 at Port Said, Egypt, with Church of England rites. Back in England, on 5 October 1930 he flew from Lympne aerodrome, Kent, in an attempt to beat Bert Hinkler's time for a solo flight to Australia. A crash on the 18th, when he was taking off from Atambua, Netherlands Timor, for the final leg to Darwin, prevented him from breaking the record. 'A friendly, jolly person, tall and very sunburnt', Hill was an outstanding rifle and pistol shot, a keen skier and photographer and a member (1933) of the Inner Magic Circle.

Hill commanded squadrons in Britain and the Sudan; rose to wing commander in 1937 and was given charge of RAF Tangmere, Sussex. Promoted temporary group captain in June 1940, he performed staff and training duties in Britain and had operational commands in the Middle East before being placed on the Retired List on 5 January 1944. For the next two years he was a ferry pilot with the Air Transport Auxiliary. In retirement in England Hill took up gliding. He died on 5 March 1975 in his home at Windsor, Berkshire. His account of his feat of 'malingering', *The Spook and the Commandant* (London), was published later that year.

Jones continued in the RAF after the war, becoming a Wing Commander in 1937 and commanding RAF Tangmere. He retired from the RAF in 1944 and then acted as a ferry pilot for the Air Transport Auxiliary. On 5 March 1975, Hill died at his home in Windsor, Berkshire.

Endnotes Chapter 13

1   *Tracing Your Prisoner of War Ancestors; The First World War, A Guide for Family Historians* by Sarah Paterson (Pen & Sword 2012).

Chapter 14

Escaping From England

Günther Plüschow

As a race the Germans are not good escapers - they don't seem to have the right outlook. As far as I know only one German escaped from England in the last war. His name was Pushtow ['sic] and he wrote a book [originally published as Die abenteuer des fliegers von Tsingtao, in 1916] which was translated, called 'My Escape from Donington Hall'. As a psychological essay it is interesting but the true escaper will find it an irritating account of haphazard adventures written from entirely the wrong angle. In the book there is an intolerable amount of sentimental wash. Pushtow ['sic] escaped from a sense of duty; he clearly did not enjoy it a bit and on reaching the Fatherland one is not surprised to learn that he fell on his knees and kissed the sacred soil.

A. J. Evans, Escape and Liberation 1940-45[1]

During World War One, Donington Hall, the mock Gothic stately home in a 1,100-acre landscaped deer park in Castle Donington, North West Leicestershire, located close to the city of Derby became a byword for easy living and lax security. The hall had been turned into a detention camp for officers early in the war. Intended as a maximum security prison, it was ringed by two barbed wire perimeter fences more than 6 feet high - the inner one electrified - with wire traps, watch towers searchlights and a guard house. Officers on both sides were guaranteed a certain level of treatment by international treaty. From 1915, imprisoned officers were held in camps reserved for them. By October 1918 the number of officers' camps had reached 73. Living conditions for officers were usually less harsh than those endured by troops. Officers had beds instead of straw sacks, specific rooms were fitted out for their meals and they were exempted from labour. In addition, there were no officers' camps in East Prussia, where weather conditions were often far worse than in the rest of Germany. One of the main burdens of camp life for officers was tedium. Their daily lives tended to revolve around sport, amateur concerts and plays, lectures, debates and reading. Officers' camps also accommodated a smaller number of other ranks prisoners, known as orderlies, whose role was to act as servants to the officers and to perform menial tasks around the camp. Orderlies appreciated that their situation was safer and more comfortable than that of their counterparts in soldiers' camps and so, even when offered the opportunity, they generally did not try to escape, knowing that if recaptured they would be sent to far worse conditions.

Donington Hall became a byword in wartime luxury. One of Donington's most striking features was its 90-capacity dining room, based in the old library. 'It was all laid out with silver service cutlery and table cloths, rather like a posh hotel. There was a good menu with a choice of options and there was a good wine list - but they could also send home for wine and other things. The local post office had to put extra staff on because so many parcels were sent from Germany. And of course they were all waited on by German privates and corporal, who were billeted in huts in the grounds. I wouldn't call it luxury perhaps but it was certainly great comfort - and the contrast with the soldiers at the front could hardly have been greater.'[2]

On top of this were homely rooms, games of football, cricket, tennis and skittles and a relaxed regime where 'the commandant did everything he could to alleviate our hard lot' according to one prisoner. New arrivals were welcomed with a guard of honour and every Friday the prisoners were lined up to be given a cash allowance - direct from Germany. Another inmate was Captain Franz Dagobert Johannes von Rintelen, a German Naval Intelligence officer in the United States, who was interned at Donington Hall for twenty-one months before he was extradited to the United States, tried and found guilty on Federal charges in New York and imprisoned in Atlanta, Georgia for three years, after the US entered the war. In America in 1915 he developed time-delayed incendiary devices known as pencil bombs, which were then placed in the holds of merchant ships trading to Britain to cause fires in the ships' holds so that the crew would throw the munitions overboard. Several were planted successfully. von Rintelen found enthusiastic support among Irish dock workers, who made much effort to sabotage British ships. However when they attempted to plant bombs on the passenger mail boat *Ancona,* von Rintelen looked for other supporters. He also organized the Labour's National Peace Council to foster strikes and work slowdowns among munitions workers to inhibit American aid to the Allies.

von Rintelen recalled holding his own 'wake' at Donington Hall following false reports he had been shot. 'The canteen overflowed that evening and the orchestra played Chopin's *Funeral March.* I drank both red wine and champagne and praised the Lord,' he wrote.[3]

The newspapers got to hear of the sumptuous conditions at Donington Hall and, fuelled by tales of brutality in German camps, called for action. Pressed during a debate in parliament on excessive privileges at the camp, Mr Harold Tennant, the Under Secretary of State, insisted the sale of alcohol was restricted to 'light wines and beers' but could not confirm whether quantities were limited. The arrival - and subsequent departure - of dashing pilot Günther Plüschow only added to its notoriety.

Günther Plüschow was a First Naval Flying Officer at Kiao-Chow, China on outbreak of war. In November 1914 he escaped in his aeroplane from Kiao-Chow during the siege and travelled by steamer to San Francisco under assumed name, sailing from New York on Italian steamer in January 1915. Identified and taken prisoner by English authorities at Gibraltar, brought to England and interned in Donington Hall Camp in February 1915. He escaped on 4 July 1915 to London and managed to board a Dutch steamer at Tilbury by night, reaching Germany through Holland on 13 July. He was awarded by the Kaiser the Iron Cross 1st Class for his successful escape. After many thrilling adventures during the first year of the war in China and America, he attempted to get back to Germany from New York disguised as a Swiss on an Italian steamer in February 1915. But he was discovered and arrested at Gibraltar by the British authorities and eventually found myself in the German officers' prison camp at Donington Hall, Castle Donington near Derby. Day and night he planned, brooded and deliberated how he could escape from this miserable imprisonment. He had to act with the greatest calm and caution if he hoped to succeed.

'For hours I walked up and down in front of different parts of the entanglements, whilst I unostentatiously examined every wire and every stake. For hours together I lay in the grass in the vicinity of some of those spots that seemed favourable, feigning sleep. But all the time I was closely watching every object and noting the ways and habits of the different sentries. I had already fixed upon the spot where I had decided to climb the barbed wire. Now the question remained how to make headway after this obstacle had been overcome. We possessed neither a map of England nor a compass, no time-table, no means of assistance of any kind. We were even ignorant of the exact location of Donington Hall. I knew the road to Donington Castle, for I had fixed it in my memory on the day of our arrival. I had also heard through an officer, who had been taken by car to Donington Hall from Derby, that the latter lay about twenty-five to thirty miles away to the north and that he had passed a long bridge before the car turned into the village. I resolved to make common cause with a Naval officer, Oberleutnant Trefftz, who knew England and spoke English remarkably well.

'On 4 July 1915, in the morning, we reported ourselves sick. At the morning roll-call, at ten o'clock, our names were entered on the sick-list and on its completion the orderly sergeant came to our room and found us ill in bed. Everything was working well. With the afternoon came the decision. About 4 pm I dressed, collected all that I considered necessary for my flight, ate several substantial buttered rolls and bade farewell to my comrades, especially to my faithful friend Siebel, whom, unfortunately, I could not take with me as he was no sailor and did not speak English.

'A heavy storm was in progress and rain poured in torrents from grey skies. The sentries stood wet and shivering in their sentry-boxes and therefore nobody paid any attention when two officers decided to walk about in the park, in spite of the rain. The park contained a grotto, surrounded by shrubs, from which one could overlook its whole expanse and the barbed wire, without oneself being seen. This is where Trefftz and I crept in. We took a hurried leave of Siebel, who covered us with garden chairs and we were alone. From now onwards we were in the hands of Providence and it was to be hoped that Fortune would not forsake us. We waited in breathless suspense. Minutes seemed like centuries, but slowly and surely one hour passed after another, until the turret-clock struck six in loud, clear chimes. Our hearts thumped in unison. We heard the bell ring for roll-call, the command 'Attention' and then the noisy closing of the day-boundary. We hardly dared to breathe, expecting at any moment to hear our names called out. It was 6.30 and nothing had happened. A weight slipped from our shoulders. Thank God, the first act was a success. For during roll-call our names had again been reported on the sick-list and as soon as the officers were allowed to fall out, two of our comrades raced back as swiftly as they could through the back entrance and occupied Trefftz's bed and mine. Therefore, when the sergeant arrived he was able to account satisfactorily for the two invalids. As everything was now in order, the night-boundary was closed, as every night and even the sentries withdrawn from the day-boundary. Thus we were left to our own devices. The exceptionally heavy rain proved a boon to us, for the English soldiers generally indulged in all kinds of frolic in the evenings and we might have easily been discovered.

'At 10.30 pm our excitement came to a head. We had to pass our second test. We clearly heard the signal 'Stand to,' and from the open window of my former room The Watch on the Rhine rang out sonorously. It was the concerted signal that all were on the alert. The orderly officer, accompanied by a sergeant, walked through all the rooms and satisfied himself that no one was missing. By observations carried on for weeks I had made sure that the orderly officers always chose the same route in order to return to their quarters, after their rounds, by the shortest way. So it was to-night. The round began with the room from which Trefftz was missing. Of course his bed was already occupied by someone.

'All present?'

'Yes, sir!'

'All right! Good-night, gentlemen.'

'And so forth. As soon as the orderly officer had turned the corner, two other comrades ran in the opposite direction and into my room, so that here also all could be reported 'present.'

'It is difficult to conceive our excitement and nervous tension whilst this was in progress. We followed all the proceedings in our minds and when suddenly silence supervened for an unconscionably lengthy period we feared the worst. With ice-cold hands, ears on the alert for the slightest sound, we lay, hardly daring to breathe. At last, at 11 pm, a lusty cheer broke the stillness. It was our concerted signal that all was clear!

'All was silent around us. The rain had ceased. The park lay wrapped in darkness and only the light of the huge arc-lamps, which lit up the night-boundary, streamed faintly towards us. The moment for action had arrived. I crept softly as a cat from my hiding-place, through the park up to the barbed-wire fence, to convince myself that no sentries were about. When I saw that everything was in order and had found the exact spot where we wanted to climb over, I crawled back again to fetch Trefftz. Thereupon we returned by the same way. When we reached the fence, I gave Trefftz my final instructions and handed him my small bundle. I was the first to climb over the fence, which was about nine feet high and every eight inches the wire was covered with long spikes. Wires charged with electricity were placed two and a half feet from the ground. A mere touch would have sufficed to set in motion a system of bells that would, of course, have given the alarm to the whole camp. We wore leather leggings as protection against the spikes; round our knees we had wound puttees and we wore leather gloves. But all these precautions were of no avail and we got badly scratched by the spikes. However, they prevented us from slipping and coming in contact with the electric wires. I easily swung myself over the first fence. Trefftz handed over our two bundles and followed me with equal ease. Next we were confronted by a wire obstacle, three feet high by thirty feet wide, contrived according to the latest and most cunning devices. We ran over it like cats. After this we again came to a high barbed-wire hedge, built on exactly the same lines as the first and also electrically charged. We managed this too, except that I tore a piece out of the seat of my trousers, which I had to retrieve, in order to put it in again later.

'But, thank God, we were over the boundary!

'Trefftz and I clasped hands and looked at each other in silence.

'But now the chief difficulty began.

'We opened our bundles, took out civilian grey mackintoshes and walked down the road in high spirits as if we were coming from a late entertainment. When Donington Castle came in sight, we had to be particularly careful. We had agreed upon all we would do in case we met anyone.

'Suddenly, just as we were turning into the village, an English soldier came walking towards us. Trefftz embraced me, drew me towards him and we behaved like a rollicking pair of lovebirds. The Englishman surveyed us enviously and went on his way, clicking his tongue. Only then, something in the stocky, undersized figure made me realize that it was the sergeant-major of our camp! We stepped out briskly and after passing the village we were favoured by chance and came upon the bridge about which we had been told. But we were at once confronted with a critical proposition. The highway branched off here in three directions and it was impossible to get any farther without knowledge of the road. At last, in spite of the darkness, we discovered a signpost; an extreme rarity in England. Luckily it was made of iron and when Trefftz had climbed it, he was able to feel with his fingers the word 'Derby' traced on it in raised letters. We now fell into a quick step and taking our bearings by the Polar star, swung along vigorously. Gradually dawn came. About four in the morning, when we arrived within sight of the first houses of Derby's suburbs, the sun rose in majestic splendour, like a crimson ball on the horizon.

'We now crept into a small garden and made an elaborate toilet. A clothes brush performed miracles and a needle repaired the damage done to my trousers. The lack of shaving soap was remedied by spittle, after which our poor faces were subjected to the ministrations of a Gillette razor. We each sported our solitary collar and tie, leaving the brush as well as other unnecessary impedimenta behind us. We entered Derby, looking veritable 'Knuts.'

'Our luck endured and not only did we soon find the station, where we separated unobtrusively, but we also learned that the next train for London was leaving in a quarter of an hour. I took a third-class return ticket to Leicester and armed with a fat newspaper, boarded the train. At Leicester I got out, took a ticket to London and when I entered the compartment I discovered, sitting opposite me, a gentleman clad in a grey overcoat, whom I must have met previously, but of whom I naturally took no notice. I believe his name began with a T.

'About noon the train reached London. When I passed the ticket collector I must admit that I did not feel quite comfortable and that my hand shook a little. But nothing happened and after a few minutes I was swallowed up in the vortex of the capital. At seven o'clock in the evening I stood weary and downcast on the steps of St. Paul's Cathedral, waiting for Trefftz. I waited until nine, but no Trefftz appeared. Convinced that Trefftz had already managed his escape on a friendly steamer, I dragged myself, totally exhausted, to Hyde Park which, to my further discomfiture, I found closed. What should I do now? Where should I sleep? I turned into an aristocratic lane where beautiful mansions were surrounded by carefully tended gardens. I was hardly able to stand on my feet and at the first favourable moment I jumped with quick decision over one of the garden fences and hid myself in a thick box hedge, only a foot away from the pavement. After I had lain for about an hour in my refuge, the French window of the house, leading to a beautiful veranda, opened and several ladies and gentlemen in evening dress came out to enjoy the coolness of the night. I could see them and hear every word. Soon the sounds of a piano mingled with those of a splendid soprano voice and the most wonderful songs of Schubert overwhelmed my soul with longing. At last total exhaustion prevailed and I slept heavily, seeing in my mind the most beautiful pictures of the future.

'Next morning I was awakened by the regular tread of a policeman who marched up and down the street, quite close to where I lay, with the bright, warm rays of the sun shining down upon me. So after all I had overslept; it behoved me to be careful. The policeman ambled idiotically up and down without dreaming of departure. At last fortune favoured me. An enchanting little lady's maid opened the door and hey presto! The policeman was at her side, playfully conversing with the pretty dear. Without being seen by either, with a quick motion I vaulted over the fence into the street. It was already six o'clock and Hyde Park was just being opened. As the Underground was not yet running, I went into the Park and dropped full length on a bench, near to other vagabonds who had made themselves comfortable there. I then pulled my hat over my face and slept profoundly until nine o'clock. With fresh strength and courage I entered the Underground and was carried to the harbour area. In the Strand huge, yellow posters attracted my attention and who can describe my astonishment when I read on them, printed in big, fat letters, that: Mr. Trefftz had been recaptured the evening before; Mr. Plüschow was still at large; but that the police were already on his track. The first and third items were news; but I knew all about the second. I promptly bought a newspaper, went into a tea-shop, where I read with great interest the following notice: 'EXTRA Late War Edition 'HUNT FOR ESCAPED GERMAN' *High-pitched Voice as a Clue*, 'Scotland Yard last night issued the following amended description of Günther Plüschow, one of the German prisoners who escaped from Donington Hall, Leicestershire, on Monday. Height, 5 feet 5 inches; weight, 135lb; complexion, fair; hair, blond; eyes, blue; and tattoo marks: Chinese dragon on left arm. As already stated in the *Daily Chronicle*, Plüschow's companion, Trefftz, was recaptured on Monday evening at Millwall Docks. Both men are naval officers. An earlier description stated that Plüschow is twenty-nine years old. His voice is high-pitched. He is particularly smart and dapper in appearance, has very good teeth, which he shows somewhat prominently when talking or smiling, is 'very English in manner' and knows this country well. He also knows Japan well. He is quick and alert, both mentally and physically and speaks French and English fluently and accurately. He was dressed in a grey lounge suit or grey-and-yellow mixture suit.'

'Poor Trefftz! So they had got him! I was clear in my mind as to what I was going to do and the warrant gave me some valuable points. First, I had to get rid of my mackintosh. I therefore went to Blackfriars Station and left my overcoat in the cloakroom. As I handed the garment over, the clerk suddenly asked me: 'What is your name, sir?' This question absolutely bowled me over, as I was quite unprepared for it. With shaking knees I asked: 'Meinen?' (mine), answering in German as I naturally presumed that the man had guessed my identity. 'Oh, I see, Mr. Mine - M-i-n-e' and he handed me a receipt in the name of Mr. Mine. It was a miracle that this official had not noticed my terror and I felt particularly uncomfortable when I had to pass the two policemen who stood on guard at the station and who scrutinized me sharply.

'I now sought a quiet, solitary spot. My beautiful soft hat fell accidentally into the river from London Bridge; collar and tie followed suit from another spot a beautiful gilt stud held my green shirt together. After that a mixture of vaseline, bootblack and coal dust turned my blond hair black and greasy; my hands soon looked as if they had never made acquaintance with water and at last I wallowed in a coal heap until I had turned into a perfect prototype of the dock labourer on strike - George Mine. In this guise it was quite impossible to suspect me of being an officer and 'smart and dapper' were the last words anyone could have possibly applied to me. I think that I played my part really well and after I had surmounted my inner repulsion against the filth of my surroundings, I felt safe for the first time. I was in a position to represent what I intended to be; a lazy, dirty bargee, or a hand from a sailing ship.

'For days I loafed about London, my cap set jauntily at the back of my head, my jacket open, showing my blue sweater and its one ornament, the gilt stud, hands in pocket, whistling and spitting, as is the custom of sailors in ports all the world over. On the second morning I had colossal luck! I sat on the top of a bus and behind me two business men were engaged in animated conversation. Suddenly I caught the words,

'Dutch steamer - departure - Tilbury,' and from that moment I listened intently, trying to quell the joyful throbbing of my heart. For these careless gentlemen were recounting nothing less than the momentous news of the sailing, each morning at seven, of a fast Dutch steamer for Flushing, which cast anchor off Tilbury Docks every afternoon. In the twinkling of an eye I was off the bus. I rushed off to Blackfriars Station and an hour later was at Tilbury. I went down to the riverside, threw myself on to the grass and feigning sleep, kept a lynx-eyed watch. Ship after ship went by and my expectations rose every minute. At last, at 4 pm, with proud bearing the fast Dutch steamer dropped anchor and made fast to a buoy just in front of me. My happiness and my joy were indescribable when I read the ship's name in white shining letters on the bow: Mecklenburg. There could be no better omen for me, since I am a native of Mecklenburg-Schwerin. I crossed over to Gravesend on a ferry-boat and from there unobtrusively watched the steamer. I adopted the careless demeanour and rolling gait of the typical Jack Tar, hands in my pockets, whistling a gay tune, but keeping eyes and mind keenly on the alert.

'This was my plan: to swim to the buoy during the night, climb the hawser, creep on deck and reach Holland as a stowaway. I soon found the basis for my operations. After I had ascertained that nobody was paying attention to me, I climbed over a pile of wood and rubbish and concealed myself under some planks, where I discovered several bundles of hay. These afforded me a warm resting-place, of which I made use on that and the following nights. About midnight I left my refuge. Creeping on all fours, listening with straining ears and trying to pierce the surrounding blackness, I came closer to my object. However, I perceived with dismay that the two barges which, in daytime, had been completely submerged, lay high and dry. Luckily, at the stern, a little dinghy rode on the water. With prompt resolution I wanted to rush into the boat, but before I knew where I was I felt the ground slipping from under my feet and I sank to the hips into a squashy, slimy, stinking mass. I threw my arms about and was just able to reach the plank, which ran from the shore to the sailing-boat, with my left hand. It took all my strength to get free of the slime which had nearly proved my undoing and I was completely exhausted when I at last dragged myself back to my bed of hay.

'When the sun rose on the third morning of my escape, I had already returned to a bench in Gravesend Park and was watching the Mecklenburg as she slipped her moorings at 7 am and made for the open sea. All that day, as well as later on, I loafed about London. I had by then acquired so much confidence that I walked into the British Museum, visited several picture-galleries and even frequented matinees at music-halls, without being asked questions. The pretty blonde attendants at the music-halls were especially friendly to me and seemed to pity the poor sailor who had wandered in by chance. What amused me most was to see the glances of disgust and contempt which the ladies and the young girls used to throw at me on the top of the buses. If they had known who sat near them! Is it surprising that I should not smell sweetly considering my night's work and the wet and slimy state of my clothes? In the evening I was back at Gravesend. In the little park which overlooked the Thames I listened quietly for hours to the strains of a military band. I decided to commandeer unobtrusively, somehow, a dinghy in which to reach the steamer. Just in front of me I saw one which I deemed suitable for my purpose, but it was moored to a wharf over which a sentry stood guard by day and night. But the risk had to be taken. The night was very dark when, about twelve, I crept through the park and crawled up to the embankment wall, which was about six feet high. I jumped over the hedge and saw the boat rocking gently on the water. I listened breathlessly. The sentry marched up and down. Half asleep, I had taken off my boots, fastening them with the laces round my neck and holding an open knife between my teeth. With the stealth of an Indian I let myself down over the wall and was just able to reach the gunwale of the boat with my toes. My hands slipped over the hard granite without a sound and a second later I dropped into the boat, where I huddled in a corner listening with breathless attention; but my sentry went on striding up and down undisturbed under the bright arc-lamps. My boat, luckily, lay in shadow.

'My eyes, trained through T.B.D. practice, saw in spite of the pitch darkness almost as well as by day. Carefully I felt for the oars. Damn! They were padlocked! Luckily the chain lay loose and silently I first freed the boat-hook, then one oar after the other from the chain. My knife now sawed through the two ropes which held the boat to the wall and I dipped my oars noiselessly into the water and impelled my little boat forward.

'When I had entered the boat, it had already shipped a good deal of water. Now I noticed to my dismay that the water was rapidly rising. It was already lapping the thwart and the boat became more and more difficult to handle as it grew heavier and heavier. I threw myself despairingly on my oars. Suddenly, with a grinding noise, the keel grounded and the boat lay immovable. Nothing now was of avail, neither pulling nor rowing, nor the use of the boat-hook. The boat simply refused to budge. Very quickly the water sank round it and after a few minutes I sat dry in the mud, but to make up for this the boat was brimful of water. I had never in my life witnessed such a change in the water-level due to the tide. Although the Thames is well known in this respect, I had never believed that possible.

'At this moment I found myself in the most critical position of my escape. I was surrounded on all sides by slushy, stinking slime, whose acquaintance I had made before at the risk of my life. The very thought caused me to shudder. About two hundred yards off the sentry marched up and down and I found myself with my boat fifteen feet from the six-foot-high granite wall. I sat reflecting coolly. One thing appeared a sheer necessity - not to be found there by the English, who might have killed me like a mad dog. But the water was not due to rise before the next afternoon. Therefore it behoved me to muster my energy, clench my teeth and try to get the better of the mud. I slipped off my stockings, turned up my trousers as high as I could, then I placed the thwarts and the oars close to each other on the seething and gurgling ooze, used the boat-hook as a leaping-pole by placing its point on a board, stood on the gunwale and gathering all my strength to a mighty effort, vaulting into space - but lay, alas, the next moment three feet short of the wall and sank deep over knee into the clammy slush, touching hard bottom, however, as I did so. Now I worked myself along the wall, placed my boot-hook as a climbing-pole against it and found myself in a few seconds on top, after which I slid into the grass of the park, where a few hours previously I had been listening to the music. Unbroken silence reigned around me. Unutterable relief flooded me, for nobody, not even the sentry, had noticed anything. With acute discomfort I contemplated my legs. They were covered with a thick, grey, malodorous mass and there was no water in the vicinity to clean them. But it was impossible to put on boots or stockings whilst they were in that condition. With infinite trouble I succeeded in scraping off the dirt as far as possible and waited for the rest to dry; then only was I able to resume a fairly decent appearance.

'Could I be blamed if my spirits fell a little and if I became quite indifferent to my interests? I confess I was so discouraged that the next morning I did not find sufficient energy to leave my hiding-place in time and only escaped over my fence after the proprietor of the timber-pile had passed close in front of my retreat several times. That day I walked up to London on foot from Gravesend and returned by the other side of the Thames to Tilbury. All this, in order to find a boat that I could purloin unnoticed. It was quite incredible that I could not do so; several lay there, as if waiting for me; but they were only too well guarded. I gave it up in despair. That evening I went to a music-hall, with the firm intention of blowing my last pound and then caught the last train to Tilbury. After I had passed the first fishermen's huts of Gravesend, I found a small scull. I took it with me. In mid-stream, just near the landing-place of the fishing-vessels, a little dinghy bobbed on the water. Not more than twenty feet away sat their owners on a bench, so absorbed in tender flirtation with their fair ones that the good sea-folk took no heed of my appearance on the scene. It was risky, but 'Nothing venture, nothing have,' I muttered to myself. And thanks to my acquired proficiency, I crept soundlessly into the boat one sharp cut and the tiny nutshell softly glided alongside a fishing-boat, on whose quarterdeck a woman was lulling her baby to sleep.

'As there were no rowlocks in the boat, I sat aft and pushed off with all my strength from the shore. I had, however, hardly covered one-third of the distance, when the ebb tide caught me in its whirl, spun my boat round like a top and paralysed all my efforts at steering. The time had come to show my sailor's efficiency. With an iron grip I recovered control of the boat and floating with the tide, I steered a downstream course. A dangerous moment was at hand. An imposing military pontoon-bridge, stretching across the river and guarded by soldiers, came across my way. Summoning cool resolution and sharp attention to my aid, looking straight ahead and only intent on my scull, I disregarded the sentry's challenge and shot through between the two pontoons. A few seconds after the boat sustained a heavy shock and I floundered on to the anchor-cable of a mighty coal-tender. With lightning speed I flung my painter round it and this just in time, for the boat nearly capsized. But I was safe. The water whirled madly past it, as the ebb tide, reinforced by the drop of the river, must have fully set in. I had now only to wait patiently.

'My steamer lay to the starboard. I wanted to bide my time until the flow of the tide made it possible for me to get across. I was already bubbling over with cocksureness when the necessary damper was administered. Dawn was breaking; the outlines of the anchored ships became clearer and clearer. At last the sun rose and still the water ran out so strongly that it was impossible to carry out my flight just then. But at last, happy in the possession of the long-desired boat, I slid downstream and after an hour, pulled up at a crumbling old bridge on the right bank of the Thames. I pushed my boat under it, took both sculls with me as a precautionary measure and hid them in the long grass. Then I lay down close to them and at 8 o'clock I saw my steamer, the Mecklenburg, vanishing proudly before my eyes. My patience had still to undergo a severe test. I remained lying in the grass for the next sixteen hours, until, at eight o'clock that night, the hour of my deliverance struck. I again entered my boat. Cautiously I allowed myself to be driven upstream by the incoming tide and fastened my boat to the same coal-tender near which I had been stranded the night before. Athwart to me lay the Princess Juliana moored to her buoy. As I had time to spare, I lay down at the bottom of my boat and tried to take forty winks, but in vain. The tide rose and I was once more surrounded by the rushing water. At midnight all was still around me and when at one o'clock the boat was quietly bobbing on the flow, I cast off, sat up in my boat and rowed, with as much self-possession as if I had been one of a Sunday party in Kiel Harbour, to the steamer. Unnoticed, I reached the buoy. The black hull of my steamer towered high above me. A strong pull and I was atop the buoy. I now bade farewell to my faithful swan with a sound kick, which set it off downstream with the start of the ebb. During the next few minutes I lay as silent as a mouse. Then I climbed with iron composure and this time like a cat; the mighty steel cable to the hawse. Cautiously I leaned my head over the rail and spied about. The forecastle was empty. I jerked myself upwards and stood on the deck. I now crept along the deck to the capstan and hid in the oil save-all beneath the windlass. As all remained quiet and not a soul hove in sight, I climbed out of my nook, took off my boots and stowed them away under a stack of timber in a corner of the fore-deck. I now proceeded to investigate in my stockinged feet. When I looked down from a corner astern the fore-deck to the cargo-deck I staggered back suddenly. Breathlessly, but without turning a hair, I remained leaning against the ventilator. Below on the cargo-deck, stood two sentries, who were staring fixedly upwards.

'After I had remained for over half an hour in this cramped position and my knees were beginning to knock under, there tripped two stewardesses from the middle-deck. They were apparently coming off night duty. My two sentries immediately seized the golden moment and became so absorbed in their conversation that they no longer paid any attention to what was going on around them. The dawn was breaking and I had to act at once if I was not to lose all I had achieved at such a price. I let myself down along the counter on the side of the fore-deck opposite to the two loving couples and landed on the cargo-deck. Without pausing for a moment I stepped out gently, glided past the two sentries, reached the promenade-deck safely and climbing up a deck-pillar found myself shortly afterwards on the out-board side of a life-boat. Holding on with one hand with a grip of iron, for the Thames was lapping hungrily not twelve yards away, with my other, aided by my teeth, I tore open a few of the tapes of the boat-cover and with a last output of strength I crept through this small gap and crouched, well hidden from curious eyes, into the interior of the boat. And then, naturally, I came to the end of my endurance. The prodigious physical exertions, acute excitement and last, but not least, my ravenous hunger, stretched me flat on the boards of the boat and in the same moment I no longer knew what was going on around me. Shrill blasts from the siren woke me from a sleep which in its dreamlessness resembled death.

'I prudently loosened the tapes of my boat-cover and with difficulty suppressed a 'Hurrah!' for the steamer was running into the harbour of Flushing. Nothing mattered any longer. I pulled out my knife and at one blow ripped open the boat-cover from end to end; but this time on the deck side. With a deep breath, I stood in the middle of the boat-deck and expected to be made a prisoner at any moment. But no one bothered about me. The crew was occupied with landing manoeuvres; the travellers with their luggage. I now descended to the promenade-deck, where several passengers eyed me with indignation on account of my unkempt appearance and my torn blue stockings, which looked, I must say, anything but dainty. But my 'I prudently loosened the tapes of my boat-cover and with difficulty suppressed a 'Hurrah!' for the steamer was running into the harbour of Flushing. Nothing mattered any longer. I pulled out my knife and at one blow ripped open the boat-cover from end to end; but this time on the deck side. With a deep breath, I stood in the middle of the boat-deck and expected to be made a prisoner at any moment. But no one bothered about me. The crew was occupied with landing manoeuvres; the travellers with their luggage. I now descended to the promenade-deck, where several passengers eyed me with indignation on account of my unkempt appearance and my torn blue stockings, which looked, I must say, anything but dainty. But my eyes must have been so radiantly happy and such joy depicted on my dirty, emaciated features that many a woman glanced at me with surprise. I could no longer go about like this. I therefore repaired to the fore-deck, fetched my boots (my best hockey boots, kindly gifts from the English) and though a Dutch sailor blew me up gruffly I calmly put on my beloved boots and slunk down the gangway. Nobody paid any attention to me, so I pretended to belong to the ship's crew and even helped to fasten the hawsers. Then I mixed with the crowd and whilst the passengers were being subjected to a strict control I looked round and near the railings discovered a door, on which stood in large letters 'Exit Forbidden.' There, surely, lay the way to

Freedom! In the twinkling of an eye I negotiated this childishly easy obstacle and stood without. I was free!

'I had to make the greatest effort of my life to keep myself from jumping about like a madman. Two countrymen of mine gave me a cordial welcome, though they would not believe that I was an officer and above all things, that I had achieved my escape from England. How horrible the water in my bath looked! I also ate enough for three that night. After I had bought a few small necessaries on the next day, I boarded a slow train for Germany, wearing workman's clothes. I was quite unable to sit still for long. Alone in my first-class compartment I was overwhelmed by the thoughts and hopes which raced through my brain. I ran about my railway carriage like a wild animal in a cage. At last!   At last!   It seemed an eternity; the train pass slowly over the German frontier. Germany, oh, my beloved country! I had come back to thee!'

Endnotes Chapter 14

1   Hodder & Stoughton Ltd, London 1945.
2   local historian Anton Rippon.
3   Captain von Rintelen (19 August 1878-30 May 1949) came from a banking family with good connections in American banking, having served with Deutsche Bank as well as acting as US representative for Disconto-Gesellschaft, then Germany's number two bank, beginning in 1906. He also spoke excellent English. He sailed back to Germany on 3 August 1915, on the neutral Holland America liner *Noordam*. He was arrested at Southampton on Friday 13th August, but protested his innocence so convincingly that both the Swiss Minister in London and Scotland Yard police were persuaded. At a further meeting, the head of Room 40, Admiral W. R. 'Blinker' Hall, was not and von Rintelen confessed. He returned to Germany in 1920, a forgotten man. He moved to England, where he died on 30 May 1949.

198

Chapter 15
Through the Bathroom Door

Michael C. C. Harrison MC

At the outbreak of hostilities in 1914 there were few, even amongst the experts of all nationalities, who visualised a war of such magnitude. To the majority a speedy termination seemed a certainty. As a twenty-six-year-old subaltern in the Royal Irish Regiment stationed at Devonport in 1914 I can perhaps be excused for sharing this popular opinion. I thought myself very fortunate when I landed at Rouen, on 11 August 1914 with the advance party of the 3rd Division and felt genuinely sorry for those who might not arrive before the end of the war. My regiment lost about twenty-five per cent of their strength at Mons on 23 August. Three days later, at Le Cateau, we lost the remainder of the battalion except five officers and about one hundred and twenty men. In our first two actions we had sustained more casualties than during the whole of the South African War. At the end of the retreat our first reinforcement arrived. By 19 October 1914 we had received eight lots of reinforcements, some being as strong as three hundred and fifty. Our losses and the strenuous nature of the fighting in those early days absolutely astounded me. I had begun to think that I had a charmed life, as all the original officers, except myself had become casualties.

On the afternoon of 19 October the 2nd Royal Irish Regiment attacked the village of Le Pilly on the Aubers Ridge on the left and slightly in advance of the remainder of the British Army. A French attack at the same time on Fournes, one and a half miles on our left, failed. Our attack was partially successful and left us in possession of half the village, not an enviable position, as we were now more or less isolated.

Early on the following day the Germans attacked heavily. Antwerp having fallen a few days previously they were able to mass great strength and a desperate fight raged all day.

Captain (later major) Michael C. C. Harrison of the 2nd Royal Irish Regiment served in the Expeditionary Force and was severely wounded in the left arm and left hip on 19 October 1914 during the defence of Le Pilly on the Aubers Ridge. When he was captured he discovered that from of a thousand-strong battalion the previous day, about 300 had been killed. The survivors, mostly wounded, were all prisoners. Incarcerated in camps at Torgau, Burg-bei-Magdeburg and finally, Ströhen, One of Harrison's first five attempts to escape from Germany was with Captain Henry A. Cartwright but they were recaptured. Harrison and Cartwright, who finally got clean away from Aachen in August 1917, jointly wrote *Within Four Walls*, first published in 1930.

Captain Michael C. C. Harrison's first escape attempt was to be made in May 1915 from Torgau. He and his fellow would-be escapists had collected sufficient money and clothes for their escape but on the eve of their intended escape a large fire broke out in the camp, necessitating the immediate removal of 150 prisoners including Harrison, who had previously been awarded a short-term of imprisonment for failing to salute a German officer, were immediately removed to Burg-bei-Magdeburg, 600 kilometres from the Swiss frontier and 400 from Holland. Their new destination was completely deserted when they arrived on 2 June 1915. 'So easy for an escape did this camp appear at first sight that our hopes were in no way shattered' wrote Harrison. 'It was surrounded by a wooden fence eight feet high with several strands of barbed wire on top and a high barbed wire fence five yards outside. One of the prisoners that went with him to Burg was Lieutenant (later Captain) Claude Frank Lethbridge Templer of the 1st Battalion, The Gloucestershire Regiment, who, noting Harrison's enthusiasm for escape, had roped him in on the thwarted escape attempt at Torgau.

Born 5 July 1895 in India, son of Colonel Henry Templer OBE (late Indian Cavalry) and Mrs. Henry Templer of 16, Avenue Charles Floquet, Champ de Mars, Paris, Templer was educated Wellington College and at the outbreak of war he was a cadet at Sandhurst. Commissioned as a 2nd lieutenant in the 1st Battalion the Gloucestershire Regiment in August 1914, he went to France with the Regiment three months later. At La Bassée near Givenchy on 22 December he was advancing ahead of his platoon to reconnoitre a German trench when he met a German NCO. Templer was on the point of shooting the German when he was knocked senseless to then ground from behind. He was taken prisoner and sent to the prison camp, a converted oil factory, at Hannover-Munden. Templer was confined to hospital suffering from concussion and poisoning in his legs caused by barbed wire in his final action in France. On 7 April 1915 he made his first of no less than ten unsuccessful attempts to escape, when, with seven Russian officers he was free for a week living on about half a stick of chocolate a day and got near to the Dutch border but was discovered by villagers asleep in a ditch. Templer was taken to various military prisons and eventually transferred to Burg prison camp where he and a fellow officer, Captain B. W. Allistone, began planning another escape in September but this was discovered and they were sentenced at Burg Civil Gaol to one year and one week's imprisonment 'for damage to public property and the 'theft of a plank.' In all, Templer made four unsuccessful attempts to escape from Burg Gaol. He was transferred a further three times and made another two unsuccessful attempts to gain his freedom.

At Burg Harrison shared a room with Templer and one other officer. It was most interesting for Harrison to get first-hand evidence of life in the country from an escaper's point of view. Soon the remaining twenty beds were filled up by the release of the officers who had been in prison as a reprisal for captured German submarine crews being sent to detention barracks in England. It was at Burg also that Harrison met Captain H. A. Cartwright of the Middlesex Regiment, for the first time as a prisoner. Harrison and Cartwright, who had been captured at Mons on 23 August 1914, were in the same Brigade on the outbreak of war, occupied the same barracks at Devonport and had been at Sandhurst and Malvern together. Harrison's first five attempts to escape from Germany were unsuccessful. The first, on 18 November 1915 was with Captain H. A. Cartwright but their escape ended with their recapture after they were at large for just ten days, being apprehended at Rostock where they were on the point of boarding a Danish steamer. After his third unsuccessful attempt to escape from Germany in December 1916 Harrison was sent with a few other officers - Russian and English - to the civil prison at Magdeburg about 400 kilometres to the Dutch frontier. The two men were deliberately separated by the Germans on 29 December, Harrison being very pleased to find himself once more in Torgau while Cartwright arrived at Halle prison camp, a disused factory, in the southern part of Saxony-Anhalt the same day.

At Torgau Harrison's thoughts turned immediately to escape once more but after escaping with a French officer, Lieutenant Lesaffires through a tunnel on 18 August 1916 and walking to the Baltic, 250 miles away, they were recaptured on in the mid-afternoon of 4 September whilst trying to find a small boat to row across to Denmark. Harrison and Lesaffires were returned via Berlin to Torgau.

Harrison planned another escape from Torgau civil prison but was court-martialled and removed to Magdeburg civil prison where he was reunited on 1 February 1917 with Cartwright after yet another escape attempt, this time with Lieutenant Marshall, a French flying officer of some distinction who had been captured by the Austrians who handed him over to the Germans. It was not long before Harrison and Cartwright hatched another escape, which was helped by friends of Templer making a duplicate prison key made out of an iron bedstead. On 4 March 1917, the night of the escape by Harrison, Cartwright, Marshall and two other officers, they were apprehended in mid-flight. Incredibly, the Germans did not find the skeleton key, which was used in another escape attempt on 12 May by Harrison, Henry Cartwright, Marshall, Captain William Crawshay Loder-Symonds of the Wiltshire Regiment, Captain Browning and Lieutenant Campbell. But after walking for 200 miles the escape party was apprehended on the twelfth night out and they were returned to Magdeburg.

Meanwhile, Templer, who on 1 May 1917, his civil prison sentence having been completed, was sent by train to Magdeburg camp. During a break at a country station he attacked his guard and escaped on a bicycle which he abandoned after fifteen miles. He hid in a wood for 24 hours but was recaptured and once again court-martialled. He was complimented on his 'military method of escape' and sentenced to six weeks 'very close arrest' in Magdeburg Civil Gaol. He was detained in a cell one yard wide by four yards long, ventilated by a window one foot square with the additional penalty of 'no exercise, no parcels and no smokes.' At the end of six weeks Templer was returned to Magdeburg camp and once again became involved with tunnelling and various escape attempts by fellow prisoners. Before he was able to complete his own plans he was moved to Augustabad Camp where he again escaped but after two days' freedom he was recaptured and sent to the fortress of Küstrin. Another escape attempt followed and in June 1917 he was transferred to the Camp at Ströhen, a bleak spot situated on an immense bog and several miles from any other form of habitation in the province of Hanover eighty miles as the crow flies from Holland. Templer was soon joined by Michael C. C. Harrison after his court-martial who arrived on 1 August with Willie Loder-Symonds, born in 1887 in Berkshire, Browning and Campbell, Captain Cartwright having been transferred to Küstrin on 6 June.

There were about 450 British and a few native Indian officers at Ströhen. As the camp was originally interned for reprisal purposes, the space for exercise and recreation was made as a small as possible by keeping the inner barbed wire fence close to the huts where the prisoners lived in about thirty wooden huts surrounded by two barbed wire fences four or five yards apart. Each was about ten feet high.

Sentries were posted at intervals of sixty or seventy yards on either side of these fences and there was a machine-gun turret at each of the four corners. The whole place was brilliantly lit up at night by arc lamps. Outside the camp and about twenty yards from the outer barbed wire fence there were two more huts. One was used as a guard-room and the other as a bath house, which was connected to the camp by a wired-in passage, but the gate at the camp end of this was kept locked except between eight and nine in the morning, when the prisoners were allowed to wash themselves in the presence of the entire guard. Access for the prisoners to this hut was allowed between 0830 and 0930 every morning when a portion of the guard was on special duty there. One part of the bathroom hut was intended for the use of Germans only and the entrance for this portion faced the guard-room. The other part was divided into three rooms, i.e. one for heating appliances, one containing six or eight showers and the third measuring about twelve feet by ten feet was used as a dressing-room. The entrance to this portion faced the camp and was connected to a gate in the inner fence by a wired-in passage. If a prisoner could remain concealed in the bath house until dark he would have practically no further difficulty, as he would be outside all the camp defences, that is, both wire fences, both lines of sentries and all the arc lamps.

Immediately after arriving at the camp preparations were put in place for an escape attempt from the bathroom hut by five officers. The morning roll call was just before the bath hour, but there was also an evening roll at 6 pm, quite four hours before it was dark. Harrison believed that this could probably be faked somehow or other. Anyway, now that he had got the general scheme into his head the next thing to be done was to find a companion. He soon picked out Templer, with whom he had made my first attempt in 1915 and who helped Harrison get a duplicate prison key made at Magdeburg. 'He was one of the most gallant officer's living.' wrote Harrison. 'He was glad to meet me again, but it turned out that he had already thrown in his lot with two others in another escape scheme and it was doubtful if their plans would permit of a fourth. I was delighted when he told me a day or two later that his scheme had fallen through and that he was prepared to come with me via the bathroom, provided he could bring both his pals too.'

One of these was Lieutenant Onslow of the Warwickshire Regiment; the other, Lieutenant Insall a Flying Corps VC, who had already attempted escape on two previous occasions. Gilbert Stuart Martin Insall was born in Paris on 14 May 1894, the son of Gilbert Jenkins Insall and his wife Mary Stuart. He was educated in Paris. At the age of 21 joined the Army in the University and public Schools Brigade of the Royal Fusiliers. He joined the RFC in March 1915 and was posted to the Western Front in July of that year. He was 21 years old when he was awarded the VC for his actions on 7 November 1915 near Achiet-le-Grand, France when he was on patrol in an 11 Squadron Vickers F.B.5 'Gunbus' with 1st Class Air Mechanic Thomas Hain Donald. He engaged an Aviatik two-seater and forced the German pilot to make a rough landing in a ploughed field. Seeing the air crew scramble out and prepare to fire, Insall dived to 500 feet and Donald opened fire, whereupon the Germans fled. After dropping an incendiary bomb on the downed German aircraft, Insall flew through heavy fire at 2,000 feet over enemy trenches. The Vickers' petrol tank was hit, but Insall brought the aeroplane 500 yards back inside Allied lines for an emergency landing. Insall and Donald stayed by the 'Gunbus' through a bombardment of about 150 shells while awaiting nightfall. After dark, they then set to work by torch light to salvage their aeroplane. After they repaired the machine overnight, Insall flew them back to base at dawn. Insall VC and Donald, who was shot in the leg, fell wounded into captivity on 14 December 1915 after engaging Hauptmann Martin Zander and his gunner, the petrol tank perforated by gunfire. After the German machine made off, Insall tried to return to his own lines but an AA star shell exploded underneath the aircraft and a large fragment blew through the aircraft and hit Insall in the base of the spine. Although at times he lost consciousness he was able to land the aircraft but was captured immediately. He was operated on and the fragment removed. On 23 December 1915 Donald was awarded the Distinguished Conduct Medal.

By 14 August work on a tunnel concealed by a trap door in a corner of the dressing-room which took four days to saw through two planks, were well advanced and it was decided that an escape attempt would be made on the 20th. But another pair had hit on the same idea and were making a trap-door in another part of the dressing room. Harrison wrote: 'We interviewed them at once and found out that they'd come upon bricks underneath and were proposing to make yet another trap-door. We couldn't have the whole floor covered with trap-doors, so we decided it would be far safer to make additional room for the two of them in our compartment. This did not delay us as long as we expected for at the same time Onslow fell out.

But a few days later Harrison had another shock. On 16 August Lieutenant Gerald Featherstone Knight, of 12 Squadron RFC[1] made a successful and highly ingenious escape from the bathroom which was to be used by Harrison, Templer and Insall and it was feared that this might have 'cooked' their own plans. However, Knight had covered his tracks well. He had gone into the bathroom with the crowd and stood in a recess in one wall about ten inches deep and one foot wide. He had brought in with him, under his coat, three long canvas frames whitewashed the colour of the wall and made to fit into each other and into the recess. These he built up in front of himself unobserved and stood behind the camouflage for twelve hours. Although several Germans entered the bathroom during the day he remained concealed and escaped that night. Knight was awarded a Military Cross in 1919 for his successful escape.

By 19 August sufficient space had been made for five people and Harrison decided to go next day but he knew that as soon as they were missed from roll call on 20 August, the guard would immediately be ordered to make a thorough search of the whole camp. The disguise to their trap-door had proved good enough to pass the daily routine search, but it might well be detected in the intensive search that was bound to take place directly the authorities knew that five officers were missing and since they should still be lying concealed under the floor waiting for darkness they would have a good four hours in which to find them. It was out of the question to bluff the 6 pm roll call for so many absentees so they decided to try and make the Germans think that they had escaped some other way and Lieutenant Onslow volunteered to cut the barbed wire fence on the other side of the camp.

The next problem to consider before they left the camp was how they were to get to the frontier. They decided to walk by night keeping clear of roads and tracks as much as possible and lie up in woods by day. Among other things they would take a supply of garlic to rub on their heels in case they were chased by dogs and some pepper for the same purpose. Pepper would also be useful if they had 'a difference of opinion' with anyone on the way. As they were only going to walk at night, clothes were not of great importance. Harrison would wear his Grenadier Guards coat that he had worn in 1915 for an escape as a German officer. He had worn the same coat eighteen months later for his daylight escape from Magdeburg prison when he was dressed as a smart civilian. He now cut a bit more off the length and used it as an ordinary workman's coat.

They learnt from other prisoners in the camp who had been recaptured on the Dutch frontier that all bridges over the River Ems were guarded and also that there was a chain of sentries on the frontier itself, so they decided to enter Holland fairly far north where the frontier ran due north and south and the Ems was parallel to it about six miles inside Germany. They did not expect to find the frontier there clearly defined on the ground, but their map showed a dyke parallel to it and just inside Holland. They decided that they must swim the Ems. If a reconnaissance of it was made one night they should be able to get across it early the next night and thus have the maximum amount of darkness in which to cover the most difficult part of the journey. They did not like the idea of having to lie up for the day between the Ems and the frontier.

Soon after 0800 on 20 August 1917 Harrison, Insall and Templer and the two others who had been allowed to use Harrison's trap-door, entered the bathroom attired as usual. As soon as the room was crowded they slipped through the trap-door one by one. By 0830 the trap-door was sealed on top of them with a solution of our seccotine and dust, by a friend who proposed escaping by the same means at some later date. At 0900 they heard the bathroom being cleared. About 10 pm they heard the Germans above making the routine examination of the floor. As their absence had not yet been detected there was no reason why the trap-door should be discovered now any more than on the previous day. Nothing of interest was likely to happen until they were missed at the evening roll call at 6 pm. Several times Germans had baths immediately above but at last the bugle was sounded for the evening roll call and presently an eruption of bellowing from the camp told them that they had been missed. The whole guard was immediately turned out on to the parade ground about five yards from where Harrison lay. 'The Commandant himself arrived on the scene and stampeded up and down in front of them, shouting out orders and despatching them to various parts of the camp. Some came into the bathroom, but as they entered fresh guttural explosions from the Commandant resulted in them doubling back to their parade ground beside me. Evidently the cut wire had been found and from where we lay we could hear the Commandant order various patrols to go out into the country to look for us. It is quite an unusual experience to be an eye-witness of the scene that takes place in the camp after your own escape has been discovered. Soon after dark we heard several shots fired, presumably indicating that some of these patrols had bumped into each other. The guard remained very active till after 2 am and we had almost made up our minds that we would have to stay where we were for another twenty-four hours, but by 0230 all seemed quiet. We then crawled back through the trap-door into the bathroom, carrying our boots. It was a great relief to get fresh air and freedom again after lying in a cramped position for over seventeen hours on the damp ground under the hut. We collected our kits and took up positions of observation at the various windows, from which we could see the nearest sentries.'

Harrison unlocked the lock of a door on the side furthest from the camp with great care but all was clear. With the camp arc lamps it was just like daylight outside the escapers passed out, still carrying their boots. They took what cover they could from the shadow of the hut. When about fifty yards from the camp the five escapers put on their boots and divided into their respective parties, Templer and Insall going with Harrison; the other two going on their own. Beyond the fact that this latter pair was recaptured, Harrison knew nothing of their adventures.

The three escapists walked 150 miles over a period of nine nights. To save weight they carried no tinned food. It is remarkably easy to keep going for quite a long time on biscuits, meat tabloids and other concentrated food, but escaping prisoners cannot carry bulk and the lack of this is bound to tell on the system in time. Beyond a little chocolate for munching at night they had practically no food other than porridge, bacon and billtong, which is dried meat, used largely in South Africa. They took with them, however, a Tommy's cooker, which is a miniature saucepan and a solid methylated spirit stove all in one. Their intention was to loot vegetables every night and make a stew the following day. On this diet they hoped to reach the frontier in the best possible condition, for they knew the hardest problem of all lay in getting across it successfully. Harrison wrote: 'If you try to cross a frontier in a starving condition you will probably make mistakes and get caught and we therefore decided that the main thing was to look after our health as much as possible.'

At 2345 on 3 September the three escaped prisoners reached the Ems. Templer and Insall wrapped their clothes tightly inside a waterproof, which they cut up and put the bundles into their rucksacks. Harrison put his clothes and boots into his sack. They all kept their hats on their heads with watches and com passes inside. Before entering the water they listened to make certain that no patrols were approaching. Soon after midnight the three men were dressed again on the western side. It was going to be light at 0500 and they had only six miles to go to the border with Holland. They all made it across at 0430.

They had breakfast at an inn at Terhaar before being handed over to the Dutch military for removal to a quarantine camp at Enschede. Lieutenant Gerald Knight, who had escaped from Ströhen via the bathhouse four days' earlier, was also there and he was delighted to see them. Templer, Harrison and Insall got mixed up with a quantity of German deserters at the camp and it was eleven days before they were put on a boat at Rotterdam. A day or two later they reached England. Later, the successful escapers were summoned to Buckingham Palace, where His Majesty honoured each of them with a private interview.

On 29 March 1918 Claude Templer, now a captain, asked to rejoin the Gloucestershire Regiment now fighting at Gorre, a small French village just north of Bethune. He arrived on 19 April just after the 1st Battalion had suffered losses during a recent attack on Festubert in the Artois region. On the evening of 4 June Templer led a raiding party consisting of two other officers and 100 other ranks on enemy's outpost and support lines west of Auchy-les-Mines. Although one soldier was killed, one was reported missing and one officer and six soldiers were wounded the raid was successful and the company took two prisoners. As he returned across No-Man's Land with his men to their own lines Captain Templer was struck by a stray shell and killed. A war poet, only a third of his manuscripts were eventually returned from Germany. He was a month short of his 23rd birthday.

Lieutenant Insall went on to achieve the rank of Group Captain, Commanded RAF Uxbridge and served in WWII. Group Captain Insall VC died at Scrooby, Bawtry Yorkshire on 17 February 1972.

M. C. C. Harrison rejoined his old Battalion in France in December 1918, transferring to command the 5th Battalion, Royal Irish Regiment in the Army of the Rhine in 1919. He then became an instructor at Sandhurst 1920-24. Wounded twice he was mentioned in despatches three times and also was awarded the Brevet of Major, Italian Silver Medal for Military Valour, DSO and MC and bar.

Endnotes Chapter 15

1   Knight, who was flying B.E.2c 2502 departed at 0815 on 9 November 1916 at Cambrai was seen to go down near Mory, a victim of Oberleutnant Stefan Kirmaier of Jasta 2 for his 9th victory of an eventual 11. Kirmaier was shot down and killed on 22 November in battle with 24 Squadron.

Chapter 16

Rendezvous with a Submarine

Hermann Tholens

Hermann Tholens, Korvettenkapitän a.D. entered the German Navy in 1900. He was taken prisoner in the first days of the war when the German cruisers Köln, Mainz and Ariadne and the destroyer V-187 were sunk during the Battle of Heligoland on 28 August 1914. Tholens was second in command of the Mainz and was in the water about an hour after she was sunk. He was then picked up by a Royal Navy destroyer and taken on board. The first ten days of his captivity was spent in the naval hospital at Chatham and from there he was taken to Dyffryn Aled PoW camp, a late Georgian country house with twenty-five bedrooms smack in the middle of the famous Hiraethog (Denbigh Moors) near Llansannan in north Wales. This camp, which held almost 100 German naval officers until it was returned to private ownership at the end of the war] was one of the best guarded of all prisoner-of-war camps in the whole of Britain, probably because most of its inmates were submarine officers but 'A happy home for Huns' is how one Canadian newspaper described it. Some of its inmates, unused to the rigours of Welsh country life, took exception to the inadequate plumbing and sanitary facilities! But the camp was deemed by the Red Cross to be well run and the camp commander praised for treating his charges with respect. Prisoners were allowed to play cricket in the park of the 25-bedroom home and were given cooked breakfasts, cigars and wine, according to some reports. In fact locals complained the PoWs were having an easier time than people who lived in the nearby villages. An early escape of German officers was on 4 April 1915 Hans Andler and Hans von Sanders Leben. Reports of 'the chase' occupied a large quantity of newsprint. They made their way westward and were captured near Harlech on Sunday 11 April by PC Nathaniel Davies. The two went up before the Blaenau Festiniog Magistrates the next day and were handed over the Denbigh Police.

It was cold and damp on the evening of 16 August 1915 when Walter Wood, accountant to the Llandudno Urban Council, left the town's County Club. Outside, he was buttoning his coat up against the weather when a man dressed in civilian clothes approached him, offered him a polite greeting and started walking with him down Lloyd Street. Fearing that he was about to be the victim of a robbery, the accountant turned and ran back to the building in which he had spent the evening. He burst into the lobby followed by half a dozen soldiers, excitedly, shouting 'We've got him; we've got him'.

Before being taken into custody, Laura Jane Jones, who had followed reports of three escapees from Dyffryn Aled PoW camp in her job as a telephone operator, was walking along a street in Llandudno with her daughter Beti when she was stopped by a 'handsome man'. The charming stranger complimented the mother on her beautiful baby before reaching down into the pram and bidding them good day. It was only later that Mrs Jones realised the man had left his Eiserne Kreuz (Iron Cross) with her daughter.

For two days hundreds of soldiers had been searching for three German prisoners of war who had escaped from Dyffryn Aled PoW camp in Llansannan. Kapitänleutnant Hermann Tholens' thoughts had turned to escape when he first arrived, but at six feet two inches in height he believed this would make it difficult for him to move about English ports and dockyards undetected. So he decided to try to arrange to leave in much the same way that he had come; that is to say, by means of one of his own ships of war. The coast of Wales was only a few miles north and it seemed to Tholens that if only he could break camp and get there, he might arrange for a German submarine to meet him and take him off.

'This plan for a rendezvous needed, of course, very careful and accurate arrangement; but I talked it over with a fellow-prisoner, my friend, Kapitänleutnant Heinrich Julius George von Hennig, who had been captain of U-18, [and himself rescued from the sea by the Royal Navy off the Pentland Skerries, after his submarine was sunk[1]]. We made a careful investigation of the camp defences and decided that if we could get our Admiralty to send a submarine to a certain part of the coast at a certain time; we could keep our side of the bargain and be there to meet it. At Christmas 1914 some of the prisoners of our camp who had lived in England before the war were exchanged by special arrangement against a like number of English prisoners from Germany. By one of these I sent a secret proposal to the Commander-in-Chief of the German submarine flotillas.[2] My proposal was this. My friend, von Hennig and I undertook to get out of our camp and reach an agreed point on the Welsh coast at an agreed time. Would it be possible for one of the submarines operating in the Irish Sea to be detailed and sent to meet us there? We proposed the most westerly point of the Great Ormes Head as a rendezvous and a Saturday and Sunday during a new moon as a time of meeting. Our signal would be an electric pocket lamp waved in a circle. The answer to this proposal was given in several letters, in what I can only call 'disguised language.' It was really very easy. Our friends thanked us for our letters and said that the wedding of Mrs. So-and-So would take place on 14 August. We quite understood what that meant and after a further exchange of letters we knew that a submarine was to await us at the proposed point during the nights of the 14th and 15th of August 1915.

'Now for our part of the job; reaching the rendezvous. We must reach it, for a second chance was not to be expected. And unfortunately, while our negotiations were being made with Germany, the chances to get out of our camp had diminished considerably. In March two of our fellow-prisoners had made a vain escape, with the result that our camp was now guarded during the nights by six sentries instead of by two. The equipment of the camp had also been augmented by four searchlights, which were posted at the four corners and made the nights all round it as light as the days. At the same time the number of roll-calls had been doubled and extra rolls had been introduced.

But where there's a will there's a way. These new orders dated from the middle of June and according to them the searchlights had to be lighted at 9 pm, which was also the time for the six night guards to take up their stations. Two of them were stationed in front of the house, one at each side and two again in the back. By the middle of August, the time of our rendezvous, the days, of course, would have become much shorter than they were in June, when the above order had been issued. So we agreed that the best time for our breaking away from the camp would be a little before the searchlights were lighted and the night guards took up their stations, as it would be already pretty dark then.

'Our plan was this. We intended to get through the two fellow-escapers, for we had added by now a third [Kapitän Hans Werner von Helldorff] to our number. Our next obstacle was the first of the two entrance gates, which led through the barbed wire fence which surrounded our prison. If the gate could not be opened, we should have to cut the barbed wire fence next to the room from which we started and endeavour to crawl through it. Thus our preparations had to consist in cutting one of the iron window bars and in removing the hanging lock from the aforesaid entrance gate as soon as possible before the time fixed for our escape. Further we had to procure a pair of clippers for cutting wire, a map of the coast, a compass, an electrical pocket lamp. Plain clothes were still in our possession, as we had been allowed to wear them during the first two months. When this had been forbidden and our plain clothes had to be delivered, of course we kept some of them back and concealed them beneath the floors of our rooms.

But one thing was imperative. All our preparations had to be done in absolute secrecy, as some of our orderlies had passed the greater part of their life in England and so were in very close connection with our warders. Under these circumstances if our fellow-prisoners had learnt of our preparations we would probably have been betrayed.

'On the date of our escape, everything was in order and nobody except us had the least idea about our intention. At 1900 in the evening we were in possession of the hanging lock of the entrance gate and by 2030 it had not yet been replaced by a new one. Sharply at 8.45 we stole through our window, crawled very, very slowly to our gate, only twenty yards from the nearest sentry and one or two minutes later we were outside the camp. Half an hour before we left, we had informed two trusted friends of our intentions and they promised to help us. One of them was to replace the cut iron bar and the other distracted the attention of the sentry, who was stationed in front of the house, by troubling him with some very important question.

'On the top of a little hill about one hundred yards away from our prison we made a first short stop to ascertain if we had aroused suspicion. We gave a last look to the house, which had enclosed us one long year, hoping never to see it again; and then started off on our march. We had to cover about twenty miles to reach our meeting place. And this had to be done within the next twelve hours, as we should certainly be missed at the daily roll-call, which took place at 9 o'clock in the morning and then, of course, the telephones would work and soon all authorities in the neighbourhood would know that three prisoners of war of Dyffryn Aled were at large. So we marched off at good speed and by 0400 in the morning according to our map we were not very far from the sea. From four till six we took shelter in a small wood, thinking that it would not be good to be seen about at such an early time. At 0630 we reached the seaboard. A very supreme moment! A little later we entered the town of Llandudno. It was now 0730 and our warders would just be enjoying their breakfast as usual without any idea of all the trouble which the day had in store for them, so we felt quite safe. We strolled along the streets, crossed a large training field in the middle of the town and admired at our leisure the exercises and drilling of a whole army of soldiers. Before leaving the town we resolved to have a last good English breakfast. We took this in a nice little restaurant near the sea. Then we set off again and soon made our way to the lighthouse on Great Orme's Head. When we reached this, we looked for a nice spot, where we could shelter all the day and perhaps the following day too. For we had arranged, you remember, that the submarine should wait for us on two consecutive nights.

'On 4 August U-38 left Wilhelmshaven to meet us and took her course through the North Sea to the Shetlands, where she arrived two days later. From there she sailed through the Atlantic along the west coast of Scotland and Ireland into the Channel and then into the Irish Sea. South of Ireland she sunk some hostile ships with contraband. But in the Irish Sea she made no further attacks in order not to arouse unnecessary suspicion. [U-38 had been making her way to the North Wales coast since leaving the North Sea naval base of Wilhelmshaven on 4August and made her way down the west coasts of Scotland and Ireland. After torpedoing a number of merchant vessels U-38 headed north through the Irish Sea arriving 50 miles off the Great Orme on the evening of the 13th]. At midnight on 13 August she had reached a point fifty miles north-west of Great Orme's Head, where she was to await U-27, which had been sent for the same purpose and to make it as sure as possible that one boat would be ready for us at the fixed time. Here Kapitän Max Valentiner U-38, who was a special friend of ours, proposed that the other boat should return to her business in the mouth of the Channel, as from now on one boat would be sufficient.

'U- 27 therefore went off to the south while next evening, 14 August, U-38 slowly approached the Hook of Great Orme's Head. When she sounded about thirty yards, she turned off her diesel motors and started the electrical engines. At the same time the boat was flooded; that is to say, some of her tanks were filled with water, so that if she grounded she could get up again by blowing out the water. The weather and the sea were quiet. There was no traffic and no patrol boat. At one o'clock in the morning she sounded ten yards and stopped her engines. The lamp of the lighthouse on Great Orme's Head showed very high up. The distance from the shore could not be more than a hundred yards. But the rocks of the coast could not be made out, for it was absolutely dark. All the crew was intently on the lookout, but no sign of life could be perceived. The small collapsible boat of the submarine was all the while kept ready to row ashore. Hour by hour passed, but nothing happened.

'Now to return to us. At 2200 on the night of the 14th, when it was absolutely dark, we left our shelter beneath a couple of brambles and carefully made our way to a point which we had marked in the morning where it would be possible to climb down the high rocky cliff of the coast. But in the dark we missed the place and could not find our way down. If any of you know the Great Orme's Head you will remember that it is a very difficult place to climb down on a dark night. So we resolved to give our signals from above on this night, rather than to risk some broken arms or legs and so perhaps spoil our chances of being taken on board by our friends on the following night. As we signalled and looked out over the dark sea we thought we saw a periscope, but it was only the mast of a sailing boat, peacefully rowing home after her day's labour. Later on we made out a light, slowly approaching the shore. But this, too, did not belong to our keenly awaited friends, but to some other boat, which soon disappeared round the Hook, probably heading for Llandudno. So the night passed.

'It must be understood that as well as the difficulties and dangers of the rocks, we were also in great danger of being detected by the coastguards, who were constantly patrolling the road which led along the cliff and round the lighthouse. At daybreak on the Sunday we carefully revised our position and especially the possibilities to climb down to the shore. We found that our position was right. We were on the most westerly point of Great Orme's Head, just halfway between the last houses, which bordered the coast and the lighthouse. Our distance from the lighthouse, which was on the most northerly point of the coast, was no more than a thousand yards. But the part of the coast between us and the lighthouse was extremely rocky. So we again carefully marked the spot, from which we would be able to clamber down to the shore. This was our last chance; we were not going to miss it a second time.

'Then we took up our quarters again in our small nest beneath the brambles and tried to sleep a little. But our excitement was too great and sleep was impossible. Up to now we had been successful in all respects. We had broken out of our camp. We had safely reached the shore, crossed the town of Llandudno, passed the coastguards and found a good shelter in the immediate neighbourhood of the rendezvous. Somewhere down below our friends were waiting for us. We couldn't fail now. We lay awake, waiting for dusk. Our shelter lay within a prohibited area and was, therefore, safe from surprise. The only creatures about seemed to be some cattle, which were grazing the meadows between the road round the peninsula and the sea-border. Suddenly we heard the loud barking of a dog in our immediate neighbourhood. Soon after we heard his master's voice calling him and luckily he was a most obedient dog. But his master had to pass our hiding-place again and so half an hour later the dog gave tongue a second time. Happily it was just before supper time and the master seemed as obedient to his wife as his dog was to him. Thus he did not bother to look for the reason for his dog's excitement. Of course our own excitement and fright had been tremendous, but it had served to give us new confidence for the night to come and had made us forget the thirst which we had suffered from all that hot August Sunday.

'This time we left our shelter before it was dark and got safely down to the coast. At 10 o'clock we began to give our signals; a circle with our electric lamp. It was a wonderful night I remember; absolutely dark, with no moon. The sea was quiet and only a light breeze was blowing. If the U-38 was there - surely she was there - she would certainly make out our signals at a distance of at least two miles. But we got no answer. We began to think that she must have had some mishap and had not been able to reach the rendezvous in time, if need be we would wait for her a third night in spite of our hunger and thirst but meanwhile we flashed and flashed our light. There was no reply. In desperation we then risked making a large fire from bits of drift wood from the shore and every ten minutes during the last hour of darkness we waved a large log of flaming wood in a circle. We made our signals as far north as the rocky coast allowed. But no answer came. How disappointed we were! I can't put that into words at all. We hid again when day broke, intending rather hopelessly to try again the next night. But we had to give up the plan, for a strong gale from the north sprang up in the afternoon and soon the sea was too rough to make any such embarkation possible.

'What had happened? During the day the U-38 had lain grounded some miles away. On that Sunday she had come to the surface again and approached the coast. Max Valentiner knew from the previous night that there was no danger from patrol boats, so he approached the shore this time early enough to get as close to it as possible. That was our bad luck. For there it had been all the time waiting for us; but closer in than we'd expected and just hidden from us by a projecting ledge of rock. It had been waiting for us there not more than 500 yards away, but had not been able to see our signals.

'In the evening, after the gale had made it useless to wait for the submarine a third night, I left my friends, who couldn't speak English. My intentions now were to reach London and smuggle on board some Dutch or Scandinavian vessel.'

'After buying a packet of cigarettes, Tholens went into a café in Mostyn Street in the Love Lane area of Llandudno where waitress, Nellie Hughes, served him a cup of coffee and piece of cake. He left the coffee bar and outside the Tudno Hotel was approached by Police Constable Morris Williams who said he looked very like a certain Kapitänleutnant Tholens, who had escaped from Dyffryn Aled three days before. The German replied: 'Right you are. I want to be arrested.'

Unable to locate the other two fugitives the authorities staked out the railway station but no men matching the descriptions entered the concourse. To be sure the London-bound train was stopped at Colwyn Bay and every compartment searched but to no avail as von Hennig and von Heldorf had just entered the offices of the Silver Motor Company in Llandudno. They asked for a car but when staff tried engaging them in conversation the Germans departed abruptly.

That evening, around the same time the innocent council accountant was being harangued, cab driver, Alfred Davies was on his way to pick up a fare from the Pier Pavilion. He noticed two men standing under an ornamental lamp in North Parade in the pouring rain. He pulled over and asked if they needed a cab and understanding that they did, he opened the door for them and they climbed in. In broken English they asked to be taken 'to the colonel' so he took them to the headquarters of the London Welsh battalion who were billeted in Gloddaeth Street.

The following day all three escapists were taken back to Dyffryn Aled PoW camp in an ambulance belonging to the London Welsh and were subsequently put before a military court held at Chester Castle. They were sentenced to 84 days imprisonment in Chelmsford Gaol, without hard labour. Heinrich von Hennig remained in Llansannan until early 1918 when he was moved to neutral Holland for internment. After the First World War he continued his naval career until retirement in 1931. In April 1940 he re-joined the German Navy.

In September 1917 Tholens was sent to Switzerland and interned there until May 1918 as part of a prisoner exchange. In 1931 he joined the Nazi party and during Hitler's reign served with the rank of Obergeneralarbeitsfuhrer (Upper General) in the regime's state labour service - an agency which helped militarise the German workforce and indoctrinate it with Nazi ideology. Tholens died in 1967 aged 85.

Endnotes Chapter 16

1   One of 329 submarines serving in the Imperial German Navy, launched in October 1914, on her third mission, on 23 November U-18 penetrated the fleet anchorage of Scapa Flow via Hoxa Sound, following a steamer through the boom and entering the anchorage with little difficulty. However, the fleet was absent, being dispersed in anchorages on the west coast of Scotland and Ireland. As U-18 was making her way back out through Hoxa Sound to the open sea, her periscope was spotted by a guard boat. The trawler *Dorothy Gray* altered course and rammed the periscope, rendering it unserviceable. U-18 then suffered a failure of her diving plane motor and the boat became unable to maintain her depth, at one point even impacting the seabed. She was rammed a second time by *Dorothy Gray* and eventually, von Hennig was forced to surface and scuttle his command just outside the Hoxa Gate. All crew members, except one, were picked up by HMS *Garry*.
2   The plot hatched by Tholens was with the assistance of the ex-German Consul from Manchester, Kapitän Theodore Schlagintweit who had broken his parole rules so he found himself at Dyffryn Aled where he took charge of mess supplies and purchases. As an ex-consul Schlagintweit was repatriated to Germany with other ex-consuls in late February and it is suspected that he took the idea of the escape plan to the German Admiralty. Letters followed, supposedly from some relation and the final signal was a letter to tell Tholens that some cousin was to be married on a certain day.

Chapter 17

An Unconducted Tour of England

Heinz H. E. Justus

The first English camp Oberleutnant A.D. Heinz H. E. Justus of the Hanoverian Fusilie (73 Regiment who fought on the Somme, Vimy Ridge and in Flanders 1915-1917 after being captured at Langemark by Irish Guards on 31 July 1917, was Colsterdale in North Yorkshire. At the start of the 20th Century Breary Banks in Colsterdale, west of Masham was created as a village for construction workers and by September 1914 land in the village was made available for army camp, but as the construct workforce departed, every significant building in the village was leased to the War Office. The Leeds Pals battalion trained there. From January 1917 it housed German officer prisoners of war; the last departing in 1919. Justus, who joined the German Army as a Fähnenjunker (Ensign) in the 15th Hussars on 4 August 1914 and who was sent to Western Front that October and after few weeks, to the Russia Front, 'hoped it would be taken in good part when he said that he did not want to stay there.

'I tried several times to get through the barbed wire and I also took part in one of the tunnelling schemes which was, however, discovered by the British just before the tunnel was completed. Then one fine day I hit upon the idea of just walking out through the gate disguised as our English canteen manager, who was about my size and figure. His name was Mr. Budd. I wonder if, by chance, he may read these words and if he still remembers it all. So evening after evening I started observing closely his every movement on leaving the camp and noticed to my satisfaction that the sentries never asked him for the password. Everybody knew Mr. Budd too well for that. This was also, of course, rather a drawback; but my idea was to do the thing in the evening after dark. I'd been informed, I think quite wrongly, that every male passenger in those war days was supposed to produce a pass or other document when booking a railway ticket, particularly when travelling to London and as I didn't feel like walking the whole way there I decided to travel as a woman.

'We had private codes between the camps and our people at home so I sent a message to my mother asking her to send me every conceivable thing which I should need for this disguise. After some time I received news that a wig was arriving camouflaged as tobacco; that all sorts of fake jewellery, a compass and similar handy things had been sent off in marmalade jars, or baked in a cake and, last but not least, that I would soon receive a large quilt with a skirt, petticoat, veil, some sort of a hat, silk stockings and a nice silk coat all sewn up in it. I had asked for everything in black, even the necklace and brooches, as I wanted to look like a poor widow so that people on the trains wouldn't speak to me as freely as if I were dressed as a giddy young girl.

'Then I heard rumours of Mr. Budd being transferred to some other camp, so I couldn't afford to wait for the arrival of these mysterious packages and began collecting an outfit in the camp. My skirt was made out of an old blanket and the hat and muff were mostly composed of parts of fur waistcoats. We had plenty of fancy costumes in the camp, beautiful wigs, hats and so on, but they were all under 'word of honour' not to be used except for theatrical purposes and so of course I couldn't use them.

'Then the great day arrived and I put on all the clothes, man and woman's mixed together, so that I was able to change from one to the other with a few slight manipulations. I approached the gate disguised as Mr. Budd with a false moustache and a pair of spectacles, worn exactly the way Mr. Budd wore them. My cap, mackintosh and bag were also exact replicas of the ones with which Mr. Budd used to leave the camp every evening. Even the most pessimistic of my friends thought I really was Mr. Budd when they saw me. Mr. Budd was in the habit of leaving the camp about 8 pm and I had timed my attempt for about ten minutes to eight. Meanwhile a few friends of mine would keep the real Mr. Budd busy in the canteen until shortly after eight and as the sentries were usually changed at 8 o'clock sharp I was sure that the new sentry would not be surprised to see the second and real Mr. Budd leaving camp. So off I went straight to the gate 'Then the great day arrived and I put on all the clothes, man and woman's mixed together, so that I was able to change from one to the other with a few slight manipulations. I approached the gate disguised as Mr. Budd with a false moustache and a pair of spectacles, worn exactly the way Mr. Budd wore them. My cap, mackintosh and bag were also exact replicas of the ones with which Mr. Budd used to leave the camp every evening. Even the most pessimistic of my friends thought I really was Mr. Budd when they saw me. Mr. Budd was in the habit of leaving the camp about 8 pm and I had timed my attempt for about ten minutes to eight. Meanwhile a few friends of mine would keep the real Mr. Budd busy in the canteen until shortly after eight and as the sentries were usually changed at 8 o'clock sharp I was sure that the new sentry would not be surprised to see the second and real Mr. Budd leaving camp. So off I went straight to the gate gaily smoking my pipe as if after a good day's work at the canteen. A few yards from it I shouted 'Guard,' as this was the way Mr. Budd used to announce himself day by day. The sentry called out, 'Who's there?' 'Budd,' I answered. 'Right,' he said and opened the big door. I walked slowly down the street from the camp towards Masham station. I had about a two-hour walk before me; but I hadn't gone more than fifty yards when I espied our Commandant coming towards me. Within a fraction of a second I had torn off the moustache and spectacles as, of course, I didn't want the Colonel to address the false Mr. Budd. As I passed him I just said 'Good evening,' and so did he.

A little further on I decided to change into a woman. This was only a matter of a few seconds. I exchanged Mr. Budd's cap with the woman's hat and veil which I carried in my bag and took off my mackintosh, which covered a navy-blue civilian jacket, trimmed with all sorts of lace and bows. My skirt was hitched up with a leather belt round my hips so I had only to undo the belt to release the skirt. Luckily for me skirts in those days reached down to the ground, so my leggings were completely covered by the skirt and couldn't be seen in the dark. I met some Tommies on the road and they all behaved very decently ; they all bade me ' good evening,' and none of them insisted on starting a conversation with the very reserved woman who did not even reply to their 'good evening.' Only once I was a bit troubled, by a shepherd's dog, but he soon withdrew when the strange woman took something out of her muff and sprinkled it on the road. It is very important for an escaper always to carry a box of pepper to defend himself against dogs.

'I'd been walking now for quite some time, making good progress towards the station of Masham, when I noticed three soldiers following me and overtaking me. One of them was equipped with a rifle with fixed bayonet and I knew that this must surely be a sentry from the camp as there were no other military in the neighbourhood. I at once thought of throwing away my bag which might so easily give me away, but anything of that sort would immediately have aroused suspicion. The soldiers came steadily closer and closer until finally they overtook me. They then stopped and said 'Good evening, miss. Have you by any chance seen a man with a bag like yours? A prisoner of war has escaped and we are out looking for him.' Well, I tried for a time, really only for a very short time, to speak in a high voice, telling them please not to bother a decent young girl by starting a conversation with her, but all they said was might they have a look at the bag I carried. I refused, of course, but it was only a matter of another few seconds before I realised that it was all over with me. I was found out. I then learned that my escape had been discovered owing to the sentry not being released as usual at 8 o'clock. So you can easily understand that a mysterious situation occurred when shortly after 8 o'clock a second Mr. Budd appeared and asked the same sentry to be let through the gate. The ensuing confusion was quite amusing, of course and the bell was immediately rung, but unfortunately I hadn't heard it.

'Well, there was nothing for it but to be escorted back to the camp. One Tommy carried my bag, which was not, however, due to gallantry on his part towards a lady, but mainly because he feared I might throw it into the small river we had to cross. I would, however, not have thrown it away as a good deal of my money was in it, which later in the same evening was returned to me by the British, as they never suspected that the small package of Gillette blades did not contain razor blades but six English pound notes folded to exactly the size of a safety razor blade wrapped up in the original Gillette paper and envelope.

'There was, of course, great excitement amongst the British officers. The Commandant, the Assistant Commandant, the Adjutant and several other officers had all assembled in the guardroom anxiously awaiting news of the escaped officer and you cannot possibly imagine the funny faces they made when the door was opened by my escort and in walked a woman wearing a white fur hat. I think the first thing that happened was that everybody burst out laughing. Then the Commandant said that it was not at all customary for a young lady to undress in the presence of so many gentlemen, but that in this particular case an exception to the rule must be made. I could not, however, undo the knot of my petticoat tape, which my friends had tied too tight. I therefore asked if perhaps one of the gentlemen would be kind enough to help undo the thing and the Adjutant very kindly drew forth his pocket knife, which finally settled the question.

'After a few weeks' confinement before trial a court martial was held. I got thirty-five days and was sent down to Chelmsford Detention Barracks (CDB). From Chelmsford I was taken to Holyport, a camp near Bray, Maidenhead. This was the best camp I'd been in as regards personal comfort, but it was a very depressing place for an escaper. I took part in several schemes of digging tunnels there and twice I tried to crawl through the barbed wire entanglement. The second time I was caught right in the middle of it; it had taken me more than four hours to get there and again I had the thrilling experience of a court martial.

'So I was quite relieved when one fine day I was told that, together with forty-nine fellow officers, I would be taken to another camp, which was 'an officers' camp [at Lofthouse Park] near Wakefield. You can imagine that when the Holyport officials were asked to send fifty officers to some other place, they didn't miss the opportunity to get rid of their 'bad boys.' Well, when we left Holyport, everybody, of course, was very carefully searched, but we had quite some experience already in smuggling and so when we boarded the train in Maidenhead I had in my pocket a civilian cap, a compass, several maps of England and English money, any single thing of which would have sufficed to bring about another court martial. I was wearing an ordinary English mackintosh which was supposed to resemble a German army coat as there were shoulder-straps sewn on to it. I removed these, however, as soon as we were in the train and when I turned up the collar of the rain-coat and put on my civilian cap my disguise was perfect. On my legs I was wearing ordinary brown leggings which, especially in those days, were worn alike by civilians and people in any army of the world.

'My idea was to get away from the transport in the general rush and turmoil either at Paddington Station, where we would arrive, or at King's Cross, where our train for the north would leave. But it didn't prove to be easy at all and I was greatly disappointed when our train left King's Cross for the north. The only chance now was, of course, just to jump out of the train and I studied the situation rather carefully and without saying a word about it to my comrades. We were travelling on a corridor train, with always about six officers in one compartment and one sentry in the corridor to watch two compartments. So it would be necessary to cover the sentry's field of observation for the moment of the jump. But it would be impossible to do the thing in broad daylight and the one great fear I had was that we would reach our destination before sunset. It would be necessary too to find the right place for the jump. The train, of course, would not have to be going too fast and there would have to be no houses or people by the side of the track. So I passed the next few hours in a rather nervous and excited state. It was about a quarter to six when, after a short stop, we left the station of South Elmshall. The train moved very slowly but was speeding up every second; there were fields on both sides of the track and as it was sufficiently dark already it was quite clear to me that the time had come to do the trick. My fellow officers were, of course, very much surprised when I asked them all of a sudden to stand up right away and place themselves before the door and the windows of the corridor so that the sentry would not be able to see me jumping out of the window. They were sporting enough to do exactly what I asked of them and a few seconds later I found myself on a meadow by the side of the track. The tail lights of the train disappeared into the dark and I was free, absolutely free; nobody who hasn't been a prisoner can possibly imagine what this really means.

'The first thing to do now was to put on my civilian cap and I then turned down the collar of my tunic. The German officers' uniforms are so made that the collar fits high round the neck, so in order to hide the German tunic collar I had to roll it down and as I wasn't in possession of a white collar and a tie I just wound a handkerchief round the neck. This didn't look so very smart but it served the purpose. I now walked the short distance back to South Elmshall and proceeded to Doncaster, whence I wanted to take a train up to London. My general scheme was eventually to go to some seaport on the west coast and to smuggle on board some neutral ship, preferably a Spanish one, as I had learnt that language in the camps. I had decided on Cardiff but I thought I would go to London first because it would certainly be easier for the first few days to hide in a big city than in a small place.

'I arrived in Doncaster at about a quarter past seven in the evening and found out that there was no train to London before 4.50 or so, I think it was, in the morning. Well, this was really a nuisance, but all I could do was to just make the best of a bad business and I started out from the station to have a look round the town. There were big signposts advertising a show with the name of You Are Spotted, which was indeed a rather apposite title for a play from the point of view of an escaped prisoner. I decided to have a look at it. At about half-past eight I made for the theatre, which I deliberately entered a little late because I preferred to take my seat only after the lights in the auditorium had been turned out, as I couldn't even take off my rain-coat and I had no collar. So when I came in, the show was already in full swing and I was greeted from the stage by a chorus of about twenty or thirty girls waving Allied flags and singing the most exciting rag-times. I can hardly describe my sensations at all this. About three hours ago I was still a prisoner of war and I couldn't help smiling when I noticed that my neighbour to the right was an English Staff Officer. When the lights went on after the first act he looked at me a little longer than I liked at the moment and there I heard him say to his companion that I was rather a strange-looking fellow. But that was all and nobody kept me from enjoying the rest of the show more than anybody else in the; house. When the thing was over the band of course played God Save the King and I wondered what my neighbours would have said if I had joined in and sung the German words to it, as we have the same tune for a German patriotic song.

'Finally the time arrived for me to go to the station. They didn't ask for passes or anything and I soon had my ticket and at about 9 o'clock in the morning I arrived at King's Cross, the station which I had left the day before under rather different circumstances. The first thing to do was to buy a good collar: and tie and also a waistcoat to put over my tunic. I then started out for a nice walk through London. Trafalgar Square was one of the few places I remembered from a short: visit I paid to this country as a boy in pre-war days, but I was very much surprised indeed to find that it all looked different now. Trafalgar Square in those days was turned into a devastated French village, probably for some Red Cross collection or a similar purpose ; there were trenches, shattered houses, barbed wire, shell holes, guns and all that, all of which I inspected with the eye of an expert. I then strolled down the Strand and after a while I went to the matinee of a show called Going Up at the Gaiety Theatre.

'After this experience I again wandered around the streets of London, had supper at some small restaurant and then began to think about where to go for the night. I passed a man in the street who looked rather a rough and the right sort of fellow probably to ask for some information of this kind, so I offered him a cigarette and started a conversation. I told him that I was in London for the first time and could he suggest some convenient lodgings for the night where they would not ask for passes, as sometimes you didn't exactly want to give your real name.

'He gave me the tip to go to some small hotel near one of the big stations where they probably wouldn't be so very strict, but still he wasn't quite sure if I wouldn't be asked to show papers there, too. I told him that I had been to the Gaiety in the afternoon and speaking of theatres he said that I should by all means go and see the extraordinarily fine play, The Hidden Hand at the Middlesex Theatre. It was awfully good, about the War and the Germans and spying and all that. I said I would certainly go and I did. It was the third time that I had been in a theatre within twenty-four hours and I very soon realised that this was a very, very thrilling play indeed. But after a while I came to think that it was a little too thrilling perhaps for a man in German uniform, even if his military attire was covered by a raincoat. It was the most anti-German performance in the world and the whole atmosphere around me didn't seem to be very pro-German. I really wondered what would happen if by some chance or other somebody would find out that there was a German officer right in their midst. They would probably have torn me to pieces and when the lights were switched on after the first act everybody seemed to look at me in a very suspicious way. All of them, just a few seconds ago, had been told from the stage all about German spies and all sorts of nice things about the nice Germans. I fancied I could hear them whisper to one another, 'Do you see that funny chap in a mackintosh? Everybody has taken off his coat, why hasn't he? 'Well, nobody of course said such things, but after all I thought it might be just as safe to leave the house after the first act, which had given me already a complete run for my money. When I went down the stairs I tried to look just as ' Allied ' as possible and I remember quite distinctly that I whistled the Marseillaise in order to be taken for a Frenchman, or at least for a man with, strongly anti-German feelings.

'It was about time now to think of going to a hotel. If after all they asked for a passport or something I would just say I'd lost mine and the only consequence would probably be that they wouldn't give me a room. But at all events they would be desirous to know my name and so I decided to adopt for the night the name of Albert Georges, which could be either French or English and I thought it might be a good idea to perhaps say that I was a Frenchman if they asked too many uncomfortable questions. The first two or three hotels were full up, but in the next one they said, 'Yes, there was a small room and would I please fill in this form here.'

'Very well, then, my name was Albert Georges, last address: Southampton. Street? Well, I hadn't thought of that, but I think I wrote Queen Street, hoping that this would be the name of a street in Southampton. Nationality: French. 'Oh, you are a Frenchman,' the young lady at the hotel said. 'There are special forms for foreigners,' and so she handed me a great big piece of paper with innumerable questions to be answered. Not only did they want to know absolutely everything about myself, but they wanted to know also all about my parents and where my grandfather had been born and a thousand questions of that sort. I became quite dizzy and all the time, in order to think of some new name or date, I pretended I couldn't very well write with those extraordinary nibs; in France, of course, we had quite different nibs and all that. Finally I got through with it. I was never asked for a passport and I smiled when I was shown into my room. But when I was in bed I became uneasy; had I said King Street or was it Queen Street and what was the number of the house I had given and what did I say was my great-grandfather's uncles' first name and what age had I given? Imagine the consequences if for some unforeseen reason or other they asked me again for one of the many dates and names I had given and if I didn't remember then the date of my own birthday or something. Well, I switched on the lights again and wrote down on a piece of paper whatever I remembered of all the many dates and names I had given, but I was glad that nobody came to compare my present notes with the ones I had given downstairs.

'I had a very good night's rest and felt fine and cheerful when I left the hotel next morning. There was a Red Cross day on or something and soon I was stopped in the street by a kind elderly lady who insisted on selling me a little Union Jack which she tried to pin on to my mackintosh. However, the pin wouldn't go through and the trouble was that she always stabbed against the Iron Cross which I was wearing on my tunic. I thought of telling her I was sorry to say that at the moment the Union Jack didn't go so very well with the Iron Cross, but I didn't. I just took the flag out of her hand and fastened it myself on a spot just above my decoration.

'I now wanted to get rid of my tunic at the earliest possible moment. I had already thought of throwing the thing into the Thames, but it was a brand new one and it was quite probable after all that one of these days I would find myself back again in a prison camp, where I would miss the nice uniform very much. So I decided just to send the tunic by parcel post to the Commandant of my old camp, Holyport, as wasn't sure about the exact address of the new camp near Wakefield. I suppose that the Holyport Commandant was much surprised to receive that parcel. I read a few days later in all the papers that he had got it all right. I now proceeded to buy a pair of trousers and a jacket and at last I looked like a real civilian and I was now able to take off my mackintosh. The following night I again tried to register as a Frenchman. I went of course to another hotel, but the young lady there said that no foreigners could be admitted before they had registered at the police station. She told me where the police station was and I promised to be back in a few minutes but of course I never returned. I just became an Englishman and spent the night at one of those small hotels near Waterloo Station.

'There was much influenza in England in those days and when I woke up next morning I didn't feel very well, but still I didn't pay any attention to that and I decided to go to Cardiff in the evening. I was still in possession of a nice sum of money to carry on for quite some time, including a bribe or two to help me to get on a Spanish ship in Cardiff, but I thought it might be good to get some more funds before leaving London, so I decided to sell a valuable platinum and diamond ring I was ' wearing. My mother had given it to me as a talisman for the trenches and as I didn't much care for such a showy thing I had accepted it on the clear understanding that I could sell it again once it had done its good work at the front. So I went to offer it at a jeweller's shop, in Fleet Street I think it was and said, I wanted fifty guineas for it. The man said that it was really a very fine ring, but would I produce some proof or something in order to show where it came from. I said my father had given it to me the last time we were in Paris. 'Oh yes' of course he didn't doubt a bit that everything was perfectly in order and quite all right, but you see these days now you had to be very careful buying things like that and finally he asked if he might have a look at my registration card or something of that sort which I had never heard of before in my life. I said yes, certainly, but after going through all my pockets I said that I must have left the thing at my hotel and I would go and get it. Everything seemed to be quite all right except that the man didn't seem to care about returning the ring to me. He knew that there was something wrong and he disappeared once more to talk the matter over with another man in the back of the shop. For a second or so I thought of just dashing out of the place, but then the man came out again and said, 'I'll give you seventeen guineas.' I protested, of course, but both of us very quickly realised that it must be either yes or no and so I accepted and then beat it just as fast as possible. The only thing I failed to understand was why on earth he had offered me seventeen guineas. I would just as soon have accepted seventeen shillings.

'I now went to Cardiff by train, arrived about 9 pm and went to the Royal Hotel. I gave my name as Allan Hinckley, who was an American opera singer in pre-war days in Hamburg. I told the porter right away that I had my luggage at the station and if anybody had asked me for a passport or something I would just have said that I had that in my suit case. After having written my name in the hotel book I asked if they could send somebody to the station to get my luggage, but I said this, of course, only for show, as I really didn't have any luggage at all and when the porter said of course he could send for it, I said, 'Well, I think after all I'll leave it just where it is ; I've got to go back to London anyhow early in the morning and I'd like to turn in right away.'

'I felt very miserable when I awoke next morning and I was quite sure now that I had the real 'flu, but I set out in order to see if I could spot a Spanish ship somewhere. I had no idea where the port was and somebody told me that there was a place of the name of Penarth, which was right on the open sea. I went there in a taxi, but was awfully disappointed to find a deserted pleasure resort with no ships whatsoever leaving there for Spain. I went to a small hotel and had a whisky and soda in the deserted lounge. I sat quite by myself by the fireside and read various articles which had been published in the Press about my escape. One paper had a big headline: *Masquerading Hun Officer in Woman's Dress.* Apparently Scotland Yard thought I was doing the same thing again. While I was reading this a British officer came in, accompanied by ladies. They all sat down quite close to me in order to g warm at the same fire and immediately started talking about the war.

'The officer had just come from France on short leave and one of the girls said rather embarrassing things about the Germans; I mean embarrassing for a German officer who sat impersonating a harmless civilian in the same room. She said these Germans must be really frightful people and she was sur that they all were the greatest cowards in the world and many other delightful things. The British officer, however, had a rather different opinion. He said that he hadn't noticed that the Germans were cowards; he had just come from the Western Front, where he had been stationed opposite a Prussian Guards division and he had a great respect for them. Well, I tell you, when this officer spoke I very nearly butted in. I felt like saying to him, 'Now, look here, I'm a German officer myself, let's talk things over for an hour or so and we can toss for drinks anyhow. Later on, of course, you must hand me over to the police, but that cannot be helped and I don't want to miss this opportunity of comparing notes with a decent fellow from the other side of 'No Man's Land.' But I did nothing of the kind as it would have been the immediate and abrupt end of my escapade and I had still faint 1 hopes of getting away to Spain some time and somehow.

'My Penarth excursion had not improved my health at all and I felt very, very miserable indeed when I was back once more in Cardiff. I went to another hotel that night, the Queen's, where I registered under the name of Henry Hughes and I told the people there exactly the same story about my luggage. Everything went quite all right except my health, as I was very sick indeed next morning. My temperature had gone up in an alarming way and I felt absolutely run down. But I carried on for another day. I went back that night again to the hotel and the porter was much surprised to see me again, but I had given very liberal tips in the morning and everybody was very kind to me; the whole staff knew already that the so-called Mr. Henry Hughes was very much under the weather.

'The following day was one of the darkest in my prisoner-of-war history. I felt so ill that I was at last obliged to go to the police station and give myself up) I was too sick a man to carry on with my plans, which after all required perfect health and perfect nerves. I was sent back next day to the new camp, Lofthouse Park, where I got the right medical treatment and when I had recovered there was the usual court martial and the subsequent 'vacation' at good old Chelmsford prison. I got fifty-six days this time and my tunic, which I had sent to the Commandant at Holyport, was returned to me here, in perfect condition.'

Heinz Justus spent Christmas 1918 in Chelmsford Prison and was sent back to Germany in July 1919.

Chapter 18

A Winters Tale

Major Jocelyn Lee Hardy DSO MC and bar

'J. L. Hardy has an illuminating passage in his book, I Escape![1] He was one of the most persistent and daring escapers of them all; in fact he was known to the Germans as 'that maniac Hardy'; and after one of his many attempts he was sent to a camp in Augustabad in the North of Germany.'

Captain Joe Randolph 'J. R.' Ackerley (4 November 1896-4 June 1967) In June 1915 Ackerley was sent to France. During the Battle of the Somme on 1 July 1916 he was shot in the arm and suffered shards of a whiskey bottle becoming imbedded in his side from an explosion. After lying wounded in a shell-hole for six hours, he was rescued by British troops and sent home for sick-leave. Promoted to captain, he soon volunteered to go back to the front. In May 1917 Ackerley led an attack in the Arras region where he was wounded in the buttock and thigh. While he was waiting for help, the Germans arrived and took him prisoner. As an officer, he was assigned to an internment camp in neutral Switzerland, which was relatively comfortable. Here he began his play, *The Prisoners of War*, which expresses the cabin fever of captivity and his frustrated longings for another English prisoner. Ackerley was not repatriated to England until after the war ended.

Jocelyn Lee Hardy was born 10 June 1894 in Kensington, London. His father was a wool merchant from County Down, which may be why, when he left Sandhurst at the end of 1913, he joined the Connaught Rangers, gaining his commission and joining the 2nd battalion at Aldershot in January 1914. He went to France on 14 August and first saw action on the 24th when his unit acted as a rearguard to cover the retirement of the 5th Infantry Brigade in action at Le Grand Fayt. By 26 August Hardy and a group of nineteen men led by a Captain Roche found themselves cut-off and took shelter in a house being used as a makeshift hospital in Maroilles village. During the night a large force of Germans entered the town and the next day Hardy's group were discovered and made prisoner, one of 286 men listed as 'missing' in the action. Hardy was sent to Halle prison camp.

'In the winter of 1915 we still knew very little of the science of escape' wrote Hardy. 'We had no secret communications with home and hadn't yet learned to make ourselves false passports; we were lucky if we possessed the copy of a map out of a railway timetable and my German at that time was also far from good.

'Halle was a hard place. I believe I am, with one exception, the only prisoner that ever broke out of it. It was a shockingly bad camp and yet there were practically no attempts made there, because one simply could not see where to make a start. It was an old machine factory; just a large courtyard, surrounded by workshops in which we lived and it was situated well in the middle of the town. It was bare and ugly and dirty. There were plenty of sentries inside the camp and sentries in the streets around it and more sentries in the munitions factory that adjoined it. At nights the whole place was a blaze of light and sufficient lights were kept burning even in our sleeping quarters to prevent any nocturnal schemes. For months I looked in vain for an opportunity and then I found that in my interminable march round that courtyard my eyes were drawn more and more to the roof of a building in the German section of the camp. The camp was shut in by buildings on three sides. Those on two sides were occupied by prisoners; the third was a long, two-storied building, which contained the guard room and the parcel room on its ground floor and the German quartermaster's stores and censor's office upstairs. Prisoners were only allowed here one or two at a time for the handing out of parcels and to prevent any unauthorised person being there a high barbed-wire fence had been put up with a gate in the centre, at which a sentry was stationed. When you went for a parcel the sentry allowed you through the gate and you walked down a short passage into the parcel room from which there was no other exit. Half-way down the short passage was the staircase which led up to the next floor. Here, on a landing, were the two doors of the other rooms I've mentioned, the censor's office and the quartermaster's stores. The door of the quartermaster's stores was kept locked. On the further side of this building, between it and the street, was a small narrow garden, lit at night by a bright arc lamp and fenced with high railings. There was practically nothing growing in this small garden - just a sentry.

'Now if, I thought, I could get on to the roof of this building, let myself down into the little garden and then scale the railings (while the sentry obligingly turned his back or slept) I should find myself in the open street and free. If yes - it certainly was an if - but, as I've already said, no one, so far, had managed to escape from Halle. There was a way on to the roof, I knew, through a skylight in the quartermaster's stores, but the roof looked very exposed; could one show oneself on it? Was it possible to cross that garden, so brightly lit and so open, under the nose of its sentry? And to scale the railings too? Besides, I had only seen the garden side of the building once, as I was brought into the camp and wasn't familiar with its layout. Well, there was one way of knowing whether these things were possible and that was by trying; but I confess to a sinking sensation whenever I looked at that bit of roof.

'First of all I had to devise a means of getting into the quartermaster's stores, where the skylight was. I might manage that by pretending to be on a visit to the censor, who, as I've said, lived on the same floor. Prisoners were allowed to visit him during working hours and I should therefore have to hide myself in the store room from the time he knocked off until it became dark enough for me to make my attempt. The stores were locked, so I should have to pick the lock and I should have to do it quickly and quietly, as someone might easily come out of the censor's office opposite at any moment. Harrison told us he had a weakness for sardine openers when lock picking. I liked the thin strong wire that is used for stiffening an officer's cap. I got myself a couple of bits and started practising on every available lock in the camp and in time I got so good at the job that I felt the particular lock in question would have no terrors for me.

'This was my second attempt to escape from Germany and I decided that this time I would put my German to the test and travel by train. I had no other choice, with the weather bitterly cold and a distance of 300 miles to the frontier. We had heard that it was very dangerous to travel openly within forty miles of the frontiers, so I chose Bremen as my destination and planned to go on foot from there westwards and try to cross into Holland through the marshes near the coast.

'I don't remember fixing a particular day beforehand, but I must have done so. Only one friend, Captain A. M. Cutbill, Adjutant of the Suffolk Regiment, knew of my plans and I proposed to do the stunt alone. I used to lie awake at nights and worry over it. I used to picture myself cornered in that garden like a rat, dodging about while a frightened and furious sentry blazed away at me. I know I was more frightened of this particular attempt to escape than of any other I've taken part in, but the chance was there and I was determined to take it. The day arrived. I dressed myself in my room, my uniform over civilian clothes. I owned a compass and a small map of the country between Bremen and Holland and was taking what food I could conveniently carry in my pocket. I had a civilian shirt and cap, dungaree trousers and a Norfolk jacket. At about three o'clock in the afternoon Cutbill and myself presented ourselves before the gate and showed the sentry two letters which we said we wished to hand to the censor. He let us through and as soon as we were in the building we crept quietly up the stairs, passed the censor's office on tip-toe and reached the store-room door. I produced the two small wires and shoved one into the lock. My friend held it and braced while I pushed in the second and felt for the bolt. I was in a frantic hurry, expecting every moment that the door behind us would open and some spotty little clerk would see us and give the alarm. At last I felt the bolt slip further and further and suddenly the door opened under my hand. I said goodbye to Cutbill; went in and closed the door and picked the lock too from the other side. The stores, I found, were divided into two rooms, so I had yet another locked door to tackle. This went as easily as the other and I was now in the little room from which my adventure was to start. I looked round first for something with which to let myself down from the roof when the time came. It was too high to jump. I found some old leather straps which I plaited together into a rope and then sat down to wait for darkness. I had a sleep, read some ancient German newspapers and was feeling quite all right when suddenly I heard a key in the outer door. Oh Lord! I was caught. The sentry must have reported that whereas two officers had gone up only one had come down. I knelt down and looked through the keyhole. To my immense relief, instead of several sentries I saw one German NCO and a number of orderlies, who were carrying bedsteads out of the room. I felt very thankful for the locked door between me and them.

'At last the fatigue party cleared off, locking the door behind them and left me to myself again. At about six o'clock it began to get dark and started to rain.

All the lights outside had been switched on. I judged the moment had come. The old hands shook a bit as I pulled a couple of packing cases into the middle of the room, climbed on to them and pushed open the skylight. Then I scrambled on to the roof. In a moment I was back again and closed the skylight behind me.

'The thing was impossible. Never had I realised how impossible it was. The fact that prisoners weren't able to go too near the sentries' beat had prevented my realising that at least three of them had a direct view of my roof and there was an arc lamp immediately over the skylight. It was as bright as day there and the sentries had probably seen me already as clearly as I'd seen them. I stood there quite dumbfounded and feeling absolutely desperate. I'd burned my boats behind me with a vengeance, for no one was allowed in this building after 4 pm If I tried to get back I should be arrested and everything discovered, including the fact that the senior British officer had reported me present at roll call. The others would think I'd funked it. I did funk it. What on earth was I to do? Then suddenly I saw a chance. The rain outside had now turned into a downpour. The sentries would probably be sheltering in their boxes. It was a risk, but one worth taking.

'I jumped for it. My hands gripped the edge of the trap door. One heave and I was up, standing in the deluge on the roof. My surmise was correct. Not a soul was to be seen in the courtyard of the camp. I made fast my rope, took a pull on it, threw myself clear of the gutter and slid down. The rope broke and I landed in a sitting position in the garden about four yards from the sentry, who stood in his box. Next moment I was on my legs again and bolting for the railings. I expected every moment to hear a shout behind me, but my man had bowed his head to the beating rain and saw nothing. The railings must have been easy. I don't remember them. I was in the street. There was no one about and turning to the left I ran with my head in a whirl. I was already soaked to the skin, but in a state of absolute elation.

'Now it had been my intention to break out without leaving any trace and I'd meant to tie something on to the end of my rope and throw it back on to the roof. But the breaking of the rope had made this impossible and I felt certain that as soon as the rain stopped and the sentry came out of his box, he would see the end of the rope hanging there and give the alarm. The rain had already stopped, so I must therefore take it that my escape was now known. There were several people about in the streets again and I realised that whatever I did, I must get out of Halle quickly.

'I felt I must look a very suspicious figure, dripping wet as I was and, for one moment, I hesitated at the station entrance, but it was the only hope, so I hurried to the booking office and asked for a fourth-class ticket to Berlin. The clerk looked me up and down, drummed his fingers on the ledge and asked what I was going to Berlin for. I thought of saying I was going there to work. Probably he thought so too and was merely going to offer me a cheap workman's ticket. But escapers see a hundred subtle traps where none exist. I said: 'My father has died and I'm going to his funeral.' He gave me my ticket at once, with a sorrowful look and I went up on to the platform. I looked pretty young at that time and I used to put on a very bad limp, half close one eye and open the other in a glassy stare. This gave me the appearance of an imbecile, but was held by my friends to be a great improvement on my natural expression.

'I hadn't long to wait before a train came in and I hopped straight into a fourth-class carriage. I had no idea in which direction it was going. All I knew was that I had got to get clear before the camp telephoned my description to the station police. Off we went, but after about two hours the train stopped in a place called Kothen, where an inspector got in and examined my ticket. He made the usual sort of bawling row when he found I was in the wrong train, called me an idiot and made me buy a ticket back to Halle. I dared not argue with him. He seemed surprised that I had the money for the ticket He pushed me into a carriage full of soldiers and there I sat staring at the notice opposite me. Vorsicht Beim Gesprach. Spionen Gefahr! ('Watch your words. Danger of spies!')

'How nice for me. I felt very small among those troops. When we got to Halle I sat well back and pretended to be asleep and let the train take me on to the end of its journey; Leipzig. Here a new difficulty arose. I couldn't leave the platform without passing the barrier and I dared not show my wrong tickets, which were bound to lead to an awkward discussion. One ticket from Halle to Berlin, one from Kothen to Halle and here was I at midnight in Leipzig. The station was emptying and I began to feel rather conspicuous. I badly wanted a smoke but I had no matches, so I tried to get a light off the tail lamp of a train. Apparently this was verboten because I was hauled up by an official and a little crowd formed. Up came a policeman, who asked for my papers and I produced my two tickets. In the following confusion and whirl of conversation, in which everybody joined but myself, he forgot about the papers. I looked anxiously from face to face. I stood all crooked. The large eye glared, the little eye blinked. In broken sentences, in muttered phrases, I killed my father again in Bremen and set out to his funeral.

'They were sorry for me. Even the policeman was sorry. We all trooped off to the barrier, where my tickets were taken from me and I was told that there was a train leaving for Bremen at five o'clock next morning. I went and sat in a large general waiting room, which was warmer than the platform. After about half an hour a policeman came in and asked someone for his papers. This was awful. I couldn't get up and walk out of the place. I thought of referring him to the inspector, but before he came round But to me, he started having trouble with a German working man with a certain amount of drink on board. There was a terrific shouting match which ended in a battle and the policeman rushed off with his prize. After this I kept on the move till my train was in and then got settled in a corner and pretended to fall asleep. We pulled up in due course at a large station and I put my head out of the window. Was this a nightmare? It was Halle again. But all went well. During the whole of that journey no passports were asked for and at six o'clock in the evening we ran into Bremen.

'I think I lost my wits completely in Bremen. I walked and walked. I had to keep going, because it was infernally cold, but I must have gone in circles because I couldn't get out of the town. There were nothing but bridges. All bridges were guarded, that was the sort of thing that prisoners believed in those days. By about nine o'clock that night I began to feel pretty done. I had no great-coat and there was a biting east wind blowing and snow began to fall lightly and lie unmelted on the ground. I went back to the station and decided to go by train a few miles further westward, risky though it might be. I took a ticket to Delmenhorst. It would at least be warmer in the train and I thought I might find a haystack or barn out in the country where I could rest for the night. I discovered a radiator, which I froze on to until my train came in.

'We reached Delmenhorst at midnight. It was pitch dark outside. I walked briskly out of the station as though I had some definite destination and I set off in a westerly direction. I did about four miles in what I believed to be the right direction, but there was such a fierce wind that I couldn't keep matches burning long enough to read my compass. However fast I walked, I could not keep warm and I was dropping with sleep and generally feeling awful. At last I came to a cottage with some sheds behind it, but I was routed out of that by a dog and his barking brought lights into the windows. I bolted down the road.

'I kept leaving the road then and crossing fields, because I thought I saw straw stacks, but when I got there I would find clumps of pine trees, through which the wind whistled. I would have given anything for a greatcoat. I turned back for Delmenhorst. Trains were good. You couldn't freeze to death in a train. the station was closed for the night. I went and sat in a graveyard with my back against a tombstone. Too cold. The whole place was frozen. I wandered about like a lost dog and found myself on the railway line, followed it up and reached the station that way. I climbed up on to the platform and looked to see if there were any fires in the waiting rooms. There weren't. But there was a lovely stove burning brightly in the telegraph office. The door stood open. The room was empty. I hesitated. It was a lovely fire! I would go in and stop there just long enough to get the frost out of my hands. But it was surrender really and in my heart of hearts I knew it. I threw my chances away because I hadn't the guts to stand the cold that soldiers on every front were putting up with and because I was alone.

'I hadn't been there long when an official came into the room. He stopped with a jerk at the door and looked me up and down in astonishment. Um Gottes Willen, woher dann? said he. I stood there like a fool. The lovely warmth of that fire; I could hardly keep my eyes open. I thought 'Woher?' Does that mean 'Where are you from?' or 'Where are you going to?' I said: 'Give me a minute to get warm and I'll tell you who I am.'

'All right,' he said, 'rest here a bit;' and he went out and locked me in. There were windows. I could still have made a bolt. But I shouted: 'I'm an escaped British officer' and I lay down on the floor and went to sleep.'

In the spring of 1916 Hardy found himself in Magdeburg camp and escaped once more but was recaptured and after a week in Stralsund prison 'without a smoke - awful' he were sent back to Magdeburg, where he spent three months in cells measuring four foot by twelve foot. Escape from Fort Zorndorf was virtually impossible but nevertheless Hardy made several attempts and one nearly succeeded when, with two others, he almost got out disguised as a German soldier. On another occasion he managed to break away from his guards while being marched to the kommandatura and got as far as the train before being recaptured.

On 1 January 1917 Hardy was promoted to the rank of Captain. After another nine months in this camp, he was transferred to Schweidnitz in Silesia. Within a short period of his arrival he broke out with Captain 'Willie' Loder-Symonds. Carrying forged police passes they climbed a wire fence, scaled a glass topped wall and caught a train. They were able to travel across Germany via Dresden, Leipzig, Cologne and Aachen and then by tram to Richtericht and the safety of Holland within two days of getting out of Schweidnitz. A fellow prisoner wrote of this escape; 'Hardy had, together with another officer, just escaped over the frontier. They were in a camp in Silicia and had travelled over 500 miles through Germany. After escaping, in some civilian clothes, which they had managed to get into the camp, they walked to a nearby railway station and Hardy, having learned to speak German fluently since his captivity, bought a ticket at the railway station for Berlin. The first part of their journey was uneventful, but after leaving Berlin, they were asked for their passports and Hardy, who had helped us to make the passports at Fort Zorndorff and had made for himself and his comrade passports, had an anxious moment while the official was examining it. But after turning the passport over several times, the official was satisfied and gave it back and they were safe again for the time being. A little later however, Hardy's comrade was taken very ill, no doubt from the effects of his long imprisonment and for some time it looked as if the people in the carriage would notice something wrong, as unfortunately he could not speak any German. At several other places along the line they had to leave the carriage and in some cases had to change trains to get away from one or other who had become too inquisitive. In the end they arrived at Aachen, when again their passport was examined and as before, the officials were evidently satisfied that it was bona fide and let them pass. After leaving the station at Aachen, they boldly walked through the town and hiding themselves in a forest near the frontier, they managed to crawl into Holland during the night. Nobody was more pleased than me to hear of Hardy's escape, as he had made many attempts and certainly deserved to succeed.'

On 5 March 1918 Hardy boarded at boat at Rotterdam after 3½ years as a PoW. The boat sailed a week later and Hardy returned to England where he was received by King George V at Buckingham Palace on 18 March. In April Hardy transferred to the 2nd Battalion Enniskillen Fusiliers in France. Captain 'Willie' Loder-Symonds was killed in a flying accident on 30 May aged 32, having joined the RFC on his return to England.

On 1 August Hardy was awarded the Military Cross on the Ypres front for leading a fighting patrol which engaged a group of enemy soldiers, killing one and causing the rest to flee. Hardy then used rapid fire to silence one of two German machine guns firing on the patrol before he was wounded by a grenade. Hardy ordered the rest of the patrol to retreat back to their lines whilst he remained to drag his badly wounded sergeant back 200 yards to safety. In the wording for his decoration it declared 'Throughout the operation he set a splendid example to his men and also obtained valuable information as to the enemy's dispositions'. On 2 October Captain Hardy led a counter attack near

Dadizeele during which he was shot in the stomach and received such severe wounds to his leg that it had to be amputated. He was evacuated back to England and was still in hospital when the war ended a short time later. He was fitted with an artificial limb and his resulting rapid manner of walking to disguise this earned him the nickname 'Hoppy' Hardy'.

On 1 November 1919 Hardy married Kathleen Isabel Hutton-Potts in London. On 30 January 1920 he was awarded a bar to his Military Cross and the DSO 'in recognition of gallant conduct and determination displayed in escaping or attempting to escape from captivity'. From April 1920 he ceased to be employed by the Military Intelligence Directorate officially due to 'ill health caused by wounds'. He was posted to 'F' Company of the Auxiliary Division Royal Irish Constabulary (ADRIC), seconded as an Intelligence officer based at Dublin Castle, retaining his Connaught Rangers uniform. He later stated that he worked for Scotland Yard which was the recruiting centre for ADRIC and to whom the information he gathered was relayed for analysis. Despite his wounds Hardy was to lead raids on various IRA locations including Vaughn's Hotel in Parnell Square. His main role however was interrogating prisoners in Dublin Castle who had been captured with weapons or seditious documents of any importance. Hardy had experienced several such interrogations himself as an escaped prisoner of war and he was often aided by his colleague Captain William Lorraine 'Tiny' King MC. On 10 June 1920 Hardy was awarded a Mention in Dispatches.

Hardy became a hated figure for the IRA who regularly accused him of brutality whilst interrogating prisoners. Hardy was one of the targets for the IRA's attempt to destroy British Intelligence by killing a large number of intelligence officers in their homes on 21 November 1920 which would come to be known as 'Bloody Sunday'. Once again he escaped death as his would-be killers were unable to locate him.

In November 1922 Hardy was placed on the army half-pay list and in April 1925 he retired from the army on account of ill-health caused by his wounds. He worked for Lloyds Bank in Pall Mall, London and later went into full-time book writing and farming, at Washpit Farm near King's Lynn in Norfolk. Hardy died of natural causes on 30 May 1958 in Hammersmith. He was buried on 5 June at Wells Church, Norfolk leaving an estate of £57,000 on which £19,000 duty was then paid. In the foreword for Hardy's autobiography *I'Escape!* Sir Arthur Conan Doyle pays glowing tribute to Hardy stating that 'a more gallant gentleman never lived.'

Endnotes Chapter 18

1   The Bodley Head.

Chapter 19

The Great Escape

I suppose you will have heard that Wood and Rogers have been in Holland a long time. Am looking forward to my turn.

Lieutenant Thomas Frank Burrill, a fighter pilot shot down in his Airco D.H.4 in April 1918, in a letter to his sweetheart Lucy dated 14 May 1918, with reference to the successful escape of Captain Joseph Nelson Octavius Rogers of the 8th Battalion, Durham light Infantry and Wood, just two months before a mass bid for freedom was made through a tunnel from Holzminden detention camp (Internierungslager) in northern Germany which the British had dug using just pieces of cutlery. Burrill made no mention of his role, which is likely due to the letters being vetted by the Germans, but in September 1918 he asked Lucy to send him newspaper articles about the camp and the escape effort.

Thomas Frank Burrill was born on 27 April 1886 in Masham, Yorkshire. He was commissioned into the Montgomeryshire Yeomanry Cavalry and in 1916 was attached to the RFC where he gained his flying licence on 24 August 1916. After completing his training in December 1916 he was posted to 57 Squadron RFC in France. The squadron suffered heavy losses supporting the British offensive at Arras. On 3 April 1917 Burrill shot down a German aircraft whilst on an offensive patrol between Arras and Cambrai. The last entry in the log is his first combat flight on 6 April as on his later patrol that day he was shot down along with his gunner Private Smith by 21-year-old Leutnant Heinrich Gontermann of Jasta 5, a 39-victory ace with the 'Bavarian Military Order of Max Joseph' and the 'Pour le Mérite'. On 30 October Gontermann, a non-smoker, social drinker, patriotic and religious introvert, took off in a Fokker Dr.I. He had not yet recovered fully from a bout of dysentery but he was anxious to try his new aeroplane, despite misgivings about it. After a few minutes, he tried aerobatics at 700 metres altitude. He pulled out of the second loop and dived into a left turn. The upper wing collapsed and broke completely off. His Fokker plunged into the ground. Gontermann was pulled from the wreck alive, though with severe head injuries after slamming into the machine gun breeches. He was taken to the Jasta's medical bay, where he died from his injuries several hours later. Some sources say his death occurred the day after his accident. Gontermann was only one of several German pilots killed testing the new Dr.I. As a result, Fokker was accused of shoddy construction and directed to change production methods for the manufacture of the aeroplane.

On the day Burrill was shot down, 57 Squadron suffered another four losses. Originally sent to a PoW camp at Karlsruhe before being transferred to various other camps, he ended up at the infamous officers' PoW camp at Holzminden near the small town on the Weser near Hanover and about 100 miles from Holland. A former cavalry barracks, it consisted of two four-storey barrack blocks, known to the Germans as Kaserne 'A' and Kaserne 'B' and to the British as 'A' House and 'B' House. Each had an entrance and a staircase at each end - the near one for the officers and the far one for the orderlies. Also there was a basement floor with cellars and a flight leading down to them. The ground floor, the first floor and the second floor were all much the same, officers' rooms opening out on to a corridor. On the attic floor there were two or three officers' rooms at our end, then (partitioned off) the English orderlies' quarters, the luggage room and finally the orderlies' staircase. This part of the attic floor - the orderlies' quarters and luggage room - was out of bounds to British officers; hence the partition. The whole of the basement floor was also out of bounds: so was the orderlies' staircase. It was barricaded off at the end of each of the other three corridors and we were not allowed to use the only other means of getting to it - the orderlies' entrance.

The camp was used to incarcerate British and British Empire Offizier Gefangenenlager from September 1917 until December 1918 and held about 250 officers. Many of them, like 23-year old Lieutenant Brian Horrocks, who tried to escape Holzminden a number of times and was awarded a Military Cross for his efforts, would become well known later in their careers.[1] The senior British officer of the camp was Colonel Charles Edward Henry Rathbone DSO RNAS, born 17 February 1886 at Trieste, Italy. Many of the officers in the camp came from the RNAS and the RFC. Lieutenant Frederick W. Mardock RNVR, an observer who, with his pilot Flight Lieutenant Francis Joseph Bailey RNAS, flying a Short Admiralty Type 830 seaplane, were shot down on 24 July 1916 by a U-boat north of Zeebrugge and were picked up by a German TBD and interned in Holzminden. Bailey was transferred to The Hague in June 1918 under the prisoner exchange scheme.

Other prisoners included 34-year-old Captain David Benjamin 'Munshi' Gray, born 29 July 1884 in Assam, India; late of the 48th Pioneers, Indian Infantry, before transferring to 11 Squadron RFC he had been shot down on 17 September 1916 by the celebrated ace Oberleutnant Oswald Böelcke for his 27th victory; 22-year old Lieutenant Algernon Frederick Bird, 61st victim of Baron Manfred von Richthofen; 25-year old 2nd Lieutenant Christopher Guy Gilbert, 31st victim of the 'Red Baron' and 23-year old Captain William Leefe Robinson VC, to name but a few.

Originally from Norfolk and a member of 2/5th Norfolk Regiment prior to transferring to the RFC, Lieutenant Bird was shot down and captured on 3 September 1917. He recalled 'We had covered our allotted beat once and had just turned to repeat the process when an enemy machine was seen some way below us and, a flight commander indicated his intention of diving. I followed suit and by this time another enemy machine having appeared proceeded to attack him. It then became clear that we were involved in a scrap with a large number of the enemy. While chasing my particular opponent I took a glance over my shoulder to find myself being followed by two triplanes which I at once took to belong to an RNAS squadron with whom we occasionally cooperated. The next thing that I knew was that I was under a fusillade from machine guns at very close quarters; my engine cut out and I got one under my right arm which momentarily knocked me out. On recovering I found that I had got to do all I knew if I was to stand a chance of reaching our lines. The two enemy triplanes were making wonderful shooting practice at me and my machine was being hit times without number, the splinters flying from the two small struts just in front of the cockpit and from the instrument board. It was impossible to fly straight for more than a few moments at a time before they got their guns on me and my progress towards our lines was very slow compared with the height I was losing for my engine was a passenger only.

'It began to be quite obvious that I should not succeed in regaining our lines as I was now within a few hundred feet of the ground and, looking for a place to put my machine down I found a field in which a German fatigue party were digging trenches. In this I eventually landed hitting I believe a tree in the process: all the while my assailants had kept up a heavy fire whenever they could get their guns on me.

'Upon my machine coming to rest it looked as if the trench digging party were going to finish the work that their airmen had begun but fortunately for me an officer drove up in a horse and cart and took charge, taking me to the HQ of a K.B. section where I was searched, my flying kit removed and my wound dressed. This later proved to be very slight.'[2]

On 2 December 1914, Christopher Guy Gilbert was commissioned into the 1/6 Service Battalion of the Dorsetshire Regiment which went to France on 13 July 1915. After serving in the trenches, Gilbert transferred to the RFC and served with 29 Squadron at Le Hameau. On 25 March 1917 Gilbert flew his Nieuport Scout as a fighter escort for an F.E.2b doing a dawn photographic reconnaissance. There were a number of two-man escort patrols planned that morning and he and a Lieutenant Owen took the first slot at 0705. The Nieuport was a new aeroplane for Gilbert and he thought that as it was a short flight he would be back in time for breakfast. He decided not to dress, but just put his coat on over his pyjamas. In Von Richthofen's report he says that at 0820 he was flying his Halberstadt D.II and saw aeroplanes over German lines. Owen had to return to Le Hameau as he was experiencing problems with his carburettor. Gilbert carried on alone over the enemy front-line. Von Richthofen thought this was the last aeroplane (unaware that others followed at later times) and opened fire. The Scout came down near Tilloy-lès-Mofflaines just south-east of Arras. Gilbert was pulled from the burning Nieuport by German soldiers and taken prisoner - still wearing his pyjamas. He was in hospital for a while and Von Richthofen sent flowers and fruit to him. Gilbert made a number of attempts to escape from the prisoner-of-war camps, but never quite managed it. He was repatriated in December 1918. He lived to be 80.[3]

Qualifying for his RFC certificate at Ruislip, Cecil William Blain, born 7 October 1896 at Hooton, Cheshire was commissioned directly into the RFC and he was posted to 70 Squadron which flew Sopwith 1½ Strutters. With his observer, 2nd Lieutenant C. D. Griffiths, they and Captain W. D. S. Sanday and his observer, Lieutenant C. W. Busk and another pilot, Lieutenant Mase and his observer, they claimed two Albatros two-seaters forced to land on 6 August

1916. The following day Blain and Griffiths were shot down and taken prisoner.

2nd Lieutenant Stanley Stuart Beattie Purves MC RFC, born on 29 June 1893 in Kirkcaldy to Mary and Alexander Purves, a draper, had been a SPAD pilot on 19 Squadron at Fienvillers in France. Tragedy struck the family when in 1896 his mother died and the young Purves was brought up by his father. In September 1914 he enlisted in the Scottish Horse Regiment, a Yeomanry Regiment. On 29 May 1916 he attended a medical board at the Military Hospital Perth, was passed fit for service and seconded from the regiment to the RFC. On 27 December 1916 he was posted to 19 Squadron which at the time was in the process of changing its B.E.12s for a full complement of new SPAD VIIs. On 19 March 1917 Purves was engaged by three Albatroses over Cambrai- Ste Quentin. His aileron control jammed due to a Bowden cable from the trigger fouling some pipe fittings, he went into a spin for about 500 feet discovering the trouble. On opening up the throttle the engine was very feeble and he tried to reach the French Lines, but the engine gave out, he could not continue to glide as the enemy was on his tail and he went down landing near Homblières. On landing he managed to rectify the fault but was pulled off the SPAD by German troops before he could get away. Two Germans claimed the victory, Hauptmann Paul von Osterroht (KIA 23 April 1917) from Jasta 12 at 0840 hours near Roisel - Templeux and at 0910 hours Leutnant Kurt Schneider from Jasta 5, also at Homblières.[4]

Purves and another prisoner, 2nd Lieutenant John Kiel 'Jock' Tullis RFC, a Glaswegian born on 26 October 1894, who was shot down and captured on 6 September 1916 flying a 70 Squadron Sopwith 1½ Strutter (A668) became firm friends at Holzminden.[5] Purves was billeted in Block 'B' and Tullis in Block 'A' and Purves managed to bribe a guard to let Tullis join him.

At Holzminden also were twenty British orderlies, who as batmen looked after the officers. Despite this consideration, Holzminden was no Donington Hall. Because of the grim conditions the PoWs called the camp 'Hellzminden' and the camp commandant, Hauptmann Karl Niemeyer, had an appalling reputation for cruelty. He was a really vindictive character who made life particularly difficult for the airmen. Torture and summary execution were not unknown at the camp.

Captain William Leefe Robinson VC was reputedly singled out by the notorious commandant who swore to make the British pilot suffer for causing the death of Hauptmann Wilhelm Schramm, commander of Schütte-Lanz SL-11, whom Niemeyer claimed had been a personal friend. Robinson had shot the SL-11 down on the evening of 2/3 September 1916. On 5 April 1917 Robinson and his observer, 2nd Lieutenant Edward Darien Warburton, a self employed farmer from Te Kuiti in New Zealand who had landed with the Main Body of the Mounted Rifles in May 1916[6] were shot down flying a 48 Squadron F.2A (A3337) in an action described as 'similar to a cavalry charge ' and the Germans scattered the twin seater Bristols in less than two minutes. The victory was credited to Vizefeldwebel (Vice Sergeant) Sebastian Festner of Jasta 11 who was flying an Albatros D.III. Festner had scored his first two victories in February that year and followed these with ten victories during

'Bloody April'. He was killed in action on 25 April 1917, near Oppy.

Captain Robinson was captured alive and was transferred from prison camp to prison camp where his escape attempts ended in failure each time. 2nd Lieutenant Warburton was later reported as being held at Scharmstedt, Provinz Hanover until his repatriation back to the UK at war's end and then back to New Zealand. Robinson had a harsh time in captivity and he made several attempts to escape, being moved around several camps. He was kept in solitary confinement at Holzminden for his escape attempts. It is thought his health was badly affected during his time as a prisoner. Robinson was repatriated in early December 1918 and was able to spend Christmas with his friends and family. However, this freedom was short-lived. Weak and sick he contracted Spanish influenza which was sweeping the world at the time and Robinson was one of the 150,000 in England alone who died, on 31 December 1918 at the Stanmore home of his sister, the Baroness Heyking. He was buried at All Saints' Churchyard Extension in Harrow Weald with great ceremony. Thousands turned up to line the route of the procession, which was led by the Central Band of the RAF and a fly-past of aircraft dropped a wreath which was laid on the grave.

Niemeyer was one of a pair of twins: his brother, Heinrich, was Kommandant of the camp at Clausthal. The brothers had lived in Milwaukee, Wisconsin, for seventeen years until the spring of 1917, when the United States entered the war and as a result Karl was able to speak English. However, his language was filled with idiomatic errors and slang terms: it was described by one prisoner as 'bar-tender Yank' while another stated that Niemeyer 'talked broken American under the impression that it was English'. The prisoners constantly ridiculed him and nicknamed him 'Milwaukee Bill'. One error, which became notorious, was his assertion that 'You think I do not understand the English, but I do. I know damn all about you.' He boasted that Holzminden was escape-proof. *'You see, yentlemen,'* he would say, in his Americanised English, *'you cannot get out now, I should not try. It will be bad for your health,'* and the prisoners allowed him to think that they agreed. Lieutenant Hugh George Edmund Durnford, born 1886 in Kensington in London, the 32-year old adjutant at the camp, late of the Royal Field Artillery, who was taken prisoner on 5 August 1917, wrote: 'Perhaps what jarred most in him was that he was so hopelessly infra dig and behaved more like a tiresome camp Feldwebel than a Commandant. He was a busybody. He prowled and pounced. He burst into our rooms in the morning to rout us out of bed. He kept us all on the jumps, including his own people. No one trusted him and he was so cocksure and blatant that he wasn't even an object of pity in his solitude. Even his own puppy didn't like him. He used to walk round the camp and the only time he was ever seen to end down was when he stooped to coax the puppy away from English officers, with whom it was always making friends.'[7]

In November 1917 thirteen prisoners[8] at Holzminden devised a plan for a mass escape by 100 men, to take place in the summer of 1918 under the noses of heavily armed German guards through a tunnel of only sixteen yards, six feet deep and just eighteen inches in diameter. The tunnel was the brainchild of 30-year old Lieutenant William Gourlay Colquhoun of Princess Patricia's

Canadian Light Infantry (who was exchanged to Holland in February 1918) and it began under the orderlies' staircase in the cellar of Kaserne 'B'. Beyond the camp perimeter was a field of rye. The plan was to dig out far enough to exit the tunnel in this field so that the officers would be hidden from the German sentries.

According to 'Jock' Tullis, a Tunnel Committee was formed to select the men who were to follow the 'working party'. A decision was taken that preference should be given to officers who had escaped before and who had refused to go to Holland on the Neutral Country exchange which was an agreement that after eighteen months captivity officers of both countries should be allowed to proceed to Holland where they would have to remain until the end of the war. The next group to be allocated a place were officers who, in the eyes of the experienced Committee would 'put up a good show' if they did get out.

The tunnellers dug using spoons, sharpened cutlery and tools stolen from the camp and they used bed slats to shore it. They designed and made an ingenious ventilation system, fake uniforms and official papers. But the plan was tinged with a lot of bad luck. They initially planned to dig [an underground tunnel] only a short distance, but their plan was scuppered by a guard who got suspicious. So they then had to dig another, longer tunnel. You could only crawl down it - when you had gone in you could not go back. But they stuck with it, amazingly. There were thirteen men involved in the digging and others standing guard. It was agreed that the diggers would leave first and would be followed by 'the ruck' - any other men who wanted out.

In the first two months of its construction, between mid-October and mid-December 1917, the tunnel had reached to about fifteen yards in length. They were under the wall and outside of the camp. Lieutenant Hugh Durnford was not one of the tunnellers but described near enough, at second hand, what it was like, how it was dug and sensations as he emerged. 'There were many difficulties and risks besides those which were encountered underground. I was adjutant and it was my job to try to get to know what was in the German mind and to sense whether there was any fresh trouble afoot. Then, in the later stages, I had to keep the peace of the camp at all costs and make everything take second place to the completion of the tunnel and when the bubble burst I had a good deal to do, so perhaps I'm in the best position to tell you the whole story.

'I do not claim a record for the Holzminden tunnel. It measured over sixty yards and it took nine months to complete. It may not have been the biggest tunnel, but it was certainly the most successful in the war. But its main interest is as a monument of teamwork and resource and for the fact that it was dug under the nose of a Commandant who openly boasted that he had made his camp escape proof and that no one could possibly get out of it.

'Each shift consisted of three men. They entered and left the chamber in the garb of orderlies, which consisted of civilian coats and trousers with a band sewn into the arm and a stripe sewn into the trouser seam. This was the distinctive badge of prisoners at large on the land or in the mines or elsewhere. Their working clothes were kept in the chamber. Now, obviously, the one moment at which they could not possibly afford to be caught was when coming through the trap-door. If they were spotted at any other moment, the worst might still, possibly, be averted. Of course if they were detected as officers in orderlies' clothes there would be alarums and excursions and almost certainly a search. And if the Commandant got a second scare, would he overlook that tell-tale hole in the planks again? So the risk was great either way. But as it happened the luck held. The working party was never spotted and never challenged as they made their chancy passage from door to door, back to their own rooms. The patrols were too wide awake. This was the sort of thing. When the relief hour was due, the patrols, loafing at the orderlies' entrance, waited till the sentry had turned his back and then gave the 'all-clear' signal, which might be some snatch of a song or a password. The workers slipped the bolt, squirmed through the trap-door and came out into the open with the quick military step of three orderlies walking abreast. Once they had gained their own door there were many bolt-holes and they were fairly safe. Remember that the hours of work were limited by daylight and by the periodic roll calls or 'appels.' Remember too that each shift worked to the last possible moment and that any hold-up in the tunnel or base-chamber might have meant three officers missing on 'appel': and that this routine went on day after day for three or four months without intermission. You will then get a clearer idea of the teamwork. The average sentry wasn't a bright lad and was unlikely to recognise any particular officers out of 500. But the German personnel included many who were good at faces. A collision often seemed inevitable and only by skilful diversion on the part of the flanking patrol - after the manner of matadors in a bull fight - was the German attention persuaded to wander.

A pump consisting of bellows home-made from wood and the leather of a flying officer's coat had to keep the air tolerably clean at the tunnel face so that the tunnellers could breathe and the candle can stay alight. It is fixed on wooden uprights and discharges its blast into a pipe of tin tubes made out of biscuit boxes which came in parcels from home. The pipe was sunk in the tunnel floor and grew, of course, with the tunnel. Later on, as the twists and irregularities of the tunnel increased, the rope and basin method to remove stones and earth gave place to merely filling sacks with the earth and stones and pulling them out from the face.

One day, because of some alleged injustice to German prisoners in England, the prisoners were now to be cut off games, walks and exercise and be subjected to four 'appels' a day instead of two. This was depressing for the tunnellers, as it meant a much greater restriction of working hours. So henceforth they would work from indoors again and through the night.

By the end of June 1918 the end of the tunnel was estimated to be still ten or so yards short of the rye. With harvest time approaching there was a danger that the crop would be gathered before the tunnel was completed. Just short of the rye field was a row of beans that afforded a degree of cover. Though not as good as that provided by the rye, the tunnellers, fearing that they would miss their chance, decided to use the screen of beans to shield their exit from view. By mid-July the tunnel was ready; it had taken nine months to dig and extended sixty yards out from the basement of Block 'B'. This was about ten yards within the outer walls of the camp so the tunnel exit was effectively fifty yards beyond the camp wall.

On 24 July at 2100 hours the doors of Block 'B' were locked and the British officers went to their rooms. At 2200 hours the German guard did his rounds closing all of the windows in the corridors and until he was well clear of the build it was unsafe for the escape to commence. At 2215 hours Lieutenant Walter Butler who had done the lion's share, had been chosen to go down first and cut out, left his room and made his way up to the attic with the next two men on the escape list. They passed through the hole in the attic into the Orderlies' Quarters before descending to the tunnel's entrance. Butler entered the tunnel and he wriggled and bumped his way along the tunnel for the last time. By 2330 hours he broke the surface with a large bread knife with the other two working as his team, before pushing his kit through first and then crawling up, much to his satisfaction, in the beans. Though the sentry was quite near and the arc light appeared to be throwing everything into strong relief, he was aided by rain and shortly after he and his companions had crossed the river and were well away. All was going according to plan. The remaining members of the tunnellers gathered on the Officers' side of the attic to await the signal to proceed. The remaining members of the tunnellers move quickly through the hole in the attic, down and into the tunnel. Within a matter of minutes they had all passed through the tunnel and were away. It was Captain Hugh Durnford's job to regulate the departure of all those after the first twenty, so as to avoid unnecessary noise and movement. 'All the escapers were lying ready dressed on their beds and I summoned each as his turn came and sent him through to the orderlies' quarters where he was taken in tow and escorted to the tunnel mouth.'

Ensuring that the plan was strictly adhered to, Durnford went around the rooms warning the next men on the list to be ready. He went to see 2nd Lieutenant Louis 'Swaggie' Greive DCM 24, of the 23rd Battalion AIF from Wagga-Wagga, NSW and was told that the tunnellers were away; all was going to plan. At 0030 the next batch of nine escapees climbed through the hole in the attic. They were led by Colonel Charles Rathbone, 33-year old Captain Peter William Lyon MiD of the 11th Battalion, Australian Imperial Force from Korang Vale, Victoria and Lieutenant John Keith Bousfield RFC in the Royal Engineers in 1915 who made a number of reconnaissance flights over enemy positions, but was taken prisoner of war in early 1917 when his aircraft was brought down behind the German lines. By 0115 hours they too were away. At 0110 hours Durnford began his rounds a second time, assembling those next on the list. The first of these began to go through the tunnel as planned one hour after the previous party had exited. Only three had gone through when the orderly on the Orderlies' side of the hole in the attic reported a hitch to 'Swaggie' Greive and he would let Greive know when it was all clear.

With no news having been received from the Orderlies' Quarters by 0300 hours, Durnford agreed that Captain Frank Sharpe, who was one of those due to go through, should climb through the hole in the attic and see what was going on. After quarter of an hour Sharpe returned to report that there was no one about and that the tunnel was empty. In the absence of the orderlies it was decided to send the next five officers through at five minute intervals led by Captain Sharpe. When none of these returned it was assumed that the tunnel was still clear and the next half-dozen were passed through the hole in the attic again with about five minutes between each.

'Jock' Tullis and Stan Purves were billeted with Captain 'Munshi' Gray; one of the tunnel working party who departed earlier in the evening. Tullis and Purves were summoned around midnight. After saying a few good-bye's they proceeded to the tunnel entrance where they tossed to see who would go first, Purves won and started to worm his way through, followed closely behind by Tullis and then the next man. The week before the escape they had spent a lot of time studying the best route to follow, preparing their food packs and clothes. They were not part of the 'working party' that had designed, surveyed and constructed the tunnel; they were part of a group of men who were selected to follow the working party out. Tullis and Purves' provisions included ships biscuits dipped in melted dripping, stoned dates, a large amount of chocolate, meat cubes, Plasmon oats (as advertised in the *Illustrated London News*) which were compressed and mixed with Horlick's Malted Milk, soup cubes, tins of sausages, trench cookers, and wax blocks with a wick in the middle to cook their one hot meal each day. The provisions were divided into daily rations and tied up in waterproof bundles so that when crossing rivers they would remain as dry as possible. Clothing for the journey was also prepared. Tullis carried two pairs of socks, warm under clothes and a silk shirt. He had to find a way to keep his clothing dry when crossing any water and he treated his Burberry coat with a thick coating of melted fat rubbed into the fabric; to test the efficacy of the arrangement, he tested it by putting his boots, clothes and food packs in the coat, then wrapped them and tied with string and tested in a tin bath of water and all were found to be dry after fifteen minutes immersion.

One of the last of the prisoners waiting to escape, 27-year old Captain George Guyatt Gardiner MiD of the 13th Battalion, AIF from Randwick, NSW subsequently returned to report that the tunnel was blocked. It transpired that someone had got stuck in the tunnel and was urging those behind him to back up and let him out. Those behind however, urged him to go forward and thus the tunnel had become impassable. It became apparent that the tunnel had become blocked at the bottom of the slope to the final exit. This had been caused by a landslip as the officers had exited the tunnel, which although only small in scale was enough to make it impassable. With dawn approaching it was decided that everyone should return to their beds. With ordinary luck, if they had all succeeded in getting safely back to their rooms, the secret would have been kept from the Germans until morning 'appel' several hours later: which would have meant so many more hours' grace to the successful escapers. But just then, the Commandant of all people, put in one of his unadvertised appearances, out for an early morning stroll. He ran into two mud stained officers at the staircase entrance and the secret was out.

'But', wrote Durnford; 'the extent of the escape did not dawn upon the Germans until the roll had been called. It was a delicious moment when the fat and good-natured Feldwebel in charge of Barrack 'B' reported to the

Commandant that no fewer than twenty-nine officers including Colonel Rathbone were missing. That moment repaid many an old score. The air was charged. We who had held ourselves in for many weeks now laughed loud and long. Loud and long laughter was always the most certain method to annoy. And you may be sure the Commandant responded. We were all shut up at once in the barracks and the place became alive with secretly amused and delighted sentries. Emergency rules were posted up and recited, forbidding any officers to do practically anything except breathe, under penalty of the cells, which were, of course, at once filled. Several shots were also fired. We organised a sort of passive resistance mutiny in the hope that there might be an enquiry from headquarters and the Commandant would become discredited as a gaoler and as a keeper of order: but it didn't come to that and after a hectic week things got back more or less to normal.

'If the tunnel had been fully occupied for every minute between 1015 and 0600 when the last entombed officer had been pulled out, feet foremost, from the ruins there is no doubt that many more than twenty-nine would have at least got clear of the camp. Whether a larger number would have finally escaped is a different question. The orderlies purposely left the tunnel clear for much longer than the scheduled time so as to give the better chance to the first twenty who were the real tunnellers. It was for these, after all, that they had worked so loyally and ungrudgingly for many months, without any hope of ulterior benefit for themselves and not for any Tom, Dick or Harry who pressed for a free passage at the end.'

Of the 29 men, nineteen were apprehended. Captain Frank Sharpe and Captain Bernard Porter Luscombe who had been the last two out of the tunnel, had been at liberty for just two and half days and had been caught passing through a village at night about fifteen miles down the River Weser. After ten days Lieutenant Frederick W. Mardock RNVR, Lieutenant Colin Laurence RNAS, Walter Butler and Captain William Henry Langren of the West Yorkshire Regiment were brought back to the camp. Butler had stolen a bicycle and was caught on it while passing through a village. The others had been taken in the vicinity of the Ems, fourteen days after the escape, Captain Philip Norbert Smith was recaptured just three miles of the Dutch border.

'Jock' Tullis became stuck in the tunnel for a while and had to loosen a rock that was stopping him. Once he reached the end of the tunnel he crawled along the track made by earlier escapees across the corn field. Tullis and Purves stopped for a short while to get their breath and then set off towards the River Weser. Shortly after they were joined by Captain Edward Wilmer Leggatt RFC, born in 1892 and who was shot down and captured on 9 August 1916, who reached Dutch territory on the night of the 6/7 August. Leggatt left the party some time after crossing the river, but unplanned, they met up again when near the border. They crossed the Dutch border after fourteen nights on the run and were interned in a quarantine camp at Rijks on 8 August and after a nine day stay in Holland they crossed to England by ferry.

Also making their way to Holland safely on foot were Somerset-born 2nd Lieutenant Harry James Bennett, who had been shot down on 2 Squadron RFC; Lieutenant Bousfield RFC; Colonel Rathbone and Lieutenant Pierre (Peter)

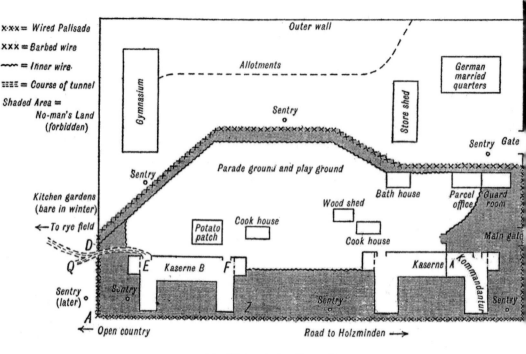

x·x·x = Wired Palisade
xxx = Barbed wire
〜〜 = Inner wire·
ΞΞΞ = Course of tunnel
Shaded Area =
   No-man's Land
   (forbidden)

Outer wall

Allotments

German married quarters

Gymnasium

Sentry

Store shed

Sentry   Gate

Parade ground and play ground

Sentry

Bath house

Parcel office   Guard room

Kitchen gardens
(bare in winter)

←To rye field

Wood shed

Cook house

Main gate

Potato patch   Cook house   Cook house

D

Q

E   Kaserne B   F

Kaserne A

Kommandantur

Sentry
(later)

Sentry

A

Sentry

Sentry   Sentry

Z

← Open country

Road to Holzminden →

'The Holzminden Tunnel'

Clifford Campbell-Martin MC CdeG, an Anglo-Indian officer of 25 Squadron RFC who couldn't swim (between them and ultimate freedom lay three rivers) - and the three 'main' diggers: Captain 'Munshi' Gray, 2nd Lieutenant Cecil Blain and Captain Caspar Kennard of 16 Squadron RFC who, on 9 October 1916, had been shot down during his first flight over the German lines around 4.15 in their B.E.2c (4494) with Air Mechanic B. C. Digby. These three serial escapists were great friends. One of them spoke excellent German, so en route to Holland they pretended he was a German guard in charge of the other two. One of them pretended to be insane in order to avoid rousing suspicion, as they made the 150 kilometre journey through Germany. They made it to the neutral Dutch border and from there they had safe passage back to Britain to be greeted as heroes.[9]

All those who were recaptured were kept in solitary confinement until early September, when they were released from their confinement to await court-martial. This trial took place on 27 September and the officers, who were charged as a group, were represented by a lawyer. A representative of the Netherlands Ambassador in Berlin also attended the trial to act in their interests. They were found guilty by the court and each sentenced to six months imprisonment, to be served in a fortress, on a combined charge of mutiny and damage to property. As it transpired the sentence was never carried out, as the military situation in German had so deteriorated it was becoming obvious that the war was in its closing stages.

Colonel Charles Rathbone, whose escape had particularly agitated the Commandant, rubbed it in by sending a telegram from Holland. *Having a lovely time stop If I ever find you in London will break your neck stop.*[10] Lieutenant Hugh Durnford showed this to the Commandant just as he was himself about to be removed as a suspected character to Stralsund Camp, where a few weeks later, in October 1918, he was lucky enough to escape to Denmark, for which he was awarded the MC for his successful escape. Durnford too could not resist the temptation of sending him one himself.[11]

At the 11th hour of the 11th day, we will remember them.

Endnotes Chapter 19

1   In World War II Horrocks was a British army general. Another famous inmate at the camp was future Hollywood film director James Whale, a Second Lieutenant in the Worcestershire Regiment. He went on to direct the film *Frankenstein*. Michael Claude Hamilton-Bowes-Lyon (25), brother of the future Queen Elizabeth, The Queen Mother, was also incarcerated at Holzminden.

2   Algernon Bird was eventually repatriated on 14 December 1918 when he returned to Norfolk to work in the family firm of flour millers and merchants in Downham Market. He died on 24 August 1957. Thanks are due to his son Peter who posted this account on the internet on 10 November 2008.

3   Thanks are due to Karen Ette.

4   Schneider died on 14 July 1917 following combat with a RFC squadron.

5   Tullis' observer, 2nd Lieutenant J. C. Taylor was also destined to escape captivity, on 27 December 1917.

6   On 24 August 1916 he was reported sick, suffering from Enteritis and was sent off the Peninsula to hospital in Malta and was then hospitalised in the UK to recuperate. In April 1917 he was discharged from the NZEF to take up a commission in the RFC and trained as a navigator.

7   The Tunnellers of Holzminden.

8   Lieutenants Frederick W. Mardock RNVR, Lieutenant Colin Laurence RNAS; Captain David Benjamin Gray RFC; Lieutenant Walter Butler, Captain William Henry Langren, Lieutenants David Wainwright RN, Neil Macleod, 2nd Lieutenants Cecil William Blain RFC and Caspar Kennard RFC, Lieutenants Robertson, Lieutenant Andrew Mearns Clouston, Royal Newfoundland Regiment; Lieutenant Arthur Morris and Lieutenant Robert Milner Paddison, Duke of Cornwall's Light Infantry.

9   Blain was awarded the Air Force Cross as per the *London Gazette* of 3 June 1919. On 22 January 1919 he was flying a Camel (C1588) at Martlesham Heath aircraft testing and experimental centre when the port wing cracked in level flight at 450 feet and he side slipped in and was killed. He was 22-years old. Squadron Leader David Benjamin Gray OBE MC died aged 58 on 8 November 1942.

10   Rathbone was awarded a bar to his DSO on 16 December 1919 'For gallantry in escaping from captivity whilst a prisoner of war.' He died on 21 December 1943.

11   Durnford died on 6 June 1965.

Afterword

An Aerial Victory Of Peace

Ernest Protheroe

I went into a public 'ouse to get a pint o' beer,
The publican 'e up an' sez,'We serve no red-coats here.'
The girls be'ind the bar they laughed an' giggled fit to die,
I outs into the street again an' to myself sez I:
O it's Tommy this, an' Tommy that, an' 'Tommy, go away';
But it's'Thank you, Mister Atkins,' when the band begins to play
The band begins to play, my boys, the band begins to play,
O it's 'Thank you, Mister Atkins,' when the band begins to play.

'Tommy Atkins', used to refer to a common soldier in the British army was used quite widely and rather contemptuously in the mid 19th century. Kipling sums this up in Rudyard Kipling's poem *Tommy*, one of his *Barrack-Room Ballads* (1892) in which he contrasts the mean way in which the soldier was treated in peace time with the way he was praised as soon as he was needed to defend or fight for his country.

In July 1918 the British 'Press Baron' and owner of the *Daily Mail*, Lord Northcliffe, offered a prize of £10,000 for the first flight across the Atlantic, which aroused much interest on both sides of the ocean and as soon as conditions permitted there would be no lack of aspirants for aviation fame and fortune. Finally, in the spring of 1919 there were five British aeroplanes in Newfoundland making ready for the attempt; the weather conditions were bad and more than one machine was damaged in preparatory trial flights. The weather indicated a west-to-east crossing as being the most favourable and Newfoundland was chosen by most of the teams because of its proximity to the British Isles, although one crew, Major J. C. P. Wood and Captain C. C. Wylie, in their Short Shirl, decided to try the opposite route. They made a trial flight from Ireland in April 1919 and crashed into the ocean, putting an end to their challenge. The £10,000 prize money lured several sets of aviators with their aircraft, support teams and sponsors to Newfoundland and by early 1919 it was clearly going to be a race to see who could be ready first. Meanwhile, three US Navy Curtiss flying boats were preparing for the task of crossing the Atlantic in stages by means of a soundly-organized plan in which the attendance of naval vessels all along the route reduced the element of risk to very small proportions. The NC-1, NC-2 and NC-3 all crashed in the attempt, but starting first, the NC-4, piloted by Lieutenant Commander Albert Cushing 'Putty' Read (so-named because his face rarely showed any emotion) actually made the first aerial crossing of the Atlantic in stages, taking eleven days. He and his crew - a navigator, radio officer and two engineers - crossed over to the Azores, 1,381 miles in fifteen hours 19 minutes; the second stage, Azores to Lisbon, 1,034 miles in nine hours 42 minutes and the third stage, Lisbon to Plymouth, 895 miles in five hours 1 minute. Although it was intended that this flight would carry an official commemorative mail, it was taken off to save weight and no official mail was carried, although one letter was flown unofficially.

The sporting attempt of Harry G. Hawker and Lieutenant Commander Kenneth Mackenzie-Grieve was in quite a different category. Their Sopwith Atlantic aeroplane with a single Rolls-Royce 'Eagle' engine of 350 hp had a flight duration of about 25 hours at a speed of 100 to 110 mph for about thirty hours. They proposed to fly through the night from St. John's to somewhere near Clifden in Ireland, a distance of 1,880 miles. Word coming to St. John's that the Americans had already set out on the venture afflicted Hawker with the fear that he would be forestalled and on 18 May the Royal Aero Club in London received a telegram from the official starter of the race stating: 'Mr Hawker and Commander Mackenzie-Grieve in the Sopwith Rolls Royce Biplane began the transatlantic flight this afternoon at 6:45pm from Mount Pearl flying field, St. John's, Newfoundland.' In the face of unfavourable weather reports the Sopwith aeroplane got away, climbed well and disappeared into the fog of the Newfoundland Banks. As Hawker and Grieve passed over the Newfoundland coastline, the undercarriage of the Sopwith was jettisoned to decrease weight and improve airspeed.

Hawker and Grieve's red light was sighted by the cable ship Faraday at 4 am Greenwich time, on the morning of the 19th only a few miles off the regular steamer track, but from that moment the aviators were lost to a waiting world. By 24 May nothing further had been heard of them and it was only reasonable to assume that the heroic attempt, greatly daring, had greatly failed. Mrs. Hawker alone refused to give up hope; expressing her disbelief that calamity had waited upon her husband.

On 25 May word came unexpectedly out of the unknown to Lloyds signal station at the Butt of Lewis. The Danish steamship Mary, passing at a distance, spelt out with flags the laconic but electrifying message: 'Saved 'hands' of Sopwith aeroplane.' The Admiralty took steps to intercept the Mary, with the result that Hawker and Grieve were taken aboard the destroyer Woolston and they told the dramatic story of what had occurred.

'Everything', said Hawker 'went well at the start. The sky was quite clear for the first four hours and then we encountered heavy cloud banks and flew into a storm with rain squalls. Trouble did not begin until we were five and a half hours out from St. John's, when the temperature of the water in the radiator began to rise and we could see that something was the matter with the water circulation. The only thing we could do was to stop the motor, put the nose of the machine down steeply, with the hope that this would clear the refuse in the filter and this was successful. But it was again choked in the next hour and this brought us to about 800 miles out.

'We came to clouds, very, very high; I should say about 15,000 feet, very black, too and almost impossible to fly through. Each time we tried to climb above them we boiled badly. Coming down to about 6,000 feet we found it blacker than ever. The sun was just getting up when we reached the fateful decision to see if we could find a ship, for we knew we could not go on indefinitely boiling our water away. The wind was blowing half a gale and we were getting knocked about very badly at times.

'At last I sighted a ship close to us on our port (left) bow. We were both fairly in the fog, with the clouds low and we were almost on the top of her before we saw her. We flew alongside her at 400 feet, fired three Very distress signals and waited some time, flying across and across until she got some men up on deck. Then we went ahead about two miles and landed in front of her. We made a very good landing, although a very high sea was running and the machine floated on an even keel well out of the water.

'We watched the steamer approaching. We put our own boat out and stood by in case the machine should break up and sink, which it began to do rapidly in a heavy sea. The sea was running up twelve feet and breaking right over the machine and us.

'Our life-saving suits kept us dry and for an hour and a half we watched the crew trying to launch a lifeboat. She was only 200 yards away. After much difficulty she succeeded in getting to us and we boarded the lifeboat and were pulled to the ship by a line.'

As their wireless was not working, it was a merciful dispensation of Providence for the distressed aviators to descry a ship so speedily.

The Sopwith had remained drifting on the sea until it was located by the SS *Lake Charlottesville* on 23 May. In a telegraph to the Secretary of the Navy, Lieutenant Commander A. C. Wllvers reported: 'Near the top of the plane was lashed a brown postage bag which was marked 'Newfoundland GPO.' It contained mail mostly addressed to prominent British Peers, the Royal Family and one addressed to His Majesty the King. The mail was very soaked and otherwise damaged.' The *Lake Charlottesville* arrived at Falmouth on 28 May and the wrecked aircraft was handed over to the local Customs and Excise officials. The mail was sent to London and put into the British postal system on 30 May.

Commander Grieve's navigation of the aeroplane for 1,100 miles over the sea through unknown winds and without speaking to a single ship and yet deviating only a few miles from the prescribed track, was very different from that of the American seaplanes that flew to the Azores. He and Hawker had failed in their attempt, but they had covered 1,200 miles of the 1,800 miles from Newfoundland to Ireland and the *Daily Mail* gave them £5,000 each.

Harry Hawker was killed in July 1921 while flying near Hendon through losing control of his machine owing to sudden disability.

After the historic attempt of Hawker and Grieve to conquer the Atlantic there was something like a race on the Newfoundland side between the Vickers and the Handley Page teams in getting their respective machines ready for the next attempt. Captain John Alcock was the pilot and Lieutenant Arthur Whitten Brown RAF the navigator of a Vickers Vimy two-engined bombing aeroplane of standard Government type. Alcock was the only pilot among the Atlantic candidates who had designed and actually built an aeroplane on active service, which feat he accomplished at Lemnos. Lieutenant Arthur Whitten Brown was an engineer interested in flying before the war. Born in

Glasgow on 23 July 1886 to American parents; his father had been sent to Scotland to evaluate the feasibility of siting a Westinghouse factory in Clydeside. The factory was eventually sited in Trafford Park in Stretford, Lancashire and the family subsequently relocated there. After service in France, Brown was seconded to 2 Squadron RFC as an observer. Brown's aircraft was shot down by anti-aircraft fire over Vendin-le-Vieil in France while on artillery observation duties. He was sent back to England to recuperate but returned only to be shot down again, this time with a punctured fuel tank, near Bapaume in B.E.2c on a reconnaissance flight on 10 November 1915. Brown and his pilot, 2nd Lieutenant Harold W. Medlicott were captured by the Germans. (In June 1918 Medlicott was shot by the Germans while attempting to escape for the fourteenth time). Later interned in Switzerland, Brown was repatriated in September 1917.

The Vickers Vimy's overall length was 42 feet 8 inches and the span 67 feet. The approximate loaded war weight, including bombs, four Lewis guns, ammunition and a crew of three men, was 12,500lb. For the Atlantic voyage no alteration was made in the machine except that special tanks were fitted. Altogether 865 gallons of petrol were carried, with thirty gallons of lubricating oil to serve the two 375hp Rolls-Royce engines 2,400 miles. The speed of the machine was 100 mph. Thus, with an aeroplane of engine power proved innumerable times during the war and undoubtedly capable of flying without a stop, the mileage from Newfoundland to Ireland and in such capable hands, everything promised favourably so far as human ingenuity and forethought could contrive it; but the balance of risk was against the aviators, as was exhibited just less than four weeks earlier. Upon that occasion a most experienced and a most air-wise pilot was cheated out of success by an apparently almost insignificant trifle such as a few scraps of solder shaking loose and interfering with the functioning of the radiator. Whether Alcock would prove to be successful was on the knees of the gods.

On 14 June at 1628 GMT Captain Alcock made a daring ' get away ' in face of a 40 mph wind, probably spurred thereto by word that the Handley Page machine was getting ready to start. Climbing to a height of 1,000 feet, Lieutenant Brown set the course, which was kept until well on in the night. At dark they were 4,000 feet up. Going on steadily until between 4 and 5 am, the aviators were then in a bank of thick fog.

'We began to have a very rough time. The air speed indicator jammed. It stood at 90 and I did not know exactly what I was doing. It jammed through sleet freezing on it. We did some comic stunts then. I believe we looped the loop and by accident we did a steep spiral. It was very alarming. We had no sense of horizon. We came down quickly from 4,000 feet until we saw the water very near. That gave me my horizon again and I was all right. That period only lasted a few seconds, but it seemed ages.'

Later the machine climbed to 6,000 feet only to find fog, but higher they saw the moon and a few stars. 'We climbed to 11,000 feet. It was hailing and snowing. The machine was covered with ice. That was about 6 o'clock in the morning and it remained like that until an hour before we landed.

'We came down and flew over the sea at 300 feet. It was still cloudy, but we could see the sun as he tried to break through. It was a terrible trip. We never saw a boat and we got no wireless messages at all. We saw land about 0915 when we discovered the coast. It was great to do that. We congratulated each other. We were very pleased our job was over.'

The aeroplane, having come safely through all the dangers and difficulties of the mid-Atlantic air currents, behaved badly at the landing at Clifden and buried her nose in the ground. It would have been outrageous misfortune that could inflict injury on pilot or navigator at that moment. Happily they escaped, with but a little deafness and shock and Lieutenant Brown was ready to fly on to London later in the day.

This conquest of the Atlantic Ocean by a nonstop direct flight of 1,900 nautical miles in sixteen hours twelve minutes was a remarkable performance whether viewed in the light of the physical endurance of the airmen, or the reliability of the engines. All Britons could feel a justifiable thrill of pride in the fact that the dauntless aviators were British (In 1914, Brown enlisted in the ranks of the University and Public Schools Brigade (UPS) for which he had to take out British citizenship) and that the machine they flew was British throughout. Alcock and Brown not only won the £10,000 prize, but His Majesty the King bestowed knighthoods upon them for a feat that was a notable step forward in human accomplishment. On 18 December 1919, Sir John Alcock was piloting a new Vickers amphibious aircraft, the Vickers Viking, to the first post-war aeronautical exhibition in Paris when he crashed in fog at Cottévrard, near Rouen in Normandy. Alcock suffered a fractured skull and never regained consciousness after being transferred to a hospital in Rouen. Lieutenant Colonel Sir Arthur Whitten Brown KBE died in his sleep on 4 October 1948 from an accidental overdose of Veronal, aged 62.

In 1919 the Australian government offered a prize of £10,000 to the first aviator to fly from England to Australia within thirty days. Captain Ross Smith and his brother Lieutenant Keith Smith decided to enter the race with two sergeant mechanics, James Mallett Bennett and Walter Henry Shiers, who, after the Armistice, had been invited to act as air mechanics for Captain Ross Smith, then attempting the first Cairo-Calcutta flight in a Handley-Page aircraft. Keith, born in 1890, became an observer/navigator in the RFC and RAF during World War I. His brother, born two years later, enlisted in August 1914 and went to war with the Light Horse Brigade.

On 12 November 1919, Ross Smith, who had been awarded the MC, DFC and AFC for his military service, his brother and their two mechanics, left Hounslow for Australia on a Vickers Vimy and were the first to reach Darwin on 10 December. Their successful flight of 11,294 miles in just under twenty-eight days Ross and Keith Bennett aroused world-wide interest and acclaim. On 22 December the Smith brothers were knighted; Shiers and Bennett (who was mentioned in dispatches in World War I and was later awarded the Meritorious Service Medal for his distinguished service as an air mechanic) received Bars to their Air Force Medals. Popular opinion favoured greater recognition for the mechanics, especially after Ross Smith stated publicly that the success of the flight was mainly due to their skill and zeal.

Early in 1922 the Smith brothers decided to attempt a round-the-world flight; Bennett and Shiers were again chosen as mechanics. The crew planned to take off from England on 25 April, but on 13 April, Ross Smith and Bennett were killed during a test flight at Weybridge, when their Vickers Viking Amphibian crashed. Captain Stanley Cockerell, test pilot for Vickers, had flown Smith and Bennett as passengers on the aircraft's maiden flight earlier that day and testified to the inquest that the machine seemed to be in perfect working order. The pioneer aviators were mourned as national heroes and their bodies were brought back to Australia. Sir Keith Smith had also planned to fly with them but his train from London was late, only arriving in time to see the crash. Sir Keith outlived his brother by 33 years. In 1923 he joined the staff of Vickers Ltd as their Australian representative. He became chairman of the directors of Vickers-Armstrong (Australia) Pty Ltd and several other engineering and public companies and airlines. The historic Vimy was presented to the Australian Government after its flight in 1919. It was stored and, on at least one occasion, badly damaged, but after World War II it was restored and put on display at Adelaide Airport.

On 21 August 1919, Cockerell had flown a Vimy from London to Amsterdam loaded with copies of *The Times*, which were then sold for the benefit of local charities. After leaving school, Cockerell, who was born in Wood Green, London on 9 February 1895 became a motor engineer. The day after war was declared, Cockerell joined up as a despatch rider in the RFC. In April 1915 he became an air mechanic 2nd class and later that year was promoted to air mechanic 1st class. He later became a pilot and was credited with seven aerial victories. On 24 June 1920 he and Frank Crossley Griffithes Broome DFC (who had been his flight commander in 151 Squadron) accompanied by mechanic Sergeant Major James Wyatt MSM, rigger Claude Corby and passenger Peter Chalmers Mitchell, an eminent zoologist and correspondent for *The Times*, set out in a Vickers Vimy on a pioneering flight to South Africa in an attempt to test the air route from Cairo to the Cape of Good Hope.

Ten days after the outbreak of war, Broome had enlisted in the Middlesex Regiment. The following year he obtained a commission in the Horse Transport Section of the Army Service Corps. In 1917 he transferred to the RFC. After obtaining his pilot's licence, he was posted to Hadleigh to take part in the air defence of London with 112 Squadron. In 1918 he returned to France with 151 Squadron. He was then a lieutenant. In one week he destroyed three German aircraft, his only three victories. One of these was a giant Zeppelin-Staaken R.VI bomber he shot down over Beugny, France while flying a Sopwith Camel during the night of 15/16 September 1918, one of the only two R.VI bombers the Germans lost to enemy action in World War I and the only one shot down by an Allied aircraft. For this achievement, he was awarded the DFC on 3 December 1918.

Broome and Cockerell's pioneering flight to South Africa was sponsored by *The Times*. On the first evening they arrived at RAF Manston in Kent. The following day they crossed the English Channel and arrived at Lyon. They reached Istres on 26 January, Rome on 27 January, Malta on 29 January, Tripoli on 31 January (having been held up by storms the previous day), Benghazi on

1 February and Heliopolis near Cairo on 3 February. On 6 February they set out for the main flight to South Africa and reached Aswan. On 8 February, after two forced landings caused by leaking cylinder water jackets, they reached Khartoum. After repairs, they left Khartoum on 10 February and reached El Jebelein, 208 miles to the south. Following further repairs, they left later the same day, but were forced to land in a dry swamp near Renk. The following day they returned to Jebelein for further repairs.

On 14 February, they set off again and reached Mongalla, in the far south of Sudan the following day, after spending the night on the banks of the Nile. They remained in Mongalla making repairs until 20 February, when they took off again and reached Nimule, again with engine trouble. They began again on 22 February and reached Uganda. On 24 February they left again and reached Kisumu in Kenya. They reached Tabora in Tanganyika Territory on 26 February, but crashed on take-off the following day, writing off the machine and ending the flight. Cockerell and Corby were slightly injured. Cockerell and Broome did eventually reach Cape Town, although not by air. There they were welcomed by, among others, Lieutenant Colonel Hesperus Andrias Van Ryneveld known as Pierre van Ryneveld[1] and First Lieutenant Quintin Brand,[2] two South African airmen who had had left Brooklands on 4 February on the same journey in their Vickers Vimy named *Silver Queen* by a slightly different route.

Van Ryneveld was born on 2 May 1891 at Senekal in the Orange Free State. After matriculating at Grey College School in Bloemfontein he trained as an engineer in London and began his military career in July 1915 in the RFC.

After an exciting night crossing of the Mediterranean he and Brand arrived at Derna on the morning of 5 February. They arrived at Cairo on 10 February, but crash landed the *Silver Queen* in bad weather at Korosko in the Sudan a day later. A second Vimy was purchased from the RAF in Cairo and christened *Silver Queen II*. Leaving Cairo on the 22nd all went well for 3,880 miles but on 6 March it crashed at Bulawayo. Fortunately the airmen again escaped injury. A D.H.9., one of 100 surplus machines with spares and maintenance equipment supplied to South Africa by Britain in 1919, and known as the 'Imperial Gift', was dispatched post haste to Bulawayo where the name *Voortrecker* was bestowed on it and the two airmen continued the journey in this machine. On 20 March Van Ryneveld and Brand reached Young's Field, Cape Town after a total flying time of 109½ hours; the only one of five crews attempting the journey to successfully complete the flight. Van Ryneveld and Brand were awarded £5,000 by the Government of South Africa and the King made each of them a KBE.

On 12 July 1920. Cockerell and Broome were awarded the AFC and Wyatt and Corby the AFM in recognition of their flight. Cockerell married Lorna Lockyer in 1921 and they had seven children. He and his six-year-old daughter Kathleen were killed in the German bombing of Sunbury-on-Thames on 29 November 1940.

On 2 May 1923, Lieutenant John Arthur Macready and Lieutenant Oakley George Kelly made the first non-stop coast-to-coast flight, from Roosevelt Field on Long Island, New York to Rockwell Field, North Island, San Diego,

California with a total flight time of 26 hours, fifty minutes and 48 seconds. En route, they made the first in-flight aircraft engine repair in Air Service history, replacing a defective voltage regulator switch while the single engine, high wing Fokker T-2 Liberty monoplane churned westward. The flight also set a new distance record for a single cross-country flight; 2,625 miles. They flew through the night and near the end of the journey crossed the Rockies, 11,000 feet high. This trans-continental flight, although nearly 1,000 miles longer, was far less perilous than the Atlantic passage. Nevertheless it opened up possibilities of a flight half way round the world in about five days.

Transferring from the RNAS to the Royal Air Force on its creation in 1918, Air Commodore Charles Samson CMG DSO AFC held command of several groups in the immediate post-war period and his deep commitment to aviation, combined with his restless pioneering instincts, saw him authorise and personally lead several experimental long-distance formation flights in the 1920s. In October 1926 Samson led three de Havilland D.H.9As and two Vickers Victorias on a long reconnaissance over the Kharga and Baharia oases in the Libyan Desert. This was mainly to test the Victoria's endurance and reliability under primitive conditions of maintenance, having already flown a Victoria from Cairo to Aden in the previous month and returned safely - a round trip of over 4,000 miles. On 30 March 1927 he led four Fairey IMF two-seaters from Heliopolis, Egypt to Cape Town, South Africa, arriving there on 21 April. Four days later he set out on the return trip, arriving at Cairo on 22 May, having made a round trip of 11,362 miles without encountering any serious problems en route. These and other pioneering sorties were instrumental in founding the air links around what was then the British Empire.[3]

During the First World War the German Zeppelins had stirred the imagination in British circles and a British government programme to develop civil airships capable of service on long-distance routes within the British Empire was begun in 1919. But the dream ended in 1930 when the R 101, one of a pair of British rigid airships completed in 1929 and designed and built by an Air Ministry-appointed team, effectively in competition with the government-funded but privately designed and built R 100, crashed on 5 October 1930 in France during its maiden overseas voyage, killing 48 of the 54 people on board. Among the deceased passengers were Lord Thomson, the Air Minister who had initiated the programme, senior government official and almost all the dirigible's designers from the Royal Airship Works. The crash of R 101 effectively ended British airship development.

The German airship enterprise ended abruptly also when, on Thursday, 6 May 1937, the *Hindenburg* disaster took place as the German passenger airship LZ129 *Hindenburg* caught fire and was destroyed during its attempt to dock with its mooring mast at Naval Air Station Lakehurst, New Jersey. Of the 97 people on board (36 passengers and 61 crewmen), there were 35 fatalities (13 passengers and 22 crewmen). One worker on the ground was also killed, making a total of 36 dead. Although Max Pruss was the commanding kapitän of the *Hindenburg*, Kapitän Ernst August Lehmann, who had commanded army and navy airships during the the First World War, was the most senior

250

officer on board. He had served as commanding officer on more than 100 of the flights of the *Graf Zeppelin* between 1928 and 1936, when he commanded ten round-trip flights to Lakehurst on the new *Hindenburg*. Only on board as an observer, Lehmann was fatally burned and died the following day.

The disaster was the subject of spectacular newsreel coverage, photographs and Herbert O. 'Herb' Morrison's recorded radio eyewitness reports from the landing field, which were broadcast the next day.

It's practically standing still now. They've dropped ropes out of the nose of the ship and they've been taken a hold of down on the field by a number of men. It's starting to rain again; it's - the rain has slacked up a little bit. The back motors of the ship are just holding it just, just enough to keep it from - It burst into flames! It burst into flames, and it's falling, it's crashing! Watch it, watch it! Get out of the way! Get this, Charlie! Get this, Charlie! It's on fire and it's crashing! It's crashing terrible! Oh, my, get out of the way, please! It's burning and bursting into flames, and the - and it's falling on the mooring-mast and all the folks agree that this is terrible; this is one of the worst catastrophes in the world... It's the flames... it's a terrific crash... It's smoke and it's flames now... and the frame is crashing to the ground, not quite to the mooring-mast. Oh, the humanity and all the passengers screaming around here... I can't even talk to people whose friends are on there. Ah! It's–it's–it's–it's ... o–ohhh! I–I can't talk, ladies and gentlemen. Honest, it's just laying there, a mass of smoking wreckage. Ah! And everybody can hardly breathe and talk and the screaming... I can hardly breathe. I'm going to step inside where I cannot see it... listen, folks, I'm gonna have to stop for a minute because I've lost my voice. This is the worst thing I've ever witnessed.

A variety of hypotheses have been put forward for both the cause of ignition and the initial fuel for the ensuing fire. The incident shattered public confidence in the giant, passenger-carrying rigid airship and marked the end of the airship era.

Endnotes Afterword

1   After the war, van Ryneveld was called back to South Africa by the Prime Minister Jan Smuts in order to set up the SAAF. General Sir Hesperus Andrias van Ryneveld KBE CB MC died on 2 December 1972.
2   Air Vice Marshal Sir Christopher Joseph Quintin Brand KBE DSO MC DFC (25 May 1893-7 March 1968).
3   Samson was placed on the retired list on account of ill health in 1929. After a morning ride on 5 February 1931, however, he complained of feeling unwell and before the local doctor could be called Charles Samson had died from heart failure at his Wiltshire home in Cholderton..

Index